I OF SUN

RICHARD ARTHUR

Matador
9 Priory Business Park
Wistow Road, Kibworth
Leicester LE8 0RX, UK
Tel: 0116 2792299
Email: books@troubador.co.uk
Web: www.troubador.co.uk/matador

ISBN 9781780881751

Cover wrap image © Peter Holm
www.homezproductions.com

Typeset in 11pt Times by Troubador Publishing Ltd, Leicester, UK
Printed and bound in the UK by TJ International, Padstow, Cornwall

Matador is an imprint of Troubador Publishing Ltd

ONE

We drift into life slowly as if waking from a long dream. Memories appear like broken fragments of an unwritten book, gradually taking form as we emerge from the darkness. Bleary eyes open ever wider with each rise of the morning Sun. Eyes of brilliance, a mind of meaning, gazing forth upon a world too great to comprehend.

Life flows by in a heady haze of youthful colour, people and places, joys and pains, the future twinkling on the eternal horizon beyond. Growing within the borders of our circumstance, our lives intertwined with those around us. Stories are told, pictures of the world passed on and transformed. A human world of happiness and sadness, good and bad, right and wrong, truth and falsehood. A world of endless variety and diversity, yet one where ideas cluster to create cultures, philosophies and religions; some of which we may agree with, yet other parts leave us cold. Facts and opinions accumulate and blend, as we cling to that we find desirable.

★ ★ ★

I grew up in a regular place, a life as normal as the next. Little to do but gaze at the world beyond and wonder what it really looks like, the light on the horizon growing ever brighter. A blooming fascination with the phenomena of life – its sheer size, complexity and beauty. Ideas reverberated – about the mind, people and the world. Analysing, questioning, always wondering why, why, why?

I yearned for simple truth. An understanding of that which clearly exists, is obvious and undeniable, about which we can all agree. An acknowledgement of that which is true, that which remains unknown, and that which will never be known. The triumph of rationality and common sense over irrationality and nonsense.

As I grew into adulthood, the curiosity turned to intent. I'd lived in the same country all my life. I was bored. I wanted to break free, cross the line and step out into the world alone. Go somewhere new, somewhere I didn't know. Start afresh – without purpose or prejudice – and simply be in the world. Reborn into complete independence and ignorance to live unimpeded and free. Free from responsibility, free from others, free from myself. Free to do whatever I wanted, anytime, anywhere. That way I'd really learn what made me tick.

As far as I could see I only had one life and I wanted to live it. Really live it. Experience the world. Push myself and find out what I was capable of. I was searching for something, but I didn't know what it was. But I wanted love, happiness, joy and revelation. To swim the oceans, explore mountain tops and jungles, and conquer the cities. Dreams of parties under the stars, falling in love on the beach, epiphanies at dawn, beautiful people and friends for life. Bright lights, hard liquor and neon jungles. Crazy days and endless nights, journeys to new frontiers and the beauty of nature, forever seduced by the lure of the unknown. Chance meetings, road warriors, mad men and mystics. Expectations satisfied and the thrill of the unexpected. The crazy, impossible dream to go everywhere, meet everyone and do everything. That was what I wanted – I wanted it all – everything and nothing.

★ ★ ★

I woke up at 6am in my old bedroom in my old family home. I'd moved out a few years before but the bedroom remained. I'd grown up in this room. My old familiar bed, furniture and wallpaper. The same as it had always been.

Cold outside, early spring, the Sun barely above the horizon. I lay there for a few moments in the dead calm of dawn, dark shadows unfurling in the silence. After a lifetime of waiting, the day had finally come. This was it. I was leaving today. Alone into the world. I lay still for a moment, surprised at how calm I felt, not nervous or excited as I thought I'd be. I felt nothing. Just a quiet acceptance, a readiness for action. Just for a moment. Then I got up. The time is now.

Goodbye to my family and home and everything I'd grown up with. Daylight wound slowly over the dark morning plains, the rooftops of the city gradually emerging through the fields. Round the shadowy metropolis to the airport, gateway to beyond. A silent breakfast in the faceless crowd looking out over the drizzle-grey tarmac. Time to leave. My final footsteps down the tunnel and onto the plane. No turning back now. And with that kick of acceleration, soon all that I knew disappeared behind me in the thick clouds.

The trip I'd been dreaming about for so many years was finally upon me. I could have gone anywhere, but I'd chosen Southeast Asia. It looked like the place for me. The other side of the world. Lots of strange, new countries on a map: Indonesia, Malaysia, Thailand, Burma, Laos, Cambodia, Vietnam. I barely knew one from the other, but they all sounded tropical and exotic, full of promise and adventure. Tropical beaches, lush jungles, rolling mountains and steaming cities. On a whim I'd chosen to fly to Kuala Lumpur, the capital of Malaysia. The long peninsula north through Malaysia and up into Southern Thailand looked like the perfect runway into the mysteries of Asia.

It was my first time there and I had a one-way ticket. There was no going back. All or nothing. No time limit, no plan, no clue what I'd do when I got there. I'd saved enough cash to keep me going a while but it wasn't much. I guessed I'd travel a bit, find somewhere I liked and get some work. Until then I was just going to hit the road. Only I who made the decisions about what to do next. That was the plan.

Cruising high towards the tropics. Meals, toilets and movies. The long wait as the flight dragged on into the night. A line on the map, speeding through time and space, night quickly turning to day again.

The ocean below soon burned a brighter blue than I'd ever seen before. Land approaching. Bright green trees and fields. That swooping descent, ground rising, the angel of dreams coming into land. Then that thud of undoubtable certainty. The plane swung round, Kuala Lumpur International Airport looming like a vision of the future – all stainless steel and glass domes.

I stepped into a new continent, the biggest of them all. Elevated train ride to the main building and through Immigration. I grabbed my backpack from the belt and gazed around the huge glass arrivals hall. Outside a wall of eager taxi drivers waited to pounce. The plane ticket in my pocket was now a useless scrap of paper. This was it now – on my own in Asia. No idea where I was going, let alone when I was coming back. This was exactly what I'd wanted. And now I'd got it.

★ ★ ★

Where do we begin this search for simple truth? Perhaps by acknowledging that which clearly exists. What simple things in life can we all agree on?

Two aspects of life are instantly apparent to us all – the world and I. One is unique to me, about which only I know. The other is there in everyone. Yet they exist as one – two sides of an equation. The world exists and you exist in it.

We live in a very complicated world alongside billions of other people. But by standing on the shoulders of our ancestors, we have developed a clearer picture of it. The makeup of the world is learned in a gradual progression over many generations. The wonders of nature are learned through science; the wonders of mankind through history. By looking back to the beginning of time and moving forward to the present, we can get a clearer idea of the big picture – the world we find ourselves in.

And I? The human mind is so everyday to us all, yet so mysterious. The brain and the mind can be studied externally through neuroscience and psychology respectively. But another method of understanding is through this very means itself – delving deep within one's mind to uncover its essential properties and structures.

Our whole experience of the ever-changing world is filtered through our body and brain to our consciousness, flowing through time like a river. A bewildering fusion of phenomena – sights, sounds and sensations in synergy with our emotions and thoughts – remembering, learning, judging, reasoning. The brain performs countless operations subconsciously while only the most pertinent issues rise to consciousness. It continues every moment of our waking lives and even echoes in our sleep.

What can we say about the complicated and intertwined phenomena of the mind? Well, our thoughts are our own and we can think about virtually anything. And we are always feeling emotions – sometimes strongly, sometimes more subtly – both positive and negative. And we are always judging things and deciding what is good and bad.

But we are not merely conscious, thinking, feeling beings. We are active beings, living and doing things all the time. In terms of our place in the world, it is our actions that define us. Every moment of our lives we are always, necessarily *doing* something.

And so some questions arose in me. Every moment of your life – why do you do what you do? Why are you doing what you are doing now? And why did you do everything that you did before this? In essence, what causes our actions? Do we really control our thoughts and actions? Or are we controlled by our human nature or other external forces in the world?

And what about our emotions? What are they and why do they exist? And finally our judgements and values – what we think is good and bad? How do we decide? What does 'good' really mean?

These complex questions about free will, action, emotions and values seem to be very different, yet I suspect they are closely related, since they are bound by the same human consciousness through which they all flow.

By going alone into the world, free to do as I pleased at all times, it was these questions I wanted to investigate on my journey. And so it began.

★　★　★

The automatic glass doors opened and it hit me like a sledgehammer to the face – the heat – a thick wall of humid fog consuming me like a heavy blanket. I was met by a line of grinning, expectant faces. I approached a pleasant-looking old Indian man and haggled a fare into town. I got inside the clapped-out motor and we were off.

The driver was excited. The Formula One Grand Prix was in town. "Hello my friend. You want a ticket for the race this afternoon? I can get for you." A sudden unexpected opportunity. I entertained the possibility for a moment, but I had more pressing concerns on my mind. Like where I was going.

Not sure how I was feeling yet – excited or nervous? I stared out at the rich green jungle and fields of rubber trees planted in endless rows by the side of the road. Vegetation more lush and verdant than anything I'd seen before. The opening chimes of *Apocalypse Now* rang in my head. Was this the beginning for me or . . . ? Napalm rising through the mind's eye.

I woke up in a dirty sweat on the back seat as the city loomed into view. Dusty roads, frantic traffic, colourful old buildings by the side of the road, gleaming towers behind. Everything was foreign, strange and exotic. Suddenly we'd arrived and I was out, stumbling through the busy streets and markets of Chinatown; the heat weighing down on me, noise and clamour, people rushing by in every direction, Malay, Indian and Chinese, dodging the weaving crowds, kerbs, gutters, shop fronts and market stalls. Need a room. Saw a sign and a door leading upstairs to a cheap hotel. A dingy old room with a plastic air-conditioner on the ceiling, a dusty window opening onto the next building and creaky wooden furniture.

I opened my backpack with its detachable day bag and looked at the meagre possessions I'd brought with me – sandals, trainers, one pair of jeans and some basic clothes, a guidebook and a little first aid kit. The only technology I had was my old camera and a little plastic digital alarm clock. I'd packed light. No mobile phone. I wanted to cut myself off – untouchable, invisible, alone. Hold onto these final moments in time before the mobile phone's ubiquity took hold. And no music. No home comforts. No escapism. I wanted to hear all the sounds of this new world and immerse myself fully. I set my alarm for 7pm.

★ ★ ★

The piercing alarm was beeping before I knew I was asleep, throwing me into a black room in a strange new country on the other side of the world. It took me a few moments to remember where I was. And even then it was just an idea. My first night in Asia. I had to go out.

Chinatown was quieter now, heat subsided, the market stalls all shut down, people eating noodle soup from stalls in the streets. Lines of red lanterns bobbing up and down over the roads in the warm evening breeze. A large rat scurried along the kerb and into a drain. I noticed a young Western guy sitting with a bunch of locals drinking beer at a little table. I wondered what they were talking about. Another lone traveller on the road like me. But he looked like he'd been here a long time and knew what he was doing, whereas I was fresh off the plane.

So what now? Where to turn? Where to go? Left, right, forwards or backwards? A little panic set in. I was completely alone in a foreign land. No one to guide me, advise me, influence or chide me. My choice was of no consequence to anyone but myself. Absolute freedom. A silent wall of sound enveloped me and choked me for a moment, invisibly, intangibly there. Everything was totally up to me. There was nothing I could do but cut through it and walk on, for it was nothing and I was someone.

I was hungry and thirsty. I decided to walk to the Golden Triangle area where the bright lights of the city were supposed to be. The streets were surprisingly quiet. Leafy roads, not a pedestrian in sight. After trudging along the side of the road up a few hills and sweating my shirt through, I soon worked out why. The Petronas Twin Towers came into view, rising into the dark night like two sparkling white, bejewelled sceptres, their height and design a wonder to behold. A bridge connected the towers about halfway up, their tiers rising ever smaller up its jagged exterior as they reached into the sky like two shooting stars. I was in a new world.

I found the Golden Triangle with its gleaming towers, shopping centres and entertainment venues. There was a cluster of flashy sprawling discos and bars packed out with a mix of international punters. There was a buzz in the air. The Grand Prix crews were out celebrating. I was about to enter a packed bar when suddenly a tiny little fear hit me. I suddenly changed my mind and carried on up the street.

The feeling surprised me. Although I liked to party, I'd never really been out on my own before. I was always surrounded by friends. The absolute certainty of my new solitude suddenly hit me. Panicked questions flooded my mind. What would I do when I got in there? Sit and drink on my own all night? Start talking to people? For a split second the idea of getting the first flight back home entered my head. A stupid fearful thought. Walk tall. Keep going. I was alone now, so I'd have to push myself into new situations. I'd already taken the leap into the deep end in coming here, so now it was time to start swimming. I saw an outdoor restaurant and made myself sit down and eat some meat and sauce on rice and drink a couple of bottles of beer. I felt a little liberation as I sat there and overcame my fears. But it was strange to be alone all this time. Each minute felt like a little eternity. I hadn't had a proper conversation with anyone since I left home. I wasn't used to being alone like this all day. Alone with a constant feedback of thoughts and feelings sifting through my mind and nobody to share them with. No companionship. No escape. Just me, myself and I. I'd better get used to it quick. This is the way it's going to be now. My head is my home and the world my garden.

Two beers worth of contemplation turned to resolve and I returned to the bars. I entered a swanky little place, lounge house music, all dimmed lights, sofas and marble finish. I sat at the bar and sank more beers, paying Western prices. I drank quickly because there was nothing else to do and I felt better drunk. Thoughts slowed, tensions melted away. I got chatting to some engineers from a Grand Prix team, but I seemed to be more interested in them than they were in me. They left and I sat alone again, wondering what to do next.

I was about to leave when two dolled-up young Asian girls entered and sat at the bar near me. My worries were suddenly replaced by a greater urge. A few furtive glances later and we were chatting in broken English. They said they were students from mainland China. I'd never met any Chinese girls before. I was quite taken by the pretty one, Pandora. She was tiny, in a tight-fitting, little black dress, cute with high cheekbones and a huge smile, her thick black hair set against her white porcelain face. She looked exquisite, a picture of otherworldly beauty. And she was smiling at me too. I was just grateful for the company if anything, but maybe, just maybe . . . They eventually left but agreed to meet me at the nearby Rock 'n' Roll Café tomorrow at 9:30pm. I couldn't believe my luck.

I wandered round all the next day, getting my bearings and waiting for nightfall, which announced itself with a dramatic lightning storm. A taxi driver asking seedy questions took me to the Rock 'n' Roll Café, a theme-bar full of old Western guys and young Asian girls. I drank at the bar, nerves jangling. Pandora and her friend eventually arrived. I got them drinks and we chatted. They knew the young guys working behind the bar, all jokes, winks and nods. What was going on here? I needed to break the tension, so I tried taking beautiful Pandora for a dance. We shuffled uncomfortably with the other couples for a while until I tried to kiss her. She turned her head away. Too soon?

She led me to a club, some big theatre-sized place full of young locals, 160BPM dance music playing, hard as nails but cheesy as hell, full of sped-up pop remixes. I'd grown up listening to dance music, but I'd never heard anything like this. I held her hand worming through the crowds, until I found a quiet dark corner. Suddenly Pandora leapt on me, kissing me passionately out of sight. This was it! I'd arrived! Asia! I held her close up against me, not wanting to ever let her go. But she finished her drink and was gone again, leaving me with a phone number on a scrap of paper. I trudged back to my room, lost and found, tantalised and confused.

The next morning I decided to move somewhere cheaper, something I'd have to get used to as I couldn't afford air-con rooms if I wanted my money to last. The guesthouse rooms looked like a series of wooden boxes, with nothing inside but a bed on a metal frame and a ceiling fan that wobbled so much it looked like it might come off at any moment and carve me up in the night. Some young monks were staying there too, washing their huge brown robes in plastic bowls. I didn't know where they were from as I thought Malaysia was a mostly Muslim nation.

I explored the streets – to the grass and fountains of Merdeka Square, where Malaysia gained independence from the British Empire, through to Little India and KL Tower. After three attempts I eventually got hold of Pandora from a phone box. We met at 7pm and she invited me straight to her place. We sped off over some flyovers to the 24th floor of a skyscraper somewhere. It was a nice apartment. She led me to her little bedroom, anticipation building like the clouds before a storm. Without saying a word she suddenly and very calmly took off her top and skirt, her white underwear exposed like exquisite ribbon. Tension broken, I grabbed hold of her. I'd never felt skin like it. So tight and smooth like marble. I kissed her sweet lips and we fell on the bed. I pulled the white underwear from her body and we made love in the early evening as her Britney Spears collection played out around us.

Later we went to her local supermarket full of strange food products, and she made me some noodle soup with big shitake mushrooms. We chatted and I told her I might come back to KL and find a job here. It seemed like a cool city. And then at 1am I got up and left, vowing to return. I kind of meant it. I don't know why I left so quickly. She was gorgeous. But I wanted to hit the road.

★ ★ ★

The monks woke me at dawn washing their robes. I had mosquito bites everywhere and red friction sores all over my feet from the expensive sandals I'd bought back home. I got my bag together to leave town. Everything was in English at the nearby bus station. I decided to take a bus to Penang, the only place on the board I'd heard of.

Four hours north through the alien landscape of roads, jungle, signs and modern architecture, sat between two friendly men, one of Chinese, one of Indian descent. There were sizable communities of people from both nations in Malaysia, though the majority were ethnic Malay, making it a melting pot of Asian cultures in one country.

We eventually crossed a long bridge to bustling Georgetown on Penang Island in the northwest of Malaysia, full of beaten-up, chalky, colonial buildings, with peeling paint and wooden shutters. Market stalls on the side of the road sold food and cheap household products, as rickshaws and motorbikes zoomed down the narrow streets, Chinese signs everywhere. The island was once an important colony of the British Empire and was still bustling today.

I tramped around with my backpack till I found a cheap dormitory bed in a travellers' hostel with about ten other people in the room. I met the first backpackers of my trip. It was a shock speaking to them after being on my own for what felt like weeks already. There was a good-looking young couple from different European countries who'd met each other here in Asia. Tanned skin, tattoos, dreadlocks, tatty clothes, beads and necklaces. They'd been travelling for a long time and had seen things I had no clue about yet. I was strangely envious of them, meeting on some paradise beach and travelling the world together.

They had a mysterious aura; like they belonged to some secret club I wanted to be a part of. They'd already done the things I wanted to do, explored the mysteries that lay ahead and fallen in love on the way. I told them I'd just arrived three days ago and that was the end of the conversation.

I looked around Georgetown with a middle-aged Canadian hippy who gave me some tips, such as not to trust anybody, to stay off the tourist buses because of the thieves in the baggage compartments, and to check the bottled water in case it had been refilled with dirty water from the tap. He sounded kind of paranoid to me. I was bored.

After a restless night in a bunk bed sleeping with ten strangers, I got up early, found a map of the island and hired a bicycle. It was a wonky old woman's bike, and as the heavy traffic out of town streamed past me, I began having doubts about the wisdom of my trip. I cycled west along the north coast of the island, past the big hotels and urban beaches. The traffic calmed down so I decided to carry on, south into the interior of the island, up into the hills, past a reservoir and through lush forests and fruit farms. And then down the other side, free-wheeling for miles, weaving down twisting bends through the jungle, the buzz of adventure spurring me on.

Had some delicious curry in a friendly Indian restaurant and then went onwards through busy towns, before taking a wrong turn up and down another hill, until I was on the south side of the island somewhere. I kept pushing that gearless, rickety death trap north along motorways, past the rush hour traffic, trucks, cars and teens on motorcycles, on and on, sore arse, aching legs, smoke and grit on my sweaty, sunburnt face, all the way back to Georgetown – about 70kms in all – watching the sunset by the old fort with a weary grimace.

I didn't know what to do with myself at night again, wandering around but not connecting with anyone. That lonely feeling was following me like a shadow. Not talking to anyone all day, I ended up having full blown conversations with myself in my head. Sometimes I would imagine chatting with specific friends from home, imagining their remarks about whatever situation I was in, imagining our jokes and chuckling to myself. I thought back to all the mad-looking homeless people you see talking to themselves, and quickly found a new respect for the lonely of the world and their sad burden.

Best to keep moving, follow the Sun, keep the shadows at bay. The next morning I took a large car ferry across the cloudy sea to the nearby mainland town of Butterworth, letting the warm morning's sea breeze flow through me. I was headed for Kota Bharu, a town on the northeast coast of Malaysia, to explore the nearby beaches and islands that people had recommended. But at the bus station in Butterworth I was told I'd missed the bus. "No more today," someone said. "Get a bus to Alor Setar and catch another one from there," another said. I didn't know any better, so I did. At Alor Setar, I was told that the next bus to Kota Bharu was in three days! Stuck in some town I had no intention of going to, I felt my anger and frustration building. What to do? I looked at a map. I was near the Thai border. Let's do it. Why not? A new country. My anger turned to excitement again as I got a taxi to the border of Thailand for the first time.

* * *

I guess most people's first vision of Thailand is arriving at the airport in Bangkok and driving into the city. Not me. I filled out some forms and was stamped out of Malaysia and into Thailand, crossing the Sadao border checkpoint in Thailand's far south. The difference with Malaysia was distinct. The big wide road with dusty shop fronts either side was much busier and more chaotic than Malaysia. Big trucks and cars pumping down the street, motorcycles weaving in between, some with side-cars selling food, all of them kicking up big clouds of dust and smoke from the street. It seemed like a wild, crazy, lawless place, full of chancers and bandits, like some vision of an Oriental Wild West. I liked it. This was the Wild East. It seemed like a land full of promise and adventure, not as orderly and efficient as Malaysia. I knew little about the place other than it was famous on the travellers' circuit for its beautiful beaches, islands and legendary parties.

I picked a white bottle out a shop's fridge, a strange-tasting soy milk, and looked at my guidebook. I decided to head for the city of Hat Yai not far to the north. Taxi to the bus station and onto a *songtaew*, literally meaning 'two rows' my book told me – a truck with two benches on the back for passengers to sit facing each other, covered by a thin metal roof.

It was a prosperous bustling border town, lots of Malays and ethnic Chinese doing business with the local Thais. Walking the streets was a far more hectic experience than Malaysia. Vehicles zooming past in every direction, people jostling through dark, covered markets, before coming out into the blazing bright Sun again and avoiding hitting a speeding motorcycle or food hawker. Exotic spicy fumes emanated from Muslim, Chinese and Thai restaurants everywhere. Lots of well-used, old shop houses and freezing cold 7-Eleven convenience stores on every street corner. Inside, an automatic 'ding-ding' sound and a chorus of young women behind the counter all saying hello in Thai, "*Sawasdee kaa.*"

I went to some dank old backpacker centre. The receptionist handed me a key for a dorm room. "This your room." In the room was an English guy Martin. He was 30-something; been teaching English in Bangkok for a few years, and was now in Hat Yai. He seemed happy for me to tag along with him around town, as I listened to his torrent of advice, piss-takes and Thai language with the locals. "That's a squat toilet. After you take a shit, pour water down your back and scrub it off your arse . . . Don't live down here mate there's nothing to do, you're better off starting in Bangkok . . . This place is full of Malay blokes getting their end away from over the border . . . *Moo daeng thao rai?* . . . Watch out for the local blokes, they're all trained in Thai boxing and five of them'll gang up on you if you start anything . . . You're a *farang* now mate." "What's that?" I wondered. *Farang* was the Thai word for Westerners I learned, and they used it a lot to talk about any they came across.

14

Martin had this gaunt frame, harrowed face and slightly mad look in his eyes like he'd been here too long. But he was doing what I wanted to do, so I stayed with him as we hit the beers and he ran around trying to sort out various problems with his girlfriend, old school, guesthouse, money and so on. He didn't seem too happy in his current predicament living in a shit-hole guesthouse in Hat Yai, but at the same time I was drawn to his street swagger and experience amongst the people of this foreign land. I wanted a slice of the action for myself – to be able to swing through the trees and vines of the jungle freely like him. He told me there was lots of work for foreigners teaching English in Thailand. There was certainly much less English written and spoken here compared to Malaysia, the local language looking like an incomprehensible maze of squiggles. I could tell you needed experience to get by here, and I had none. The place had an electric urgency to it, a mad buzz that had me hooked. Stumbling from bar to bar, we met a young Swedish guy who'd been bumming round town for three weeks, some funky-looking Japanese guys, pretty bar waitresses and plump sunburnt Irish girls, before stumbling home happy after my first night in Thailand.

★ ★ ★

I checked my emails the next morning and saw that a friend of mine from home, Adam, who was already over here, was arriving in a place called Krabi today. A few friends from home were travelling around the region already or were planning on coming later in the year. Most of them had these round-the-world ticket deals, going from Bangkok to Australia, maybe New Zealand or Fuji, and onto USA and Europe. Maybe I would go round the world too. But not yet. I got a ticket for a minibus to Krabi from the tour shop outside my guesthouse, chatting excitedly with the other young travellers on board. I'd just turned 22 and it was time to shine . . .

We drove for four hours through towns and dramatic hills, all foreign, all intriguing, and came to Krabi Town, getting off the minibus on a street next to a river estuary leading out to the sea just beyond. Inland in the distance were strange-looking rock formations topped with green vegetation. Long-tail boats, long wooden vessels with massive engines that swivelled round with a propeller at the end of a long metal bar, chugged down the river past the swampy undergrowth. On the road were dozens of young Western kids in hippy and surf gear, getting in and out of minibuses and *songtaew* trucks, struggling with their huge backpacks, some boarding big white ferry boats docked in the harbour area by the riverside. There was a buzz of excitement in the air. On the other side of the road were lots of restaurants with English menus and tour shops selling tickets to various strange-sounding places whose names I couldn't pronounce: Ao Nang, Railey Beach, Ko Phi Phi, Ko Lanta, Phang Nga, Phuket, Trang, Ko Samui, Ko Phangan, Ko Tao . . .

This was it! I'd found the famous backpacker trail of Southeast Asia here in Krabi! This was the place to be, full of cool people, paradise beaches and beautiful *ko*, the Thai word for island. Things were on the up!

I guess people have been travelling since we could walk upright, but at some point in time it became cool, as young philosophers, poets and beatniks hit the road in search of adventure and everything else that came with it. The spark lit the '60s hippy movement and soon people were taking off overland on trails across America, Europe, the Middle East, India and the Himalayas. Some made it all the way to Southeast Asia, telling tales of paradises lost, found and ruined. Back then the air was heavy with poetry and big ideas. Nowadays no one gives a fuck about all that. It's all booze and sex. Me? I love it all. The world had moved on but legends of undiscovered backpacker enclaves remained. Full moon beach parties, jungle raves, hidden ruins, travellers' settlements. Did they still exist here in this new century or had I missed the boat? All I knew was that I was real thirsty.

I got a fan room in a dusty attic on the corner near the port. I put my trunks on and strolled happily down to the river and through a park with locals picnicking in the shade. I kept ambling on towards the sea waiting for my paradise beach to appear, but it didn't. I couldn't find any beaches, just more rocks and streets as the estuary widened. I went back into Krabi Town. It was small and quiet, more laid-back than Hat Yai. I killed time, checking my emails every hour. My friend Adam and I didn't have mobile phones, so the only way to meet was by emailing, agreeing on a time and place and hoping they were there.

I eventually met Adam in an Italian restaurant, grateful to see a familiar face. He was looking strong, healthy and jubilant. Suddenly I was no longer alone and could share my experiences with someone else. We talked non-stop for hours, full of questions and stories, two hungry guys eager to pool our knowledge of this foreign land. He'd been here a while now and was having the time of his life, telling tales of breathtaking beaches and exotic women. I wanted it all too, but I wasn't quite there yet. He told me that the beaches weren't here in Krabi Town after all. The next day we caught a *songtaew* truck for a half hour ride through amazing rock formations, jungle and rubber plantations, Buddhist temples and Islamic mosques to Ao Nang, a beach resort down the coast.

It was a pretty little place, with small guesthouses, convenience stores, pharmacies, diving, kayaking and tour shops, tailors and little Thai restaurants everywhere. Street vendors tended stalls either side of the wide road which led down to a long sandy beach on the town's front.

I moved into Adam's double room, took off the expensive sandals that had been rubbing my feet apart, and got some cheap flip-flops with a little rubber thong between my two toes. Instant relief. We went to the long stretch of Ao Nang Beach and swam in the warm waters. But it was an overcast day, the colours dark and shadowy. At the end of one side of the beach a huge imposing wall of jagged limestone cliffs rose up vertically. On the other side of the vertical cliffs, completely cut off from the mainland, was Railey Beach. Mysterious shadowy islands bobbed tantalisingly on the horizon, far out to sea.

There wasn't much going on at night, just some restaurants and empty bars. But strolling up the road inland we saw a tiny alleyway of little wooden bars with fairy lights hanging off them. Entering the alleyway, we were suddenly greeted by a wall of young Thai women standing up and appearing from the shadows. "Hello Mis-tah, welcome, have beer, lady, handsome man, come in!" There were dozens of them, young beautiful brown-skinned girls with little dresses and big wide smiles, all beckoning us into their bars. It was like some tantalising, illicit hallucination. But it was real and I'd never seen anything like it in my life. My heart stopped, sank into my stomach, did a 360, and rose back into my chest in a knot. Were they barmaids or something else? I didn't know, but I was just as scared as I was excited. We panicked and retreated like little whimpering dogs that were just snarled at by a bigger beast.

We found an Irish bar down another quiet side-street called Shamrock, an open-sided wooden bar with a few wooden chairs and tables, and a scratchy pool table. That was about it, but it was fun and friendly, with tourists and locals mixing inside like old friends, just like a good bar should be. We were welcomed warmly by the boss, Sally, a funny young Thai woman and her friend, a drunk local guy who called himself Jackpot. We drank the local beers, Beer Singha and Beer Chang, meaning Elephant Beer. Both had a kick to them, some saying Chang was 6.4% alcohol, others saying it was actually a lot more. Soon the drinks were flowing and people were passing round colourful little plastic buckets full of a Thai rum called SangSom, a bottle of energy drink and Coke; a dozen straws sticking out the top, people banging their heads together to suck up this strange concoction. It tasted sickly sweet, but with a hell of a kick. I felt a surge of positive energy, mad banter flowing out my mouth like Niagara.

Next thing we're in the back of a truck with Jackpot, Sally and her Irish boyfriend, too drunk to think twice, driving through the dark forests to Krabi Town. A disco full of local kids, Thai rock music playing with different singers jumping to the stage, before more full-blast, 160 BPM, Asian techno-pop kicks in. Drinks, dancing, girls and confusion. Back in Ao Nang and they reopen the bar for us, Jackpot dancing like a drunken mystic, free SangSom buckets, tequilas and madness till dawn. I was sold.

* * *

Adam was starting a scuba diving course the next day, so he wasn't supposed to drink anymore. It sounded like something I'd like to do one day, Thailand's tropical waters being some of the best in the world apparently, but I had more exploring to do first. From my emails I knew another friend from home named Rachael was in Ko Phangan. This was the island famous for its backpacker scene and Full Moon Parties. It was supposed to be the biggest party around and it was coming soon. I decided to check it out. And the idea of meeting my beautiful friend Rachael on a tropical beach sent my imagination spinning. I emailed her and said I was coming over.

I bought a ticket from a tour shop all the way to Ko Phangan. A group of us backpackers were driven back to the riverside in Krabi Town, and then transferred to a bigger bus with more tourists on a long drive across the southern peninsula of Thailand to the town of Surat Thani. From here another long wait and transfer to a little port on the coast, with masses of backpackers with different coloured stickers on their t-shirts showing their destination. There were hundreds of people coming and going all over the place. It was well organised and well trodden. I felt like I was in the hub of things now. I was still the new kid, but I was feeling more confident and chatty, gradually finding my travelling feet. I met people from Holland, Germany, England and some cool record producer from L.A. We exchanged stories and backgrounds, them telling me about places to go in the region. The American told me about a mystical cave in Trang province that you swim through in blackness until emerging at a hidden beach surrounded by rocks. It sounded like a fantasy, but he swore it was real. A car ferry took us over the sea, tiny islands shimmering hazily on the horizon as the Sun descended into a velvet cushioned blanket, sinking cold cans of beer with my new buddies.

Ko Phangan appeared as a row of growing horizontal lights in the night. We disembarked on the dark sandy shore. I had directions for a certain beach, Ao Thong Nai Pan Yai on the northeast coast. I tried to memorise it and say it to the local taxi drivers like I knew what I was on about. After five attempts I was led off and put on the edge of a pickup truck, squashed tight with tourists in the front, back and sides. We soon veered off the main road and onto a rough trail of dried muddy tracks winding up and down through the black jungle. We had to concentrate to stay in the vehicle as it swung round the dark bumps and bends, just flashes of yellow sand and green foliage appearing in the headlights. Everything was kind of dangerous and reckless here but nobody seemed to mind. It was all very carefree and exciting as hell.

We arrived late in the night. I stumbled along the pitch-black beach with my backpack, the shadows in the sand and scant light playing tricks on my vision. It was quiet, just a few little bungalows and restaurants along the side of the beach, little groups of travellers here and there. I found the bungalows I'd been sent to.

Searching through the palm trees and shadows, I found Rachael lying in the sand and dancing lights. She was with her pretty friend from home that she was travelling with. They were with another male friend from home I'd never met before. They were all my age. They were sitting in the sand with some German guys they'd met, wacked out and giggling on weed and mushrooms. I said hello and they murmured and giggled. We were on different planets. I tried to converse as best I could before Rachael led me away to a little wooden bar in the sand down the beach.

She wasn't as stoned as the others and I was pleased to see her again so far from home on this dark, tropical night. Far from home, but old feelings travel well. We caught up and exchanged stories for a couple of hours, as I basked in her warm smile.

I wasn't sure of the sleeping arrangements but they were expecting me and I was put in her bungalow. It was a dilapidated little wooden shack with wobbly steps up to the veranda; inside a small double bed under a dirty mosquito net, full of sand, spiders' webs and the buzz of little insects in the shadows. A toilet next door with no flush, just a bucket of water and plastic scoop, little gecko lizards scampering around the walls. It wasn't pretty, but I was happy lying there in the dark talking crap excitedly as she fell asleep.

Arriving somewhere at night for the first time is always a bit bewildering, but the trade-off is the sweet surprise in the morning when you see where you are for the first time. I awoke in the dark windowless shack and opened the door to find myself right on the beach. The perfect beach. The beach you dream of when you're stuck in a sad place, and you close your eyes and try to imagine what paradise looks like. Golden white sand, so fine it squeaks under your feet as you step through the palm trees and hammocks to the sea, the surface blinding bright from the Sun's reflection, glimmering in the still blue waters lapping softly onto the shore. Long sands, a gently curving bay, rocky outcrops at either end, the trees a brilliant green, handfuls of quaint wooden bungalows set in the palms behind.

I got chatting to Guy, their friend from home, over breakfast. A good-looking guy with a dark brown tan from their travels. He seemed okay, but was a bit cool and moody, not smiling or joking with me at all. It seemed a strange set up, this handsome guy travelling with two pretty female friends for months on end. But Rachael said he had saved the two of them from all the weirdos they'd met on the road, as they told me tales of Cambodia and Laos, these two wild countries to the north. I liked to hear about all these places, feeling sure I would go there too eventually; but I felt that disconnect again, like the new kid in school that no one wants to speak to.

We swam in the warm shallow seas as the midday Sun beat down hard. The surroundings exceeded my imagination. Then someone suggested some magic cookies which were readily available here apparently. It seemed pretty safe on this beach miles from anywhere. We ate some but it didn't seem to have much effect.

Later on, my curiosity led me off alone in my flip-flops and swimming trunks. I took the road behind the beach up to the next bay. I thought my bungalow was basic, but the locals were living in tiny shacks of corrugated metal and wooden sheets away from the coast. They seemed content enough though, waving at me as they nibbled on food and chatted together.

I got to the next bay. More bungalows, palm trees and scrubland leading to golden sands and the illuminous turquoise sea. Just a few people lazing around in the shade. I dived in the sea to cool off again. I could see my feet pulsating in the shining sand below, little blue fish nipping around through the ripples. It was truly sublime here. I smiled as the Sun beat down on me like a divination. It was the same Sun as back home of course, but it felt different here. Closer, hotter, more alive.

To the right were some giant boulders lining the headland. I decided to scramble on the big grey rocks back around the hill that separated the two bays. The Sun beat down on my back as I clambered up and down the huge rocks like a little boy on holiday. I reached a point where I could no longer continue on the rocks, so I jumped into the sea to swim the next part. I quickly learnt that swimming with flip-flops didn't work, dragging me down like dead weights. I kicked them off and held them in my hands anxiously, but it was still hard to swim, the throbbing waves urging me towards the spiky rocks. I threw them onto a rock and swam on.

My heart was pumping now, reality suddenly getting a little more real. As I got further round I still couldn't see the first bay, my head reeling from the Sun's rays and the sweat and the swimming, and the . . . oh yeah, the cookies. They were hitting me hard now as I swam along the outcrop of rocks, both bays out of view now, no possessions on me, nobody in sight. Panicking and dizzy I tried to pull myself out the water, but the waves sent me flailing around onto the sharp rocks and encrusted shells. I dragged myself onto a dry rock on all fours, red blood pouring down my leg, just me and a cut leg in some trunks in the searing Sun, stuck on the rocks with a belly full of hash. I'd fucked up. I realised it at that point, half-baking to death, my mind deep frying with the increasing realisation of the decreasing fortune of my present reality. I tried to get a grip of myself but it wasn't working.

Then a sign! A fisherman chugged by in his long-tail boat. I waved at him desperately. He saw this lost tourist and pointed up the hill behind the rocks. I went back over the rocks to retrieve my flip-flops. I still couldn't see either bay, but eventually I did see a little trail going up the headland above the rocks. I pulled myself up through the mud and trees, body exhausted, nerves frayed, and saw some local women in a building on the hill top. I don't know what I looked like to them, clambering out of the jungle, but to me they looked like angels. They gave me some water and patched me up before I went back the sensible way, shocked at how quickly my afternoon stroll had deteriorated into danger. This was no theme park.

In the evening we drank and smoked more on the beach, but I still felt a tension in the group, knowing it must be my recent arrival. Later I saw Guy rubbing Rachael's back as they sat closer and closer together. Something must be going on between them, but I didn't know what it was exactly, or how long it had been going on for. Nobody told me anything. Why did they put me in her bungalow? I guess I didn't know her friends well enough to stay with them. Or what? Maybe they hadn't thought about it as much as I clearly was. It was playing tricks with my mind and I wasn't getting on with these German guys either. Damned weed! That's the thing about the weed. You start seeing the world in four dimensions – the usual three plus a new dimension of hidden meanings that weren't there before. After hours on the beach I felt a social claustrophobia, so I went off alone to the fairy lights of the beach bars, surly, confused and paranoid, and sank some Beer Changs and tequilas with the first group of pisshead blokes

I met. They passed me more reefers till I was well and truly shipwrecked in this confusing new world – body a mess, head-fucked and heartbroken. Fade to black.

I opened my eyes to the sweet sight of dawn breaking over the sea, flaming colours simmering through the misty haze. I was lying in an empty hammock tied between two trees. I got up, still frazzled, and stumbled back in the soft light to the bungalow. Rachael was lying alone on the bed naked under a sarong. But it wasn't what I wanted to see the morning after the night before.

Over breakfast the three of them giggled about skinny dipping in the sea together last night as we ate more cookies. My stupid little dream was over. I tried to enjoy the sea and beach games but my nerves were fraught, nothing to say to anyone, nobody wanting to speak to me. The day dragged on in this surreal, tense, stoned wonderland, Eden without Eve. Still no explanations. I wanted to get out of there, but had to wait another day until the Full Moon Party. I lay next to her that night in silence staring at the blackness above.

We hired some motorbikes the next day. I'd never driven one in my life, but Guy showed me the controls and took the two girls on his bike while I worked out how to drive mine. It was just a little 100cc motorcycle, with four gears you could click through without a clutch. We headed off along the twisted mud road. This was the end of the dry season so there were huge long ruts that had formed on the slopes which the bike would slip into and you'd be forced to follow like rollercoaster tracks. Not to mention all the loose rocks, sandy patches and occasional puddles of mud. Guy said it was one of the most treacherous roads in the whole country, but I got the hang of it. Pretty much like riding a bike.

It felt good to get off that illusory beach, straight-headed again, flying along on two wheels through the forest and hills, the warm air flowing around me. We reached the concrete road and headed to Thong Sala, the main town where the boats came in. Then to Hat Rin, up and down some of the steepest roads I'd seen in my life, to check out the scene of the Full Moon Party that night. The whole little village of guesthouses, restaurants and bars was packed full of tourists, mostly young Western backpackers getting ready to party. We drove back before dark, passing some young English guy at a waterfall. He was so happy here on this island he seemed enchanted, walking the jungle with a big stick and a dog he said he'd bought.

The full moon rose over the sea, so bright here in the black wilderness night, thousands of stars shining bright back through time. We waded through the sea to the speedboat we'd booked, rounding the island quickly, excitedly, the dark shadows of the beach behind us now. Hat Rin's beach emerged from the purple horizon lit up like a horizontal firework as the boat passed the headland. It was bigger than I expected, a whole beach of large bars set into the beachfront, all playing different musical styles to thousands of people flying around in various states of undress, wide-eyed, buckets in hand, bright UV paint everywhere, some dancing, some splayed out on the sand. This was the famous Full Moon Party of Ko Phangan. I'd made it. I folded my jeans up to my knees and hopped off the boat into the waist-deep water. I waded to the shore, my jeans heavy with sea water and wet sand.

Guy got some white diet pills from a pharmacy, basically just amphetamine pills people took to stop themselves eating, I was told. Then we were offered some mysterious yellow things by some experienced party sergeant. Kids' candy in the land of the lost party people. So off we popped, wandering around, drinking SangSom buckets, through bars of house music, psychedelic trance, hip hop, drum n' bass, the beats all rolling together in a giant musical babble. Happy to be here, relaxed, getting on better now, I sat down with Guy in a bar getting our breath back. Feeling woozy, I suddenly saw that we were the same – two young guys on holiday – no need for bitterness. We chatted like old friends who'd never met, rushing through all the stages of friendship we'd missed out on. He explained that he and Rachael had been falling for each other for a while now on the road, but had been holding back because they were travelling together as a three, and didn't want to cause any troubles but they could only hold back their feelings for so long, and I was happy and I could see they were mad for each other, a beautiful couple falling in love on the beach, and she was my friend and he was my friend and we're all good people and I was happy for them both and happy for myself here, young, free and limitless, no need for sadness, fear and bad feelings, and oh my God, check out that fucking bass line!

We jumped up and hit the floor, dancing, chatting madly, on and on, and then I was alone, lost and found, elation and joy, new friends everywhere, all expressing our inner souls on this beach, searching the maze of people come together under the gaze of the flying night Sun. Then I found the real meat – techno – the king of the beats, and I was up on some stage on the beach thumping and swaying in waves, hours like minutes, mind-bending 303 acid hooks driving into my psyche, and always that primordial beat, bang-bang-bang-bang, the cave man's drum from the beginning of time . . . and oh fuck I know this track, 1st Bass – *Slam Me Down*, bass like thunder, searing hi-hats, whooshing and rushing on and on and on till . . . break, break, break, break, *bang*! On and on, don't ever stop . . .

The shadows decayed, sweet kisses of light emerging from the sea like the fingers of God, until a massive bulb of pure energy broke forth from the waters, the red Sun rising majestically over the ocean in an array of flaming hot colours over the relentless pound of roaring future techno. I had a moment of overriding clarity and vowed to return here as soon as heavenly possible. The others found me and dragged me off stage to get the 7am speedboat back. I contemplated the alternatives before remembering that jungle road. We went back together on the speedboat, flying along Heaven's waters in the brilliant morning rays, the olive greens and azure blues alive with the energy of the great Sun. I was happy, we were happy, everything was good. Rachael and Guy sat in each other's arms dreamily. Rachael's pretty friend lay her head down on my lap as we cruised back along the island's edge.

26

I waved the young lovebirds and their friend off on their journey south the next day. I was on a solo journey and it was time to find my own path again. One day chilling out on the beach before shaking the sand out my backpack. I remembered I was supposed to be looking for a place to find work. I decided to get a ticket to the capital city Bangkok. The German guys also told me about a city called Chiang Mai in the mountainous north which sounded interesting. I imagined an ancient walled city in the foothills of the Himalayas.

At Thong Sala, me, the Germans and the enchanted English kid, who'd now given his dog away, met some other young English guys, one called Matt from London. We were all travelling solo and got on easily. It seemed pretty normal for guys travelling on their own to just start hanging out with each other with no questions asked. We drank and joked on the sunny boat back to the mainland. Everyone laid-back and friendly. A two hour wait at another backpacker cafe in Surat Thani, dozens more stickered-up backpackers in bright shorts and t-shirts.

I was put on the back row of a packed bus with everybody complaining and fighting over their leg-room and reclining seats. Eventually people settled down and plugged into their gadgets as some inaudible VCD started. I was next to an attractive German woman as we made the long journey north up the peninsula of Thailand through the night. The seats at the back of the bus didn't recline and the two of us only had one blanket to combat the freezing air conditioning. But I didn't care, because I was going to Bangkok for the first time, that exotic Oriental metropolis, young, free and happy. I chatted to the girl, getting along well with our shared blanket. Then dozing on and off, time moving slowly through the night, past petrol stations and mysterious twinkling temples, hours passing, orange lights and white lines flashing by forever, merging into a hypnotic blur, the signs slowly counting down the kilometres to Bangkok.

★ ★ ★

*

Going back to those simple truths we can all agree on. The two aspects of life which are at once instantly apparent – the world and I. We have already introduced some questions about the human mind. What about the world? Over millennia of human history, what have we learned?

We all observe and interact with the world on a personal level, learning and discovering how things work. Through scientific observation, theory and testing, scientists also study the world and discover the causes and effects of things, and sometimes calculate physical laws which appear to be universally true.

On a large scale we can talk about the cause of movements of gigantic objects in space – planets, stars and galaxies. On a small scale we can look at the causes of change in atoms, the tiny units of matter of which the world is composed – a nucleus of neutrons and positively charged protons, surrounded by a cloud of negatively-charged electrons. We can even go beyond this and study subatomic particles.

And so it appears that every event in the Universe which happens in time is due to another event which occurred before it – it has a cause. And in turn this will affect other events in the future – it has an effect. These causes and effects occur in physical proximity in space, and are necessarily sequential in time; every event being determined by a preceding cause, which in turn was preceded by another cause, and so on and so on. Thus, this chain of causation links all events in time and space together, acting like the glue of the Universe.

There is only one way the Universe was in the past, with every event determined by its cause and so on. At any time we can imagine 'What if . . . ?' this possible event had occurred instead of the actual event, and the effects it may have had. But the fact is this never happened. There is necessarily only one way the Universe ever was at any time in its history. There is only one chain of events that has occurred in time up to the present.

So if one had a full understanding of the laws of physics, it should be theoretically possible to look back in time and understand the various causes of the various events throughout the history of the

Universe. Through an understanding of its causal chain, its form at any time in the past could also be known. This is the history of the Universe.

And if we look forward in time we are sometimes able to predict future events through understanding causality in the past and applying it to the future. However these predictions are not always correct. If the future is necessarily determined by the past in a causal chain, does that mean there is only one way the future can possibly be? That is, necessarily predetermined by the past? Or is there an element of unpredictability? Does the almost infinitely complex web of causal events happening in the Universe right now have an element of random chaos? And so, is the future *not* predetermined? Can anything happen next within the Universe's physical laws? Or is the future ultimately unknowable since it does not yet exist?

★ ★ ★

I opened my eyes. Dawn in a grey city, traffic on a busy road. The German woman's head lay on my lap, centimetres from my throbbing hard-on. The bus suddenly stopped, a Thai man shouting "Bangkok, Bangkok," at the front. We filed out the bus as I rearranged myself, bleary-eyed and confused. We were parked on the edge of a wide road, long shadows arching over the street as taxi drivers touted for fares. No idea where I was. Our bags were thrown out of the storage compartment and I began shuffling off with the herd.

Then I saw Matt from the day before getting off another bus. He said Khao San Road was just through this alleyway. I knew the name. It was the famous backpackers' centre in Bangkok, where the travellers all came when in town. Through some dirty alleyways and we soon arrived, a crowd in tow, a long street with lots of metal shutters locked down, dead neon signs and electric cables hanging in the sky; a few road sweepers dusting the tarmac, handfuls of tired backpackers and a few drunks who hadn't made it home yet.

We had a breakfast beer together in the big Centerpoint Bar, open 24 hours, with tables going out into the street. Time to get a room. There were dozens of signs for cheap-looking guesthouses. I entered a doorway for the promising-sounding Happy Guesthouse. Upstairs was an empty internet shop, except for a gang of ladyboys sitting there who all turned around as I entered. I'd never seen any ladyboys before but I was pretty sure that was what they were. They were all tall and too butch-looking to be girls, sat around in faded makeup and tiny skirts. I avoided eye contact and quickly got a room for just 150 Thai baht. I found the tiny room, locked the door, dropped my bag and passed out.

Beats, crowds, engines and horns blaring, I woke up a few hours later in a room slightly larger than a coffin, hot wind blowing on me from the wall-mounted fan. Took a few moments to remember where I was . . . travelling, Thailand, Bangkok. The walls were a faded white with grime and graffiti everywhere. The door hit the bed when I opened it, giving me just enough room to squeeze out. Down the corridor were shared toilets and shower cubicles – hot, wet and dirty. I guess you get what you pay for.

Outside it was busy now, lots of tourists and Thais milling around the long street, shops, guesthouses and restaurants either side of the road and market stalls in front of them, people weaving their way around, through slow moving motorcycles and *tuk-tuks* – large three-wheeled motorcycle contraptions with a large passenger compartment on the back and a metal roof. Mostly young foreigners everywhere in shorts, beer t-shirts, beach wear, ethnic gear, tattoos, henna paint, piercings, braided hair, shades and beers in hand. This was Khao San Road.

I quickly bumped into Matt, a fast-talking, half-Indian lad from London. He knew his way around, leading me around the back-streets and alley-ways that led off Khao San Road. Through the throngs he told me about his trials and tribulations with a married Thai woman he was in love with who'd gone back to her husband in Spain, all the while passing by various women working in the noodle stores and massage parlours that all knew him. "Matt-hew, Matt-hew," everywhere we went. I liked his style and upbeat banter, dodging round the streets having funny little chit-chats with all the local girls in broken English. He told me he fancied this one on the orange juice stall and this one waitressing in the bar and so on. There seemed to be a lot going on here. I liked it. There was a mad buzz to the place.

We ordered some 15 baht *pad Thai*, stir-fried noodles cooked on a giant wok from a mobile food stall. "*Pet nit noi,*" said Matt. "What's that then?" I asked. "Spicy little bit," he translated. He could speak Thai? He showed me all the condiments to put on top – sugar, chilli powder, fish sauce and sour vinegar. It was delicious – amazing new flavours in every new dish I tried.

He then took me back to the road we'd arrived at that morning, Ratchadamnoen Road which was parallel to Khao San Road, the four large spires of the Democracy Monument in a roundabout to the left. The traffic was manic – cars, trucks, brightly-coloured taxis, motorcycles and *tuk-tuks* competing for any gap in the congestion. We crossed over and came to a massive parade ground where people were playing with kites high above us. In the distance were the magnificent steep rooftops of the Grand Palace, great golden temple spires reaching into the sky.

In the evening I wandered the area observing all the people. Mostly young travellers from the West, but some Japanese and African guys about too. Lots of Thai youngsters taking in the sights and sounds as well. Apparently this is where they came to watch the crazy *farang* at play. I was looking for the remnants of the old hippy trail. There was more braided hair and fisherman pants than you might see elsewhere in the world, but real old school hippies were few and far between. The odd one would float past like a mirage – middle-aged, faded tattoos, leather skin, huge hair and the thousand-yard stare. I wondered where they hung out in the region.

I bumped into Matt again and he took me to the large Wanderers Bar on one corner of Khao San Road, a cavernous, air-conditioned,

US-style bar, full of people playing pool and watching sports on giant TVs. Then a taxi to RCA, a street full of pretty young Thai kids dancing to more manic Asian techno-pop, all the customers dancing around their high tables with their bottles of whiskey and handbags. Back at Khao San Road in the early hours, I went off alone, ever the eager little neon barfly.

I lifted my head off the table, early morning in Centerpoint Bar, people having breakfast all around me. April Fool's Day. I slept it off in my room and was out again, getting sucked into the frantic energy, checking out all the people, eating *pad Thai*, emailing, navigating the back-alleys, taking it all in. Matt left town. I got on better with him than any other people I'd met so far, but everyone was doing their own thing here. New friends would come and go quickly I guessed.

By evening I'm drinking big Beer Changs from the bottle in some sinister little alleyway off Khao San, playing pool with local guys on a torn-up outdoor table. Inside the alleyway was Backstreet Bar, a dark little hole for those in the know. Me and a fake shirt-selling Manc hit the tequilas, eyeing up exotic Israeli girls in Wanderers Bar. Outside on Khao San, the streets were full of ladyboys now, marching along the sidewalks, little black dresses and high heels, calling to scared-looking young men from the shadows, like some scene from Ancient Greek mythology. They were taller and more glamorously-dressed than the real women here. Some were marching up and grabbing innocent guys' crotches in the street and shouting obscenities about asses, cocks and sperm. I headed to the safety of my white box.

★ ★ ★

An old family friend named Bob lived in Pattaya, a big resort town down the coast. I decided to visit him, and took a minibus from a Khao San tour shop the next afternoon with some other solitary males. After an eternity in the Bangkok traffic, we got onto a motorway and after a couple of hours I got out at a long bay in a busy town at night. All I had was Bob's address. I showed it to a tubby Indian tailor, who told me it was on the other side of town near Jomtien Beach.

His friend kindly took me on the back of his motorbike through the busy streets, bars everywhere. A long road curved along the urban coastline, hundreds of street walkers and seedy-looking guys strolling past the palm trees or sitting together on concrete benches in front of the narrow strip of shadowy beach. Off this main road were dozens of side-streets with endless outdoor beer bar complexes. The place was huge. There must have been thousands of girls working here. Most of the customers were middle-aged Western guys. I'd never seen anything like it. I was shocked, disgusted and fascinated in equal measure. This was another side of Thai tourism I hadn't seen before – a destination for international sex tourism.

We went up a steep hill and down to some quiet condominium buildings in the scrubland. I knocked on the random door in the condo building. Luckily Bob was there with his grey barnet and beer belly, slightly shocked to see me. He invited me into his large one room studio. He was living with his Thai girlfriend who was older than me, but at least 20 years younger than him. Her English was as bad as his Thai, but they seemed to have developed their own hybrid language which only they understood. Her cute little three-year-old daughter from her Thai ex-husband was staying there too, running around and playing games.

After catching up we squeezed onto his moped and headed back down the steep hill into Pattaya. Past Arab Town and Boy Town to some go-go bars, where girls danced on stage, some in skimpy outfits, some naked, some performing lesbian sex shows for the guys looking on in silence. To the pink strip lights and beer bars of Central Pattaya, hundreds of them screaming in the street like wild birds of prey, trying to drag me off the motorbike as Bob slowly edged through the crowds. "Hello welcome! Where you go? Handsome man! I want to fuck you!" grabbing each other's tits and giving blowjob gestures with their tongue in their cheek. There seemed to be ten girls for every man in town, waves of dark little girls in even littler skirts luring the guys into the endless bars, with classic rock and Thai pop music blaring out. There were girls everywhere, girls on the beach, girls in the streets, girls in the bars, girls in the discos, girls in the massage parlours, on and on and on, everywhere you looked.

Then to the traffic-free promenade of Walking Street – guys from 18 to 80, hand in hand with local girls, some with gay guys, some with ladyboys, great flashing neon signs for go-go bars and discos everywhere. Every sexuality and proclivity was catered for. Nobody seemed to give a shit what you did here. It was like some kind of wild sexual revolution. I was lost for words, being just two weeks from the sensibilities of home. The town seemed to be a huge open meat market of flesh for sale; a giant palace of Dionysian debauchery.

Inside more go-go bars, hot girls grabbing me with shouts of "Young man!" Pulling me in, sitting with me, purring in my ear, pulling my hand onto their body, grabbing my crotch. But I couldn't do it. Not here like this, with all these sex tourists molesting and licking the girls like overgrown kids playing with little dolls. I looked on, sometimes repulsed, sometimes amused, sometimes tempted by the friendly pretty little things, with their exotic brown skin, long black hair, tight slender bodies, high cheekbones and alluring dark eyes. They were beautiful, it was true. But were they all just acting it up for the guys? They couldn't enjoy being molested, abused and fucked by all these different guys every day. Was it all just for money? Had they come here of their own will or been forced, financially or physically? I had no idea.

The next day Bob showed me the beaches which were pleasant enough, but too developed to compare to those I'd seen in the South. I was getting hooked on the slices of red hot chilli in fish sauce that came with every rice dish, pouring piles of them on my fried rice. We then met various expats Bob knew, most with humungous beer guts, some looking like tough old pirates with long hair, piercings and tattoos everywhere. They seemed like mad men to me, too far gone in this shaggers' pleasure ground. I felt ill, my stomach turning from it. It was all catching up with me.

I got on a public bus back to Bangkok, glad to escape, shocked to know that such a place even existed. My stomach turned again. I'd been having terrible diarrhoea in Pattaya, but now I was stuck on a bus flying down the motorway. My stomach was soon in tatters, pangs of churning rot inside me. Clenching my arse, trying not to let the liquid-acid shit spray out – please not here on a packed bus on the motorway. Couldn't even fart for fear of what might come out. Minutes like hours. Damn signs counting down to Bangkok in slow motion. Bubbles and burns. Hold, hold, hold . . .

We came into Bangkok but the road went on forever, the never-ending traffic creeping along at a snail's pace as the molten fire burnt inside me. We eventually reached the bus station, sphincter tightly gripped. I grabbed my bag, scrambled to find three baht to pay for the toilet, before exploding a torrent of hot brown spray all over the wet squat toilet.

Another hour on a bus across town to Khao San Road. Living cheaply like this wasn't always easy, but I didn't mind too much. The newness and adventure of it all kept my spirits high. Besides, I didn't know where or when I was going to find work. Not sure I really wanted to work just yet either. So I had to make my money last.

★ ★ ★

At one end of Khao San Road was a large, red-roofed temple complex around which ran another street, Soi Rambutri, a *soi* being a smaller lane off a main road. Some called it Khao San Two or Temple Street, pretty similar but more laid-back and funky, with temporary street bars running all the way down the side of the temple walls, bigger bars and guesthouses opposite. I found a room with a big white double bed. I looked at it. I was hot, sweaty, hung-over and horny. Perhaps part of me had enjoyed Pattaya more than I cared to admit.

I drifted into restless horny afternoon dreams. Out again, the sweet promise of the night luring me on. Found a little music pub down a side alley. It was different from the travellers' end of the street. Mostly young Thai university students. I got chatting to a group of five girls, really cute with fair skin and big hairdos, more Chinese-looking than the girls of Pattaya. More shy and polite too, but with basic English. 'Good girls', to use a phrase I'd heard the expats use. We smiled and chatted a while until I got one girl's mobile number and they all left.

More dehydration, dry mouth and diarrhoea in the morning. It was becoming hard work. Checking my emails every day, I knew Adam was back in town. I tracked him down and we wandered the streets together. We kept bumping into people we'd met down south the week before. It seemed that everybody travelling the country intersected here at this one crazy street. Adam told me about a place called Nana Plaza, full of bars and girls. We took a taxi along with the laid-back Swede from Hat Yai and the Irish guy from Ao Nang.

We turned the corner to see a three-story open courtyard of red neon lights and girls everywhere. Around the sides of the courtyard were walkways in front of dozens of bars, like some shopping centre of flesh. Girls screaming at us and dragging us in their bars with all their force. Once three of them got hold of you, you couldn't get away. Before you knew it, you were thrown through the thick black curtains and into the musty go-go bar, girls in bikinis, short skirts, uniforms and leather gear dancing on stage, disco lights and mirrors everywhere, other girls sitting with the ogling guys on soft padded seating round the edge.

We explored every floor, beer-soaked, dim lights, feeling more comfortable now, the disgust I felt in Pattaya fading. Some would sit with me. Little chit chat. "What you name? Where you come from? You very handsome man!" And then the illicit touch, the hand on my thigh, mine down their lean back, their knee, their thigh, skin smoother than silk, that killer smile, gyrating on my crotch, dick twitching, gstring and ass bouncing, horny like a dog now, the cup of the breast, the temptation, the promise, the ease, the prize . . .

Another day in the relentless humidity of Bangkok. I saw Adam off before exploring with the Swedish guy. To MBK, a big shopping centre in Siam Square in the middle of Bangkok selling everything cheap – clothes, CDs, DVDs, mobile phones, technology and handicrafts. Back at Khao San, I had a traditional Thai massage with a young girl, grinding my muscles hard into the floor, whispering sweet nothings in my ear. Everything was for sale here.

Then bar to bar again, talking crap to anyone that would listen, smiling at the girls, loving the buzz, the energy, the madness of the place. I was getting good at it now, just like Matt. Ambling round on my own, chatting to everyone, no more nerves and worries. My confidence was growing. I could move around, get by and have fun on my own now. It was all just a simple matter of will. I just had to overcome my little fears and do it.

End of the night, stumbling drunk down Rambutri trying to get home, I sat in one of the street bars by the temple wall. Quiet now, just a few lone men drinking in the shadows. A pretty girl called Daeng worked there, pouring my beer, sitting with me, rubbing my hand with ice, smiling, no need to speak much. She was 22 like me, cute eyes, a shy but cheeky grin and a mop of thick black hair. I slipped into a luxuriant sea of warm pleasures looking into her smiling eyes. "Watch out for that one mate," some idiot tourist remarked. But I ignored him. I wanted her and she wanted me. By 5am, everyone had left, the tables were folded up, and Daeng followed me over the lane to my room. Just like that. I was smitten.

I went to a travel agent the next day. There were dozens of tour shops in the area, offering cheap bus tickets and flights around the world. The girl in the shop started flirting with me. This place was crazy! Women flirting with me everywhere I went! Could I live and work here in Bangkok? I liked it, but it was a bit too much! I got a ticket for the night train to the northern city of Chiang Mai.

That afternoon I met up with the shy student I'd met a few days earlier, along with a load of her friends. They were all students at Thammasat University, near the parade ground of Sanam Luang and the Grand Palace. They showed me round the campus, but we didn't have much to say to each other. Suddenly she said goodbye and jumped in a taxi. I strolled round Sanam Luang under the kites. A huge procession was going past on Ratchadamnoen Road, full of fantastic floats, dancers and elephants in colourful paint and dress. I felt a sense of being in a proud nation, with a strong sense of self-identity, the only country in Southeast Asia never to have been colonised. But it was time to go. I grabbed my bag, saying goodbye to various girls on Rambutri, *tuk-tuk* to the station, found my train, and soon we were off into the night.

★ ★ ★

I awoke to the beautiful sight of light morning mist over tropical hills as the train wound through the jungle. It was a good old-fashioned train, chugging along slowly, the toilet just a hole onto the tracks. The windows pulled down, so you could stick your head out and feel the world rushing past your face. Morning rose in the quiet countryside. Green paddy fields clothed the hills, the occasional worker stooped over or sitting in ramshackle wooden shelters in the fields, great trees rising up through the river valleys. The train kept stopping in the middle of nowhere, food vendors coming in and shouting everyone awake with drinks and bits of meat on sticks. But I didn't mind. Not with all this beauty around me.

I daydreamed through the morning – going into the jungle and back in time. Coming out of a dark tunnel, I was suddenly smacked across the face by a wall of water coming through an open window. I looked around shocked, the whole carriage laughing at me. This was my first taste of the Songkran festival, a Buddhist religious festival that apparently involved everybody throwing water on each other. It wasn't due to begin for another week yet I thought, being in the middle of April at the height of the hot season. Perhaps those modern trains aren't so bad after all.

As we came down the hill into town, I pictured myself sitting on the train, a stranger in a strange land. I liked this new romantic notion of myself, the lone wanderer arriving in town to mix things up a bit, a man with no name, crossing frontiers, making things happen.

I arrived in the city, much smaller and quieter than Bangkok. Was this to be my new home? A *tuk-tuk* took me to Suthep Guesthouse, a pretty wooden place with local art everywhere, a large courtyard and cheap rooms. The place appeared to be run by a middle-aged ladyboy and her family, though I wasn't quite sure. The other guests were friendly but were quieter and much more sedate compared to those I'd met elsewhere, hanging around all day, reading, playing cards and drinking fruit shakes.

I explored the peaceful streets lined with beautiful old temples and traditional houses, many made of wood in the local Lanna style, with steep, intricately-carved wooden roofs. Outside every building were ornate spirit houses, built like miniature temples elevated off the ground, highly decorated with fresh offerings of food, drink, incense and flowers. They served as homes for animistic spirits to keep them from living in the human dwellings.

I carried on, past the moats and remains of crumbling brick walls that formed a large square around the old town. Past Thapae Gate on the east wall, various tourist restaurants, handicrafts and tour shops advertising treks into the mountains and hill tribe villages. It all seemed a world away from Bangkok and the beaches of the South.

By evening I was at the Night Bazaar, where all manner of locally made handicraft were sold to well-heeled tourists. I bought a cheap white shirt and a tie and trudged the long walk back to my guesthouse in the old town. That sinking feeling had returned. That old loneliness from Malaysia had found me again, trudging the streets alone all day, a stranger in a strange land. I wasn't used to it, that all-day silence.

Thoughts came into my head, but as I had no one to share them with, they'd evaporate, never taking physical form beyond the neurons in my brain.

The next day I woke up the freshest I'd been since I arrived in the country. Chiang Mai seemed a liveable city, so I got hold of a list of language schools, put my new shirt on, hired a motorbike, got a map and sped off. I felt that rush of freedom from being on the bike again. It felt natural to me, but I had things to do.

Finding my way wasn't easy. Any locals I asked would look at the map like it was of some Martian rock formations. But I found three language schools, entering them apprehensively, turning up unannounced hoping for work. The first said I needed some experience. The second gave me a written application test which I couldn't do very well. The third told me to dress up a bit smarter. They all said the supply for English teachers in Chiang Mai outstripped demand since so many foreigners wanted to live here. And the wages were far lower than Bangkok. In truth I didn't really fancy it either. All the talk of grammar, teaching methodologies and schedules was killing my buzz.

The throttle was burning a hole in my hand too, so at 4pm I shot off out the city, the wind pulling against me. I'd seen a road on a map that went around Doi Suthep, the big mountain that loomed to the west of the city. I went north for a few kilometres and then took a left down a winding country road and up into the hills. I saw a wet patch of road up ahead in a village, kids playing, buckets of water, Songkran again, surely not . . . *bang*! Buckets of water hit my face like heavyweight punches as I zoomed along. Nobody seemed too concerned about innocent people coming off their bikes. I should've been angry, but instead I couldn't stop laughing! I laughed at the glorious madness of this new upside down world I was immersed in.

The road weaved round the hills and forests, past waterfalls and along a serene mountain side, the Sun setting in the mist ahead. I danced with the bike, bobbing left and right around the bends happily, till it struck me that it was going to be dark soon. I was a novice on the bike and I'd never driven at night before, and here I was stuck on the other side of Doi Suthep Mountain.

My nerves rose with the darkness, my hands tightly clenched as I navigated the thin mountain road in the black, looking to the occasional light from any source to guide me round the shadowy bends and pickup trucks rushing out of the darkness from nowhere. It was tricky but I concentrated and made it back okay.

I bummed around the guesthouse the next day. The outrageous ladyboy boss appeared to be married to one of the guys, but I wasn't sure who the younger members of the family belonged to. It was all very confusing. But they were all friendly and cracking jokes all the time. I got chatting to a few other backpackers in the guesthouse, keeping those stupid lonely feelings at bay. Everyone was very warm, relaxed and friendly. I decided to sign up for an all-inclusive three day trek the next day along with some of the people I'd met.

★ ★ ★

We loaded our bags into the back of the big truck early in the morning. Then shopping for supplies at a supermarket, kids trying their best to drench us with massive water guns. I took in my new companions in the group. There were couples of various ages, from the UK, Holland, Belgium and Canada, and some lone guys from the USA and Australia; about fifteen in all, plus two local guides. None of us seemed to have much in common on the surface. I stood up on the little metal platform at the back of the truck and hung on tight where I could see the city die away into the country.

First we went to an elephant camp in the forest. Pairs of us sat on the back of the great animals. It was slightly worrying at first being so high up on the largest land animal on Earth, but despite the wobbles the elephants moved surprisingly delicately. Apparently thousands of elephants once worked in construction and the military, but now work and numbers had dwindled, tourism being one of the places where they could make money and support their massive upkeep costs.

The truck soon went off-road up a dirt track, and eventually we were dropped off at the end of a trail into the jungle. I didn't know what to expect. Soon we were hiking up through the undergrowth along narrow trails, tough going in the humid summer Sun. Trekking in a long line, I tried to stay near the front away from the crowd to take in the scenery better and avoid all the chit-chat. We climbed uphill past great trees and bamboo woods, crunching through the dried leaves, over gnarled tree roots, sunlight breaking through the canopy, insects clicking and whooshing past, the forests alive with invisible sounds. I spoke to our guide Gon about the jungle, hill tribes, his work and asked him what the Thai words were for everything I could see. He was about 35 with a small body and pot belly, but bounded up the mountain quicker than any of us.

We eventually reached a large clearing free of foliage. On the other side, perched on a ridge, was a village of basic wooden huts. As we approached along the muddy ridge, caked in sweat and dirt, dozens of grubby little kids came running along to greet us excitedly, smiling and taking our plastic water guns from Chiang Mai. I couldn't believe how many kids there were up here in the wilderness, over 1000 metres high. It was like some valley of lost children. We reached the Lahu hill tribe village and the long dorm hut they'd made for the frequent groups of backpackers. The Lahu were one of various tribes that had migrated south from Tibet and China over the last few centuries. These groups were now nationless people living in remote hill areas of Burma and Northern Thailand, Laos and Vietnam.

I looked round the village. It was basic – wooden huts thrown together on a ridge, big drops either side. But they had a drainage system and a few TV aerials. The people were small and tough-looking, but with friendly smiles and a beguiling curiosity. There were cute young kids in dirty clothes running around everywhere, playing and laughing. Chickens, dogs and pigs sniffing around in the dirt and undergrowth. We said hello to all and saw the simple school and shop they had. I'd never seen anything like it, this rustic village up on the misty mountain ridge. It was the poorest place I'd ever seen in my life, cut off from the modern world, a simple way of life that all civilisations had emerged from – people living off the land, sustenance farmers of the forests. And yet their way of life seemed to have such an intrinsic beauty, untouched and unburdened by the madness of modernity, the people happy and strong, a good life, people of the earth, pure and simple. Then I remembered there were groups like us coming through the village every few days. Were we destroying the very way of life we'd come to visit?

As the day fell the village was blacker than night, just a few lights inside the huts and our torches to guide us along the muddy paths. We all ate dinner together around the camp fire and some kids came out in traditional black and red costumes to sing and dance for us. We were swigging local Mekong whiskey from the bottle. I stood up to buy more drinks from the shop up the hill, but Gon warned me it might be dangerous. Inside our dorm hut some guests were having traditional massages from the local women. I had one from an elderly-looking woman, lying in the corner of the dark hut on my front, listening to the indecipherable sounds of the Lahu language as I swigged the last of the whiskey. A final smoke outside by the embers of the fire, as storm clouds rolled and hollered beyond, a mysterious gong echoing from the invisible hills. I'd never felt so far from home in all my life.

The mountain chill woke me at 6am. I got up excitedly. Only the assistant guide was up. He told me of a fight and gunshot in the village last night. Not quite the idyllic country life I imagined then, but I was still enthralled by it, as I peered around the lanes alone before the others were up, cocks singing their morning call in the thick swirling clouds of dawn. Up to a monk's house and the water tanks at the top of the village, saying hello to the three generations of women in the shop, their faces differentiated only by age. The others emerged, looking less polished than the day before. We had coffee, breakfast and continued.

Part of me wished they would go on without me. I imagined living in the village with these people, learning all I could from them as I explored the forests and joined their community. These great people of the land, living as all our forefathers once did, retaining an essential link to nature that has faded and virtually died for us modern urbanites, fiddling with our mobile phones and digital cameras, worrying about our creams and sprays. I felt some strange connection to them. Though we could not speak, our common humanity still allowed for smiles, jokes and an exchange of information. We still had the same wiring in our heads and hearts despite all the differences. Meeting these people, the furthest removed from home I'd ever met, touched me more than I'd expected.

I was pleased when I saw that we were being joined by some people from the village. An old man with three dogs and a big stick led the way. Three girls were going with Gon to see the Songkran festival, and a smiling 16-year-old deaf and mute lad tagged along too. Our new group continued down the other side of the hill, along valleys, through patches of bamboo and banana trees, the sounds of cicada bugs cutting through the undergrowth like whirling sirens. The old man and the young lad went off ahead at their own speed with the dogs following. I decided to test myself and try to keep up with them. I could just about manage it but they were half my size and hopping along easily, whereas I was practically jogging, huffing and puffing in a desperate sweat, and concentrating on every step so not to twist my ankles on the rocks. We descended a green open valley to a village of the Karen tribe. I sat in a wooden shelter with the two Lahu men in purple, surrounded by the red-robed Karen tribesmen for 15 long minutes, feeling pleased with myself, until the others caught up and my little mountain fantasy ceased to be.

We went on through sparse poppy fields to a waterfall. Most of the poppy fields had gone now since the authorities cracked down on the opium trade in the Golden Triangle area to the north, bordering Laos and Burma. More kids from the Lahu village arrived, splashing in the waterfall's pool below and we bounced on the trunk of a great fallen tree. Nearby was our purpose-built camp of sturdy huts.

As night drew, I watched the bright glow of fireflies hovering around the canopy and the gushing rhythms of the waterfall in this serene corner of nature. I heard noises coming from one of the huts and entered to see Gon and about half of the tour group sitting in a ring, quietly drinking and smoking. A tiny old hill tribe man with a tight wrinkled face lay huddled up in the corner, feeding pipe after pipe of opium to the tourists. I had never come across it before. My turn came and Gon told me to lie on my side and suck as the old man lit up the long metal pipe. I waited for the rocket launch, but it didn't come. Quite the opposite. I sank down onto the floor, relaxed and calm.

The tourists took it in turns sucking on the smoke for hours. Everyone relaxed and friendly, listening to Gon's strange stories. He said he used to be addicted to opium but had quit, before lying on his side for another blast. "Same same but different . . . " he smiled as he got up, eyes glazed. I'd heard this phrase a few times from the locals. "Same same but different, not same, same same but not same. Different meaning." My head spun, trying to make sense of his words, the country, its ways and peculiarities seemingly impossible to comprehend. If I could understand the difference between same same but different, and same same but not same, perhaps I would be some way to understanding the culture of this perplexing country. Maybe . . . I wanted to know the reasons why it was so different here. Their smiles, openness and friendliness, the relaxed attitudes of the people, the lack of aggression or confrontation, their apparent disregard for danger. Everything was so different, so bewitching here . . . and I loved it.

I slept like a baby and was the last one up the next day, still hazy from the hut with the old silent pipe stoker. Descending the mountain we jumped along the rocks of a dry river bed, until we reached a path above a steep lush valley, a river running below. The path descended smoothly to the riverbank where we reached a rafting centre.

After some shots of sweet intoxicating rice whiskey, I went down with a couple, flying through little rapids, avoiding rocks till suddenly I was flying head-first into the spikes of a broken tree stump sticking out of the water. I moved my head out the way at the last second. Another close call. These close calls seemed to be pretty regular occurrences out here.

We then transferred to long bamboo rafts that floated two inches under the water once we boarded them, and glided down the lower section of the river, trying to steer with long bamboo poles. As the river opened and the waters calmed, more and more local people appeared, smiling happily, wading and splashing water at us gently from the river, greeting us for the real start of the Songkran festival, marking the beginning of the lunar New Year.

★ ★ ★

Squeezed into the truck driving back together, thousands of Thais with huge containers of water lined the roads all the way back, throwing buckets and hosing down passing motorists. Whenever the traffic stopped moving we were attacked by smiling families in bright shirts pouring water on us, kids firing their water pistols. Pickup trucks full of water containers and people were driving round too, attacking each other and groups on the side of the road. Thai country music and pop blaring out from all over the place, people necking whiskey and beer, dancing round freely. The whole country was having a water fight and partying together. Everyone happy, smiling, having fun everywhere you looked. We were in the Land of Smiles and it was infectious.

Once in Chiang Mai we had to abandon our vehicle because of the endless crowds. The streets were overrun with jubilant people playing around, shooting water guns, smearing white paste over each other's faces and avoiding the water containers full of ice which were being poured down people's necks when they weren't looking, sending their bodies into spine-tingling spasms in the 35 degree heat. We got out and zigzagged through the crowds like sitting ducks. But after three days sweating in the jungle, it was a sweet relief to be soaked in the searing hot Sun of the tropics.

Back at the guesthouse, the owners greeted us warmly, feeding us more rice whiskey as we watched the procession of people parade by. Occasionally an elaborately-decorated float would come by with a Buddha statue, the Thais falling silent and gently cleansing it with water, reminding us of the religious basis of the festival, that of cleansing the ills of the previous year, paying respect to others, and merit-making for the coming year. I gazed at all the smiling, happy people, dancing and partying together as one, playing in the water, always greeting each other by holding their hands together by their face in a prayer-like motion called a *wai*, signalling mutual respect. It was all so . . . idyllic. Something was happening to me. I was falling in love. Not with a person, but with a country. I could feel my grand travelling plans evaporating. I didn't want to go anywhere else. I was in love with Thailand, in love with everything about it. At that moment of consecration I vowed to stay in the country until Songkran next year.

Three days of Songkran madness ensued. Booze for breakfast, the party already in full swing. Me and the others from the trek would load up and hit the streets. Bottle of Mekong whiskey in my back pocket and a water pistol in my hand. Dancing the streets, getting soaked by hoses, buckets and water pistols, chalky white paste splattered all over me, slipping around in my flip-flops, grinning ear to ear like a big kid as my childhood dream of a massive water fight had finally come true. Across to the large square in front of Thapae Gate in the middle of town, people in every direction, soaking wet, splattered in paste, grinning and dancing, kids swimming in the moat and dragging water out in buckets to fill their huge water guns. A stage was playing hard house, four to the floor, people jumping and dancing together in joy, girls on guys' shoulders, people hugging, hands wandering. My memories faded with the setting Sun, jumping on the backs of random people's motorbikes, laughing and drinking with anybody I saw.

On the final afternoon at the Thapae Gate house stage, a pretty young Thai girl was dancing with me, protecting me from her horny young gay friends. Her name was Nok, 19 years old, beautiful and elegant with long black straight hair and a wide smile. We danced and drank and joked, my mind spinning around my body from the Songkran exhilaration. Next thing I was on a motorbike with her and her comedic little friend Bow, back to my guesthouse, through the courtyard, everyone looking at us, in my room, Bow disappears, and me and Nok are all over each other, kissing, ripping off wet clothes on wet flesh, her beautiful young body, mad, wet, drunken, passionate sex.

I lay there dazed for a moment in post-coital stupor, a gormless grin on my face. It didn't get any better than this. O blessed land! I was in love! Bow returned and we were off again, to Nok's older sister's condo she shared with her polite young Japanese boyfriend. And then to Space Disco, a tacky but fun place, a mixed crowd of locals and foreigners. I held Nok close to me, memories hazy, Bow going off with a Swiss guy she knew, till eventually Nok came home with me again.

I awoke in my new wonderland with the beautiful Nok in my arms. Smiling, joking, kissing, chatting. I couldn't keep my hands off her. She spoke English well, with a slight American twang from the teachers at her language school she said. She was a waitress in a restaurant near Thapae Gate. She was charming, polite, passive and sweet. Bow came round again and I lay back listening to them chat together in their floating Northern Thai dialect, tones rising and falling in sweet symphony. It sounded like sweet bird song to me that morning. I loved it here – the simple beauties of life sprinkling down on me like a sparkling fountain of mountain dew.

Apparently the Swiss guy had rebuffed Bow's advances the night before, but she was still infatuated. Funny little Bow, yapping, scrapping and joking like a naughty little poodle! We spent the whole day driving on their motorbike; to restaurants, their place, the Swiss guy's place, her sister's place. It should've been boring but it wasn't. I was just happy to be here in this beautiful land with a beautiful girl in my beautiful new life. They told me their full names, Thai people tending to have very long full names but short nicknames which they are usually known by. They talked about Chiang Mai and Songkran and the mysterious mountains beyond. They talked and talked and I listened.

The next day started the same – panting, lusty sex in the intense midday heat, the fan whirring uselessly as sweat rained off my face onto Nok's glistening honey body. We were happy and relaxed together, lying in each other's sweat-soaked naked bodies. We caught up with Bow and her guy, but she was piss drunk already, a sloppy, angry drunk. But she was Nok's best friend so she was part of the deal it seemed.

We went to a quiet beer bar complex near the Night Bazaar, seedy-looking bar girls and ladyboys mingling around. They all knew Nok and Bow. My thoughts began diverging from their previous course of blind contentment. Another little disco by the moat, full of hookers, ladyboys and Western guys. I don't like it. Nok wants to dance to some boy band crap. I don't want to, so she turns her nose up at me, that sweet smile turning to a nasty sneer as she goes off and dances near a load of guys. Meanwhile Bow is shitfaced, can barely stand up, the straight-laced Swiss guy struggling to cope with her. I'm angry, bored and jealous. I try to dance but Nok tells me to sit down and look after her bag. What the fuck! I nearly walk off, but . . . something keeps me there. At 2am I grab Nok and we all stagger to my room bitterly, the Swiss guy carrying the unconscious Bow on his shoulder, much to the shock of the card-playing backpackers of Suthep Guesthouse. He dumps her on my bed and storms off. A shitfaced Nok suddenly perks up. "I want to go to Space," she slurs. I look in disbelief at the monster she's transformed into. In the end only the arrival of Bow's sobs and wails stop her.

I didn't sleep well, pushed to the end of the bed by the two little devils. Bow left quickly in the morning and I argued with Nok, her only explanation being that she was drunk. I wasn't happy, seeing her for who she really was for the first time. But I forgave her and we screwed again all the same.

People had been telling me about nearby Laos as some kind of serene, unspoilt, travellers' paradise. I wasn't sure I'd even heard of it before I came to Asia, but it sounded intriguing. I went to the Immigration Office with Nok and got a 10 day extension to the 30 day visa I'd received when I crossed from Malaysia.

Sober now, I felt a little embarrassed walking around with this stroppy Thai girl, past the staring eyes of the other backpackers. In the eyes of some, a Thai girl and Western guy together meant only one thing – prostitute and sex tourist. I didn't feel like that was us, but their stares and frowns still made me question myself. I was sure Nok wasn't telling me everything about herself. The same Western boys' names kept cropping up when she spoke to her friends, clear as crystal in amongst the words of a language I didn't understand. And her English seemed slightly *too* good as well. Too fluent, too well practised I thought. As we waited for my passport to be returned at Immigration I told her straight. "I don't trust you." An hour of tense silence ensued.

That night in some outdoor hippy bar, the dreadlocked waiter clearly knew her intimately as well, joking and flirting with Nok in Thai. Another ex it seemed. A pretty young friend of hers named Nut was with a handsome Australian guy. He'd been in Thailand for two months which gave him exactly double my experience. He was trying to decipher their long animated conversations too, the occasional word he thought he knew in Thai, *farang* this, *farang* that, boys' names and bits of English thrown into their stories, like "Oh my God," and "Hello, what your name?" and "You're very beautiful!"

I kept hearing the word 'butterfly'. I asked the Australian guy what it meant. He told me in hushed tones around the crackling fire, as the girls watched us suspiciously. "Butterflies are girls that fly from man to man, like a butterfly from flower to flower. They're not working girls; they just do it for the fun of it and whatever else happens to come their way. Have your fun mate, but you can't trust 'em." He'd confirmed my suspicions exactly. Now I thought about it, she'd jumped into bed with me only two hours after we'd first met! Does she do that with every guy she meets? She'd told me I was only the second guy she'd ever slept with. Suddenly it seemed ludicrous! But I wasn't giving her any money. What did she want from me? Did she really just like me for who I was? I thought so, but . . .

Nok behaved herself the rest of the night, but began questioning me the next day about my conversation with Nut's boyfriend. She suggested I get a job here in Chiang Mai and then we could live together. My mind was reeling from the events of the last few days – the whirlwind romance, the flip side of the coin and last night's realisations. A pang in my heart told me to cut my losses and run, but soon we were making love again and again, the uncontrollable passions of youth too great to resist, used condoms and greasy bits of packet strewn all over the floor.

Lust spent, my mind turned again and I confronted her, demanding to know the truth about her life. We argued and she took off the ring on her finger from an old boyfriend and threw it away to show her love for me. We shut up and made up, going for a romantic evening dinner in a beautiful wooden restaurant by the river. I knew I was an idiot falling for her again and again. I knew she was a butterfly, but she was so damn good at it. When the smiles and purrs returned after the arguments and silence, it melted my little heart every time.

The next day I found myself stuck at her sister's condo in another gaggle of girly chat, the drunk Bow showing off to me in English, telling me about all her boyfriends around the world. Nok was cringing in silence, winking at her to stop, but Bow thought it was hysterical. The atmosphere with her older sister and her silent Japanese boyfriend was tense too. He never said a word to anyone. I couldn't follow a word of any conversation or the strange Thai TV shows. I asked myself what I was doing here, another mug being led around by these little crap-spouting teens.

Some more friends from home were arriving in Thailand. I decided to make a break for it. Late afternoon I told Nok I was leaving to meet my friends in Bangkok. Luckily she accepted my decision calmly. I checked out and waited at the guesthouse with Nok for my bus to arrive. She was getting annoyed at me as I could hardly contain my excitement at leaving. I quickly kissed her goodbye outside the guesthouse and told her I would come back for her. The bus dropped me off at another guesthouse. Another two hour wait and I was on the big VIP backpacker bus out of town, free and happy.

The long drive into the night again, the city giving way to the rhythmic passing of the motorway lights, and soon the blackness of the natural world. I looked out into the faint night, more long hours of contemplation. Just over a month since leaving home now. From Kuala Lumpur to the beaches of Southern Thailand, the steamy metropolis of Bangkok and the misty mountain tops of the North. I felt like I'd been away for so long and done so much already. But in fact I'd barely even begun. I'd had some adventures, some ups and downs on the tourist trail, but I wanted more. I wanted to get involved, to scratch the surface. I had a strong feeling things were going to go a whole lot higher yet. I'd wanted adventure and I'd got what I wanted so far. You usually do get what you want in life. What you really want.

★ ★ ★

Our Universe expanded into being from a state of extreme heat and density with unknowable power and force. Gravity and other forces separated and the density and heat inflated exponentially – billions of light years in trillionths of a second – in a plasma of quarks, gluons and other elementary particles. These particles became matter and anti-matter, and as the Universe expanded and cooled further the energy of the particles decreased; matter dominated over anti-matter and within its first second of existence the nature of the Universe was set – as space-time, matter, energy and the physical laws that govern them. Quarks and gluons combined to form protons and neutrons. Protons and neutrons combined into deuterium and helium nuclei, protons forming into hydrogen nuclei. Gradually electro-magnetic radiation decoupled from matter, the electrons and nuclei forming into hydrogen and other atoms, and the radiation photons travelling transparently, light pouring forth unto the Universe.

It continued to expand homogenously, until tiny quantum fluctuations led to slightly denser areas of matter attracting other matter in their gravitational field, circulating into giant gas clouds of particles, plasma gases, and atoms of hydrogen and helium. Some of these areas then collapsed under their own gravity, creating massive balls of plasma as the first stars were born. Thermonuclear fusion in these stars created heavier new elements of matter like carbon, oxygen and iron, and radiated energy and light into outer space. Stars clustered together from these clouds of matter forming giant galaxies. Black holes of massive gravitational force were formed, pulling more matter in. Gravity brought these galaxies together into gigantic galaxy clusters, billions of stars in each. And between these stars and galaxies lay huge areas of space, this space increasing as the Universe continued to expand.

TWO

Dumped my bag in some horrific sweatbox with concrete walls, graffiti and mosquito meshing around the roof, like the VIP suite at the Bangkok Hilton. Did some figures of eight up Soi Rambutri, around the temple and down Khao San Road, saying hello to the orange juice sellers, massage girls and travel agents. Saw the sexy Daeng, the lubricious girl I slept with last time, promising to meet her later. I took my friends from home out for dinner, before stumbling round Rambutri in the early hours searching for Daeng. I found her sat on some blond, body-building Germanic guy's lap, both looking happy about it. So that was that.

I investigated Rambutri the next morning looking for a better room, and came across Papaya Guesthouse. The front had a nice, Old West-style restaurant and bar with plants and a fish pond. A few familiar-looking long-termers were propping the bar up with their shabby clothes, stubble and vacant red-eyed stares. The rooms were windowless wooden coffins with stained old sheets and a wall-fan. That came as standard at this price. But the building was more homely and quieter than Khao San.

More laps, *pad Thai* and emails, before seeing my friends off on the bus to Ko Phangan. They were going down for the next Full Moon Party in a few days' time. It seemed to be every new arrival's destination of choice.

I'd arranged to meet that crazy English guy Martin from Hat Yai. He had experience so seemed like a good man to know. He was just as intense and bitter as before, but obviously still liked it here. He took me to his favourite bar on Rambutri which I'd never noticed before. East Gate Bar had a restaurant downstairs but if you walked through it and up the stairs at the back there was a dark grungy wooden place, with seats and a pool table inside, and a long outdoor balcony bar overlooking the *soi*. The bar was in the middle of the balcony so everyone sat around it facing each other. Good design for the solo piss artist because everyone ends up chatting to each other after a few drinks. It had a sociable, boozy atmosphere, Thais and foreigners mixing freely. Local hustlers, some ageing tarts and mad-head backpackers. Most of the crowd had a bit of a mad edge in their eyes in fact.

Hours flowed by, from the bar to the urinals and back again. Martin gave me the low down on teaching in Bangkok and various other areas that impinged upon his paranoia. Eventually I'm wandering around outside, looking for Daeng again to no avail. One of her colleagues that looked uncannily like Alice the Goon from the Popeye cartoons sat me down and got me a beer. I was drifting in and out of consciousness, waking up to finish my beer and spout crap to my fellow crap-spouters. A friendly hand took pity on me and led me down an alley to some rough slum housing behind the main street, up some stairs and into her room. She smiled, made some kind of nasal snort of approval and lunged at me with a gummy kiss, saying said she'd be back in a bit. I collapsed on the pillow.

Morning. I was next to Alice in a dingy white-painted wooden room. Alice seemed rather pleased with last night's catch, giggling and prodding me as I lay incapacitated in her lair. I briefly considered a response, but she wasn't really doing it for me. Then another woman from the street bar comes in and they start chatting away happily as my head spins. Next thing, some starry-eyed moon child Canadian girl comes in, all stoned grin and fake dreadlocks, quickly followed by some skinny drugged up English nutter. They all started skinning up as I lay there in my pants. The English loon went to pass me his joint. "No thanks mate." I got up quickly, clothes on, pocket check, down the rickety stairs, through the corridors, adjoining rooms in all directions with Thai guys sitting around in pants, and made my escape into the streets, laughing with relief.

The next night I decided to check out the famous Patpong area.

Apparently the go-go bars in the area were developed to cater for American GIs on R&R during the Vietnam War. Straight out the taxi there were Thai guys coming up to me. "Hello Mister. Pussy show, ping-pong show, banana show, dart show . . . " The place was packed full of tourists; not just sex tourists but curious tourists of all ages. The street had a heaving market right down the middle selling all kinds of knock-off gear – clothes, accessories, handbags, luggage, DVDs, metal weapons and novelty crap. Either side, dozens more go-go bars, same as the others I'd seen, but full of in-your-face touts outside. Inside, the girls more predatory, asking for drinks as soon as I got in, bills higher than they should be. In fact the more I looked at the girls, the more certain I was that half of them, or possibly all of them, were ladyboys. I couldn't quite tell. They all looked about six foot tall up on stage, with legs forever and massive silicone breasts. Time to split.

Another dry mouth, coffin lid hangover. My head jangled over the alternatives. Let's get out of here. Full Moon's coming. Another time-wasting afternoon and I was on the bus south again. I got chatting to an interesting guy, a true independent spirit, who told me of his travels down the archipelago of Indonesia. It sounded like a dream trip, off the beaten track, hopping from island to island, from Bangkok all the way to the Pacific. He also told me about meditation retreats he'd done in Thailand. Two weeks spent living simply in the temple grounds, helping out, studying and then all day meditating. I knew nothing about it. I didn't know visitors could do such things. He said they had to sit on the floor alone, trying to clear the mind, or think of nothing, or not think. I wasn't sure exactly what it was. He said that after a while meditating, distant long-forgotten memories would reappear, and withheld emotions were unearthed, breaking out in waves of uncontrollable tears and then hysterical laughter. I was amazed and kind of intrigued at the same time. Perhaps there were powers of the mind I knew nothing about yet.

★ ★ ★

After another rough night on the dark bouncing bus, I'm compensated at dawn by the morning ferry floating over the warm tropical seas, pristine islands and bright colours shining. Back to the islands. I found my companions on a shallow-watered beach on the south coast of the island, happy to be around old friends and relax in their easy company on the tranquil coast.

It didn't last long, that short respite. The next day, back of a pick-up truck, up the steep curves to Hat Rin. The Full Moon Party was here again. Got hold of some party ammunition and we were off again, bar to bar, on the beach, dodging the crowds, losing each other, losing ourselves, UV suns painted on my arm and back and a garland of purple flowers around my neck.

Down to the beach for sunrise but it was cloudier this time. My friends went home. I only had 50 baht and a diet pill in my pocket. I could've gone home with them of course. But I didn't. Not now. I was getting used to being alone now. No . . . more than that. I enjoyed it. I was starting to get good at it, in fact. I carried on alone.

I'd heard the real party didn't get going till the morning when all the drunks had gone home, leaving the hardcore party people to carry on. I found a bar just off the beach playing early '90s piano house – K-Klass, *Break Of Dawn* by Rhythm on the Loose and Gat Decor's seminal *Passion*. I was happy on my feet, dancing in the rising sunlight, seeing the smiles on people's faces turn from dark orange to yellow and then a bright, toothy effervescence.

Some Thai guy came over and bought me a beer. He seemed cool. We were all the beautiful, groovy, morning party crew dancing together to the bouncing beats and life-affirming piano chords. Said his name was Noddy; little stubbly guy in a vest.

About 10am I went up to Chicken Corner in the middle of Hat Rin village, tanned travellers with no shirts trying to drive off-road bikes through the crowds. I jumped on the back of a Swede's bike, who took me up a dusty hill following the beat, up to a large bar on the edge of a cliff. This was the legendary Cliff Top Bar I'd been told to head to. A big open-sided wooden auditorium overlooking the shining blue seas across the water to Ko Samui. This was where the cream of the crop came to face off the day after the Full Moon. The party crew, the mash heads, the fucking hardcore! Everyone off their face, staggering around, dancing or swaying from foot to foot, blissed-out couples all over each other, others drinking and smoking on the floor, people passed out, strictly for the nutters, the blessed and the damned. Straight in, everyone's your best friend. "Alright mate, what's your name, how ya doin'?" shaking hands, hugging and kissing, everyone knows everyone, dancing round with the sea and the sky and the non-stop psychedelic beats, digital waves sending minds into mental worm-holes.

Saw Noddy again. I could tell he was gay, but he kept coming over and handing me Heinekens from time to time, telling me not to worry about it. Then he stuffed half a pill in my mouth when I wasn't looking. I told him I didn't have any money on me and I wasn't gay, but he just laughed and went off dancing with his friends. So I carried on. How could I leave? I was in the best club in the best country in the world, loving every second of it with all my new friends. That strange familiarity the E gives you with everyone, dancing together for hours like you've known each other all your lives, but you've never spoken to them. I looked at girls dancing and fell in love with them, their eyes and forms. I could feel their thoughts and emotions. My eyes flitted uncontrollably. Some smiled at me, but I was too mashed to form words now. Every so often, another little acrid pill would appear in my mouth with another ice cold Heineken. So I carried on, hours and hours, nowhere I'd rather be, no need to leave, darkness fell, night again, what day is it? Hazy, eyes closing, consciousness fading, just the beat and the bass and the worm holes for company now, drifting out to inner space . . .

Consciousness snaps backs like a stun gun. I'm lying on a bed in a dark bungalow. Noddy's next to me, naked with a rock-hard little prick! "It's okay, don't worry. You take a lot," he whispered, trying to coax me down a new avenue. Realisation hits me like freight train. I sit up quickly, taking in the situation. My clothes are still on. I looked at his prick and his horny, stubbly, drunk face and knew for a fact that I definitely felt nothing. I jumped up, out the door and looked around. I was in an alleyway, just off the beach, music going, still in Hat Rin. And I still had that 50 baht in my pocket. Just enough to get me the fuck out of there on a truck, over the hills and down the coast.

I woke in the dark feeling like death regurgitated. 24 hours non-stop peak time will do that to you. I lay there motionless in the gloomy, pre-dawn silhouettes, fan spinning, big-winged insects buzzing around the ceiling, flashbacks from last night hitting me like bolts of lightning, only the sound of the waves outside keeping me sane. Shit. Not only could I not trust anybody I met, but I couldn't even trust myself when I was off my head like that. I didn't know what I was doing. Massive memory gaps and blackouts are one thing when you're with your friends back home, but another thing here alone in a strange land. The Full Moon Party was a dangerous place. Thousands of wasted young people playing about on a dark beach on a little island. Fatalities by various means were not uncommon. I had to look after myself better.

I sat under the grey clouds of morning, staring out to sea for two hours, a melancholy haze descending over my throbbing head, throbbing with the beat still pounding away. It had been raining at some point, the sand dull and wet. The world was weighing down on my shoulders. I'd fucked up.

Luckily my old friends were still here. But I was the old hand now, showing them round the island. We got motorbikes and drove around, through rustic fishing villages, over hills to waterfalls in the jungle and hidden beaches, the wind blowing away some of the pain of the morning. But that night I fell into a fretful sleep, waking regularly in cold sweats, head still throbbing hard.

No better the next day. Every time I moved my head it felt like my brain was crashing into the side of my skull. I'd really overdone it this time. And my visa was going to expire tomorrow. People told me it didn't matter too much if you overstayed your visa; you just paid a fine of 200 baht per day you overstayed. I didn't want to take any chances though. I said goodbye to my friends, took the bike back to Thong Sala town and got a ticket for the night ferry back to Surat Thani on the mainland. Hours to kill in town, nothing to do, wandering around slowly, feeling ill and pitiful. A couple told me about a dengue fever outbreak on the island which sent my head sideways. What the hell is dengue fever? It didn't sound nice whatever it was.

Eventually boarded the open-sided ferry boat, with narrow numbered bays on the wooden floor for us cheapskate backpackers to lie in. I lay there for a moment waiting for the boat to depart, when my stomach suddenly rolled like a capsized ship. I got up, stepping over the web of limbs and rucksacks on the floor trying to get to the toilet. Going to make it, going to make it . . . I came to a big plastic bin with no bin liner in it and threw up violently inside. I would have felt bad or apologised to the people sitting nearby but I was too ill to care by now. I lay there on the wooden floor all night, slipping in and out of a feverish consciousness. Long hours rolled by.

Before dawn, the masts of moored fishing boats moved across my vision outside as we reached Surat Thani. The crowds filed out the boat. I was a broken man, head still pumping. Yet again taken to some fucking cafe in Surat Thani to wait and wait for our transit buses. I'm finally put on a minibus back to Hat Yai. It was a long journey south, cooped up trying to withstand relentless waves of nausea and ignore my aching head. A beautiful Italian woman sat next to me. We spoke a while but the effort of conversation brought me within a retch of vomiting every time I opened my mouth. The fields of neatly planted rubber trees went on forever, the gaps between the rows flashing by like the stuttered animation of a flick book – disjointed, unnerving, unreal.

Hat Yai. I get dropped at some dirty guesthouse, dump my bag, and march straight off with a grim determination, getting wrong directions around town in the searing midday Sun. Finally find the bus station and get on a cheap open-windowed bus to the Sadao border checkpoint. It keeps stopping everywhere, picking up people every few minutes, exacerbating my dull rage and surging brain pains. Patience snapped, I suddenly get off on the side of a busy road and jump on a motorbike taxi to the border crossing, the speed bumps rattling my head and heaving my stomach. Something was deeply wrong.

Four stamps – out of Thailand, into Malaysia, out of Malaysia, into Thailand. Back on the bike, another bus to Hat Yai, and another motorbike straight to hospital. I was imagining something horrific, but the hospital was like a dream. Big, clean, cool and modern. Within minutes I was with a doctor. A blood test confirmed I had dengue haemorrhagic fever – the worst kind apparently – a tropical disease spread by infected mosquitoes. He suggested I stayed the night. I was in no position to disagree. One last journey to the guesthouse, pay the damn bill for nothing and back to the sanctity of the hospital.

I had my own room in the hospital, my first air-con since Kuala Lumpur. It felt like a palace compared to the rooms I'd been staying in. I was hooked up to a drip and various pills. The first meal they brought in was some greasy-looking fried rice with a fried egg on top and some processed meat bits. I tried one sliver of tomato from the side salad and threw up all over the floor. Pretty nurses came in and out all day, the highlight of the day being the four-handed bed baths.

It was good to finally relax in comfort, but I still felt terrible. Alone with my thoughts and reflections all day, emotions came and went. I almost cried for myself in self-pity. Alone in a foreign hospital with some tropical disease; the fact that nobody knew where I was. But the tears wouldn't fall. They never did.

More drips, injections, pills and vomit. But I was okay. I recovered, the medicine worked, and after two nights and lots of paperwork I was told I could leave.

★ ★ ★

After a day sorting out my documents I decided to go somewhere quiet to recover. I remembered that first ferry to Ko Phangan and an American guy telling me about a secret beach. I took a minibus to the nearby provincial town of Trang, then a local bus through the pristine green countryside to a little fishing village, long-tail boats colourfully adorned in cloth chugging through the still lazy waters. I got directions down a dusty trail to a bungalow resort on Hat Jao Mai Beach on Thailand's southwest coast.

The owner took me to the most basic little wooden huts they had. Mine wasn't much bigger than a dog kennel on stilts, with no electricity, but it was standing on a little slice of paradise – a quiet, tree-lined sandy beach with limestone cliffs to the right, studded with green vegetation, and the simmering waters of the Andaman Sea beyond. Barely a soul in sight apart from the odd fishing boat passing by. There wasn't much to do but read, swim, splash through the waves and chat to the handful of other travellers there. They were all nice, pleasant, sane people. We talked about Thailand, the culture and language.

My guidebook too mentioned certain unique facets of Thai culture. It talked of the importance of 'face', the need for people to save face above nearly all else, and hence the importance of keeping calm and not overly displaying one's emotions. The laid-back attitude exemplified by phrases such as *mai pen rai*, literally meaning 'it's nothing'. Also the value of *sanook*, or 'fun', to be had even when doing mundane tasks. And of reciprocal *pee-nong* relationships, or 'elder-younger' relationships. That elders will support younger family members, friends and colleagues in many ways if the younger person shows their loyalty and obedience. It also said that people would be rewarded for how close they came to fulfilling these Thai cultural ideals. I was fascinated by these passages and read them over and over. They read like the rules of a game, a game that I was playing, and the clues to uncovering some of the secrets around me.

Next morning I surveyed the mosquito bites all over me before our group took a long-tail boat trip to nearby Ko Muk Island. The boats were long and narrow, but their massive engines turned the propeller fast enough for them to cut through the sea quickly. Sun blazing, blue sea shining, our small group approached the high rock walls of Ko Muk, no beach in sight. The boat stopped and we were told to swim through the Emerald Cave in the side of the cliffs. The entrance was already crammed with Asian tour groups in life jackets, swimming in long lines together, screeching excitedly.

The ocean faded behind me as I swam into the cave, darkness soon enveloping me until I could see nothing ahead. I kept swimming forward blindly, going by the sounds of the crowds till there was nothing ahead or behind me, just pitch black and the sensations of the water. The effect was ominous, like some metaphysical nightmare, just oneself floating in the nothingness, the water and the screams of others.

I carried on, following the whooping sounds till a vision emerged ahead, shadows expanding into beams of light. Bright colours bloomed and an oasis came into view up ahead – gentle waves lapping onto the soft sand with drooping palm trees behind, the whole scene surrounded by steep imposing cliffs on all sides. Like a beach in a giant rock bowl. I felt dizzy with awe, these natural wonders blowing my mind, pulling me further and further away from the past into this seductive new world. I swam back through the dark cave, starry-eyed and fearless this time.

But after another quiet night on the idyllic beach I was bored stiff. I needed some action. I guess I preferred the storm to the calm. Looking at a map there was Krabi province to the north and Satun to the south. Satun was supposed to be even quieter than here. So the obvious place to go was back to Krabi. I'd only spent two nights there before, so I decided to check it out properly this time.

So back I went, till I was again strolling along the street by the river estuary in Krabi Town. Suddenly I heard my name shouted behind me. What? Who was it? I turned around. It was Sally in the back of a *songtaew* truck – the owner of Shamrock Bar where me and Adam had gone last time we were here. She remembered me! So of course I got in and went with her back to Ao Nang, the small beach resort town down the coast. She seemed pleased to see me again, telling me to come and see her in the bar tonight. A rather plump, single woman of 30, she spoke good English and had a very chatty and amusing disposition, though kind of nutty with it.

I went to the same place that I'd stayed at with Adam, the cheap but clean Mermaid Guesthouse, located in a row of four-storey townhouses on the main road near the beach. They put me in the same room we had before. A balcony at the end of the corridor high above the street gave great views of the street and the vertical cliffs of craggy limestone beyond. I lay down on my bed in the big empty room. Suddenly here I was back in Ao Nang again. What was I doing here? I hadn't really planned to come here.

Causation's a funny thing. Some say everything happens for a reason. Others that the world is completely random. Either way, it can have a funny habit of throwing you off your expected path from time to time.

★　★　★

It seems logical to assume that the laws of cause and effect apply to everything in the Universe. Every event in the history of the Universe must have had a cause before it.

Yet how about life on Earth? Does it work in the same way for living things or do they have a life of their own? In particular human beings. We seem capable of agency to a higher degree than other animals. Do I, do you, do we human beings have free will over our thoughts and actions? Are we self-determined? Are our thoughts and actions our own? Can we do whatever we want at any moment in time?

Or are they determined by other causal forces? Is any feeling of free will merely an illusion? If we believe that all events in the Universe are causally determined, then surely this must apply to human beings too? Otherwise it would appear that causality does not apply to humanity – that we exist as some kind of causal black hole in the

Universe, consuming and negating all external attempts at influence. A world causality cannot touch, a universe unto itself.

Many believe this to be implausible. Throughout history there have been many who believe our actions are determined by outside forces, and are not freely willed by ourselves. Some are religious, some scientific.

Some people believe all our actions are determined by God. Some attribute this to God being omnipotent or omnipresent. Or that by virtue of God's omniscience our behaviour is known in advance. Some believe that the whole Universe's nature is already pre-determined by God. Some believe the Universe itself has mental properties. They see the Universe holistically as a giant mind in itself, of which our minds are tiny rippling currents. Some call this the mind of God. Others give it no name.

Some believe our behaviour is biologically determined – that our inherited genetic makeup determines who we are and what we do. Others, that our behaviour is psychologically determined, perhaps that we always uncontrollably follow our strongest natural desire. Others believe it is culturally determined by the social environment we live in. Many believe a complex combination of these factors determines our behaviour, as illustrated in the debate over nature versus nurture. The thing linking them all is the belief that factors outside people's will cause them to behave in certain ways.

★ ★ ★

Ao Nang, *ao* meaning bay, was a holiday resort of small hotels and guesthouses, with one long road that ran through town and alongside Ao Nang Beach and the quieter, undeveloped Nopparat Thara Beach, the two divided by a giant rocky outcrop. The beachfront road was quite upmarket, lined with international restaurants, tailors, pharmacists and tour shops. The road then went inland away from the beach where my guesthouse and those girlie bars were, hidden away down side-streets. Down another of these was Shamrock Bar.

I'd finished my antibiotics by now and was feeling fresh. A little too fresh for my own good perhaps. I found Sally and she kindly invited me for dinner with some friendly tourists she knew. They were a mixture of holiday makers and travellers who liked beaches and booze and the conveniences of staying in a small town. I think I preferred this to the hippy-bungalow scene of Ko Phangan too. I liked putting my jeans on at night and hitting the town, rather than being stuck in the middle of nowhere, rolling round off my head in the sand.

We headed down to Shamrock, where all the boozy tourists would amass over the course of the evening. The atmosphere was very drunken and friendly, everybody mixing freely, joking and playing around. Sally's friend Jackpot was there again, a quirky local man from Krabi Town, dancing around in drunken zigzags, speaking fluent English in a strange drawled out Cockney accent. They were both kind and friendly to me, shoving tequilas and buckets in my hand to pass around to the other customers. They took me under their wing. I remembered the advice in the guidebook.

I returned again early the next evening. The bar was empty, but Sally stuck a beer in my hand and invited me to walk around town with her handing out flyers for the bar to pretty girls and drunken guys, meeting everybody and pulling in customers. It sounded like a great idea to me. Since there was just one main road, you kept seeing the same people every day.

Back in the bar she started giving me more free drinks here and there, as I helped her entertaining the customers with my pool playing, jokes, banter and crazy dancing, the drink orders flying in from the happy punters. I seemed to be on to a good thing.

After a few days it was officially my new local. Staying put in one popular bar seemed to be a great way to meet people, instead of going from bar to bar by myself. A smartly-dressed Thai guy in his late 20s with a thin tache called Bird worked there sometimes too, always obsessed with trying to get his hands on a Western girl, but rarely having any luck. I also got friendly with two English guys – Nick, a local dive instructor, and Rob, a DJ from London on a long holiday. We'd hang out there for hours, drinking knock-me-down Changs and pick-me-up buckets, hunting round town for some action. Sometimes we'd drive round in Jackpot's truck to the discos of Krabi Town or the deserted Nopparat Thara Beach for Changs on the beach at dawn.

One morning I found myself asleep on the pool table, the last person in the bar. Sally tried luring me up the wooden ladder to her bed in the roof area, but I resisted, deciding not to jeopardise the more important relationship with my new local.

I'd go to the other bars with anybody I met too. Ao Nang Bar down on the front, and the surreal, hippy-style Moon Bar down on the beach, trance music, shrooms and an afroed guy that looked uncannily like Jimi Hendrix. There was also the little *soi* of girlie bars I'd been to that time before and another cluster of girlie bars called Spicy Park, hidden away round the back of the shops on the front.

By day I'd wander round, chatting to all the locals on the way. The staff in Mermaid Guesthouse at breakfast. Down to the minimart, the guys in the kayak shop, the young guy in the internet shop, the Indian tailors, the funny drunk man with the liquor stand, the dodgy-looking local in black shades, sitting round and sharing a beer sometimes. Everyone was so laid-back and friendly that it brought me out of myself, no inhibitions anymore, everyone was my friend. I loved the Thai people. They were so relaxed and welcoming. I felt like I could go over and chat to anybody and everybody, they were all so happy to chat to me back. Nobody was offended, suspicious or prejudice. It felt like home. My new home.

One day I got a long-tail boat around the headland to Railey Beach. There were about five beaches there separated by massive limestone rocks and cliffs. People kayaking, rock climbing and even base jumping off the vertical cliffs. I saw a path leading up tree roots on one slope, going high up into the rocky jungle. Then the path descended steeply down a canyon to a hidden lagoon, surrounded by cliffs and dripping stalactites on every side. I was in an exotic wonderland beyond my wildest expectations here in Krabi province, landscapes I'd never imagined existed, making new friends every day. It was like being in a movie. My imagination kept flying on towards the eternal horizon, seduced and blinded by the glory of the Sun. Things were good those first days in Ao Nang.

★ ★ ★

One morning I came downstairs to the guesthouse restaurant, chatting briefly to the friendly women that worked there as usual. As I was leaving I noticed a cool-looking dude about 30 years old, in shades and a purple sarong sitting alone at a table. "Heeey maaan," he said to me in a stretched-out Californian drawl. I said hi and was about to carry on, when suddenly I changed my mind and joined him at his table. He was some kind of artist from San Francisco, just hanging out in Ao Nang a while as he travelled round Asia very slowly. We were on the same wavelength, one that I'd found harder to find out here than I'd expected. A lover of beauty and freedom. To say the guy was laid-back would be an understatement. He was so laid-back he was barely conscious.

"Call me Mr Blue," he said. "Hey. D'ya wanna Diazepam?" I had no pressing engagements that day, so I said yes, popping the little blue pill down my neck. Why? I don't know. Intrigue, curiosity, that little Dionysian glint in my eye. I don't know why. But I was always going to say yes. Besides, I'd never tried one before, and I wasn't one to say no. They were sleeping pills, but Mr Blue told me you could stay awake on them and ride the buzz. "They only cost a few baht each from some of the pharmacists in town maaan."

We ambled down the road to a kayaking tour shop on the beachfront and had a few beers on a concrete table with the Thai guys working there. They told us about kayaking trips around mangrove swamps and caves. By now it was raining again. It was the start of the rainy season, thick rolling masses of dark grey clouds and torrential downpours coming down for a few hours every afternoon, rain water flowing down the main road like a river. But Mr Blue didn't care.

He suggested more Diazepam, handing me another two. He had four, popping them back like mints. He said they weren't that strong. My head was starting to float a few inches above my body. I felt light and giddy, calm and happy, not a care in the world. A grin poured down my cheeks with a sloppy giggle. We noticed the storm clouds had kicked up some big waves, so we ran over the road through the pummelling rain, onto the beach, across the wet sand and dived into the rolling surf, getting tossed around like rag dolls in a washing machine, wave after wave in the pouring rain, laughing like teenagers off our heads.

Evening set quickly. The streets dried out but our heads kept rolling. We went to Shamrock and I grabbed some flyers to hand out, hunting for pretty girls and whatever else came our way. After scaring a few innocent tourists we went back to our guesthouse and as luck would have it there were three pretty Thai girls having dinner there. I smiled and gave them a flyer before going upstairs to shower.

Next thing, Mr Blue's banging on my door to wake me up. "Whatever you do, don't lie down maaan!" he laughed. The girls were still downstairs. They invited us to a night market where we had some more concrete table drinks.

I was chatting with the youngest one, a cute shy girl called Dear as best as I could, despite her not speaking much English. Mr Blue was chatting up the sexy eldest one called Lek, while we left their loud, comedy friend Jeab to it, jabbering away to everyone in a loud cackle. Drinks flowed, more pills may have entered the equation but memories were dissolving fast into the night. Blurred glimpses of Shamrock and the beachfront, mysterious hours lost under a blue cloud.

I don't know what happened that night, but I woke up the next day fully clothed next to Jeab. She was a couple of years older than me; a local girl, from somewhere in Krabi province. She was small and dark-skinned, kind of cute, but had a forceful intensity to her, a loud voice and scary laugh. I didn't really fancy her, but somehow we'd ended up together. She said she liked me but didn't want to have sex because we'd just met. She wasn't that kind of girl.

The next few days were a blur. I followed Jeab to the little house she shared with Dear, Lek and another young girl Noi. It was inland, on the edge of town where the locals lived. The four of them rented a basic, one bedroom terraced apartment with a small front room and a kitchen area and bathroom at the back. They welcomed me into their home warmly and we all got on well, everyone relaxed and friendly. We ate and drank and I had a pocketful of my new blue buddies too. I vaguely remembered having sex with her that night in the bedroom of their house. Just one flash memory.

I hung out there all the next day too. We sat on mats on the floor of the front room. I made an effort not to point my feet as is polite in Asia, struggling to sit cross-legged for long periods without my legs seizing up. They also taught me not to step over people, food or even cushions as this was also rude here, the feet being spiritually impure, and the head sacred, so I wasn't to touch people's heads too. We chatted and taught each other Thai and English words and I helped them cook too – exotic spicy salads and strange vegetables with dips I'd never seen in the restaurants. We lazed about, watched Thai TV and played with the little kitten that wandered in from next door. We drank water from a communal metal bowl as little Dear swept the floor and did all the other chores. I grew to like them all as friends, appreciating their warm company, and felt lucky to be living with real local people and learning so much from them. I didn't want to just hang around with backpackers all the time, going to all the same places as everyone else. I wanted to scratch the surface. I wasn't too keen on Jeab being my partner of the four of them, but it was too late for that now.

Apart from Dear, I eventually worked out that the other three worked in the beer bars of Spicy Park behind the shops on the beachfront road. I'd drive them to work, the four of us squeezed on their one motorbike, one perched in front of me, and two squeezed in behind as I tried to keep the bike in a straight line. All the *farang* expats in town watched us incredulously as we veered slowly down the road laughing together. It was low season now with all the rain, so there were barely any tourists around.

I wandered round the tight cluster of interlinked bars in Spicy Park. Jeab waitressed in Dream Bar, though she hardly talked to me most of the time, always some little problem or issue between us. But I didn't care. Me and Mr Blue were playing pool with young Thai guys, Connect Four with the bar girls, more little blueys floating down with SangSom sets, pouring our own glasses from the bottle. Mr Blue was doing 20 or more pills a day. We floated through the hazy maze enveloped in the ever-thickening fog, staggering round the bars, jelly legs, goofy grins, giggles and bendy pool cues, happy and sociable, spilling my guts out to all and sundry. Everyone was my friend now, not a care in the world, the warm blue blanket soothing and sweet.

I still had my room at Mermaid Guesthouse, but I was staying at the girls' house every night now, either borrowing their motorbike, or hitching lifts on people's bikes to get there and back. Waking up each morning in the dingy little windowless bedroom with Jeab next to me and a stack of bags in the corner with the four girls' possessions. Dear slept on a mat in the front room, the other two staying with their boyfriends usually. I still had a soft spot for Dear, but it was too late for that now. Jeab was the dominant female of the group and everyone knew it. Poor little Dear. She looked like an angel, running round doing all the housework, cooking and sweeping the floor all day while Jeab lazed around. I wasn't sure why she lived with them.

In the afternoon Lek and Noi would return and we'd eat together. I'd joke with them both about last night, teasing them, calling them butterfly girls, but I liked them as friends too. Dear and Noi were still so young, both in their late teens I guessed. I wanted to take care of them and protect them from the nastier guys out there. "Be careful. Some men not good here," I warned them. "Why three girls work in bar and Dear stay home and clean the house?" I asked in my new broken English. "You know Cinderella?" I asked, which sent the stepsisters rolling round the floor with laughter. But I felt like they were all my sisters. They'd taken me into their home and I was happy living with them, appreciative of their caring female companionship.

Away from the tourist strip, the locals out here in the village were mostly Muslim. As evening came, the darkness set in and the Muslim call to prayer would echo out across the neighbourhood from the local mosque's loudspeakers. The hypnotic, rhythmic chants sounded so foreign and beguiling to me. Enticing yet unnerving, the sounds of time's culture far removed from home. I was falling further and further away from everything I knew.

Noi, from the Northeast of the country, was seeing a young Swedish guy named Nils. Very warm and open guy, but he was in love with Noi and it was killing him. The older Lek was seeing a Swiss man. He was cold and wary of me, so we didn't speak much. Me and Nils chatted together in Spicy Park one night trying to get to the bottom of things. Jeab told me she never went with customers, she was just a waitress. Noi had told Nils the same. It was hard to believe though when we saw them chatting and flirting with all the customers in the bars. Although we were seeing them, they told us to keep our mouths shut in the evening as they had to entertain the customers. The bars were nothing like as seedy as in Bangkok or Pattaya. But still questions wrangled, and all we knew was that we didn't know shit.

"She's so young," Nils explained, passionately heartbroken. "I don't give her any money, so she must just like me for who I am. And when I'm with her, and kiss her, it . . . it feels so right. I can't believe she would go with old guys for money. It's not possible." I remembered the two-month Aussie's advice in Chiang Mai. "Whatever you do, don't fall for them," I told Nils pseudo-knowingly. The truth was I had fallen for them too. Not for Jeab, but for all of them in some strange way. They'd looked after me, taken me into their home. Lek told me I reminded her of her lost brother. There was a mutual fondness there. And the idea that these young girls I'd grown so fond of would sell themselves to any guy, any night, fat old sex tourist or whoever else, filled me with self-consuming rage. They insisted they didn't though, so I tried my best to believe them. Maybe they were just looking for boyfriends or only went with young guys like us. We just didn't know. The truth remained a mystery. But we wanted to know everything.

One evening me and Nils drove Jeab and Noi through the rubber tree plantations to the small shopping mall in Krabi Town. "I want that t-shirt," Jeab demanded, pointing to an expensive brand. I hated her for asking me in such an aggressive way and refused. But somehow she spun my reaction back on me, making me feel bad for being so mean and not caring about her. How did she do that? It was like magic. But perhaps she was right. It was just a t-shirt after all. And I didn't want to anger her, didn't want to lose my access to the girls. So I bought it. Sometimes I wished I'd ended up with any of the other girls instead of Jeab. If only I could remember what had happened that first night. She could be cute when she wanted, but she was hot-tempered, loud and aggressive.

But I wanted more. Without her I wouldn't be able to hang around with them all in their home. And I wanted to be with them, understand their lives, see the picture from their perspective. I didn't just want to travel around with the herd and take pretty photos. I wanted to get involved. I felt privileged, like I'd broken through the tourist veil and was really accepted by the Thais as one of them. And it felt good to be part of a family, here alone on the other side of the world.

That night I dragged Mr Blue out of his room, where he'd been caked out for two days and hit Spicy Park again. Diazepams, Changs, SangSom, banter and pool, the same as every night, everyone's my friend. Hours evaporate in the tropical heat. Suddenly Jeab, who I'd obviously not been paying enough attention to, is hit by a mystery illness and demands to be taken home. I didn't believe a word of it but we drive back anyway and sleep.

Wake up with a jolt suddenly after very little sleep. It had been happening a lot recently. Only 6am. We're in the bedroom, little Dear in the living room as normal. Jeab's groaning in agony. I don't know what's true and what's not anymore. Then she's lying with her ear on my chest, asking questions about whether I like her or not, why I'm here and what I think she does for a living. My heart beat's going faster and faster, pumping messages in her ear. I stammer out some vague responses, unsure what to say, unsure what to think, barely able *to* think. She's testing me, listening to my heartbeat to check if I'm lying or not. Is she? I don't know. I got to get out of here. I don't even like this girl. What am I doing? Claustrophobia creeks and lurches over my body, my heart cracks and that rush kicks in. That same rush that had dragged me out of every place I'd been to so far – that mad, unstoppable yearning for freedom.

Despite her protests I get up, grab her bike keys, slam the door behind me, pull the throttle and accelerate down the road and along the coast as fast as the bike will go. I necked a beer and cigarette down on the long serene coastline of Nopparat Thara Beach on the far side of town, my head still racing but alone at least. Tiny, glistening waves rippled up against the shore, the benevolent Sun climbing into the pure blue sky. It was beautiful, so beautiful here. So what am I doing? What am I *doing*? . . . Gotta get out of here. I returned the bike, threw some paracetamol at Jeab and told her I'd be back. Hitched a ride to my guesthouse, grabbed my bag, jumped on the 20 baht *songtaew* to Krabi Town and I was out of there. Freedom. I could have laughed out loud. But I didn't.

★ ★ ★

Ko Phi Phi was another of these legendary backpacker islands I'd heard of but not yet been to. Just two hours from Krabi by ferry boat. Time to check it out. I boarded the ferry in the river estuary, loading up with young backpackers and their backpacks. I necked two blueys and sat on the roof deck outside slurping Chang. Two hours on the open sea passed, chopping through crystal waves, stunning rocky islands, the sky ablaze with heat and light. My heart was burning with a passion for life and yet I was cooler than Fonzie, chatting up two beautiful blonde Swedish girls – laughing at my jokes, amazed by my stories, Ao Nang a distant memory. This was the land where you could do what you wanna do, be who you wanna be, and anything was possible.

We approached an island, perfect beaches, palm trees and jungle rising up into the hills. Passing around the tip of a headland, the centre of the island suddenly swung into view, a huge swooping bay, beaches everywhere, a massive wall of spectacular limestone cliffs beyond; and to the left another huge rocky island, rising out of the sea like a giant crown. It was beyond anything I'd ever seen in my life. It was glorious! I laughed out loud on the boat, and the people loved me for it!

The boat moored at a concrete pier and us new arrivals strutted down towards a village, dozens of touts trying to get us into their hotels. I passed a 7-Eleven and turned right into a tight rabbit warren of little alleyways, not a car in sight, just pedestrians and bicycles filing past. There were tour, dive and massage shops, internet cafes, restaurants, sandwich and pancake stalls, jewellery, art and handicraft stores, bars and guesthouses. Beautiful young tourists everywhere, pretty girls in sarongs and bikinis, and tanned muscular guys in trunks. The local guys were lean and dark, the younger ones covered in tattoos, going by on little BMX bikes in bright football shirts, saying "Beep, beep," everywhere they went to avoid crashing into people on the busy little lanes. I kept going a long way till the street ended at a hill.

I got a room and went straight out again, completely lost wandering the winding alleys, till I came to the most beautiful beach I'd ever seen in my life – a vast, circular bay, steep cliffs at either end, endless golden sand and palm trees; hundreds of people relaxing on the sand, eating and drinking on wooden tables, having fun, playing volleyball, swimming in the shining waters, banana boats bouncing along and people paragliding through the air dragged by speedboats. It was pulsating with natural beauty and human joy.

I waded into the shallow sea, the water hotter than a bath tub.

Unbelievably hot. I dived forward and glided underwater till the warm sea, the mother of all life enveloped my soul. I surfaced a man reincarnated, floating anew in this primordial soup, this illustrious theatre of dreams, my old brain oozing out of my ears into the salty waters of this vivacious new world. A smiling Thai man was waving at me from an anchored speedboat, beckoning me over. I swam over and pulled myself up the metal ladder at the back. Two wiry little local guys in vests were smoking a bamboo bong on board. "Hello my friend!" They grinned yellow smiles and passed it to me. "Is it okay? I don't have any money on me," I said, a little unsure of the situation. "Don't worry," they smiled, so I took the bong, inhaling the toxic bliss. My head span 360, the sweat and colours intensifying around me, consciousness oversaturated. It was almost too much to take. This place was beyond belief! The locals smiled. I jumped off the boat, swam back and lay on a deckchair merrily wasted in the searing heat, head reeling, brain melting, face grinning, because . . . because . . . I knew I'd found it. This was it. I'd found what I was looking for. Paradise, the Promised Land! This was it. Forget the rest. *This* was it! *This* was paradise!

Night fell and the streets were packed with beauty and youth. Stunning Scandinavian blondes and tanned Latino brunettes out drinking and partying. It was like Beverly Hills, Copacabana or Monte Carlo, except everyone was serenading past tin-roofed wooden shacks in dirty alleyways.

I saw a Thai kickboxing match going on and entered a courtyard. It was a big bar, decked out with red, green and yellow paint, fake vines and flashing lights, people on wooden benches sitting around a boxing ring, two hard-looking Thai guys knocking the crap out of each other. This was the Jungle Bar. I saw Nils and his friend there. We hit the SangSom buckets, toxic energy, fluids and rum, the hard juice running through our veins like sweet gasoline, power surging like an electric current. What a rush! I was hooked on the things. Feeling more and more like Superman with every sip. We discussed the situation in Ao Nang in intense depth, happy to have escaped, but the confusion still unresolved. We constructed a mission to find out the truth. Sweat was pouring from my body in the intense humidity, replaced only by the savage magic of the liquor, the boxers attacking each other in a flurry of punches, knees and kicks while the crowds roared.

Jungle Bar had two boxing rings. One in the courtyard downstairs by the front bar on the street, and another upstairs, in the middle of a big open-sided disco perched on the side of a hill, dance music blaring out. From there concrete steps ran down to Lucky Star Bar, which transformed into Lucky Star Disco once the live band had finished, and next door to that was Predator Bar, a funky dusty little place all decked out in bamboo, people grooving round.

Nights of madness ensued. Couple of cheeky D's, round all the bars, Sangers flowing like the Amazon, two for one deals, tequila and sambuca, and free buckets at midnight in every bar for ten minutes. Free buckets? Insanity reigned! Me and the other wreckheads would get one bucket in Jungle at 12, neck it, run down the stairs, force our way through the crowds and try to get two more from Lucky Star and Predator Bar before 12:10am. Everyone high as kites in the muddy alleyways, dancing like loons, gibbering like madmen, the next generation, the holy doomed, the possessed, the bearers of the prophecy!

A bang on the door. Some new friends dragged me up after two hours' sleep for a boat trip I'd agreed to the night before. The word hangover didn't quite do justice to how rough I was feeling. Dreams moulding into consciousness, flashbacks and voices in my head, still drunk as hell, pleasure tinged with pain, aches and dehydration like a Death Valley drought. I staggered through the streets following them and collapsed on a big wooden sightseeing boat.

When I came round again we were cruising around the crown-shaped island I'd seen when I arrived. This was Ko Phi Phi Leh, the sister island to the main inhabited island of Ko Phi Phi Don. High cliff walls scarred with gashes and colours from millennia of erosion, reaching vertically out of the sea and into the sky, topped with drooping patches of glowing green bushes and trees. It was majestic, yet surreal. Too amazing to be real. We stopped the boat in a bay and I jumped into the crystal clear waters, suddenly plunged into an underwater world with a rainbow of glowing tropical fish.

I saw a hole in the cliffs at sea level leading through to some land on the other side of the cliff walls. I swam over, trying not to be swept into the sharp rocks by the swell of the waves channelling through the funnel. Timing my movements with the ebbs and flows of the waves, I carefully made it over the spiky rocks and through the hole in the cliff. It opened up into an area of sandy jungle, steep rock faces either side. I edged through a patch of trees and over some sand dunes till I was hit by yet another breathtaking sight – a bay of bright turquoise water and white sands, ringed by picturesque green and grey cliff walls almost entirely on all sides. This was Maya Bay, 'The Beach', made famous by the movie shot here. It was an adaptation of the book *The Beach* depicting a community of backpackers living in a secret island paradise. In choosing this beach as their primary location, the filmmakers had immortalised the place, effectively declaring it the most beautiful beach in the world. It was hard to disagree with that. And now Ko Phi Phi was booming.

Our trip carried on to more beaches and islands, though I had no idea where I was – diving off the boat, snorkelling, drinking and chatting to everyone, intoxicated by wonder.

But I was starting to realise something wasn't right – I was losing it. As ecstatic as I was all the time, my brain wasn't working properly. I barely had any memories of anything. I couldn't remember what I'd done an hour ago. It took me two hours to get ready in the evening simply because it took me that long to plan out, remember and execute the simple procedure of getting showered, changed and ready to go out. I just couldn't do it without forgetting some vital step along the way. I couldn't think properly, my mind racing round in ever-increasing circles. I'd wander round the village, sweating like crazy, no idea where I was going, the locals giving me funny looks, people I'd never met before coming up and saying hello to me. But I was still up for it. I couldn't wait to go out at night again, even though my body was deteriorating and I was losing my mind. I had an insatiable thirst for the night. I was so up for it, it scared me. One little sip of that sweet liquor of life and everything was okay again. It all made sense! I was the man of the night! Tuned in, fully absorbed! An animal! A beast! A fucking juggernaut!

I woke up in a tiny wooden shack next to one of the Thai girls from Predator Bar, my head clanging like Notre Dame. We rolled around a bit, but she wouldn't take off her tight denim shorts. "No. Can not!" She was giggling, plucking my paranoia strings. What's in there? Was she pretending to be a ladyboy? Or was she really a he? I didn't know what was going on anymore. She looked like a girl, but I . . . I was losing it.

That evening I noticed some Canadian girls on the street corner handing out flyers for Lucky Star Bar. "You *work* here?" I asked. They did. Apparently they just handed out flyers for a few hours in the evening and danced in the bar. 200 baht a day, free accommodation and free alcohol all night. "Are you friends of the boss?" "No, we just turned up and got the job," they replied. I couldn't believe what they were telling me. You could *work* here! You could live in paradise, surrounded by beautiful women and get smashed on buckets every night for *free*! This was beyond comprehension! Finding paradise was one thing. Finding out you could live there for free was beyond paradise. It was a gift from God!

I went to Lucky Star and got chatting to an Irish friend of the boss, who'd been there a while. It was all true. He said I could come and work there anytime. He had the satisfied grin of a man who'd made it to the top and was enjoying every minute of being up there. I wanted that grin. I sat there entranced by dozens of blonde, buxom, tanned Scandinavian valkyries dancing round the pit in front of the stage, tempting me through the gates of Valhalla. "I've never been to Scandinavia," I said. "Ai! You should go!" the Irishman laughed. All this

– the booze, girls, life on Paradise Island – all this could be mine! My own slice of paradise.

A plan was forming in my head. The football World Cup was coming up next month. I would come back and work here on Phi Phi while that was going on. The perfect storm. How could I put on a shirt and tie and get a teaching job when I had this amazing opportunity to live in Heaven at my fingertips? It wasn't going to happen. Not in a million.

But I was spending a fortune here, and Ao Nang was still running through my head for reasons I didn't fully understand. The next day I followed the signs up the hill to the viewpoint on the mountain side, overlooking half the island. I hadn't realised it before but the village lay in between two bays on a narrow isthmus of land running between the cliffs on the west side and the mountain I was on to the east. From here I could see the high cliff walls, the village in the middle and the seductive Andaman Sea stretching out either side, Ko Phi Phi Leh floating majestically in the background. It was the most beautiful sight I'd seen in my whole life. I left the island knowing beyond a shadow of a doubt that I'd be back.

★ ★ ★

I didn't know why I was going back. A love of the land? To see my friends? Unfinished business? I didn't know.

I got the same room at Mermaid Guesthouse, rang Jeab and went straight to the girls' house for dinner. I was pleased to see the four of them again, but the reception was frosty. I wasn't sure what was going on, not daring to even touch Jeab or meet her steely gaze. I played it cool. "Why you come here?" she asked me. "You want to fuck three lady huh?" at which, her, Lek and Noi started gyrating on the floor in unison, laughing their heads off. It depressed me. That wasn't what I wanted at all. Did I? "I work tonight. You don't come," she tells me. Mind games sprung into action like a pinball wizard on multi-ball.

Does she want me back? Do I want *her* back? What am I doing here?

I headed back to Shamrock. Sally, Jackpot, Bird and Nick were there. Great to see the old gang again. A couple of buckets and I'm running round, playing pool, chatting to everyone, telling jokes, dancing about, the life of the party. But the girls and that question were still smouldering under my drunken cover. I tried to ask Jackpot about them, whether they were good or not. He was unwilling to say anything, but looked at me seriously. A diver friend of Nick told me they were trouble and to stay away from them. Maybe he was right, but they weren't bad people, I was sure. I went for a piss.

I opened the door on the way out and suddenly there's little Dear. What's going on? Had she come to see me? My hopes leapt for a moment. No. She beckoned me outside and down the street where Jeab was standing alone in the shadows of night. "Give me your key. I stay your room tonight," she orders me. Alarm bells start ringing. She had that crazy look in her eye. I didn't want her in my room, no way. I'd be back in her grip again. I refused. She said we were finished and stormed off. Somewhat relieved I went back to the bar where I was met by a huge cheer from everyone. I laughed too. They all knew I was hanging round with the wrong girl and were pleased I'd got rid of her. Good bunch there in Shamrock. Me and Bird went to eat noodle soup at the night stall run by the jolly Thai guy who looked like John Lennon. Noi turned up at one point and told me that Jeab was in love with me. I went home alone. I liked this town, but it was too damn small.

My hangovers were getting worse and worse. Waking up early in the morning after just a few hours' sleep, lying there rotting in bed for hours, body too exhausted to move, mind racing round uncontrollably. I had a sore throat, cough, sweats and chills, my limbs aching randomly. Pain was building up. But eventually after a few hours surfing the waves of nausea and tides of self-doubt I would emerge standing . . . and wanting more.

I crawled downstairs and saw Rob, the cockney DJ. We went down the beach to sunbathe, discussing women excitedly. A lot of Western guys weren't into the local women, but I seemed to be growing more and more fond of them, as was he. What was it? Their laid-back attitude and lack of pretence were refreshing, though it may have had more to do with the availability and sheer quantity. There seemed to be friendly, cute girls everywhere you went. Perhaps the language barrier was more of a bridge, enabling us to have simpler, natural interactions. I wasn't sure exactly, but there was definitely something in that seductive smile. Something extremely desirable but also double-edged. You never knew what was on the other side of it.

Later that afternoon, I persuaded Sally to let me and Bird drive round town on his bike flyering to girls. Simple business of course, for where the girls go the guys are sure to follow. Bird was obsessed with getting hold of one, but was too nice a guy to pull it off. There'd been some kind of sexual event with an Irish girl a few months before which he was still going on about. He was definitely ready for number two now. A lot of the dark, muscular Southern Thai guys I'd seen in the tourist areas had Western girlfriends. Most of them had tattoos and long hair, and cool jobs like boxers, fire jugglers, rock climbers and DJs. But Bird was from Bangkok and couldn't quite pull off the beach stud thing; too excitable and nervous. Though his English was good, he'd work himself into such a fluster that his sentences would descend into an unintelligible mess. We scooted round, handing out flyers for tonight's big party, but in the end it was just the usual boozers that turned up. I never could work out where all those hot girls on the beach went at night.

Changs, Sangs, tequila, spliffs and a mushroom shake, and I'm off like a rocket, king of the hill, man of the people, dancing like a champion in Shamrock. Suddenly Dear's there again, poor little Cinderella, caught in the middle. But I'm not so pleased to see her this time as I know what's coming. She pulls me down the street where Jeab waits for me in the same spot, this time sobbing hysterically, tears running down her face, snot coming out her nose, pulling on my shirt,

I OF THE SUN

pleading from the bottom of her heart to come back, telling me how much I mean to her, and how much she loves me. A flash of panic cuts through the rising tide of inebriation. What have I done? I didn't think she really liked me all that much. But I see the terror in her eyes, just wanting me back and nothing else. She can't be faking it, it's impossible. I felt terrible for her, sorry I'd broken her heart, but I couldn't go back to her. She was crazy. I calmed her down, and eventually walked her back to Dream Bar to dump her with her friends.

I escaped back to Shamrock a free man and the party continued till dawn, a big crazy rabble of party nuts. I laughed out loud. I felt so alive! Travelling round paradise on my own, all my old inhibitions gone, new friends everywhere, Mr Popular, a success story, a man with his destiny in his own hands. I'd done it! I'd come here and made my dreams come true. I even felt that . . . I had finally become the man I'd always wanted to be – cool, confident, funny, charming, a man of action, capable of doing anything I wanted. I'd made it! It was all real now.

Still something in my head though. Something pulling me back again and again. Noi had invited me to the beach the night before. There was never any doubt in my mind that I would be there waiting for them. I . . . I cared too much. I cut through the lunchtime undergrowth and headed down in the late afternoon. I waded into the dark sea, and soon saw the girls cruising past on mopeds, waving at me without stopping. I was confused but went for a swim, always keeping an eye on the beach road. I saw Jeab and Lek appear with two Western guys. I joined them for an uneasy half hour, Jeab calm now, the two guys seeming just as confused and paranoid as me. She invited me back for dinner.

I changed and hitched a lift, pleased to be allowed back just as a friend. This was what I really wanted, wasn't it? The atmosphere was even tenser than before though. The girls were virtually silent in fact. Jeab gave me a little figurine statue of a cherub next to a chicklet trapped in a glass orb. My mind started racing. Then she showed me a pencil-drawn portrait of herself. She said she'd had it done earlier today. The drawing was sad and mournful. Sad because she loved me, she said. She kept saying it, but I wasn't feeling it. I was just feeling more and more confused. Deeply confused. I looked at the objects again. The cherub, the orbed chicklet, the portrait. Hidden meanings percolated. The situation was getting strange. Surreal even. I didn't know what was going on anymore.

Then she told me they all had to leave the house because they had a problem with the owner. They wouldn't explain what the problem was, but judging by their sad looks I decided they weren't lying. They didn't know what they were going to do, or where they would go. I didn't know if they were expecting me to do something, but I promised to help them move house in a few days. I felt terrible for them all, suddenly seeing the sadness behind the smiles for the first time. These poor girls, from poor homes, wearing fake plastic grins every night for leering Western sex tourists, selling themselves to the highest bidder just to survive and support their parents. It pained me to think about it. Surely they didn't. Did they? A deep melancholy drew over me. I wanted to help them more, but how? I had nothing.

Later I went to Shamrock in a deteriorating mood but it was empty. So I went to Spicy Park. The three of them were paired up with guys already. I didn't care about that though, I just cared about them. Especially little Dear, stuck at home on her own cleaning up after the others. I drank bucket after bucket, charged up but angry, playing pool with the surly local guys, not speaking to any tourists. I felt different now. I wasn't one of them, but I wasn't one of *them* either. Some tourists tried to befriend me, asking me questions about the girls, but I told them nothing. I was on their side now, not the guys'. I hated them in fact. The stupid, drunken, gawky bastards, with their stupid jokes and wandering hands.

It was getting too much, so I stormed off to Ao Nang Bar nearby and sank more beers round the pool table. A large group of rough-looking, local boatmen with long hair and black eyes were drinking in there. A confrontation erupted between them and some drunk Italian idiot. My nerves were on a knife edge so I jumped up in the middle to stop it for some reason.

Later on Jackpot arrived with some local friends. I stupidly charged up and asked about Jeab again. I couldn't stop myself. He didn't want to say anything, but I kept pressing him, till he gave in and slowly uttered, "She's an experienced girl." That was all I needed to hear. So it was true. She sold herself just like the others. It was the confirmation I was looking for. I'd got the answer I wanted so much. Everything made sense now.

A bit later, me and Jackpot are checking out a table of pretty Western girls. I smile, lean over and hand them a flyer for Shamrock from my back pocket. Suddenly there's shouts, chairs screeching, people standing, uproar. The gang of locals are shouting at me with vicious intent and start surrounding me, violence looming any second. I suddenly realise what I've done. Handing out flyers for a competitor inside their bar. Shit. I'd heard stories of murders down here. People could be ruthless if you angered them. But I'm saved by Jackpot, who speaks to the gang in their Southern dialect, and stops them kicking the fuck out of this stupid little prick. Lucky for me he's a proper local, known by everyone. He calms them down till they're seated and I apologise to everyone. Tensions reverberate round, fucked up, drunk, angry and confused, mind and body deteriorating fast. I decide I'd better leave soon while I still can. A moment later I suddenly see Jeab and Dear outside getting on their motorbike. I quickly escape.

Back in her bedroom again, early dawn, Jeab lying next to me asleep, grey shadows shifting round the room, the sound of drizzle outside. I was in a terrible, terrible mess. Really bad this time. My body shaking against my will, freezing cold one minute, then sweating all over the next, over and over, coughing and snivelling, Jeab waking occasionally to hug me and calm me down before falling asleep again, my mind racing round uncontrollably for hours and hours, flashbacks, images and voices alive in my head as real as last night. Jeab's evil cackle and orders flying round the room, her moments of quiet tenderness, her kiss, and her tears, her apparent love for me, poor Dear sleeping outside on the floor, the funny, cunning Lek, little Noi, so young and kind, the endless parties, booze and drugs, Jackpot's words echoing round my mind, experience, experience, experience, it was all true, all lies, the locals, half a dozen or more, wanting me dead, dead, moments from oblivion, the intervention and apologies, all round and round again, clear as day, the girls' faces burning through my eyelids, their words echoing in my ears, Jeab's screaming at me, but she's lying next to me, breathing gently, calm and soft now as she slept. God what was I doing? Here again, I didn't even like Jeab, not like this, but . . . but I loved them all, all four of the girls like . . . like they were my sisters. God I loved them, wanted to take care of them and protect them, protect them from all the evil of the world, men like me, stupid, big-dicked, horny idiots. But I couldn't, I was helpless, fucking useless, these poor girls, my sisters, selling their bodies every night for every damn fucking man that paid them. The realisation of the truth was sheer agony now. I loved them but I was one of them, I hated myself, I *hated* myself. I was crying now, wailing uncontrollably, like a baby that had lost its mother, like a mad man condemned to death, crying for these girls, crying for every woman that ever sold herself to a man, vowing to myself never to do it again, I thought of my . . . Oh God, what have I done? Screaming in silence now for no sound would come out, my face taut with pain, body convulsing, I'm sorry, so so sorry, sorry for ever using you, sorry for hurting you, Oh God, where am I? What am I doing? Rain was clattering on the tin roof top as the call to prayer sounded again, mystical chants from another world. I'm lying in bed with a girl I don't love, living with a group of prostitutes in a little house in a village on the other side of the world, what the fuck was I doing? I was so fucking alone, lost, choking so much I could barely breathe. Jeab was awake now, but she didn't understand, didn't care. "You crazy! You drink too much, I tell you already!" I had to get away from here, I was completely losing it now, I knew it but I couldn't stop it, couldn't bring myself back from the brink, it was too late, I was falling, I'd gone mad, this was it, but I couldn't even stand up, crying and shivering, my body tingling all over. I suddenly swung myself over off the bed and stumbled out the room, Dear was hunched in the corner looking scared. I wanted to hug her, for her to hug me, but it was useless, she couldn't help me, the poor girl. I left her alone and hunched over into the kitchen area away from them both. I collapsed on the floor in the corner, and cried, cried for every woman in the world and every pain ever suffered, my home and family I'd left and deserted, and I cried for myself, lost, so lost here, miles from home, hopelessly lost and confused, alone on the other side of the world, out of control, alcoholic, drug-abused, ill, broken and wounded, I was having an emotional breakdown but I couldn't stop it, I couldn't stop the tears, they kept coming, an hour or more. Hadn't cried like this since I was a baby, all the pain of all the years pouring out of me like a river. It came and it didn't stop.

After a long time, gasps turned to sobs turned to murmurs as I gradually calmed down. Dear had turned the radio on full blast in the front room to drown out my suffering. Jeab came out in her underwear and looked at me, kind of confused and disgusted at the same time. She hugged me a little but she didn't know why I was crying. It wasn't helping and she went back to her room.

Then, the tiny little kitten that lived next door appeared from round the corner. Patchy grey, feeble little thing. It tottered over to me, shaking and whimpering. It let out a raspy little yelp, rubbing its tiny head on my leg for affection. I stroked it and cared for it, looking at the face of this beautiful, helpless, little creature. The tears stopped. I wiped my face and slowly stopped shaking. Eventually I was okay again. I think that little kitten very nearly saved my life.

I returned to the bedroom and lay there for hours, completely exhausted but calm now. I had no more tears to shed, all emotion exhumed. Too lonely to leave, but too tired to sleep. I couldn't speak to anyone about it.

The rains stopped and I heard Lek and Noi turn up later in the afternoon with some of the guys from last night. Jeab joined them. I listened to them all turning on the bar chat in the front room as I lay in the dark bedroom with the door shut, alone and confused, not knowing who I was anymore, brain still not working properly. Eventually I came out and said hello. The guys looked at me strangely, trying to work out who I really was. I didn't know myself. After they left I got myself together and went back to my guesthouse room.

Early evening I went to Shamrock and gave out some flyers with Bird. I didn't tell him anything about what had happened. All the locals were looking at me though, staring. They all looked familiar but I was never sure if I knew them or not. I thought they were all my friends but now I realised I had no idea who any of them were. How *stupid* I was! Do they all know what I've been up to? About the flyers, the girls and the near-beating last night? It's only a small town. Does everyone know each other or not? Do they all talk about what I've been doing the night before, drunk, crazy and out of control? What am I doing, charging round asking people questions about their friends and neighbours? It was terrible behaviour. What have I done? The paranoia and exhaustion were getting too much. I felt like I was in danger. I went back to my room and hid.

I lay in my empty guesthouse room trying to sleep, but my mind was still racing uncontrollably. Outside the van with the loudspeakers advertising the Thai boxing was going by every ten minutes, "*Muay Thai, Muay Thai,*" and the crazy twisted psychedelic music that went with it, twisting my brain into an ever tighter knot. It sounded evil, like the chants of some cannibal tribe out to get me. Can't stay here. I got up again and had a few quiet beers in the corner at Shamrock, trying to keep calm and drink myself to sleep.

Around midnight I went to an internet shop, and heard someone call my name softly. It was a gentle-looking Thai man. He looked familiar, but I couldn't be sure who anyone was in this little town as I was so drunk all the time. I knew everyone and didn't know anyone at the same time. But they all knew me. I racked my brains and eventually worked out we'd met in Spicy Park before. A friend of the girls I think. Couldn't be trusted. But we talked and he seemed nice. He came back with me to Shamrock with his girlfriend who appeared to be a ladyboy, though I wasn't sure. It was quiet that night. He passed me a joint as I tried to calm down, my reactions still edgy. I was having trouble even understanding him, but he was calm and gentle, despite my initial paranoia.

I settled a bit as we chatted about our backgrounds. "Do you have any children?" I asked them innocently, and they both giggled. Then he said it: "Don't worry. Thai people are very friendly." Instantly, something clicked in my head. He was right. They were friendly and relaxed. Nobody cared what I was doing. I was just another tourist in town. Why was I taking everything so seriously? It was crazy. Just relax. Everything's okay. With that realisation I felt my paranoia disappear like a drowning man's sudden gasp of air. I felt my old self returning, sanity regained, my crazy, bucket-fuelled alter ego spiralling off like a released balloon.

I spent another couple of days in town, hanging round with Rob, Nick and Bird, drinking but not like before. I decided to stay off the buckets. It was a good idea. Only sometime later did I work out what had sparked my breakdown that morning. A few people told me that the rum and energy drinks I'd been drinking every day for the last two months contained various kinds of amphetamine-like substances. Amphetamines are renowned for their bad comedowns, and I was hooked on the stuff every night. That might explain the life-affirming rushes I was getting, the mad energy, only sleeping a few hours a night, the mind-bending comedowns in the morning, not being able to eat in the daytime, and the withdrawal symptoms in the evening till I drank some more. I wasn't sure if it was true or not, but there was something going on. Maybe it was just the booze and caffeine. Oh, and the sleeping pills, blanking out my memories and emotions. When you take shit, you feel messed up the next day, but at least you know why. You sweat it out and get over it. This was a very subtle beast though, creeping into your consciousness, altering your moods and thoughts in different directions without you knowing it's there. You just think you are genuinely going mad. That's what I told myself anyway.

As promised, I decided to help the girls move out their house. Closure maybe. It seemed like the right time for me to go too, as my visa was about to run out again. I returned to the house tentatively. The three other girls had already left. I helped Jeab load all the furniture, it all being Jeab's, into her male friend's pickup truck. As the Sun set through orange skies and purple clouds, we drove inland for nearly an hour, into the jungle and stunning limestone mountains, to a small cluster of houses in the dark forest. We came to a poor dusty old house with a cement floor and wooden walls. Her parents came out in simple, cotton clothes. They looked older and frailer than I'd expected. I said hello and *wai*-ed them, putting my hands together and bowing slightly. They said nothing. We unloaded the furniture and left.

We drove back to Krabi Town, everyone talking calmly. Jeab seemed normal again. Maybe I was the one to blame for all of this. I'd wanted the company of the group to which I was admitted more than the source of the introduction. She was a means to an end, and a person should never be that. But we were okay now.

They dropped me off outside a guesthouse in town. Jeab looked at me sadly through the window as the truck pulled away, taking all my troubles and pain with it. I wasn't sure what had happened to me there in Ao Nang. But it was over now. I was alive and I would continue.

★ ★ ★

Footsteps crunched on the gravel path. I was crossing a little wooden footbridge over a babbling brook, an oak tree's long branches hanging down, a ford to the right where the brook ran over the road, the green fields and trees of the countryside beyond, a fresh breeze cooling my face. I was home. Then the streets of the city where perhaps I should be, going forward, furthering myself. And my family speaking to me in my dreams. I don't know what they said. A long sleep, taking me far

far away on subconscious trails of memories and thwarted desires.

I woke up in a hot little shed in a garden, not sure where I was. But I knew I was still here. A guesthouse in Krabi, that's right. Ao Nang was over now. I was alone again. She was gone. It was all in the past. But I was still here. Ready for the next chapter.

I remembered my plans of travelling around Asia, getting a good job somewhere. But that was all slipping away now, swept away by my love for this land, the beaches, cliffs and jungle, brilliant nature, women, wine and song. And I was free again now. A little smile rose on my lips. Despite everything, Ko Phi Phi hadn't been forgotten.

★ ★ ★

Was the Big Bang the beginning of the Universe? If we assume that the known laws of physics can be applied to all parts of the Universe at all times, then the Big Bang and inflation theory explain the development of our Universe from its earliest known form, just after its creation, as best as we currently understand it to be.

Assuming it's correct, it still does not explain the initial condition from which the Universe came to be. It seems we cannot go back any further. It may be beyond the realm of our existence to understand the beginning of the Universe before its attributes of space-time, matter and energy were set.

And so, the biggest question of them all remains unanswered and possibly unanswerable. What is the ultimate cause of the Universe? Where did that original mass and force come from? Did it expand from a tiny singularity of infinite matter and energy? Or is the Universe a causeless event? Is a causeless event even possible? Or has the Universe actually existed for eternity? Or did everything, all matter and energy simply come from nothing? Nothing, and then suddenly everything, appearing from nothing? If so, then why is there anything at all? Why not simply Nothing? No Universe, no matter, no energy, space or time?

But clearly there is not Nothing. There is a Universe. So what great event or force caused the Universe to be? Did God create the Universe and set its laws into being? Or was it some other great force we do not know of?

Perhaps there is a physical explanation. Did the Universe come about from a great contraction of a previous universe to a singularity which then expanded into this Universe? If so, then where did that previous universe come from? Or does the Universe constantly reform itself through great cycles of expansion and contraction?

Or is our Universe merely a 'bubble' universe that was created from an event in another universe, like a giant black hole? And so is the Universe a single unit of existence, or merely a drop in the ocean? Are there other universes existing with a causal connection to ours? Or do other universes exist in parallel, on another plane of being? A Multiverse of parallel worlds, perhaps unconnected, perhaps connected spatially beyond observability, or connected temporally, coming into existence as new events create possible new worlds. Is there even an Omniverse of universes comprising every single possible universe that could have existed, through every single possible change that could have occurred, expanding exponentially as every possible event creates infinite new universes?

It's all possible. But of course, it could all be something else entirely.

THREE

Back to Hat Yai, sharing a nasty dorm room with a freelance photographer and some old guy travelling the world busking on his guitar. Interesting stories from them both, but unfortunately our room stank. I mean really stank of fetid shit. We all suspected each other, but nothing was said.

I was grateful for the relative normality of life in Hat Yai, getting my head back together, no more SangSom or Diazepam, chatting to the girls in the tour shops, pacing the streets, seeing a movie in the shiny mall, and eating lots; once in a Muslim restaurant, a poster of Osama Bin Laden staring down at me.

As night fell I looked up past the city streets and saw the full moon shining bright through the warm drizzle, remembering past glories and pains. In a tacky theme bar I met an old US Vietnam veteran living in the city, chiselled face, baseball cap, cigar-chewing. "What you doin' there boy?" he demanded. Quite a few retirees living here who didn't like the tourist areas of the country, he told me. The guy was hardcore, like Robert Duvall in *Apocalypse Now*. "I'm 67 years old and I'll still kick your ass in an arm wrestle." He wasn't wrong.

I didn't feel much like chatting though. I just wanted to sink beers and stare at the neon lights dancing on the rain drops and puddles outside. So that's what I did. I reflected on what had happened in Ao Nang. All that serotonin, adrenaline and over-confidence, fuelled by the stimulants, Diazepam and alcohol meant that I was far from balanced. An alter-ego born, fed, loved, crippled and destroyed by a far mightier world, a world whose laws were set into operation long before this greedy soul was set loose in the playground. I could only be grateful that upon self-destruction it was I, the I of old, who crawled out the other side. I'd emerged deflated, emotionally exhausted, exhumed of all juices of the heart, operating in auto-pilot, just the occasional pulse of feeling to remind me I was still alive. But alive I was. Yep, still here, thank God. A little bruised and battered perhaps, but still me. In one piece, still holding on, wide-eyed and hungry. Though with perhaps a little more caution and wisdom than before. What doesn't kill you makes you stronger. Sounded about right to me. And I felt stronger now. Because if you don't learn from your mistakes in some way then you're fucked in the long run. You can do what you want in life. You've just got to do it. Simple as that. Despite everything, I couldn't shake off my belief in the capacity for free will. To will to act on ends chosen by oneself and oneself alone. And now I wanted to act again. I wanted to make things better. The World Cup started in a week. I had a plan to chill out somewhere quiet till then, wallow round in self-pity and so on, but now I was bored out of my wits. I wanted to get back on it! I got the bill.

Minibus through the karaoke bars of Padang Besar to another border crossing, four stamps, back to town and a minibus to Krabi. I decided to return to Ao Nang to fix things before heading to Ko Phi Phi to find work. Face my fears, confront the past, see if everything was okay, restore my name and . . . well I guess I liked it. But I was determined to control myself, get fit, recover and do things better this time.

★ ★ ★

Although many have argued against Man's capacity for free will, throughout history, many have argued in a variety of ways to show that we *do* have free will, we *do* control ourselves; usually arguing within the context of causality.

Some believe free will is possible since the non-physical mind doesn't behave in the same way as the causally-determined physical Universe. That the mind, consciousness, or soul, exists in another mode of being, and we have free will over it.

Many believe a causally-deterministic Universe is compatible with free will, stating that a person's choices are their own, and are not directly due to external forces. That despite often having conflicting desires, it is always oneself that makes the ultimate decision upon which to act on, not any external force.

Some think there is a combination of both determinism and free will in our minds. Maybe we flit between instances or periods of naturally-determined, animalistic behaviour, and periods of self-determined behaviour, using the power of our mind.

Some have highlighted the difference between two related concepts of free will. That of voluntary action or controlling oneself, and that of origination – being the first cause of one's action. If one's will is free then perhaps one must be the first cause of one's actions.

Some break down the decision-making process into two parts – the free generating of alternative possibilities, and the choosing, or willing of the option. The first part is down to indeterminate chance, the second down to determined choice, say some. Others say the chances are determined and only our choice is free.

But despite all of these complicated theories, people have always had problems explaining how such a free realm can exist in a world of cause and effect.

★ ★ ★

Straight off the *songtaew* and there was the laughing Bird on his bike. "You back already?" He told me about his most recent near-misses with Western girls and his business ideas for moving to nearby Railey.

I patrolled the strip again, saying my hellos, determined to get it right this time. Since it was low season, the guys at the kayak shop said I could have a free trip if I found three customers. It was quiet at night. I just cruised in third gear, no more buckets. But I soon found some lads for the kayak trip.

The next day, Krabi's easy charms swept me away again. We were taken to the sea cliffs and mangrove swamps of Ao Thalane. Working my paddles through the choppy sea, feeling strong and alive, rejuvenated by the Sun's rays. The guide, another of these buff Southern gigolos, got talking to me about women and power, power to do what you want in life. Back in town, we went jogging down Ao Nang Beach, smiling at the ladies.

Back at Shamrock, Jackpot showed us a flyer he'd written for his new business. "Haven't got a Scooby's what to do next?" it read, "Come on Jackpot's Magical Mystery Tour around Ao Nang!" He wanted to take groups of unsuspecting tourists off on long-tail boats for deserted beach parties. Seemed like a ruse for him to get hold of impressionable young blondes to me. I edited his flyer all the same.

Later we went to the bar where I'd nearly got a beating the week before. After a few handshakes it seemed my reputation was restored. I played pool with the young boss of a new language school in Krabi Town. Said he needed teachers. Suddenly the opportunity of living and working here in Krabi had appeared. This beautiful place where I felt so at home. I got his number and then ventured into Spicy Park, ever curious. As I crept about I heard my name called out by various faces I vaguely recognised but couldn't quite remember through the haze. Faces that knew more about me than I did. Unsettled, I quickly left.

Another couple of days getting stronger, swimming in the sea, jogging down the beach, playing frisbee in the Sun, getting tanned and healthy. I enjoyed helping out the locals, finding customers and writing their adverts for them in return for drinks or little favours. I was so well known around town that people were approaching me for help. An Indian tailor came up to me on the beachfront. "Hello my friend. I know about you. You are the excellent salesman! You find me 20,000 baht worth of customers for my suits and I give you free suit!" he told me in my trunks and flip-flops. That was pushing it a bit though.

Sometimes me, Nick and Bird squeezed on a bike and cruised round looking for some action. But the nights in Ao Nang never quite lived up to their promise. The bars were all dead later on. It was low season. Time for the next step.

I watched the opening game of the World Cup in Shamrock one hot afternoon. Anything was possible and a new challenge lay on the horizon. I'd repaired things here and was feeling strong and confident again. Bird had been talking about coming with me to Ko Phi Phi to find work. I wasn't sure about it, wanting to tread my own path, but he was so enthusiastic and friendly that I couldn't really say no to the guy. He'd only been in the South of Thailand for a short time himself and seemed eager to find his own place too. He got on with everyone and spoke good English. So why not, I thought. So off we set, back on the ferry to Paradise Island.

★ ★ ★

I sat outside at the back of the boat watching the dream become a reality. Could I really pull this off? The young Thai boat-hands with their tattoos and pendants were popping pills and drinking cans of Chang in fits of giggles, as a few tourists sat dangling their feet off the side of the boat. The island grew from a shadow on the horizon to a green oasis in the ocean, verdant jungle covering its steep slopes, high cliff walls beyond and yellow sands glistening on the shore.

We arrived at the busy pier in Ton Sai Bay, got a room and headed off to find work. I went to Lucky Star Bar and met Jimmy, the young American boss. He said they had work. It was happening! I checked Predator Bar next door. They said I could work there, but not Bird.

We had a smoke on the beach in the fantasy dreamscape of Ao Lodalum Bay, the huge bay on the opposite side of the isthmus to Ton Sai Bay where I was baptised that first day I arrived. The perfect bay. The island was much busier than Ao Nang; a pretty young international crowd, national flags flying for the World Cup. People swimming in the warm seas, playing frisbee and volleyball, everybody chatting to each other, great laid-back party atmosphere, the perfect lifestyle on Paradise Island. Forget the rest. *This* was the place to be.

That night we checked out the other bars on the island. To Coco

Loco Bar by the rocks on Ton Sai Bay and Pirate Bar in the market, but there wasn't much going on. Lucky Star had a fun atmosphere, with a talented band of leather-clad Thai rockers doing perfect covers of classic rock tracks. But after they finished it was pretty quiet. We went to Jungle Bar next door. The downstairs courtyard was quiet now. The action was all upstairs. We climbed up the steep stairs past the glamorous-looking Thai girls working at the entrance. We emerged from under the boxing ring into the huge open-sided bar and disco, elevated on a large wooden platform looking over the island at night, two storeys high.

The boxers were knocking each other about when we arrived, throwing elbows, knees and kicks in too. The crowds watched excitedly around the ring, getting surged up on their buckets. When the boxing stopped everyone hit the dance floor on the mountain side of the bar. Palm tree trunks painted in red, yellow and green broke through gaps in the black and white tiles on the floor and a giant, gold-painted wooden cock statue was cemented in the middle of the room. This was the biggest place on the island, no doubt.

Midnight and the free bucket bell rang. I couldn't really say no now, could I? The old crazy juice ran through my veins again, the old grin, the over-confidence, the super power! I couldn't see any foreigners working there, but what the hell? I went up to the middle-aged Thai man behind the bar and asked if we could work there. He told me to come back tomorrow when the boss would be here. He then scribbled something on a pink slip of paper and handed it to me. "200 baht. Free drinks. Free room." I looked at it in disbelief, like a winning lottery ticket. This was too good to be true, too true to believe. Was I going to be the only foreigner working in the biggest disco on the most beautiful island on Earth?

Next afternoon, we went to the downstairs of Jungle Bar where the boss was sat chatting with friends. The man from last night, who did all the paintings in the bar, introduced us and we *wai*-ed respectfully. We chatted a bit and got on well. Everyone was cool and friendly.

Eventually, we were told we could work there. That was it! We'd sealed the deal.

★ ★ ★

7:30pm, we started work. *Welcome to the Jungle*. I was introduced to Ning, a pretty girl I'd be working with, all dressed in black. "Aaah, you very handsome," the boss said laughing. "You get all the girls in here okay? Good for business!" as Ning eyed me over. I grabbed my first free Chang from the bar before Ning led us around the streets, showing us where to go as we handed out flyers, advertising the drink deals, boxing, free buckets and disco.

We got chatting to up-for-it guys and pretty girls, meeting everyone. Ning told us not to flyer in front of competitors' bars, though I'd learnt that lesson already. We went up to the pier, grabbed another drink and headed back, scoping everything out, the streets alive with the World Cup atmosphere.

After a couple of laps we were told to stay at the front of the bar to get people in for a drink, and later on for the boxing. The boxing ring and disco were upstairs on the other side of the courtyard, so far from the downstairs bar on the street that you could barely see them. We had to pull newcomers over to convince them there really was a boxing match going on up beyond the darkness of the courtyard. *Eye Of The Tiger* would play out over the island to announce the start of the boxing, and then the traditional Thai boxing music, that reedy flute sound playing twisting, hypnotic, random rhythms like a snake charmer. The boxers did a traditional warm-up dance in their headbands before the bout. I hit the buckets, everything handed to me for nothing now, crowds rising, anticipation building.

At 11:30pm the boxing finished and that was our cue. I sprinted up the stairs like a bucking bull out the chute, erupting out into the disco, grabbed another bucket and hit the floor, trying to make sure people stayed in the bar for half an hour till the free buckets at midnight. Once we got the buckets down their necks, they were ours – the floor packed with drunken madmen and woozy girls in short skirts. And that was it. Walk, talk and dance like a loon every night. The job of my dreams, sharing full-to-the-brim buckets with the punters on the dance floor, everybody plugging into the straws like suckling pigs to a sow. Bucket after bucket after bucket . . .

I raised my head. I was asleep on the bar right in front of the boss on my first night. I'd screwed up again. I looked at the boss like a man about to hear his final judgement. The boss laughed and handed me a big Chang. "Don't worry. This will wake you up!" Amazing Thailand! At closing I was given 200 baht. I staggered onto the streets, kissing some girl, falling over, talking crap, just like I knew I loved it.

I saw the boss the next afternoon and was told I'd done a good job despite passing out. It seemed I was in. I could also get a free room but there was only one left. On the left of the courtyard area was an accommodation block of ten rooms on two floors. The cleaning lady showed me room 3 on the bottom floor. There was just a small double bed, a fan and a bare bathroom, with a wooden shutter at the back opening out onto a tiny gap full of rubbish in between buildings. The water ran a soft brown from the dirty reservoir in the village. It wasn't pretty. Me and Bird would have to share the bed if we both wanted to live here. The guesthouse prices here were even more than the mainland, so we had no choice if we were going to stay here a while.

★ ★ ★

We settled into a new routine. The female staff would often be hanging out at the street front bar at lunchtime. In the downstairs courtyard, lined with coconut trees sticking out the concrete, tourists would sometimes train with the boxers, spar in the ring and hit the punch bags hanging outside the accommodation block. Sometimes I'd join the boxers playing keepy-uppy with a little wicker ball, a popular Southeast Asian game. They didn't speak much English but I thought it a good idea to be on friendly terms with them. They lived in the corrugated iron shacks perched on the side of the hill around the disco.

There were at least a dozen female Thai staff giving out flyers, waitressing or bartending, another dozen boxers, a couple of DJs, a guy called Green whose chief responsibilities seemed to be shifting ice upstairs in the early evening, sponging the boxers down and maintaining his dreadlocks, (being the only dreaded guy in the bar,) the drunk cook, some cleaning ladies, and now me and Bird. Next door was Lucky Star. Jimmy had been here a few years and had now set up the bar with the Jungle guys. So you also had the five piece rock band living there, Jimmy, a handful of his *farang* flyer staff, and another dozen local staff too. We were living in some kind of crazy, self-contained, drunken, testosterone-fuelled, kickboxing, rock and roll, hippie commune. I'd never worked in a bar before, let alone anything like this. But now the dream had come true. Living for nothing and working in the biggest bar in paradise.

I hung out with Jimmy in Lucky Star some afternoons as he got his bar ready for business. He was pretty happy with his lot, a permanent grin smeared on his face. "You must be screwing every girl on the island," I said. "Well you know, I live here and it's a small island, so I gotta behave myself. I can't go around screwing all my staff!" It seemed wise. Best not to bite the hand that feeds you. Also, it was always hard to tell who Thais were in a relationship with, as they rarely showed affection in public. I decided to get back to the Western women again. The scars from Ao Nang were still fresh.

Bird would usually hang around the front of the bar all night. He was always very polite and charming, and was good at getting families and couples in for a drink. I usually walked the streets flyering with Ning. She was in her late 20s, quite hot and quite flirty too. Moved here from the Isan region in the Northeast of Thailand, like a lot of girls I'd met. We'd patrol the streets early on, chatting to each other, me flyering to girls, her to boys. World Cup group games were playing on every TV in the village, locals and tourists alike enjoying the carnival atmosphere. I'd wait for her with my big Chang and a handful of flyers, sweating like mad as guys chatted her up. She loved the attention.

Back at the front of the bar, chatting to colleagues, meeting the tourists, keeping tabs on the pretty girls. Lots of English, Swedish, Canadians, Israelis and more – hundreds passing by every night. Infinite potential. I quickly worked out who to hit with the flyers. People who were walking slowly and looking around at everything were probably new arrivals. So straight in, explaining the set up. Different angles for different people. Polite for older people, families and couples. Mad-for-it-geezer with young blokes on the piss. Flirty with the girls. Some would grab your flyer without looking at you, while others would shun it completely, looking annoyed. It seemed there were a lot of Westerners working here as divers or running restaurants and bars who didn't appreciate the harassment. It was interesting seeing the range of reactions evoked in people from performing the same action over and over again.

There were other *farang* staff on the nearby sandwich stall corner – the guys at Lucky Star, a cool guy Mitch from LA and others at Predator Bar. We'd playfully compete, whilst gossiping about everyone going by and watching the grisly-looking stray dogs humping in the shadows.

The hypnotic charms of the mind-bending *Muay Thai* music drifted down from up the hill, the streets quiet now. Bounding up the concrete steps, grabbing my buckets and passing round the sweet amber nectar. The orange love affair was back in full swing. That dirty chemical rush! That domineering explosion of freedom! Freedom from oneself.

Crazy football fans were peaking, some climbing up the coconut trees and swinging over the crowds from the lighting rig above. I had to climb halfway up the trees to persuade them down, as well as picking up broken glasses and bottles as drunk punters danced around barefoot.

The disco had a good mixture of Westerners and locals. The boxers mingled around shirtless after their fights, Western ladies swooning over their pecs and easy confidence. Local Rasta dudes, predatory girls and ladyboys over from the beer bars of Phuket, drunk massage girls on the pull. All the pretty young things dancing and hooking up.

After a few hours of this I was usually pretty far gone, my duties slipping away as the booze took hold. Girls shaking their asses, eyes roaming, smiles, dances, this one or that, can't make my mind up, playing it cool as the booze descended, consciousness evaporating . . .

Waking up on a double bed lying next to an unconscious Bird every morning. The old rushy hangovers were creeping up on me again, waking up after little sleep, Bird snoring, body dead but mind whizzing like a wind turbine. I barely knew him really. I felt a little responsible for him, having lured him here with my tales, but I knew I could trust him. He was a good guy. But the flashbacks were getting louder. Had to get out the room.

Out onto the streets. People in the sandwich stalls and travel shops calling my name from the shadows. Tourists passing me in the street smiling, familiar faces everywhere. Just got to sweat it out. Down to Lodalum Beach, across the isthmus to the pier at Ton Sai Bay, dozens of long-tail boats anchored to the beach. Sometimes I sat and watched the tourists arrive by the boatload, fresh custom for the evening, locals hustling them into hotels and pushing metal carts of goods away into the warren.

★ ★ ★

One night I managed to stay on my feet till closing time at 3am. The music stopped and the lights dimmed as people streamed down the stairs, leaving new couples chatting and kissing in dark corners. Through the blur I got chatting to a tall, elegant Thai woman in a sexy dress I'd never met before. There was something . . . exotic about her. Pretty soon she invited me to her room. We walked the streets together past various familiar faces lurking in the closing time shadows.

We came to her room in some back-alley. I left my shoes amongst dozens of pairs of high heels outside the door and sat on the edge of the bed in the tiny dimly-lit hovel. Suddenly another woman entered the room. A different kind of woman. I recognised her. She was the famous ladyboy on the island who came to Jungle Bar occasionally. My heart lurched in realisation. They both stood blocking the door, whooping with joy at their catch. Didn't know whether to laugh or scream, suddenly trapped in a small room with two ladyboys. They were hot, but . . . The pretty one pulled down her skirt and knickers, revealing some kind of bush. I was trying to work out what it was when suddenly the one I'd come back with pulled her skirt down to reveal a massive donger swinging between his legs. Oh God! They moved towards me. I backed away into the middle of the bed. They crawled onto the bed on all fours like hungry vampires. Looking down the barrel of a gun, snap decision time. Ladyboy threesome or . . . run away! I leaped off the side of the bed, shimmied past them, out the door and shot off into the night.

Another whiskey-fuelled crippler next to the snoring Bird, flashbacks swinging through my head from last night. I forced myself up and staggered out into the burning inferno streaming into the courtyard. I saw one of the boxers sitting around. His name was Chai. He was 28, older than most of the other boxers, covered in tattoos and muscles. A good-looking, laid-back guy. He didn't speak much English, but then he didn't have to. Girls were queuing up for him every night after the fights. I went and said hello. "Last night I see you with ladyboy," he smiled. Shit! People were already talking about me for sharing a room with the rather camp Bird, and now I'm getting spotted going home with ladyboys. I panicked for a moment. Then those reassuring words from the smoke of Ao Nang came back to my head like a mantra: "Thai people are very friendly." I looked at the smiling Chai, his eyes reefer-red. He didn't give a fuck. Nobody here gave a fuck about what anyone else did. We were living in paradise. Why would you? It's all good. I explained my mistake anyway. "Okay. No prob-lem," he said. "I speak English no good. You teach me okay?"

We strutted down to the beach, girls in bikinis swooning at him from all angles. I was hoping I might get some kind of rub-off effect from hanging round with one of the island's prize studs. "I fuck her already," he'd say after this girl and that. "Good fucking!" He was a brazen gigolo, sauntering up to any girl on the sand he liked the look of and trying it on. We went to an internet shop and I wrote an email to an English girlfriend of his, asking for money for his sick mother. I was pleased to have one of the boxers as my friend now. Working with them behind me I felt practically invincible.

After the boxing, the bucket-addled would often get in the ring to fight. Usually just for fun but sometimes it would get serious. The lure finally pulled me in. I had to give it a go. I got into a tag team wrestling match with some English lads. It felt good to fight like a little kid again. But we lost after my teammate got strangled into submission. I sprained my hand but nothing serious.

Every night surrounded by women, every morning next to Bird. Always me awake first. Always him snoring. I was beginning to resent his presence in the room, and his mad paranoid ramblings about some girl he was after, and about the Thai staff gossiping behind our backs. The buckets were frying his mind. Dealing with my own paranoia was burden enough, without having to listen to someone else's crap. This was supposed to be my job in paradise, not his.

I'd have to get out that damn room, forced out into the streets, never a moment to myself. The endless hellos and morning-after conversations. Stories, shock and embarrassment. Little chats, smiles, nods, handshakes. And the longer I stayed there, the more people I knew. I met so many tourists and locals at night that I couldn't remember half of them the next day. Some people would come up and start chatting to me like we were old friends but I had no idea who they were. Random strangers who knew my name telling me stories about what I did last night. It was like being famous. Everybody knew me, but I didn't know everybody. It was fucking my head up. I told myself it was just the booze. But the voices still didn't go away, whispering little madnesses in my ear. People looking at me in a funny way. Some smiling at me one minute and then ignoring me the next. Others dropping hints about what I'd done last night. "You! Last night!" kind of thing. "What have I done?" I agonised. Did my lips move when I thought that? Faces I recognised but wasn't sure if I knew them or not. Scary-looking boatmen coming up to me and shaking my hand. Strangers calling my name. Every day, no freedom in my room, none outside, no way to escape the madness in my head. No way except one. One more drink.

★ ★ ★

The big England match came. I crossed the rainy courtyard to Lucky Star watching the game with Jimmy and the staff. Oh, and about 100 English fans cheering the place down. Big hard bunch of lads. England won. The bar erupted, singing and dancing in the puddles and monsoon rain the whole afternoon, *Three Lions* and *A Bucket Of Vindaloo*.

Upstairs again, the same songs night after night. Pink, Christina Aguilera and *The Ketchup Song*. On the floor, me and five other guys, including the two big hard-looking Thai rock climbers, are all fixated on the same girl, a gorgeous, beautiful blonde. And I mean really hot, on another level. Six guys all jiggling and shimmying around her trying to capture her attention in the bizarre world of human mating rituals. Anything could happen. Suddenly she chooses me, dancing up flirtatiously. The other guys gradually danced away and we sat in the windy corner of the disco overlooking the island.

Her name is Crystal from Canada, working as a model in Japan. She's rubbing my hand telling me I'm one of the most beautiful men she has ever seen. She even dropped the old classic: "I can make you famous in Japan." All reasoning was melting away. I couldn't believe my luck. For all my pains and labours, finally my gift from the gods! The dream resurrected. The perfect girl on the perfect island, leaving for Japan together for fame and stardom! Suddenly her friend appears in a bad mood, dragging her away. She told me to find her at the beach tomorrow.

The next day I went to meet them at the western end of Ton Sai Beach, past the little doctor's shack and the huge restaurants set up for the day-trippers from Phuket. The beach ended at the climbing wall where the huge cliffs towered out the water. They weren't there. I got chatting to the climbers. I was friendly with Joey, a young Canadian guy who'd got a job taking climbers up with these two gigantic Thai guys, both former boxers, both built like a brick shithouse. They were in the club most nights. I was friendly with them too, but we were often chasing the same women, and my bucket twinges kept me from feeling too comfortable with them.

That night, two posh English lads on their gap year between school and University were giving me the low down about the threesome they'd had with a Thai girl last night. "The best blow job I've ever had," they told me excitedly. "She was on her period, so I did her up the arse three times!" one told me with a look of wonder on his face. I was ticking boxes in my head. "Who was she?" I asked. He pointed her out. It was the ladyboy with the big prick from last week. "Did she keep her knickers on?" I asked. "What? Errr . . . yeah. Why?" he asked, his mind suddenly in vertigo. "I'm sorry mate. She's a ladyboy." Confused, they went into a corner for a few minutes, analysing their hazy drunken memories of the night before, before coming back to me like they'd seen a ghost, faces white and shell-shocked. "You've just changed my life forever," said Mr Triple Whammy in solemn sincerity, before exiting the building, and almost certainly the island on the next boat.

As much as guys may dream of such things, I didn't know any real girls that sucked dick like porn stars, loved it up the arse three times on the trot and kept their knickers on throughout. I laughed, but I felt sorry for them. I had to do it just the once, but I decided to stop telling people after that. Better to let people work things out for themselves.

In the morning I had a long swim past the anchored speedboats, trying to keep fit. Then to the climbing wall again. I found Crystal and her friend topless on the beach. Good God she was hot, long blonde hair running down her beautiful face, perfect tanned skin. Too good to be true. I sat and chatted with them, trying to ignore the whispers echoing round my bucket-head. But she wasn't the same enthusiastic Crystal I'd first met. No more touching, no more promises. I was sure she had a boyfriend or something somewhere. Two very confident girls in their late twenties working in some vague entertainment industry in Japan. There was definitely a lot to them. They were fascinated by the climbers, who were looking down at us and waving from high up on the cliff face like predatory soldier ants.

Crystal invited me for a dip in the sea. It was low tide, the sea shallow and rocky. We waded out into six inches of water, trying not to cut our feet on the spiky rocks below. Suddenly I felt a sting on the side of my foot. A rock? A crab maybe? I looked down, but the water was murky from the kicked-up sand. What was it? Suddenly a stingray emerged from the sandy water, swimming away through the rocks. A fucking stingray! Size of a dinner plate, with a long tail and a stinger at the end. I'd never seen a wild one in my life and now I'd just been stung by the bastard! Blood was coming out the side of my foot. I didn't know if it was poisonous or what. I told Crystal, expecting some reaction at least, but she didn't seem concerned, wandering off into the sea.

I hobbled off alone to the nearby doctor's clinic, the only one on the island. The staff looked at me as I drew a picture of a stingray on a scrap of paper to explain the situation. "Aaah, *plaagaben*," the doctor said. It didn't hurt too much till he started cleaning my foot with some liquid and gave me an injection right into the wound. Jolts of agony. I bit down on an empty water bottle to hold it together. But then he said I could go, warning me that the poison would still be in my system for a while.

Back down to the beach hoping for some female sympathy. Crystal told me to lie down. I lay on her sarong, the beautiful topless Crystal next to me. It should have been great but it wasn't. I was shivering as the poison ran through my veins, taking a grip of my nervous system. I think it was the poison anyway. I looked upside down at the rock climbers looking down at me from above, last night's vapours screaming mad lies in my ears. What the fuck was going on? I could feel reality loosening again. Crystal went back into the sea, bending over in various positions, splashing water over her naked body, water dripping down her perfect breasts, stomach and thighs, teasing every damned prick on the beach.

I retreated to my dank room to get a hold of myself before 7:30pm. That half hour between sunset and work was always a bad time of day. Lights fading, exhaustion rising, with the inevitability of nothing but another night on the front lines ahead of me. The early evening was the only time they played any reggae music. As I was wrestling with the demons and having a cold shower in the spider-ridden bathroom, there was Bob Marley singing his sweet lullabies around me. *No Woman No Cry.* Sometimes the water supply didn't work and everyone would be queuing up to wash in the disco toilets upstairs, pouring water from the plastic scoop floating in the large water bucket, trying not to breathe in the acrid piss fumes.

I was getting tired of trying to be chatty every evening when all I wanted to do was lie down and rest. Booze was the only way to break through. Crystal went past a couple of times, a climber in tow. The momentum had long faded now, my mood turning fouler with every sip of liquor. But I still held a candle of hope. Would she come back? Upstairs, the flyer girls got some vodka and orange buckets in. Hit the memory wall. Bird comes in our grey room and wakes me up. 6am, party over, no Crystal, raining outside, confused and gutted.

I went to an English restaurant and splashed out my meagre wage on an English breakfast, an hour of BBC World and a flushing toilet. It was high-end luxury to me, not being in that damp squat of a room with Bird mumbling incoherently about some girl he hadn't pulled. Though that was all I was doing too. My head was still reeling from last night. Maybe it was time to get out of Thailand. The place felt dangerous . . . No. One last try, the dream too great to let go of.

I went to the end of Ton Sai Beach again and found Crystal and her friend sitting outside their expensive beach bungalow. She didn't really speak much, the momentum in reverse now. I didn't know why. Suddenly, *bang*! A huge, green coconut slammed onto the stone tiles just a metre from my head. It would have knocked me out or killed me if it hit my head. Was this a sign from God? Stingray attack yesterday and now falling coconuts! The woman was a Siren, singing sweet nothings in my ear and luring me onto the rocks! Time to cut my losses.

The sexual frustration of island life was immense, hot girls on the beach by day, Ning winding me up all evening, and drunk girls in the clubs by night, the stench of sex heavy in the humid air. The disco was going crazy, all the ladyboys drunk after the Cabaret show at Coco Loco. Jumping all over the golden cock, grabbing crotches and flashing their silicone efforts. One charged over and had a go at me for telling too many tourists about their little secret. It was getting too much. Maybe it was time to leave the island.

Suddenly a statuesque Dutch girl appeared from nowhere, grabbing me for a dance. I took hold of her and kissed her. We wandered the dark alleys looking for her room, but she couldn't find it. Luckily I lived in Jungle Bar and I knew exactly where it was. I took her back, kicked Bird out, and we fell onto the bed.

I awoke in the morning as she closed the door behind her as quietly as she could. But I didn't care, I'd broken my duck and fucked Crystal out my head. The boxers cheered as I came out my room a minute after the girl, my sexuality confirmed. There was no way I was leaving the island now. Bird reappeared later, woken up by the rain on the beach. Great lad that Bird.

★ ★ ★

The island, the job, the women and the World Cup. I was caught on a runaway train of liquid oblivion. Lucky Star erupted as teams advanced into the second round, dancing round, doing the conga. "Let's get fucking Chang-ed up! Let's get fucking Chang-ed up! La-la-la-la . . . *hey*! La-la-la-la . . . *hey*!" Ning, who liked to assume the role of my immediate superior, tried to get me to stop drinking, but the train had already derailed.

By evening I felt like shit on a hotplate. I now needed a few Changs, some gulps of bucket and an energy drink, just to stoke up the old generators and be able to handle a conversation, let alone be the friendly face of a fucking cheesy disco. The buckets always saved you in the end though. And the punters needed me. I was the link-man, the top dog, the new Prince of Paradise!

The boxing stopped but the floor was dead. Time for the old bucket manoeuvre, getting a full bucket with ten straws, tempting the weak with some dance steps and sips of the holy water. Somehow it worked – the Midas touch of the SangSom. I was the grinning, bastard son of Tony Manero and The Pied Piper of Hamelin, luring the innocent to their bucket-fuelled demise. And for my labours another drunk tourist was gifted. The gods favoured me it seemed. Though sadly not Bird who had to sleep on the beach again.

By now a few other Westerners were working at the bar. A pretty diver worked behind the bar upstairs with his pecs out. A young English backpacker joined the crew and a Swedish man, Fred, a tall skinny guy of about 30, with a long hook nose and greasy brown hair. He'd worked here before so knew everyone. He was friendly with the boxers and trained with them sometimes, but by night he would drink and Diazepam himself into a wobbly stupor, chewing on tobacco-bags of snus, staggering around trying to force flyers into people's hands like some New York pimp. Eventually he was sent upstairs to wait tables as he was scaring the customers off. And Katie from England who'd also been here before. We got on well, her advice and piss-taking having a slight stabilising effect on me as I juggled the balls of madness. Another English girl, one of the boxers' girlfriends, would occasionally work too. Ning and I were good friends by now too. I would laugh at her trying to deal with the various young men she had on the go at any one time. But she would get jealous if she ever saw me flirting with other girls. And eventually I admitted to myself I didn't particularly enjoy seeing her slip off with random geezers at the end of the night either.

★ ★ ★

I was starting to explore the island more during the day. Panting up to the glorious viewpoint again to take in this little miracle on Earth. Sometimes a long swim or evening jog along Lodalum Beach, the exercise slightly counteracting the daily cycles of abuse.

Another day, I took a left at Ton Sai and climbed across rocky outcrops and smaller coves, past tiny huts perched on the rocks where local fishing families sat living together in cramped conditions. I eventually reached the magnificent golden sands of Long Beach, the shadowy enigma of Phi Phi Leh stretched on the sea beyond, its shape changing from every angle. Nearby the boats from Krabi came round the tip of the cove past the outlying rocks of Shark Point, huge tropical fish swimming in the coral, metres from the steep shore.

I'd also chat with the local guys hiring out the water sports gear on Ao Lodalum. One of them was the guy with the bong I'd met when I first came here. They were the real island inhabitants, born and bred on the islands of the Andaman Sea, unlike most of the Thais from the mainland who worked in the tourist industry. Nobody knew much about them, since they seemed to exist independently from the rest of the country. Some had moved from other islands, some were descended from nomadic sea gypsies that once lived all over the Andaman coast but had now settled here. They were Muslim and had their own Malay-related dialect which Thais could barely understand. Some were landowners collecting big rent cheques, others fishermen, boatmen, touts and handymen. Some of them just hung out all day getting loaded. They also ran the lucrative bird nest trade, collecting swiftlets' nests made of the birds' saliva in the caves and crannies of the cliffs. These were then sold and made into soups as a delicacy in Chinese restaurants. They tended to be very much of the old school. Ko Phi Phi may have been part of Krabi province, Thailand, but it was their island.

The boss down there, Mr Kit, knew I worked at Jungle and we discussed ideas for setting up beach parties. I'd bring in the customers, he'd supply the party. It sounded intriguing but I wasn't sure if I'd really do it or not. He said I could take his kayaks out for free though. I seemed to be getting special status everywhere I went.

I rowed myself out of Ao Lodalum to the next bay called Monkey Beach, then beyond the high cliffs to see the sunset which was only visible at sea, since the cliffs to the west blocked it off from the village.

It was good to escape the island and the people for an hour. Sitting in reflective silence, bobbing up and down on the soft waves and fresh warm air, dreams of paradise realised, perhaps new legendary beach parties to come – it was a lot to take in. This was it, this was the dream, to be King of Paradise. The sky and the ocean erupted in colour all around me, an electric painting of reds, oranges, purples and pinks. God it was good to be alive. I stared into the heart of the bright orange globe hovering before me on the edge of the horizon, till all I could see was the glowing impression burnt into the back of my eye.

The Sun's electromagnetic waves travelled at the speed of light, 150 million kilometres in eight minutes, entering my pupil and forming an image on my retina. This was converted into electrical signals, transmitted through optic nerves and complex neural networks to the visual cortex and other areas of my brain. The signal was then realised consciously as my visual perception, my guide through life. All was golden.

The fading aurora darkened to a burnt red as it was engulfed by the turning Earth; a spectral starburst of light waves emitted purple and yellow traces, ten million colours visible to Man, radiating across the hazy evening sky, their reflection dissolving into a glittering sheen in the warm ocean below. And it was all real . . .

★ ★ ★

People losing their minds on buckets and patriotic fervour. Chanting, body painting, football shirts and flags everywhere. It was mostly good humoured, but fights were frequent after midnight. I intervened in several drunken arguments, antlers locked, and told them to sort it out in the ring. Not a bad thing having a boxing ring soaking up the testosterone in a lairy tourist disco. This was the Jungle, where booze, sex and violence reigned supreme.

One night a crazed guy started shouting his head off at the boss. I pulled one of the older boxers over assuming he'd step in, but he just laughed. Katie told me that they didn't double as bouncers since they'd get into trouble with the police. I'd always assumed I had an army of kickboxers to back me up, but I was wrong. Suddenly I felt slightly less invincible.

Another night the diving barman got into a fight downstairs and ran up in hysterical tears, the buckets having completely consumed his soul, and started grabbing hold of people in tearful desperation till we intervened. Another victim down.

Then the new English guy was told to move into our room. We had one night with the bloody three of us passed out drunk on one bed. It was getting ridiculous. Bird had nearly lost the plot by this point from the buckets and all his recent nights on the beach. His paranoid rambles were incomprehensible. I really couldn't understand anything he was saying anymore. He was also flirting with an almighty beating by constantly chatting to the English girlfriend of one of the boxers.

With all the new staff coming in and the new bed mate, Bird decided to return to Ao Nang the next morning. I hadn't fallen out with him, but I wasn't too sad to see him leave either. It was getting too much living together. But now I was waking up next to a complete stranger.

While the tourists sunbathed on the beach every day, there was no relaxation for me. No rest for the wicked. It was getting too much. The carnival atmosphere was winding down as everyone's teams got dumped out of the cup. Another month had almost passed and I had to leave the country. I packed my small bag and boarded the boat to Krabi.

★ ★ ★

Most of the traditional arguments for and against free will take place within the context of cause and effect. They take a position on whether or not the world is causally determined, and then whether or not we can have free will within this context.

It may seem natural to assume the world is a causally determined place. But perhaps we are mistaken in believing that the world is necessarily determined by the past. There are, in fact, many problems underlying the assumptions of cause and effect.

Firstly in relation to the human mind. Due to the nature of time, we can necessarily only do things in the present. Therefore it may be impossible to know whether we could have done otherwise in any situation. Or to put it another way – we can't change the past, only the present. And we only get one chance at that. Therefore the question of whether our actions are willed or determined may be unanswerable, since there is no way of knowing what would have happened if we had acted differently.

These problems relate to the world also. Since there is necessarily only one present state of affairs, and one past from which they came, is there really any way of knowing what would have happened, had things have happened differently? Is it really possible to analyse the nature of cause and effect if it only happens once, in the present, and we can never really know how things would have been under different circumstances?

Certainly scientists can do controlled experiments, observe the results, and eventually gain a better understanding of the causal relationship between certain entities. But outside the lab in the highly complex real world, is it really possible to understand the depth of causal complexity between all things? Does it even make sense to talk of x being the cause of y, when in fact the number of causes of an event, and the number of effects it will have are far greater than this? And similarly, since every event has causes, and those causes have other causes, where do you draw the line looking back at the chain of causes of causes of events?

There are many other problems concerning any attempts at understanding the causal relationship between things. For example, what things are we actually observing as causes and effects? Are they events in time, objects, properties of objects, processes, variables, probabilities or even the whole state of affairs?

Then there are issues resulting from human observation. There are various biological and technological limitations to what we can observe in the world. Another problem is that our judgements on causality are often affected by emotion and ideology. The world is full of meaningless generalisations and dubious inductive reasoning. Another is the common human error of mistaking correlation for causation – of seeing two things happening at the same time, or one just before the other, and assuming one to be the cause of the other. Turn on the TV news and you'll soon be bombarded with various examples of this.

There is also a problem concerning scientific disciplines. Most scientists strive to better understand the causal relationships between various aspects of the world. But most of this is done within their particular realm of science. There is less crossover research done on the causal relationships between their realms of expertise – physics, chemistry, the Earth sciences, biology, the human sciences and so on. Although all experts in their field, there may not be enough crossover and big picture work taking place.

Also, throughout history, philosophy and science were two aspects of the same thirst for knowledge. Philosophy was concerned with the theory, and science the testing of these theories. Many great thinkers throughout history were both philosophers and scientists, as well as other professions such as politicians and engineers. In the West, it wasn't until the 18th Century that the two began to split into separate branches. Today, there is little academic crossover between the two. But science without philosophy may be guilty of theoretical assumptions, of being misguided and too analytical, and of failing to see the wider picture. On the other hand, philosophy without science is mere fairy tale. Both sides would probably benefit greatly by coming together again.

Scientists do amazing work unravelling the mysteries of the world. But there still remains much to be learned about causality in various fields, both in understanding the past and in predicting the future based on that analysis. A few brief examples:

Physicists have an excellent understanding of causality concerning forces and the motion of matter and energy; so much so that they can accurately predict the motion of celestial bodies many light years away and the behaviour of matter under various conditions with precise accuracy.

Chemistry too can predict the changes that take place in reactions, yet fundamental questions about the nature of atoms and subatomic particles remain, and predictions aren't always accurate.

The Earth's forces, though fairly well understood individually, are very hard to predict when interacting in the real world. Take the weather, climate change and tectonic activity.

More questions arise in biology. Although many biological processes are understood, the behaviour of organisms and ecosystems is extremely hard to predict, as are the effects of changes in the environment.

And moving into the realm of humanity, I'm not sure the word science is even applicable in attempts to study individual or social behaviour, such as in history, human geography, sociology, politics and economics. Look too at attempts in making business, economic or political forecasts. Mankind's behaviour seems to defy any attempts to shackle it with rules or laws, patterns or predictions.

Physical determinism may even have been proven wrong already. Quantum physics studies subatomic particles and shows that their behaviour is entirely random and uncertain, and hence indeterministic.

For example, electrons are subatomic particles which can also behave like waves. There is always an uncertainty about them, since we can measure the momentum, or path, an electron travels as it moves, *and* we can measure its position at any given moment, *but* we cannot know both. Hence we cannot know where an electron will be going at any moment. Its location is more of a statistical probability than an actual point in space.

Some believe this opens the door to free will – that a mind free from determinism is entirely in keeping with the nature of the Universe. Or would this mean that our will is also entirely random, chaotic and uncertain? And even if indeterminism at the subatomic level is true, is this effect strong enough to affect causation at the atomic level and above?

It may not be possible to know the extent to which events in the present are necessarily determined by the past, or are more random and chaotic. Perhaps physical causality is better understood as being a probability. It makes more sense to talk of probabilities of events occurring due to certain causes, than of definite causes and effects happening in such a complex world. We can talk of the probability of events never, sometimes or always having certain effects. Maybe everything could be explained by mathematics if only we knew all the data to enter into the equations.

Perhaps what we think of as everyday causality is just a very simplified and subjective way of seeing and understanding the world at a human level. Observable objects with close proximity in time and space, and an apparent causal connection between the two. We may often be right that these things are indeed causally connected, but be under no doubt the world is far more complex than we will ever know.

★ ★ ★

I OF THE SUN

Holed up in a comfortable room in a Chinese hotel in Hat Yai, the subsiding flood waters of drink releasing waves of suppressed thoughts, emotions and long languid dreams. I mulled over my future. I'd gone off teaching in Krabi. It was simply too small. I could try Bangkok. Or how about flying off to Japan or somewhere else? The more I saw of the region, the more I realised what I hadn't seen. The world lay before me in an infinity of possibilities and opportunities. My wings were fully stretched now. I was flying like an eagle, free will realised, ready and able to do anything I wanted in this glorious world.

So what did I do next? I spent the 12 Malaysian ringgit that I'd been carrying around for three months, turned around and went straight back again. Did I really have any choice in the matter? Old habits die hard.

It was raining, the sky a thick grey, the paths blocked by deep murky puddles. A lot of familiar faces had gone, replaced by the new. I'd only been away a few days but things changed quickly here. In some ways at least. My Jungle room was blissfully vacant for a few days before another young English lad moved in.

I bumped into Joey the climber. He dropped me a bombshell in hushed tones. He was seeing the stunning ladyboy. "She's the best-looking girl on the island, and she's had everything done." This I could confirm, but decided not to share the mangina sighting with him. Still a bit too fresh in my head. She was working, picking up tourists for cash and whatever else, but was taking care of young Joey too, buying him a TV and DVD player. I couldn't really argue with that. But it was too spicy for me.

I watched the World Cup final in Lucky Star, satisfied the best team had won. The island calmed down. Calmer, but the Jungle never sleeps.

I was friendly with all the Thai staff now. Playing 3-a-side football with the boxers in the courtyard. On the pull with Chai the boxer. The artist, the old guy we called Pablo, explaining his mad ideas to me over noodles in the local market area. One night after closing he pulled me into the karaoke bar the locals used. Inside all the Thai staff were going wild. It was good to see them all letting themselves go.

Fred was still lurching around off his head. One night, after a long afternoon of liquid training, he got in the ring as part of the show. It wasn't competitive, but after some sparring, the little Thai boxer did a roundhouse kick. Fred was too slow to react, getting a 360 degree heel to the face, breaking his nose in a spray of blood. Another night four *farangs* were fighting in the ring. Things got out of hand, ending in amphetamine-fuelled, nose-bleeding brutality, guys throwing up, hysterical girlfriends and so on.

Lots of late night lock-ins at Lucky Star. Mr America, Jimmy's birthday. He's shitfaced, taking the piss out of everyone. Ning gets a frying pan wrapped around her face by one of the other flyer girls. They were all fighting for their place in the queue to be Jimmy's girlfriend, a position none of them realised to be non-existent.

A mysterious girl approaches me in the disco. Love at first sight it seems. Amazing stuff this SangSom. She tells me to meet her on the pier in the morning to run away to the quiet island retreat of Ko Lanta together. Another morning of man-in-my-bed dread. Fuck this. I decide to make a run for it, scampering through the early morning streets, the Devil on my back, bad time to be awake. She wasn't there of course. I crawled up under a bush on the beach, quivering and confused, trying to get some sleep. The mysterious Mr Kit spotted me. He came over and started talking about the island families and police to me. More than I needed to know in my pickled state.

It seemed to be raining more and more, big puddles and wet mud everywhere. One day I made the mistake of walking around barefoot, slicing my foot open on some steel rebar sticking through the concrete floor of a shop. I was getting some kind of rash all over my body too. I was in decay. Waking up next to my third male bed mate after little sleep and more orange-glow day-mares. I tried to sleep on the beach but never could. I'd go back in the afternoon and he'd have gone out with the key, forcing me back on the streets all day, or to climb through the thin gap at the side of the building, full of rubbish and chickens, and break in through the wooden window. I'd often just end up sitting round the front of the bar punch-drunk with Fred, Chai, the boxers and whoever else, drinking beer and talking crap, laughing at the crazy life.

That night some pissed twat started on one of the big climbers. I should've left it alone but for some reason I jumped in. His friend launched into me. The climber stopped him before throwing the tourist down the concrete stairs into a mangled heap. The tourists often assumed I was a kickboxer, so I always got away with these security incidents unscathed and with a few extra drinks too. But I was still pissed off at why I was the only one trying to stop the fight. A boxer came over and tried to calm me down. "Don't worry. You work here. Nobody can touch you." My ego put my common sense to bed. Revenge was a dish served only in the dark it seemed.

I didn't really have the cash or will to stop drinking and go scuba diving. But I thought I'd try rock-climbing while I was here. I went to the shop and paid, but my friend Joey wasn't there, just the big guy whose fight I'd broken up. Same guy who was competing with me for Crystal. I kind of got on with him but he never spoke much, just smiled enigmatically. Nobody else was there, so the two of us went to the end of Ton Sai and climbed through the tree roots to the base of the climbing wall. He showed me the ropes and harnesses and I started climbing up the gaps in the vertical cliff face. Halfway up, my hand suddenly seized up from my wrestling injury a few weeks earlier. I looked down at the climber smiling up at me. If he let go of the rope between us I'd plunge to my death and nobody would ever know why. The orange whispers suddenly got me in a high altitude death-lock, hanging off a cliff with a gammy hand and a murderous climbing partner. I quickly descended, blaming my injured hand.

Katie left the island, leaving me and Ning alone all evening again, parading the streets like a couple, massage girls taking the mick out of us as we passed by. We began flirting like mad again. I couldn't stand the tension and suggested we stayed together on a vow of silence. She said no, we were just friends. That night I left the disco with another drunken teen in front of Ning. I took her back to mine, but she freaked out when she saw my sleeping bed mate and ran away. The next night Ning refused to talk to me, except to shout at me and order me around in front of everyone else.

Another week of afternoon drinking at the front bar in the rain, getting less fun every time. I decided it was time to go. My last night. Ning and I made up. She said she liked me but didn't want to get hurt as I was too young and leaving soon. After closing, I got dragged into the karaoke bar with all the Thai staff again, singing a stirring rendition of *My Way* before clowning about in the courtyard till dawn dancing to Thai country music with the boxers and flyer girls, Chai, the Rasta Green and the drunk cook.

I waved goodbye to everyone the next morning and made my way to the pier with my backpack. There I saw Ning sat under a palm tree in a sarong as the tide lapped against the shore, looking radiant and forgivable in the morning Sun. We smiled but didn't speak.

★ ★ ★

I took the afternoon boat to Ao Nang. Two hours tanning on deck in the late afternoon Sun, right past all the stunning islands on the way – Mosquito, Bamboo, Chicken and Poda. Then to the majestic peaks of Phra Nang and Railey Beach on the mainland. The Sun and the sky and the open seas. Incomparable beauty. Heaven on Earth.

A couple of nights in Ao Nang, finally in my own bed. Bird seemed shell-shocked, but on the road to recovery. He was off on his scooter trying to find a non-existent track over the sheer cliffs to Railey, to find a *farang* girl staying there that he'd kissed the night before.

I went bar-hopping with Nick. It felt very quiet after Phi Phi. This had been my training ground. But now memories walked the streets like ghosts. I saw little Dear on the street, who told me the other three had moved to Ko Samui for the low season. Heard my name emanating from various dark alleyways and bars. They had memories like elephants I swear. Met a brazen bar girl we nicknamed Chainmail, on account of the chainmail dress she wore over her bra and knickers.

She took a liking to me, following me round on her scooter the next day shouting, "I want to fuck you!" at the top of her voice whenever she passed, much to Nick's amusement. I didn't want to go down that road again though, remembering the chasm beyond the bottom of the bucket.

I was sad to be leaving the South. I'd been there for months now. I'd had the best and worst times of my life. I hadn't expected it – all the lows as well as the highs from travelling. I thought it would be one long holiday. It was, but it was also the biggest test of my life, doing it alone like this. Travelling alone but people everywhere. That's the way it is. A world of people, lives intersecting. I guess you never know what you're going to get till it comes, travelling alone without a plan in a strange land on the other side of Earth. So what next? Centerpoint was calling.

★ ★ ★

Now, almost 14 billion years after the creation of the Universe, it continues to expand, perhaps faster than the speed of light. Hence we can only observe the fraction of it nearest to us. There are many billions of galaxies in this observable Universe, and in one particular galaxy group is a large galaxy, with bars of stars revolving in spiral arms around its centre. It is composed of hundreds of billions of stars of different ages, sizes and masses. On one of its spiralling arms is a belt of stars, in which is a cluster containing one particular star, medium in size, and at 4.5 billion years old, about halfway through its life.

It is our Sun, a giant sphere of hot plasma and electrical fields consisting of hydrogen, helium and other elements. Nuclear fusion in its core converts hydrogen into helium, releasing photons which fire around inside the Sun before being emitted out into space as light and heat.

Eight distinct planets orbit around the Sun's gravitational field, formed from the remaining orbital disc of coalesced gas and dust left over from its formation – four small rocky planets nearby, and four larger gas planets beyond them. Around these planets orbit smaller moons. Countless other objects also orbit the Sun in various trajectories.

Not long after the Sun was born, a third of the age of the Universe itself, the third planet formed as rocks collided in space, gravitationally accreted and grew into a large mass. It was once a molten mass of rock, but its surface cooled and hardened into planet Earth. Another huge rock, perhaps fragmented by a massive collision, began orbiting close to the planet. The moon had the effect of steadying the speed and angle of Earth's rotation on its tilted axis. Condensing water vapour from the crust, intense volcanic activity and meteorite bombardment formed clouds, which condensed into rain, forming pools of liquid water. The Earth's distance from the Sun and its greenhouse gases ensured much of this water remained liquid and didn't boil away or freeze. The pools spread in size over and around the migrating plates of tectonic crust to form great oceans, slowly shifting in size and shape as the plates diverged and converged in great continents of rising and falling land. Around this globe formed an atmosphere of gases protecting its surface from solar radiation and retaining its heat. The hot molten interior of various elements created a magnetic field around the planet, also deflecting much of the Sun's solar wind from the Earth.

On this ever-changing world of molten rock with its thin crust, shifting land masses, seas of liquid water and ice, shifting winds of atmospheric gases and condensing rains, erosion and deposition, changing tides, seasons, climates, sea levels and magnetic fields, something else very special happened more than 3.5 billion years ago, still in the Earth's infancy. Through complex chemical processes in this chemical-rich planet, under certain conditions, something new began to occur.

This may have occurred in the sea, or in wet areas inland. Perhaps on the shores, rocks or mud where they met. Perhaps in deep sea vents where the heat and minerals of the Earth's mantle reached the sea floor. Perhaps even in the extreme heat and electrical charge of lightning. Perhaps the conditions or materials came from meteorites colliding into the Earth from space. Perhaps it was the touch of God.

Electrical activity reacting with the chemically reducing atmosphere of Earth began creating certain small organic molecules, such as amino acids and nucleotides. These later merged and organised into increasingly more complex patterns of larger molecules such as proteins and nucleic acids including DNA and RNA. These larger molecules began to aggregate and gradually began forming membranes. These formed into proto-cells and later the first cells – the very building blocks of life.

These cells regulated themselves, converted chemicals into energy for sustenance, grew, responded to stimuli and adapted to their environment. Over the course of this gradual development, the cells, or some parts of the cell, began reproducing themselves, passing on their genetic material to their offspring, and theirs to their offspring and so on; while the older cells died, their organic remains consumed by other organisms. Gradually, over the course of millions of years, life evolved on planet Earth.

FOUR

The clear skies, azure seas and fertile land were replaced by the grey concrete smog of the city. A steady drizzle at dawn. I was back at Khao San Road, Bangkok, centre of the backpackers' world, the wanderlust of the herd which sucked you in, chewed you up and spat you out again. Was I going to get a job in Bangkok? Fly somewhere new? Or hit the road again? I didn't know yet.

I got myself another shiny wooden box in Papaya Guesthouse and spent a couple of days wandering the Banglampoo area near Khao San Road, catching up on some sleep and getting back into the swing of the city. I called home and had an uncomfortable conversation telling my family I wasn't coming home anytime soon. They didn't understand what I was doing here. I wasn't sure I did either. They felt a long way away. A memory of love and security gradually fading from view. I was falling with intent, allowing myself to drift further and further away from all that I knew, desperate to see what was at the other end. My appetite, though whetted, was far from satiated.

I received an email. One that wrote my plans for me. My long emails to my old friends at home regaling them with tall tales from Asia had finally hit the spot. Two of my best friends, Charlie and Joe said they were saving up money and would definitely be out in mid September, two months from now. I couldn't believe it. They were coming. My best friends! I wouldn't be travelling alone anymore. This changed everything.

We'd grown up together since childhood before gradually going our separate ways in recent years. We'd talked of travelling the world and going on crazy adventures together since we were youngsters, staring into the stars at night, gazing into the past and imagining the future. They were my brothers. If they were coming here then we were hitting the road together. That was certain. Nothing was going to get in the way of that. This was going to be the trip we'd been talking about for ten years or more. The trip of our lives.

The last time I saw Charlie earlier that year, I blustered out something about seeing him in Vietnam. Some crazy half-idea, mere words briefly spoken. But he remembered them. And now he was coming.

I was grinning with anticipation. However, I still had two months to kill before they arrived. I'd have to hold back on my spending or make some money for when they arrived. I mulled over my options.

In the meantime, an ex girlfriend from home arrived in Thailand on holiday. We met and explored Bangkok together for a few days – Chinatown, Chatuchak Outdoor Market, the Chao Praya River, riding the Skytrain to Siam Square. It was a visitation of the past, a reminder of who I was then and now. I flirted with normality, sightseeing with the nice girlfriend. But it wasn't me. Not now. There was no going back. I was going to go forward, further into the jungle, deeper down the chasm, flying higher towards the never-ending horizon and the Sun that never waits. We said goodbye.

I hung out with the friendly Thai staff at the front of Papaya – the barmen, cooks and cleaners – good, friendly folk from the Northeast of the country. We'd drink rice whiskey, eat spicy Thai salads and chew bits of pork gristle with hot dips. There were plenty of regular *farang* drunks in the bar area too, mostly deadbeat alchies here for the cheap booze at the bottom end of Rambutri.

An older guy worked there occasionally. He told me he also worked for a modelling and acting agency, finding foreigners in Banglampoo for jobs. It sounded like a promising lead to get some cash. After a few days promising this and that, he said he had a role for me and a girl acting as a couple on a sofa watching TV. But he didn't have the girl yet. "Blonde hair, about this tall, no hippies," he told me. My eyes lit up.

So off I went down Khao San Road looking for a beautiful girl to make famous, another amazing opportunity come my way. Life felt full of achievable possibilities again. I approached various blondes, searching for my onscreen wife. "Hey! You wanna be on TV?" They all looked at me like I was a psycho and fled.

In the end we found a guest at Papaya and went to a studio early one morning. They put makeup on my face, gave me a stick-down side-parting, some thick, black-rimmed glasses and a nasty green shirt. I looked like a twat. I was starting to have second thoughts about my new career move, feeling like a pet poodle with people wiping their hands all over me. Then the director arrived and told me I was too young. They wanted a guy in his 30s, not Clarke Kent's confused little brother.

Of course I was still on the piss. Saying my hellos to the massage girls, Daeng, now waitressing in a restaurant, the travel agent now flipping burgers on a street stall. Familiar faces everywhere. I felt famous, tourists from Ko Phi Phi chatting to me everywhere I went. I never had this back home.

Funny how all us backpackers came to this huge country but all ended up going to the same ten or so places. Everywhere I went I saw people I'd met previously in another part of the country.

I bumped into an Irish lad from Lucky Star Bar, one of Ning's boys, and we went drinking in the street bars of Rambutri and upstairs to East Gate Bar, with the rickety wooden balcony overlooking the *soi*. The place was hopping with the outcasts of society – hippies, drunks, punks and whores. We sat at the bar minding our own business, as a procession of nut jobs came and introduced themselves. Number one among them was some young Thai punk with a Mohican, tattoos and self-inflicted scars all the way down his arms. His name was It. He was clearly off his head on something; intense, fucked up guy, kinda friendly, but you could see that violence followed him like a shadow. Said he'd just done three years in prison. I'd read a book about Bangkok prisons. They were not somewhere you wanted to go. A pretty girl playing pool called Horny or something; kind of alluring, but again with the stench of trouble all over her. Mad-eyed, alcoholic English teachers who all seemed to have blown their brains out living here. Then a skinny young African guy came up to us. "Hello. My name is Samuel Odobo from Sierra Leone. Where do you come from?" I told him. He looked at me intensely. "I respect you, but I hate your forefathers," he intoned gravely.

I got in touch with a teacher friend of Pattaya Bob's. He'd been here years, knew his stuff and seemed saner than the other teachers I'd met. He taught business English courses to company employees for good money. We had a night on the busy Sukhumvit Road where the expats hung out, before going to Grace Hotel in the early hours. I'd never seen anything like it. It was like the UN Headquarters of whoremongers – European, Arab, Indian, African and Asian men everywhere – along with hundreds of Thai girls dancing round the discos and bars in the labyrinthine hotel basement. The more I learned about Bangkok, the more I realised how little I knew. The city was huge, and everything was happening. Did I want to live here?

I'd half-heartedly arranged an interview with a language school, but after another 5am finish I sacked it off. Bob's friend told me I wouldn't be able to get two months part-time work anyway. Most courses were three months long.

Next night I was on the street outside East Gate with the usual types that accumulated after closing, a random assortment of rag tail drunks, meth heads and slappers. It, the punk, always led the way. He was a dangerous guy to know, but being 22 I buzzed off hanging round with trouble. We went down Khao San, past reams of drunk revellers and predatory ladyboys, and into the seedy little alleyway in front of Backstreet Bar. There was a ripped up pool table and two big concrete tables outside. It was the kind of place you could get a drink 24 hours. Down another smaller alleyway to the side were some hellish-looking guesthouses where the local ladyboys and hookers lived and plied their trade apparently.

Hours passed till a moment of clarity emerged. I stopped and looked at myself and my new gang of friends. Some obnoxious drunk Aussies, some other slobbering drunk fuck-up, a clinically depressed alcoholic teacher from England called Alan, stuck here for years, all bitter, twisted and cynical about Thailand. Then the psychotic punk It, a scattering of wasted and unwanted hookers, and some deaf and dumb middle-aged ladyboy with tear tattoos on his cheek. I say ladyboy, but really it was just a wasted gay guy in shorts, a bra and a hairy chest. I shot out the dark alleyway and into the piercing truth of morning, staggering home in between the last remaining drunks and the busloads of fresh backpackers wandering around lost in the bright morning glare of Bangkok.

Another soul-searching hangover. I escaped down to the fort by the Chao Praya River in Banglampoo, watching the boats go by in the brown water and floating tangled leaves, looking for a sign or some inspiration or something. I was going off the idea of living here, worried it would consume me like it had so many other guys I'd just met. The teaching and modelling seemed a no-go for now. But I still had two months till Charlie and Joe arrived. I didn't want to go straight back to Phi Phi to work, but I needed to get off the piss and save my cash. I was still in touch with Nok in Chiang Mai, emailing each other often. I was touched that she was still waiting for me all this time. I could go back up there for a while, chill with her, stop partying and travel round the North and Laos a bit while I'm there. It seemed like a good way to spend two months.

★ ★ ★

North on the night bus listening to a young Cambodian b-boy talking enthusiastically about hip hop till 3am. Awoken at dawn by the conductor welcoming me back to Chiang Mai, the capital of the North. The ticket here was just 100 baht from my friend at Papaya Guesthouse travel shop, but we were in the hands of the backpacker bus firms who shepherded us into *songtaews* to take us to certain guesthouses, whereupon we'd be talked into going on treks and tours. I hung off the back of the *songtaew* looking around the streets till I recognised the landmark of Thapae Gate. I jumped off the back and found a decent room at a non-backpacker hotel nearby.

Chiang Mai was an easy city to get around. The old town was bordered by a large square moat with one-way roads either side, each side 1.5km long, with some gates and corner sections of the old red walls still remaining or reconstructed. There were dozens of old temples and ruins everywhere in amongst the newer buildings. To the east was the Ping River and the modern Night Bazaar area, popular with tourists for handicraft shopping. And to the west, the large University and nearby mountains of Doi Suthep and Doi Pui, looming iconically over the city, visible from everywhere. After the South and Bangkok, it was a relief to be in the cooler air and calmer atmosphere of the North. Despite being Thailand's second or third biggest city, it was a tiny fraction of the size of Bangkok and still had a relaxed small town feel to it.

I eventually found Nok and her best friend Bow at work waitressing in a touristy place called Siriporn Restaurant near Thapae Gate in the centre of town. I expected her to be pleased to see me but she wasn't, slapping me on the arm and barely speaking to me. I wasn't sure why, having told her I was coming a couple of days before. So I sat in the restaurant chatting to her friends, the funny little Bow who I'd met before, her older 'sister' Pin with the Japanese boyfriend, the pretty Nut who'd been with the Aussie guy before, a cute, polite girl Pop and their silent ladyboy friend. Eventually the pouting princess Nok loosened up a bit and we went off round the bars and clubs again.

After three male bed mates at Jungle Bar, it felt good to wake up in a clean room with a beautiful woman by my side. No more sneaking through the shadows looking for somewhere to get my end away. The cost of living was a lot cheaper than Bangkok and the South, so my usual 150 baht a night bought me a room with glass windows, a double bed and en-suite bathroom. Nok was still quiet but we kissed and made love in the morning to the sound of bird song, soft light streaming in through the lace curtains.

She had to go to work every day, so I'd usually walk her there and hang out in Siriporn Restaurant all day, working my way through the menu, chatting to tourists and friends of Nok, reading books or learning Thai. Nok and Bow knew a lot of regular customers too. I got friendly with an interesting Thai guy in his early 30s named Aek. He worked on the tour desk at the side of the restaurant, and I'd chat to him about trekking and tourism in Thailand. Sometimes I'd look around town. Chiang Mai was often called the cultural heart of Thailand, with its temples, architecture and street markets. People came here from around the world for its handicrafts, silk and artwork. Others came to study diverse subjects such as meditation, massage, cooking and *Muay Thai*. Others, like me, just came to hang around and fuck about for a bit.

★ ★ ★

It was nice to be with Nok again, but I quickly realised I was very much on my own and outnumbered by her friends here. They were constantly gossiping and discussing every situation, men's names and the odd Thai word I knew popping in and out the conversation. Often her friends would take me off somewhere, while Nok and another friend 'showered' or 'went shopping' for an hour or something. They were clearly no angels but they all had day jobs, except the ladyboy who worked in the beer bars. However, hanging out in a pleasant town with a pretty girlfriend and saving my money seemed to be the best option, so I put up with it.

I had to bite my lip on a daily basis though. Occasionally we went to the outdoor bar where her Thai 'ex' worked, making various jokes I didn't understand. She also had another 'ex', an American guy, the only *farang* she'd ever been with, who had lived here training in Thai boxing. He'd left town and had a new girlfriend now I was told. The eldest,

Pin, was still with her Japanese boyfriend but he'd gone home. Now she had some balding, bespectacled, middle-aged Canadian hanging off her. He hadn't been in the country long, but was very much infatuated. They weren't touching or acting like a couple though. I asked Nok what was going on but she just told me Pin was clever. The poor old man was coming with us to Space Disco, looking rather uncomfortable shuffling on the spot to banging hard house with a room full of teenagers.

Nok was now living with Bow and Nut in a studio apartment opposite the moat, next to some kind of karaoke bar with pretty girls waiting outside. Another cause for confusion. One night two Danish guys came back to the room on Bow's invitation, and asked me if this was some kind of brothel before panicking and running away.

I got on well with all of Nok's friends though. Nut, who was originally from the Lisu hill tribe, worked in a handicraft shop and currently had a new boyfriend in town. However, Bow and Pop were single, with various guys chatting them up in the evenings. Bow was fiercely loyal to her best friend, but chatting to Nut and Pop alone they would occasionally let slip little pockets of information about Nok. I didn't like to interrogate her friends, but I still felt a burning urge to know the truth behind Nok's past, to separate the story from the facts. I knew she was covering things up and I felt a strong desire to know what they were. I thought that maybe in doing so, I'd learn more about the other girls I'd meet in the future. I enjoyed the investigation game I guess, determined to crack the clues to the tantalising but enigmatic puzzle of the Thai female.

One afternoon I was invited to go off with the cute little Pop, who was the sweetest and least slutty of the gang. I couldn't help flirting with her sometimes. I had to accompany her and her female friend, who was going on a date with a 40-year-old Thai army soldier. I didn't know the details, but the girl in question didn't seem too enthusiastic about it. But due to a feeling of *kreng-jai*, felt she had to accept. This word roughly translates as 'considerate', but has a stronger meaning whereby the younger or lower person in a relationship feels they must say yes to the elder or higher person's requests and demands.

The soldier picked us up and drove us round his army base out of town before going for a huge meal in a bamboo gazebo by Huay Tung Tao Lake. I was on my best behaviour as we ate on a mat with my legs crossed painfully. He ordered far more than we could eat as is customary for the host on such occasions. Moist white rice was served from a large pot and small helpings from each dish served on one's plate and eaten modestly. The famous spicy prawn soup, *tom yam kung*, served in a metallic bowl with a flat candle in the middle. Papaya salad, or *som tam*, a spicy mix of grated green papaya with chilli peppers and various ingredients. Colourful fragrant curries, fried fish, barbecued meats, dipping sauces and other extravagant dishes I could barely comprehend. It was all delicious, as was everything I'd ever eaten in the country, aside from the occasional crap served in backpacker areas.

Another day a young American friend of Nok and Bow arrived at the restaurant. I was suspicious at first but soon saw he was a nice friendly guy. His name was Brad from the South of the US. He was a very gentle, genuine guy with bleached blond hair and a hippy drawl to his Southern accent. He was very open to the world, keen on understanding the intricate cultural and religious aspects of the country. He spoke about ten day meditation courses in Chiang Mai that he'd done. For a small fee you could live in the temple wearing white robes to study and practise meditation. Just like another guy I'd met on a bus to the South once, he said all these forgotten memories and old emotions came out, and when you emerge at the end of the course you appear as if your body is glowing. He spoke with such wide-eyed enthusiasm and conviction I could only believe him. Chiang Mai was his favourite place on the trail though, and he was here now studying different styles of Thai massage. Despite our differences, we both shared a love of freedom, independence, wisdom and the road.

★ ★ ★

After a couple more nights following Nok and her friends around, various confused *farang* guys in tow, I was bored. Me and Nok were only getting on half the day too, the other half spent in stroppy silent treatment due to a snide comment or probing question from me. All my chats with Aek about touring opportunities had got me excited to go out into the countryside. Brad was up for it too, so we decided to take some motorbikes up nearby Doi Inthanon, Thailand's highest mountain at 2565m. He brought a girl with him that Nok and Co. looked down on because she worked in a beer bar.

So at midday the three of us went off on two 100cc rental motorbikes, through the traffic south out of the city and into the Sun, cruising down the valley past villages and gleaming golden temples in this land we loved, the silhouettes of mountain ranges luring us in ahead. Eventually we came to the entrance for Doi Inthanon National Park. Up and up, twisting roads through layers of forest and descending temperatures, stopping off to paddle in a rocky stream, white water spraying from waterfalls over the round grey rocks. We sat in the Sun, feet dangling in the cool mountain water, humbled by the beauty and magnitude of the environment around us. Me and Brad barely knew each other but it didn't matter. We were quickly bonded by the love of the natural world around us.

Further up the winding route we went, air cooling and sky darkening, fog forming over the ridges and peaks. We stopped off at a huge waterfall, rainbows shining through the mist and vapours. Past hill tribe villages and terraced paddy fields cut intricately down the slopes, the thick rainforest vegetation changing to fragrant pine trees, mosses and ferns.

By 5pm I felt cold for the first time in a long time, as we drove into the clouds. I think the altitude was affecting the bikes because they were spluttering and slowing down till they barely went above 10 kph, grunting uphill at jogging pace. We persevered, making it to the summit of Thailand, but couldn't see anything through the trees and thick evening clouds. It was the coldest I'd been since I arrived in Asia. I just had a t-shirt, shorts and a light rain jacket on. We circled a marble shrine in the misty forest before descending.

Instead of going all the way back in the dark we decided to stay the night in an ecotourism Karen hill tribe village we found just off the road. The Karen are a sizable ethnic minority either side of the Thai-Burmese border, famous with tourists for their long-neck women, who wear rings of metal, apparently extending their necks. In this village they were wearing red traditional costumes, entertaining a large party of Thai tourists in 4x4s. Luckily they had a riverside hut available for us.

We all spent the evening huddled round the campfire, the three groups trying their best to communicate as the Karen men played their string instruments and sang humorous traditional songs. We sat there, slightly bewildered but charmed and bewitched by the mystery of it all; drinking throat-burning rice whiskey, gazing at the unfamiliar faces flittering in the smouldering shadows, inhaling the burning moss and wood, staring deep into the glowing embers of the fire and up at the twinkling cosmos above. I had another moment when the sheer foreignness of everything makes you realise just how far from home you've come, memories and hopes dancing in the flames.

"Have you ever been to the edge and back?" I asked Brad wistfully, remembering that kitchen floor, the Thai radio, the kitten. I don't know what thoughts the question brought to his mind, but he said that he hadn't. "But the longer I stay away each time, the more I feel different and cut off from the normality of my old life," he said. The magic evening swirled to night in the smoke of the fire.

"I see snake in the river," she giggled. I awoke to hear Brad and his girl playing in the stream next to our hut. It was nice to hear them together in the crisp air of dawn. Brad seemed to be falling for her despite his better judgement. Maybe it was the mountains, drawing out warm feelings from his heart, this fellow wanderer, the willingly displaced, another man looking for his Eve, looking for his Eden. I went out into the fresh, crisp air and looked on, playing the lonely spectator again. But I didn't miss Nok. Maybe I liked being the lonely man. Who can know such things?

The head of the Thai tourist group made a heartfelt speech in the morning to everyone, thanking the Karen for their hospitality before we all left. The sky was clear so we tried one more run to the summit, but the clouds soon returned higher up. On the rough hand-drawn map of the park I had was a line apparently showing a second route down the mountain back to Chiang Mai. I wanted to give it a go. Brad and his girl just wanted to go back slowly and chill out in the warmer valley below. So we drove down to the junction and said goodbye. "Will you be okay?" she asked me. Brad replied to her, though really to me. "He's on a spiritual journey and he doesn't even know it yet." And with that they were gone. I took the side road leading off into the unknown.

On down the gradually descending mountain road, only the wind, churning grey clouds and deep green of the forest for company, the constant turns soothing and relaxing. I had no idea where I was going as the road twisted in all directions and the midday Sun hid behind the clouds. There were hardly any cars or buildings and all the signs were in Thai script. I'd only come here for a day trip and didn't have anything with me, just a handful of cash, not even my bank card for some stupid reason. But I carried on, can't go back, the ever-evolving lure of the road ahead too much to resist, relishing every lick of freedom the air graced upon me. I got to a muddy wooden village in the middle of nowhere, and filled up the tank from a wooden shack selling red and yellow gasoline in glass vats with a hand pump. A policeman gave me some dubious directions, taking me another 100km through forests, valleys, paddy fields, tribal villages, ridges and cliffs, lost as hell, loving every moment of it. The unknown was my friend now. A weak little voice in my head was telling me to turn around and take the same route back to Doi Inthanon and Chiang Mai. I had little money and no idea where I was going. I was heading for danger. But a stronger voice was urging me on, to consume every moment with vigour. Didn't know where I was till finally I hit a proper road. Took a right and carried on

137

till I saw a sign in English. I was on the road to Mae Hong Son, in the far northwest of Thailand, on the other side of the long mountain range separating this province from Chiang Mai. I'd been travelling away from Chiang Mai all day. I didn't fancy turning around as I'd have got lost on those rough mountain roads. So I decided to head north to Mae Hong Son and loop back on the main road.

Along the valley, up and down steep curving roads, sweet views of the mountains leading me on in the hot Sun. I stopped at a deserted waterfall off the main road and swam in its plunge pool, cooling my hot body, tensed up from two days on the bike. Then descended a steep mountain with stunning panoramas and entered the small peaceful town of Mae Hong Son, cut off from the rest of the country by the mountains and the Burmese border not far to the west. There were occasionally problems up here with Burmese soldiers, hill tribes, immigration and drug smuggling. Before it was opium, but now meta-amphetamines were the biggie. There were police checkpoints and frequent army trucks passing on the road. But the town remained quiet and serene.

I found a cheap little hut and drove up the steep hill in the middle of town to a temple to see the stunning views, the setting Sun sparking reflections on the two large white stupas overlooking the town. The setting was breathtaking yet an atmosphere of serenity prevailed. I went to the west side of the hill and watched the orange sphere descend over the purple shadowed hills looking out to the beyond. I stared into the glowing globe of light, absorbing its heat and light, feeling its energy warming the air I breathed, heating my skin and filling my consciousness as I stared out towards the unknown. Burma was one of the most isolated countries in the world. But I thought I could just about see it from here. I felt I was standing on the edge of the known world looking at an undiscovered land. I gazed at the border on the horizon, desolation in view, mountains ranging for miles in all directions. It was so beautiful and poignant that I felt like I was due some kind of realisation. As the Sun melted behind the mountains' edge, I waited for an epiphany or some insight or something. But none came.

About 2500 years ago, a young prince named Siddhartha Gautama was born in modern day Nepal. He is said to have lived comfortably within the confines of his palace until the age of 29, when he went out and saw the suffering of the less fortunate for himself. He then lived an ascetic life, wandering the Indian subcontinent learning about and practising meditative states, till eventually reaching a state of enlightenment meditating under a banyan tree. Here he learned that suffering exists from one's attachment to one's desires, but can be overcome by detachment from them. This understanding is not revealed divinely, but is realised by walking the path oneself. By doing so, one can escape the endless cycle of life and death, known as Samsara, and reach a state of supreme awareness free from suffering known as Nirvana. He spent the rest of his life teaching and attracting followers who anointed him the Buddha, or enlightened one, and spread various versions of his teachings across Asia and beyond.

★ ★ ★

I woke at dawn, alert in trepidation. It was going to be a long day. I paid for breakfast and filled the tank. Just 120 baht in my pocket for 300 kms of mountain roads on a 100cc bike. I set off early, north through a wooded valley, descending down to Fish Cave, hundreds of blue carp wriggling through a hole in the cliff face. And then up again through the forest, the road winding like a giant *Naga* up the mountainside.

I came to a turning in another valley and entered a hidden monastery. I was growing more curious about Buddhism and particularly meditation, though not quite enough to actually practise it. A Chinese-American man was living there. He kindly showed me round the grounds, past Buddha statues in caves and wooded glades. There were various meditation caves on the grounds. He said I was welcome to stay there anytime. I was touched by his invitation to live, study and meditate at a place I'd just turned up at on a motorbike. I felt comfortable there. Part of me felt a desire to return there one day and join them. But the part was too small to win over the majority. Too easy to pull the throttle.

I continued on, right wrist twisted back, feeling the power of the engine growl between my legs as I leaned around the curves effortlessly. The road eventually rose through the clouds and escaped the trees, weaving along the side of the mountain to a beautiful viewpoint looking out across the green textured hills. Women from the hill tribes had stalls there selling tribal clothes and handicraft, the dreamy breath of wooden flutes punctuating the wind. I welcomed the sight of a friendly face and bought a wooden bead bracelet from two Lisu girls. The road then descended steeply into a picturesque valley of villages, woods and paddy fields. At Soppong town, I drove off the main road speeding along a narrow concrete track through the woods to Lod Cave, a huge crevice opening in the cliffs, a stream running through the massive cave embedded with immaculate rock formations. No time to hang around though.

Up again, past a pretty hill tribe village winding up the steep hairpin road to another viewpoint, stark, windy and rugged this time. To save gas I turned off the engine and descended the ever-winding road for 30 minutes, down past neatly-arranged wet paddy fields and into the town of Pai. I had a spot of lunch and fell asleep briefly on my restaurant table I was so exhausted. I drove around the town a little, a famous backpacker hang-out, lots of hippies hanging out in restaurants, but I didn't have time to join them. I rode up again, the road winding left and right forevermore into the thick forest and hills. Hours passed, the bike feeling like an extension of my body by now, my mind falling into a relaxed, unthinking meditative state, as I swerved around the bends unconsciously, time passing by unnoticed, my mind more focussed on the songs I was singing in my head than the actions my body was performing to stay alive.

I filled the tank once more. Only 20 baht left. Didn't even dare buy a bottle of water in case the full tank wasn't enough to get me back. I was thirsty as hell stuck in the hot sun all day, my exposed skin red raw from sunburn, but I had to get back. I had no choice. The road flowed down the mountains again and back to civilisation, my nerves wrought, face dirty. The fuel gauge was soon getting low as I caned it down the main road. The trees were gradually outnumbered by buildings as I made it back to Chiang Mai, gasping for water, right hand numb, sunburnt but buzzing. I drove to Siriporn Restaurant and excitedly told an unimpressed Nok what had happened, another innocent little day trip gone dangerously off the rails.

★　★　★

I spent a few more days in Chiang Mai, sleeping, shagging, eating and drinking. Days spent in Siriporn Restaurant, chatting to the girls, Brad and Aek the tour shop guy. I was trying to get a bit of info out of Aek about what the girls got up to. He dropped a few hints that I wasn't the first *farang* who'd passed through the doors of her eaterie. Obviously it was a good place to work if you wanted to meet lots of transitory foreigners.

More nights out with Brad and the girls, the Canadian man tagging along sometimes. Up in the rooftop bar overlooking Thapae Gate and Doi Suthep Mountain in the background. *Tuk-tuks* in the rain to Space Disco, dancing with the Cambodian hip hop guy and more backpackers from Phi Phi.

I made an effort to learn some more Thai language. The written script looked incomprehensible to me, but I tried to improve my speaking skills. Westerners have trouble getting their tongues around it, partly because some of the letters and vowels are hard to pronounce, but mostly because it's a tonal language. Thai has five tones: high, medium, low, rising and falling. A word's meaning can be altered by the tone, so every word must be pronounced in the correct tone in order to be properly understood. There are also short and long vowel sounds which can mean different things too. For instance, the word *khao* pronounced in different ways can mean 'he/she', 'news', 'enter', 'rice', 'knee' or 'white'.

Me and Nok were still swinging between periods of affection and silence, her teenage grumps getting rather tiring. Usually I would set them off by asking her too many questions about her past. Not that I was really bothered about her past. What I was bothered about was her lying about it. I just wanted to hear the truth so I could trust her. It was hard to believe I was the second Westerner she'd ever been with, when her friends were constantly talking about boys and picking up tourists in the discos on a regular basis. But demanding the truth would never get us anywhere, sending her into a sullen silence, and me wondering what I was doing here. If I kept my mouth shut and didn't think too much then we would be happy together, making love passionately in the morning and night. But then, in these happy moments, I would feel myself falling for her again, and that was when I suffered and needed to know the truth. If I held my feelings back and didn't care about her so much, then I was happier in another way. And so we would go through these cycles every day.

★ ★ ★

I decided to travel to neighbouring Laos. I knew nothing about the place, but travellers I'd met described it as a backpackers' paradise, beautiful and calm. Nok seemed sad to see me leave, though I planned to come back afterwards. I couldn't spend weeks on end sitting round Chiang Mai.

I went to the public bus station and was the only foreigner on board for the long journey north to the border town of Chiang Khong, through rolling hills and paddy fields. The two countries were separated by the Mekong River along most of the border. The border control in the sleepy little village was virtually non-existent. Two Thai officials sat in an outdoor restaurant by the banks of the river writing down my passport details in a big log book. Then a long-tail boat across the river to Laos, whereupon I could have easily just walked up the road into town. I looked around before seeing a dark window with an official behind it and did the formalities.

New country. The town of Huay Xai, a muddy riverside place with a temple up the hill, two huge snake-like *Naga* bodies forming the sides of the staircase leading up to it. Clearly less developed than Thailand, there were no brand names here. Everything seemed to be locally made. I was disappointed at first. It was pretty dull. I'd considered travelling around the remote north of Laos from here, but decided on the easy option of getting the two-day boat to the larger town of Luang Prabang in the centre of the country.

I spent the day wandering around town, the easy charms of the place slowly rubbing off on me. The smiling kids who saw me would all shout "Hello!" and "*Sabai dee!*" at me excitedly when I strolled past, unlike in Thailand. People were riding their bicycles and playing badminton along the quiet, muddy streets, lines of young monks in saffron robes, dogs yapping around playfully. It had a certain rustic charm.

I ate my first Mefloquine pill that day. I'd chosen these anti-malarial drugs because you only took them once a week instead of daily due to their strength. They were known for giving many people who took them intense dreams, which interested me too. The information sheet stated that various other psychological side-effects were not unheard of, but I figured I'd be alright.

That night I had a dream – a gigantic tree, so large that humans looked like ants next to it. Thousands of people were climbing up the exposed roots and ascending the trunk with picks and ropes. Others were cutting at the tree with axes till large chunks of bark were falling off, taking out dozens of people below. In the mad race to conquer this tree of life, the people were also destroying it. Finally the tree collapsed, falling down towards me, killing all the people, destroying everything, gravity turning over on itself.

A humid murky morning, thick grey clouds rolling over the muddy riverbank, the jungle a dark, ominous green. I was driven to a restaurant by the river where about 50 tourists were waiting around quietly, eating breakfast, drinking coffee and smoking cigarettes. We made our way to the boat, an ancient-looking, narrow wooden cargo barge with no seats. We all crammed in and sat on the floor or on wooden beams holding the thing together. I kept myself to myself, looking out the open side of the boat or observing how the other passengers were handling the beautiful but uncomfortable ride. Lots of young backpackers, usually in couples or pairs, some relaxed, others complaining about everything and nothing, intellectual old men of the world, and a hippie couple whose young kids were running round on board, amusing and annoying the tourists in equal measure. All these random people thrown together, it inspired in me some kind of claustrophobic narrative.

Later I clambered up onto the bare flat roof of the boat with some other adventurous guys. There were no guardrails. One slip and you were in the drink. I carefully sat down and admired the untouched forests of Laos as we chugged through the eddies, whirlpools, currents and hidden rocks of the oozing, earthy-red Mekong, logs and vines popping up and down through the water like mysterious underwater denizens. It was a treacherous river. Who knew what lurked underneath its impenetrable surface?

We eventually came to the little village of Pak Beng, hanging off the side of the river bank, sandwiched between the river and thick jungle on all sides. Dozens of men came aboard to carry our bags up the concrete jetty. We got rooms in a little hotel perched on the side of the river, cut off from civilisation here in the unknown. I had a few beers with some nerdy English guys and an Australian couple before sleeping early. Not much else to do there.

Another day on board chatting to more people, kids waving happily and swinging off the trees into the river as we pass by villages and floating homes. At one point as people got braver, 20 people were on the roof. The crew ordered us down for fear of destabilising the boat and tipping us all into the swampy broth below. Flat-bottomed speedboats flew by with other tourists on the one-day fast ticket. I didn't fancy it myself with all the rocks hidden under the surface.

We eventually reached Luang Prabang, one of the biggest towns in Laos, but it still felt very small. Small but beautiful, situated where a tributary meets the Mekong. The architecture was old French colonial, pastel shades and ornate wooden buildings, temples of various eras, market stalls and palm trees, with the rivers, jungle and green hills in the background. Being a UNESCO World Heritage site the old town was untouched by modern development, sending visitors one hundred years back in time with a little imagination.

I stumbled round in a daze to the pretty peninsula where the rivers met. Teams of young men were frantically cutting through the river in brightly coloured dragon boats preparing for an upcoming race. Monks trailed the hot-baked streets in long lines. *Tuk-tuk* drivers and tourists weaved around each other in the charming old streets. However at night there wasn't a lot there. Only one bar in the centre of town.

There were no ATMs anywhere either, so I went to a bank to change some Thai baht into Lao kip. They gave me a huge brick of 5000 kip notes, each one worth about 50 cents US. It felt good having a brick of notes in my pocket for the first time. Another day walking round in the intense heat. Laos is a land-locked country, so temperatures can rise high in the daytime, scorching the earth and everyone on it, reprieved only by the regular rains. I climbed up to the temple on top of the hill, giving me views all around the town, set perfectly in the picturesque jungle.

In the evening I ran into Reggie, another friend from home who was travelling around Indochina too. It was funny to suddenly see an old friend out here in the middle of nowhere. I told him all about Thailand and he told me stories of Cambodia, Vietnam and Laos. We met some other guys, all solo male travellers from the UK, France, Germany, USA and Australia. They got into some lively debate over dozens of Beerlao, the national brew. It raged on into the night sat under a parasol near the dark river, discussing politics and history in Asia, Europe and America. I listened to everyone's rants. I avoided getting into political debates with drunks unless someone said something truly ridiculous. So I just listened. "Wise men judge not," a wise man once said.

The naughty little boy serving our beers looked on amused as a large flying cockroach buzzed around the nearest light bulb. Suddenly he caught it in between his palms in one swoop, picked its legs and wings off and ate it whole with a smile. That's when I realised these people were rather special.

Me and Reggie went to the nearby Kuang Si Waterfalls. We squeezed into a truck and bounced about through the rustic countryside, everything made of wood. An Israeli couple talked passionately about the problems in their country, and how they knew they weren't popular over here, but if people knew what the other side was doing to them they would understand them better. It was true that Israeli backpackers had a bit of a reputation. Although I'd met many friendly individuals, I'd also seen many instances of rude and aggressive behaviour from others. They'd sometimes roam in large groups, ordering locals around and questioning people curtly like they owned the place. A few guesthouses had gone as far as to ban them, while others had Hebrew everywhere and were specifically geared up to cater for them.

The waterfalls were stunning – multi-tiered pools and flows over green-clad rocks, rising up into the trees. We ascended to the right, over flickering streams and pools, wet legs and water sprays, passing drop-offs into the cascades below. At the top the water ran straight through the roots of the forest, before plummeting over the edge in translucent, aquatic sculptures. Some of us edged our way along some fallen trees which hung precariously over the rim of the falls, dangling our legs over the edge of the huge drop, toying with oblivion as young men do. We came down the far side and hopped around the rocks and lower pools, happy in this quaint little corner of natural delights. Of course there were dozens of other tourists there, clambering around the site like big kids in a play park.

Back in town, I was up to my old tricks, running around trying to get a group together to go trekking in some remote area. I got a little interest but no confirmations. The cost per person went down as the group got larger and I couldn't afford to do it alone. I remembered the tourist trek I'd done in Chiang Mai and wanted to go more extreme this time. By the next day, most people from the boat had moved on. Reggie took the boat in the opposite direction to Huay Xai. It was grey and drizzling all day and there was nothing more to do in town. I kept looking for people, but only the friendly Israeli couple were interested. For three people it would be $150 each. We needed more people but we couldn't find any. The Israeli man left me alone with his girlfriend for 20 minutes in a restaurant. I must admit I was rather charmed by her, perhaps a little envious that I didn't have a nice girlfriend by my side to travel the land and share my experiences with. Nok didn't quite fit the bill. I felt sorry for them too, seeing them get a hard time in travel shops for no reason as soon as their nationality was ascertained. It's prejudice, a pre-judgement. Judging someone before you know them based on some external factor unrelated to their actions, such as nationality, race or religion. If you're going to judge people, at least base it on what they can control. And it's wrong. I don't mean morally wrong. I'm saying it's logically wrong – judging something based on something else. It doesn't make sense. It's stupid. But it's a mistake we are all guilty of from time to time.

I abandoned my trekking plans and continued on the tourist trail, getting a bus south to Vang Vieng the next day. It was raining hard, cramped up on a packed little local bus, my knees jammed in, the locals sat on plastic stools and standing in the aisle. The decrepit bus chugged out of town slowly and weaved around the mountain bends, as we were already at a high altitude in Luang Prabang. I couldn't see much out the steamed up windows.

Hours passed till we stopped at the back of a line of traffic in the middle of a hilly nowhere. There was an issue. After a while people began getting off the bus. I went out in the continuous rain and edged along the line of traffic till I saw the problem. A landslide of thick wet mud had engulfed a section of the road, maybe 30 metres long, spilling down from the steep hillside above. I returned to the bus again as a little digger went in to clear it. Nothing to do but stare at the water drops accumulating and streaming down the glass. I started slipping into horrible, sweaty, semi-conscious mind spasms, my head banging into the misty window and the seat in front every time I dropped off. Suddenly I jumped up with a start and noticed people walking outside with their bags. I got up, grabbed my backpack and followed. The digger was making slow progress. I trampled over the footprints in the mudslide carefully with other pedestrians, dogs and slipping motorbikes. A line of *songtaew* trucks was waiting for people on the other side of the roadblock. I hopped on board. The weather cleared as I chatted to some Western girls, hanging off the back as we drifted down the green mountains and limestone cliffs towards the little town of Vang Vieng.

★ ★ ★

The quaint Laos town on the outskirts had transformed into something very different by the time the truck stopped in the centre. The place looked like a rural Khao San Road. Lots of cheap guesthouses, tourist restaurants, internet and tour shops in a lush green valley. This was clearly a place newly-manufactured for the burgeoning backpacker market. I found a comfortable room and went straight out at sunset to the river which ran past the little town, great cliffs of limestone rising up out of the ground like natural monuments.

In the evening I met up with the Aussie couple and others from the boat again. All the tourist restaurants were selling 'happy' pizzas, omelettes and shakes. People were already passing round joints in the laid-back restaurants, the easy-drinking Beerlao flowing smoothly. Nobody seemed too bothered about anything here. It was like some young hippie's fantasy town. And so we dined on happy pizzas, happy pancakes with a side of fried happy, the happiness coming in mushroom form. I was starting to get a little drunk when everything suddenly closed earlier than I was used to. I made my way home in the dark, and went to bed as nothing more seemed to be going on.

How wrong I was. The beers put me to sleep for an hour or two but now I was wide awake alright, awake in a pitch black room, tripping balls. Not sure if I'm coming up or down, my mind spiralling in fractals of memories, ideas and illusions. Try to sleep again but I ain't getting away that easily. Voices started luring me down rabbit holes, so I turned on the light just to give myself something to look at and extricate myself from my own mind for a while. No music. No TV. No phone. No air-con. Just me in a bare room, dehydrated to fuck, but there's no water. Outside is silent. 3:30am in a small town. Wasn't gonna drink the tap water here. And that brick of Lao kip had already disappeared. Just me, a very dry throat and a hyper-active mind trying to kick my sanity off its back like a bucking bronco. I was sweating, my heart pumping fast. I noticed a strange scratch on my cheek too. I had a cold shower and lay wet on my bed in the fan. After a few hours my mind could take no more punishment and I passed out. Woke up at midday, head still scrambled, sweating and thirsty. After an hour's planning, I eventually summoned up the courage to venture outside into the toxic heat and light, went to the bank and filled out some forms to get more kip on my credit card. Drank litres of water and ate before squirming off to bed again to hide from the world. I went out at night but I was still dazed and confused, little jitters of anxiety still itching in my ear.

Ventured out the next day. The town was like some backpackers' Disneyland, full of picturesque valley views, rivers, caves and waterfalls to explore and easily available drugs for sale in family restaurants – weed, opium and mushrooms everywhere. Large groups of young people would spend all day off their head, lying down in these chill-out restaurants watching DVDs. They all looked slightly pitiful lying there all day in the shade watching TV. Others would get high and float down the river on big black inner tubes to the riverside bars on an island in the river near town.

After 36 hours of confusion, I hired a bicycle and got out of town, south to a blue lagoon by the side of the cliffs, feeling good to get away from the crowds. I swam about in the pool, before noticing the stream was flowing under the rock. I dived under and came out into a cave with sunlight coming through above. I swam along the narrow channel in the blue water, rocks either side of me until they went under another dip. My danger sensors were going off again, better tuned than they used to be. I got out of there before getting sucked underwater or something else equally deadly.

I cycled down side lanes to quiet villages, buffalo bathing in ditches and puddles by the side of the road. The further I got from Vang Vieng, the more inquisitive and friendly the cute little kids were in every village. There seemed to be dozens in each village, running out to see me, choruses of excited hellos, the shyer kids hiding behind the more confident ones. I enjoyed these little trips to see the real people away from the tourist industry. Though they were poor, living in basic wooden houses, the people all seemed happy and friendly. Back in town I came to a huge disused air strip built by the Americans in the War, now just used as a shortcut for mopeds and kids playing on wooden carts.

I was more interested in adventure than drugs and DVDs. I wanted to sample the natural wonders of this beautiful mountainous country. That evening I ate in the Super Kayak Tour restaurant and got chatting with the boss, Somsak. He was a cool guy in his early 30s who spoke good English. He was intelligent and ambitious, proud of his kayak tours and newly built restaurant. He told me about his plans for expanding his kayak tours all over Laos. I liked him and fancied getting out in the country too, so I agreed to go on the Vang Vieng river trip the next day. Outside on the streets, a couple of Lao girls were lingering around in short skirts on the pickup. Just two, but between them and Somsak's ambition I could see the future development of this expanding town clearer than day.

We drove north a while before getting off at a bridge and drifting gently down the river with a few others. It was boiling hot but good to be in a kayak again. The river was soft and easy. We stopped at the shrines of Elephant Cave before tip-toeing along the muddy ridges of paddy fields to Snail Cave, an eerie multi-caverned place where civilians hid during the US bombardment. They say Laos was the most heavily bombed country in the world. Apparently the US bombed Maoists in Laos and bombed the Ho Chi Minh trail which cut through Laos on its way from North to South Vietnam, as well as emptying their remaining loads here after bombing missions.

Lunch with a chained-up pet monkey, jumps off a suspension bridge and on to Sleeping Cave. We waded through the watery entrance and into the dark with lamps on our helmets. Up a bank and down a mud slide into the river again, not somewhere you'd want to get stuck alone. Up a muddy bank on the other side of the underground stream before the roof got narrower and we eventually squeezed out of a tiny muddy gap to the outside of the cliff face, like getting squeezed out the arsehole of the mountain, covered in brown shit. The gentle little Lao guides flirted with the Western girls, smearing mud on each other's faces.

That evening I hung out with Somsak and some of his gang of young Lao guys who helped out on the tours, lugging kayaks around and loading the van. He had his little 17-year-old girlfriend, father and brother working for him too. And then he gave me an unexpected proposal. He said I may be able to help him with the expansion of his business. He would take me round the country to some unknown kayaking areas, huge underground rivers and to Si Phan Don, the Four Thousand Waterfalls area in the south of the country. In return I'd write up descriptions of all his tours on his website and advertising. It sounded like another unbelievable opportunity had come my way. I agreed to go on his second trip the next day before returning to town again soon. This was a two day trip south on the river, ending in the capital Vientiane back on the Thai border. The first day included some proper rapids, before visiting Nam Ngum Lake for the night.

The scratch on my cheek had now turned into a little scab. I packed my now grubby rucksack and had breakfast with the other guests, including a friendly guy Colin from Canada. Somsak and his guides were out in their tight black spandex outfits loading up the vans with kayaks and flirting with the girls, like some camp boy band of Lao adventure gigolos.

We drove to a rougher stretch of river. I was feeling confident and in control of the kayak as we went through three sets of rapids. I made it past the first two sets, currents sucking me through channels, white water gushing over me. I came to the third but suddenly my kayak got stuck in a ridge of rapids, waves coming in at me from three directions. My kayak was flipped over and we separated, as I was swept downstream in my lifejacket. Two of the guides came and rescued me, after I capsized them both trying to pull myself into their kayaks. After a barbecue lunch on the river, I fell straight in the water again trying to get into my kayak which was stuck in some revolving current against a rock. I clearly didn't know what I was doing. There were no more rapids though as we cruised down the gentler stretch of river, playing on our boats and tipping each other in. It was all good fun, but it wouldn't take much for something to go horribly wrong out there.

We came to a village and loaded up the van, driving past a spectacular dam which formed the huge Nam Ngum reservoir in the centre of the country, dotted with hundreds of grassy islands. We took a slow boat to some kind of giant bandstand in the lake, doing jumps from up high. Then on to an island with a dusty old house which was once the Prime Minister's villa we were told, watching the indigo sunset over dinner.

You think you'll get a great night's sleep in these quiet country settings, but the damn roosters get you every time, slapping you awake with their screeching before dawn. We spent the next day on a slow boat exploring the Japanese-built reservoir, playing in the water and visiting Mong and Lao villages where dozens of curious little kids came out to observe these strange people from another land.

Eventually evening drew in and me and Colin took a truck into Vientiane, the capital city. It seemed big, but very spread out. The city centre was very quiet and small town-like. Old French-era townhouses and shop houses opening up onto the street, a few guesthouses and tourist restaurants. But by evening there was barely a car on the road, just handfuls of people out on the dark streets. We ate near the gleaming white and gold Cultural Hall, chugging on the Beerlao. There was definitely something in those things. Everyone loved the stuff, but it had a strange edge to it. *Tuk-tuk* drivers seemed to run the streets at night. They took us to an Egyptian-themed Lao disco full of rich locals, Somsak turning up later with a group of young local girls, introductions not forthcoming.

I got out my dorm bed and looked in the bathroom mirror. The scab on my cheek had got bigger and was spreading now, patches of scab appearing from nowhere on my neck too. I guessed it was some kind of infection. But it was on my face and it was getting worse by the day. I was getting worried. I didn't fancy trying to sort it out here. Best get back to Chiang Mai tomorrow.

I had a delicious baguette from the numerous street stalls, wondering why they didn't make them in Thailand. A few sums later I realised I didn't have enough cash on me to pay for my room and transport to get over the border. I spent the whole day looking for an ATM, bank or hotel that I could get some money from. All over town I went, to the impressive banks of the Mekong River, which curves along the edge of the city, wide and majestic now with vast sandbanks. Then up to the large Morning Market and the Victory Gate, inspired by Paris's Arc De Triomphe but with a local flourish. The streets weren't that busy in the daytime either. A few people milling around, lots of school kids and monks outside the numerous old temples. It was a green and pleasant town centre, charming, quaint and peaceful. However after walking round for hours, there appeared to be only one ATM in the country which didn't take foreign cards. It was Saturday so the banks were all shut, and the hotels all said no. I couldn't get any money.

Luckily I found Colin in the evening and he said he'd lend me some cash. We were both headed to Chiang Mai where he also had a girl waiting for him. We went out to a nice French restaurant by a fountain in the centre, and to some dreary bars playing the ubiquitous *Hotel California*, but I wasn't feeling too sociable with the dark scabs growing over my face. I was starting to feel like a leper.

The next day we took a *tuk-tuk* to the Friendship Bridge spanning the Mekong River and Thai border. We crossed to the small town of Nong Khai and took a bus to the larger city of Udon Thani. I noticed the change of pace straight away, taxi drivers hassling us as soon as we entered the country, people and traffic everywhere. I was in Isan, the Northeast region of Thailand for the first time. We looked round Udon Thani a bit. Nobody spoke much English but everything was incredibly cheap. The time soon came to take the 12 hour bus back to Chiang Mai. It was dark outside as the bus ascended the remote mountains along the country's northern border. I drifted away in the hands of another.

★ ★ ★

Since there are so many problems in analysing the nature of free will within the frame of causation, perhaps we must look elsewhere in order to gain a better understanding of the problem. Perhaps we should look at the physicality of the process. If it's possible to answer the question of free will, then maybe the answer lies in the study of the brain.

We all possess a human brain, the centre of the nervous system that runs through our body. It's the most complex biological structure on Earth, constantly transmitting signals and coordinating all the actions and reactions going on in our bodies by activating muscles and secreting chemicals. It is divided into many areas, each controlling specific functions of the brain. There are around 100 billion neuron cells in our brain and nervous system. Each neuron sends electrochemical pulses known as action potentials along a transmission line called an axon. The longest axons can be a metre in length. If connected into a single line, the total length of all these axons in one human would stretch for thousands of kilometres. Each axon then connects to networks of thousands of neurons and other recipient cells in the body via synapses. Therefore, there are approximately 1000 trillion, or 1 quadrillion, synapses in a young child's brain.

Most neurons are created genetically before birth, and we lose many over the course of our lives. The brain was once thought not to grow new cells, gradually decaying towards death. However, scientists are beginning to discover that the brain is highly malleable. It can change its very structure over the course of our lives, an ability known as neuroplasticity. New neurons are created, notably in the area associated with new memories. Hence, continuous learning throughout life creates new neurons and gives further health benefits as well. Synaptic connections between neurons are also created and broken, and their strengths vary as the brain changes with our life experience. The more connections we accumulate in our brain, the greater our intelligence becomes. By practising certain actions, or changing our behaviour, we can positively reinforce the brain's capabilities in these and associated areas, building up our skills and intelligence further. Our brains are our own, to exercise and mould as we wish.

And so these neural networks are working round the clock, when awake and asleep, controlling the various functions of the body, extracting sensory inputs, transmitting signals and sensations, affecting bodily movements and coordinating them all; the mind alive with memories, emotions, thoughts, plans and language. Yet how these unimaginably complex systems cooperate through cellular networks of thousands and millions of cells is still unknown. It's a system too large and complex for us to fathom. And yet it is us – the motor which runs the show behind every one of us – the grand show of human consciousness which plays before us each day.

But is it you that runs the show? Is it you who controls what you are conscious of, out of the myriad of processes constantly going on in the brain? I believe so. If not, then who or what else? We are not merely reactionary automatons. Just sitting here now, you can choose to be conscious of what you like. Perhaps your sensory inputs – that which you see before you now in all its glory, the sound waves bouncing around you, the feel of the objects touching your body, the smells and tastes, the temperature, the motion of your body and the sensations within it. Or you can go inside. The thoughts and ideas that whirl through your mind, your memories and emotions. All of them can be explored endlessly. It is totally up to you. Your consciousness is yours to explore at will, and the options are limitless.

All the processes occurring in the brain work simultaneously, thus making our everyday actions possible since they depend upon all the brain's functions working together. Yet upon self-reflection we can control our consciousness and focus upon any of the brain's various, continuously-changing processes that we choose.

Of course, when you are busy you tend to be focused on the task at hand. And when experiencing any extreme sensation, emotion or thought, it is this which comes to the forefront of consciousness. Yet of all the processes underway in our brain at all times, it is still us who decides what we are conscious of. With practice we can steer our minds away from previously overriding emotions. For example, in facing a dangerous action, the fear may be overwhelming at first, but with practice one can calm the fear and focus on the job at hand. At a higher level, witness the mastery of fear of the tight-rope walker, the mastery of pain of the firewalker or the mastery of desire of the monk. But in practice we all have less dramatic instances of mastering, or overcoming, our emotions every day.

Can all of this control simply be explained causally? That there is a cause for every thought and action we take, which can be reduced to processes on an atomic level, the impulses of an animal driven by a genetic instinct for survival and reproduction, with no real control over itself? The answer remains unknown to science. As we saw before, perhaps it is unanswerable, since there is only one actuality which occurs from the endless possibilities of life.

But in trying to follow the flow of consciousness, something occurs to me. We naturally follow the movement or momentum of our consciousness in our everyday lives without a problem, as we perform various tasks throughout the day. And we are also able to focus our consciousness on one thing or position for a period of time. However, it seems impossible to follow the position and momentum of our consciousness at the same time. Trying to track the position of one's consciousness during the normal flow of our lives is impossible. It still works, but you can't pin down what is happening at any given moment without stopping and focusing on it completely. It can't be tracked as a series of linear events. Like electrons around the atom, it seems at odds with the very notion of mechanistic causality. Consciousness appears to dance effortlessly above the storm of the brain.

★ ★ ★

We arrived at the bus station in the early morning and split up. I got another cheap room near Thapae Gate in what resembled a horse stables. I went straight over to Nok's room half-hoping to catch her red-handed, engrappled in some early morning orgasmic rapture. Her, Bow and Nut were all asleep in their big bed together, not too pleased about being woken up either. They started to gossip straight away though as I told them about Laos and my face.

The others had to work in the restaurant, so Nut took me to a nearby doctor's, who gave me some pills and cream. My spreading scabs looked even worse when I smeared the thick white cream over them. I went to Siriporn again, their friend Pop appearing with an older

Australian guy, who she was going to marry I was suddenly told! I never really knew what was going on with these girls to be honest. The rain came down heavily, Nok not really speaking to me, as Colin came to visit with his girl in the evening.

I went to Nok's room with her after work. After some silence she eventually warmed to me bit by bit. As I dozed on her bed, she curled up against me and told me she loved me. "No you don't," I replied coldly. I followed her and the gang out to Space Disco again as usual, not really wanting to go but not wanting Nok to go without me, a stupid self-defeating reason. I stood bored in the silly disco again wondering what I was doing there.

After another similar day me and Nok were talking again. Again, the more I distanced myself from her emotionally, then the closer I felt to her paradoxically. If I allowed myself to fall for her then I knew I would suffer because I couldn't trust her. If I kept my feelings at arm's length and enjoyed her company on a simpler, physical level then I felt much happier and so would she. If I interrogated her she fell into silence and I'd grow angry. If I forgot about it and didn't care, then I didn't suffer. We were both young, passionate and jealous. I thought she might be disgusted by my face, but she didn't seem to mind. Once we were in my room, I put all the analysis behind me, stripped the clothes off her beautiful body and laid her down again.

The thick red scabs had now spread to the other side of my face, covering both my cheeks and neck. Where the sticky scabs were peeling off I could see purple scars underneath on my face. I was getting worried now. The cream wasn't working and I was contemplating the possibility that I could be permanently scarred from this horrible infection, with purple blotches all over my face. I considered letting my beard grow to hide it, but the cream wouldn't absorb through the stubble. So I shaved, painfully scraping the scabs off my face with my disposable razor, bits of scab, blood, stubble and shaving foam everywhere, my face red raw in pain, leaving bright purple scars underneath.

What was I going to do now? My various, rather tenuous, work opportunities – kayaking with Somsak in Laos, modelling in Bangkok, or back to Jungle Bar – were no longer possible with my disfigured face. I wasn't ecstatic about my current set-up in Chiang Mai, but at least I had Nok's affection, I was drinking less and saving money. I was in limbo, but here seemed to be the best option, despite feeling like a little girl's ugly pet pug. I sank into self-pity, confidence shattered, my face a scabby, bloody, blotchy mess.

I tried turning it into a positive. Perhaps losing my looks would stop me wasting so much time partying, drinking and hunting for women. Perhaps now I could move on from my shallow existence to concentrate on more intellectual pursuits. It didn't work.

I hung out with Nok, Bow and Nut in their room watching TV a lot, forced inside by the rain and my face. They explained what was going on to me. We watched music videos, the girls swooning over the boy band of the day. They told me about the high demand for half-Thai, half-Western models and actors these days, as they all fantasised about having a little blue-eyed baby.

We also watched group stand-up comedy shows, making jokes about the different regional accents of the North, South and Isan. Then about tourists catching HIV in Phuket. Though some subjects were taboo and not openly discussed in Thailand, others which might be taboo in the West (such as joking about catching HIV,) were not. The Thais would often joke about things to people's faces which most Westerners would not, such as disease, death, ugliness, stupidity, obesity, skin colour and sexuality. At first it was shocking when people laughed at others for things considered politically incorrect, but it was said in a kind of innocent way, without any menace. I think it was because nobody really cared that they were able to joke about it. They were just trivial, physical differences, unrelated to the more important matters of the soul.

One day I was exploring the old town alone, eating some spring rolls, when I saw a poster advertising some *Muay Thai* matches with *farang* guys fighting. On it was a picture of Nok's ex-boyfriend I recognised from a photo – some butch young American. I thought he didn't live here anymore. I looked at the date. The fight was two weeks ago when I was in Laos! My head reeled from all the recollections of lies, half-truths and unspoken events. I almost laughed at her audacity. I imagined confronting her with the information, but decided to sit on it for now. I passed Nut's antique and handicraft shop and went in to have a look. We chatted and she dropped another cryptic clue, "I know Nok better than you."

In the evening I looked round the Night Bazaar for presents to send home to my family who I was missing a lot. I came back to Siriporn and saw Nok in the internet shop opposite. I entered and saw her email inbox littered with messages from various men with names from around the world. She quickly closed it and we went home after dinner, talking little. I was angry but at least I knew the truth. I kept my mouth shut for now to preserve the peace.

I was due back at the doctor's the next morning, but on hearing the rain outside Nok refused to come with me. My silent contempt fermented. I trudged there alone for more medication. He tells me it's contagious for the first time. Thanks for that Doc. I ask him if it'll leave any permanent scarring behind, but he doesn't answer. Taking that as a Thai 'yes' to an uncomfortable question, I traipsed the streets despondently, the constant rain and girlfriend problems exacerbating my increasing loneliness and self-absorption. Without a better alternative I felt stuck here. Of course I could have gone anywhere, done anything, but my reasoning persuaded me that the status quo was the best option in order to fulfil my desires of saving money for a month and having someone there to do it with me.

Another morning waking to the traffic and rampaging stray dogs. Sex with Nok was getting better and better again, climaxing in an almighty thunderous shot-bolt, followed by an immediate sense of cold emptiness in that sacrosanct moment when the lust is ejaculated, leaving only the undeniable truth about that which is hanging off the end of one's dick. And the truth was that she was just a hot slut I didn't care about anymore.

My face was sorer than ever now, red raw and scarred. I couldn't move the right side of it without the skin tearing up and bleeding; couldn't smile or eat properly. I'd lost my trust in the doctor yesterday so went to a hospital with Nok. The doctor there said it wasn't herpes but a skin infection, maybe from the river water in Laos. He gave me new pills and a cream that actually absorbed into my face, unlike the battery acid the other damned quack had given me.

I got friendlier with the tour agent Aek. He invited me to his office near all the rundown girly bars on Loi Kroh Road, chatting about this and that. I was grateful for some male company. He drove me round a bit and kindly invited me to his family home to eat with his wife and young child.

Call it self-obsession, an ego in crisis, but I kept dreaming about my face, drifting into consciousness with an image of myself before it was scarred. But it was just a dream. Another painful shower and shave, another identical day in Chiang Mai. Nok finally awoke from another marathon slumber blaming me for being late for work. I ignored her as I tagged along. I ate and read before going to the market in the drizzle. Was it just me or were people staring at my face? Damn whispers of paranoia in my head. Stuck in negative, defeatist limbo, trudging round the rain-soaked, whore-trodden streets.

I went home and slept all evening as I was doing often. Sleep was escape. Escape was bliss. By midnight, I was reading in my room not wanting to go out anymore. Nok hadn't come back yet. I convinced myself she was off drinking or fucking somewhere, till she suddenly arrived in jubilant mood. Was she drunk? Had she just got laid? My confusion soon turned to joy though, seeing her looking great, telling me how much she liked me. We joked, teased, tickled and hugged, kissed and made up. I asked her why she was so happy. She just said she was happy to be with me. She curled up and fell asleep like a baby content in her father's arms. I lay there glowing in her affection. She loved me it seemed. I was the one constantly plotting in silence, not her. Was it actually I who was the villain in this whole piece?

I woke before her as usual. She looked beautiful and serene. I could feel myself falling for her again, my emotions and reason in a tug of war between my ears. But now I was starting not to care about her previous lies, forgiving her for the unimportant trivialities that they were. The new medication was working too, thank God, my face starting to clear up slightly. In the evening Nok and I looked round the busy Sunday market, admiring the stalls of textiles and wooden handicrafts, musicians filling the air with the entrancing reedy sounds of the old Lanna Kingdom. I showed the girls my photos of the South, hiding the ones of Jeab and the gang, too painful for me to even look at. They remarked on how the Southern girls weren't as pretty as them, as I dreamed of escape to the Paradise Isle. I called Somsak in Laos too, who gave me some enthusiastic but vague-sounding promises about our pioneering trip together.

We went up Doi Suthep Mountain on the edge of town one day, curving round the bends to the large temple overlooking the city. Two *Nagas* formed the staircase rising up the temple grounds where we bowed to the golden Buddha statues and were blessed by monks splashing holy water on us and tying white string around our wrists for good luck. Thai visitors made merit in the temple by honouring the monks and listening to their teachings, meditating and performing various ceremonies, such as giving offerings of flowers, ringing bells and coating statues in gold leaf. From there the whole city was laid out ahead of us, flat in the valley, gleaming like white gold in the tropical sunshine.

Nok was happy all day, but I pushed her again in the evening with my stupid jealousy, trying to catch her out. I fell asleep with her crying into the pillow. I started to think she really was telling the truth, she did love me. Perhaps it was the anti-malarials that were mixing my head up, acting as a catalyst for my paranoia and jealousy. I was supposed to take them for four weeks after leaving malaria-prone areas like Laos.

But still the shit continued. Some French guys were hanging

round the restaurant all the time. Bow was friendly with them and kept trying to take Nok along with her, as I tried to pull her away. When it was just me and Nok together I was happy with her, but once she was out with her friends, which was most nights, the flip side of the coin was revealed, and I didn't like that side so much. The gossip, the eyeing up of the men, the feeling like my presence in the group was less than appreciated.

My face was clearing up little by little. The scars underneath the scabs didn't appear to be as bad as they first seemed, just slight blotches of pigment now. I was getting better. Meanwhile, I was getting emails from friends in Phi Phi, old companions like Matt, Mr Blue and Brad passing through Bangkok, and I was still in touch with Somsak. Always thinking ahead, plotting my next move, the road beyond always luring me on.

I needed to make a decision. I got a bike the next day and went up Doi Suthep again, alone this time. It always felt good – the twist of the throttle, the rush of acceleration, searing round the mountain bends, the wind in my face, my life in my hands. Nothing gave me that sense of freedom more than riding those bikes around. I yearned for it, like a dying man in the desert. I went up high past the temple and a palace, before going along a muddy side track and edging along through the shadows of the pine trees. I reached a viewpoint on the side of the mountain looking south. I was alone there, just me and the mountains and the bright blue sky above, looking for an epiphany in the best place I could find it – alone in nature. I sat down on the grass in the Sun's warm rays and had a think. There was no epiphany, but I had to make my decision. Do I stay or go? Was I happy? No, I wasn't happy here. So I had to go. I decided to tell Nok I was leaving town and wouldn't be back. I freewheeled down the mountain, a rainbow forming over the city below me, half-seriously taking it as a sign I'd made the right decision.

Back in Siriporn, the usual shit. Me bored, Nok smiling vacantly, Bow sniping at me, French guys flirting. Fuck this shit. I was out of here. Every girl I met here, I always seemed to get the gang of friends as part of the deal. I kept hearing a word in their conversations, *jao-choo* or something. I remembered hearing it all the time with Jeab and her friends in Ao Nang. That word. I wasn't sure what it meant, but I knew it wasn't good. It took me back to the conversation about butterfly girls – by the fireside with Nut's Australian ex-boyfriend when I was first here. So what was I doing, going through it all again?

After work Nok came to my room, me all contemplative and serious. She asked me what I was thinking. It all came out. I told her about the Thai boxing poster I'd seen with her 'ex' on it. I told her about the email inbox. I told her I knew about her lies, and that I was sick of her and her butterfly friends. I told her I was lonely here. And I told her I was leaving. She protested her innocence on my deaf ears for a while before a long hour of silence in my little stable room. Then she left.

I was woken briefly by a knock on the door. It was a drunk Nok at 4:30am. In dreamy silence I allowed her in my bed and we slept in each other's arms, the gentle fondness still there.

Morning brought a calm. I escorted her to work as usual and ate. She seemed happy. Maybe she thought we were back together. I didn't think we were. I said goodbye to Aek who was working in his office again. I told him I'd broken up with Nok and was leaving town. He laughed, perhaps at my expense, perhaps pleased for me. He suddenly told me everything. He told me Nok shagged around all the time. Big-mouthed Bow used to tell him everything they got up to. I wasn't angry. I was relieved and contented to finally hear the truth for once, and felt a reaffirmation of belief in my own instincts. And absolved of my guilty suspicions. And my will hardened. I felt vindicated.

Another knock on the door in the evening. There was Nok, all smiles and kisses. She didn't get it. But I was hardened now. I said nothing about Aek's revelation, not wishing to betray his confidence, but I told her I was still leaving tomorrow. She protested her innocence, claiming she didn't fuck about. But I knew the truth now. I don't know why it mattered to me so much. It was in the past. I didn't own the girl, let alone her past. I think it was just the truth I was after, the revelation that I'd now been given. I wanted to see how far they would push the lie. Another poisoned silence ensued in that rotten room – two hours this time. She cried, inconsolable as I hugged her, before eventually falling asleep. I lay there for another couple of hours, looking at her, looking at the ceiling, looking ahead, my mind turning over. She looked cute lying there like a baby. My decision was still reversible.

I woke up before her the next morning, showered and put the cream on my face. I was looking okay again now; even the blemishes were fading. Perhaps I wouldn't be left with any scarring at all. I was cured. We all take our health for granted until it's gone . . . then again when it returns.

I lay down and cuddled Nok and she slowly woke. We lay face to face for a long time, eyes opening and closing, occasionally shifting position in a slow game of body chess. I still liked her. Maybe I wanted more than that but I knew she wasn't the one who could give it to me. Finally we came closer together and started to kiss, both wanting it as much as the other. Was I going to forgive her or was it to be the last time, the long kiss goodbye? As we sucked on each other's lips, tongues darting, I was sure of one thing and one thing only, and that was that I wanted her there and then. I pulled her skirt off, hungrier than a wolf, white knickers down her honey thighs, knees, calves, feet, legs thrown apart; I jumped in between and penetrated her hard, the dry thrust suddenly breaking into the wet, the instant gratification of that warm vulvic dip. I fucked her passionately, loving every plunge and withdrawal. As I came, exhausted and sweaty, that steel coldness struck me again right through the heart – that feeling of cold hard truth. Because that was how I felt. I felt cold. I got up and started to pack my bag, Nok watching in mournful silence.

She skipped work. I took her to her room where she suddenly collapsed on the floor in tears, hugging my legs in desperation, urging me to stay. I told her I knew she was always lying to me and that I couldn't trust her. "Why you always talk about the past?" she pleaded in her Thai-American accent. "Don't go. Give me time." She crouched before me subserviently. "I've gone already," I said. My mind was racing back to that house in Ao Nang again. I was an idiot. She cried and sobbed. "You will never know how much I love you." I nearly broke at that point. It was true. But I couldn't change my mind now. The road lay ahead of me. Always. She clung to my hand as I tried to get out of the room. She pulled and I pulled until her grip was broken and I was free again.

I paced down the street, stomping off the negativity. I passed Nut's shop and told her I was leaving. There was a look of inevitability in her face. "That's why I told you I know Nok better than you," she said.

I got my bag and returned to Siriporn one last time before my bus left for Bangkok in the evening. I wasn't sure what my next move would be, but all roads led to and from Bangkok. I could go anywhere from there. I said goodbye to Nok, Bow and Pop. Nok sat there in silence, tears streaming down her cheeks. I was sad to see her in pain, some affection still there. But I was happy, happy to be leaving; happy to have my life back in my own hands again, happy to be free. I was so happy it was an effort to stop myself from laughing in her face. I guess there's a fine line between being vindicated and vindictive.

* * *

Back in the steaming drunk alleyways of Banglampoo again. But my head was somewhere else. I wanted some nature, some purity. I didn't want to be here. Despite being knackered from all the travelling I decided to head straight back to Laos again and see if Somsak's kayaking trip was going to happen.

I killed three hours waiting around in Hualampong train station. I was so used to whiling away the hours doing nothing that I didn't care about these waits anymore. Three hours was child's play. Sweating and waiting were just part of my daily routine.

My third-class seat on a long wooden bench may have been cheap but it was far from comfortable. I was the only foreigner there, whole families with dozens of tightly-packed cardboard boxes crammed together on upright wooden benches. I sat in the corner of the carriage with a young couple, curious kids peering over at me. The couple were only slightly older than me, but that's all we had in common. The man could not have been friendlier though. The tensions of the day wound down as we communicated by pointing at sentences in my second-hand Thai phrasebook. We managed to discuss religion, politics and all sorts using this book-pointing method. He was genuinely pleased to meet me. I guessed he'd never met a foreigner before. He said he worked in Bangkok but was going home to Nong Khai to see his family for the first time in two years with his new wife. I think that's what he meant anyway. He shared his plastic bag of sticky rice and cold pork with me, smiling the whole time as his bemused wife watched us. Eventually I caught a few hours' fitful sleep on the jolting train, getting thrown around in a seated foetal position leaning against the back of the bench.

At 5:30 I gave up trying to sleep anymore. My new friend was still grinning at me. I gazed out over the murky, green, pre-dawn sky, past trees and endless paddy fields as the Sun slowly permeated the heavy fog and clouds of the rainy season. This was the heart of Isan, the highly populated but poor Northeast region of Thailand. The train stopped for a while and my new buddy bought me a can of Chang which we guzzled on the side of the tracks out in the middle of rural nowhere. Men here didn't seem to have any problems with drinking at the crack of dawn or any other time, so who was I to decline? We eventually arrived at Nong Khai station in the breezy morning drizzle, the end of the line and the gateway back over the Mekong River to Vientiane and Laos. I said goodbye to the lovely newlyweds, half-wishing I could enjoy a simple life with a good woman like that.

★ ★ ★

Over the bridge and into Vientiane. Trudged to the bus station and got a crowded, rusty bus straight out of there. Back in the country, I'd forgotten how beautiful Laos was in the Sun, all rich green fields and bright blue sky; though I was too much of a scummy mess to truly appreciate it. Back to the idyllic tourist ghetto of Vang Vieng. I got a room at Somsak's guesthouse at Super Kayak. I finally showered after two days of tramping around and lay down on the warm welcoming white sheets.

It's in these restless moments that occasionally something very strange happens. One of the strangest phenomena in all of human life in fact. My mind wanders, seemingly uncontrolled, strange half-thoughts merging into ideas, emotions and surreal visions. And instead of falling asleep in the normal manner, my dreams emerge into life there and then. The sleep is so light that I know I'm dreaming and once this realisation occurs, I'm free to do as I please within the new dimensions of this dream world. I call it dream surfing, for the dreams then come one after another in waves, and with practice it feels like I can control my actions within them.

The first time it happened to me I felt myself rising out of bed and saw my body still lying there. I took flight over the land and oceans, rising up through the atmosphere and into space. It felt divine. I eventually learned that I wasn't the first person to experience this phenomenon. It's better known as lucid dreaming – being aware that one is dreaming. The experience of entering this state and controlling oneself within it, make it quite distinct from regular dreaming.

It happens rarely, but when it does it's usually when trying to sleep when not really tired and the mind is restless. You can feel it coming on as you lie there drifting away. Sometimes your body feels like it's floating away from you, or you fall forwards into infinity or down through floors of a building, or are swung around the room by your feet. The faint shadows of your thoughts become visible and gradually morph into more concrete visions of solid objects. Sometimes, you hear the most beautiful music ever heard playing from the beyond, like a faint echo from Heaven.

Then the dreaming begins, but since I know it's all just a dream, I can do whatever I want. But even then it's not easy. My first instinct is to fly. I flap my arms and slowly rise up above the land. But it takes practice in successive dreams. On a bad day, I have trouble staying up, like a plump chicken. On a good day I fly like an eagle, soaring high, turning and twisting above the dreamscape world of the infinite with exhilarating freedom. The happier I am, the better I fly.

Sometimes my sense of touch is awoken and I can feel things clearly, objects in my hands, the wind in my hair. With more practice, more powers are acquired. With an effort I can pass through walls, swim to the bottom of the ocean, conjure up objects from my imagination and control them with my mind.

Sometimes the dreams take place in a beautiful landscape – hills or a beach. If I'm surfing at night, it's usually a dark, more sinister, urban environment, with ghostly apparitions around me. Sometimes we fight or I flee. I've even had conversations with these denizens of the mind, interrogating them, desperately trying to discover their secrets. Sometimes I get too excited and wake up. But usually after what feels like about 20 minutes of dream surfing, I slip into a deeper sleep and the lucidity ends.

What is this new world? Is it mere illusion, a tired mind rearranging its mental garbage? Maybe the experiences people take as religious phenomena, out-of-body experiences, UFO sightings, ghosts and other unexplained events may be linked to this special facet of human life. Or is it a glimpse of something higher, a portal to another world? I don't know, but if there is one thing in this world that instils in me a pure wonder and belief in some higher realm than the physical, then it is this. If dreams offer us glimpses of possible worlds, then lucid dreams let us go there.

★ ★ ★

After journeying around the outer limits of the Universe, I awoke in the heart-tugging mountains of Central Laos. I still felt exhausted, but there was only so long I could stay alone in cheap guesthouse rooms, with no entertainment other than my wrists and dwindling imagination. I came outside and breathed the sweet mountain air. It felt good. I couldn't find any motorbikes for rent, so I hired a dilapidated little bicycle and pedalled north, past the lush wet paddy fields, shimmering in the bright glow of the afternoon, past wood shack villages with kids running out to see me, waving excitedly, more sweet choruses of "Hello" and "*Sabai dee.*" The warmth of the people and land touched me again. They are perhaps the friendliest people in the world. Stunning rock formations lined the rising valley, blue mountains peering on beyond. I cycled the bitter stench of the city out of me, harder and harder over bridges and rivers, villages and schools. Eventually the road started going steeply uphill, so I turned around and came back the same way. There aren't many roads in Laos.

I waited for Somsak in the evening as his teenage squeeze and her friends giggled at me. I sat there kind of embarrassed and looked around. It was quiet now, just a few backpackers laying roots in the DVD restaurants. Eventually a woman told me he wasn't here.

A couple more days hanging round the quaint little town, wandering around in a stoned haze, bathing in the Sun's warm benevolence. I hung out in Somsak's restaurant, chatting to his family and friends, but still no sign of the boss. This crazy little plan of mine didn't seem to be happening. Then I was told he *was* here, but had been struck down by some mysterious illness. His friendly father took me up to his room where he was in bed, being nursed by his little girlfriend. The father teased his son, playing with his nipples in bed, the pampered young lord of the manor! I knew they had close families here but this was a bit much! His girlfriend looked happy. People told me there was nothing else to do out here in the fields other than grow rice and make love. Beautiful people really.

Later that day I took my pushbike over the river on a little ferry boat. I pedalled along bumpy earthen tracks into the fields, around which stood huge pillars of rock which formed the borders of this mystical valley. I came to a hand-painted sign for a cave which said it had opened two years ago. I decided to have a look and cycled down the muddy track where an old man lay in a wooden frame in the shade. He was the only person there. He had a weather-beaten face but an amiable aura. He led me through fields to a muddy track in the forest going up the side of a mountain, over rocks and tree roots. We chatted a little, though the conversation didn't go far beyond us both saying "Hot!" lots, sweat oozing out of my every pore. He gave me a head lamp attached to a huge plastic battery pack with wires hanging out of it. "I go back," he said. I tried to explain that if I wasn't back, would he come back in an hour. I don't know if he understood me or not, but he nodded and said, "No fear." "No fear," I repeated uncertainly and he left in silence.

I carried on alone up the rocky track, tree roots like metal rods, curtains of dead vine and the piercing sirens of invisible insects, battery pack banging against my sweat-soaked torso. Eventually I came to the cave entrance on the side of the mountain from where I could just see Vang Vieng through the trees. I felt I was entering the unknown, where few had gone before. I gathered my wits and entered the cave, descending a little bamboo ladder into a cavern where the Sun's rays still permeated. I was quickly covered in sticky pale brown mud, as the rocks were all damp from the dripping walls above. The large rocks in the cave were all at different levels, so you couldn't walk, just clamber between the rocks. The cavern walls were formed by what looked like undulating vertical tubes and stalactites, the intestines of Mother Earth, white and bobbly, soaked in a milky white layer of salty mucus.

I went up another short wet ladder to a platform that led into a crack and darkness beyond. I twisted the two short pieces of wire around the nodes of the battery pack as best I could, and put the elastic-strapped lamp on my head. I crawled forward into the darkness on all fours like a spider, the hard pump of adrenaline urging me on into the depths of the Earth where no man should be, until it was pitch black all around. I felt my way over the shadowy flashes of rock till I came to the top of a ledge where a long vertical bamboo ladder descended deep into a narrow pit. I couldn't see the bottom with my lamp, just the ladder disappearing over the sheer drop into the pitch blackness. Danger everywhere. But that youthful vigour, that need for discovery and adventure, that overcoming of fear, that indescribable yearning to really live that had brought me here in the first place – they all urged me to go on. "You have nothing to fear but your own fear." This sentence kept going through my head like a mantra. I turned around and edged backwards to get my feet on the ladder when suddenly there was a blinding flash of blackness all around – asphyxiating nothingness, a whiplash of fear. The light had gone. I remained motionless for a moment. I couldn't see a thing. Absolutely nothing. Just the echo of water drops and the occasional fluttering of bats' wings. I felt around and carefully slid my hand down the wires until I found the metal contacts and touched the nodes. A flickering light broke forth once more, but the wires had become disconnected from the battery pack and would only connect if I held them in position. I took one last look down the hole. It was no place for a man. Another bang of visual silence. The wire wouldn't stay attached to the node. I was lost in nothingness. A man is close to hell in such surroundings, being sucked back into the bowels of the Earth from whence he came. The fear pumping round my system was intoxicating . . . but revelatory. Because all I knew right then was that I was getting out of that cave. The instinct for survival permeates our every move, but it is fear which draws this fact to the forefront. Luckily I wasn't too far from the cavern. I managed to slowly inch my way back blindly on all fours, feeling my way along the rocks until some sunlight gradually emerged ahead in that deathly hole of hell.

I reached the light of the cavern, bathed in relief, drunk in the love of life, grateful for the Sun's God-given light. I climbed down the small bamboo ladder from the crack to the cavern floor again. Halfway down, my foot gave way and I went crashing onto the hard wet rock below. My heart was thumping madly, but I was fine. The fall was only a metre. The soggy bamboo ladder rungs had snapped clean in half. But I was in shock. Not from the fall itself, but the realisation that if I'd taken one step on that long ladder further inside the cave it would have collapsed too, plunging me to a certain death alone in the darkness. Even if I had survived the drop, it wouldn't have been pretty, lying there in pitch blackness, screaming broken bones and agony, with no one to hear me and no way of getting out; my only hope of survival an old man asleep in a field. I climbed out the cave, filled my lungs with the sweet clean air and sat by the entrance for a long time overlooking the peaceful valley, covered in mud and trembling from the adrenaline. I was pumping with that instinct for survival, that instinct which manifests itself in the innate love of life we all share deep down. The mountains looked more beautiful than ever before. I am not going to die. Not yet.

My mind turned over those words that had been going round my head from somewhere. "You have nothing to fear but your own fear." I could understand it in one sense in that the values enshrined in your emotions exist only in your own head, not out in the world, hence we have nothing to fear in the world, only that which we choose to fear. And I was beginning to see how this kind of mental state might be possible. However, to rid oneself of fear is to disrobe oneself of what it is that makes one human. Anyone of an elevated meditative mind who can achieve this state of fearlessness, is in effect elevating themselves from their own primordial instincts. They are rising above the very base characteristics of their being. They are exercising what appears to be the human mind's capacity for self-reinvention. For a critic to pass this off as mere religious fanaticism would be a gross misunderstanding. There was clearly something very special at work here – people using the power of their mind to change even their most core values, and in turn change their behaviour. There seemed to be something within the Buddhist system of thought that was closely associated with Man's capacity for free will, this Holy Grail I was searching for. For a Western mind only just beginning to understand the East, it was a revelation to realise I was still scrambling in the dust of 2500 years of history.

Nothing was happening back at Super Kayak. This trip around the unexplored wonderland was looking like it was going to be nothing more than dream. Somsak was barely speaking to me either, saying we'd maybe do it when he was better. I didn't fancy hanging around here indefinitely. The next day I was off again, riding on the roof of the *songtaew* for three hours with caged roosters and piles of green bananas, burning to a crisp and loving it. No longer dreaming, I was soaring through the mountains for real now, still alive, still flying high. Stamp, stamp and another third class train with the locals, nodding my head all night till the Sun rose over the golden fields and temple tops of Central Thailand.

★ ★ ★

It appears that every species that ever lived is descended from the same common ancestor or gene pool. The first organisms to evolve on Earth were probably simple-celled prokaryote bacteria which lacked a cell nucleus. These would later form huge communities in slimy biofilm. These different forms of bacteria were the only life on Earth, and for one billion years were living and reproducing successfully but certainly not changing quickly. But gradually, there were natural variations in the traits of their offspring. Organisms with the traits best suited to survival and reproduction in their changing environment would be the ones more likely to survive and reproduce. And the Earth's environment is a varied and ever-changing place. Over time the numbers of organisms with certain traits within a species would change. Hence there is a natural selection for advantageous physiological traits in species over time, which very slowly brings about a gradual evolution, or slow change, in the physiology of the species as a whole over countless generations. And so, over the next billion years, some of these simple bacteria gradually evolved.

Cyanobacteria, or blue-green algae, began using the energy of sunlight to feed on the hydrogen atoms contained in the water around them, releasing the oxygen atoms as waste. Photosynthesis had begun, and oxygen gradually entered the atmosphere, creating an ozone layer in the upper atmosphere, blocking more of the Sun's ultraviolet radiation from the Earth's surface, and retaining more heat on the Earth's surface, stabilising temperature fluctuations.

As the atmosphere slowly became more oxygenated over the next one billion years, more complex organisms developed under this more efficient means of energy production. Some forms of bacteria successfully merged, forming more complex eukaryote bacteria, with cell nuclei and organelles in their cells.

After another billion years some species began to reproduce sexually, with female and male genders evolving in different ways. Species' cells began to cooperate and merge to such an extent that they grew into various multi-celled organisms of increasing complexity, such as amoebas, algae, plankton, slime moulds, fungi, sea weeds and sponges. A separation developed between plants, which gained energy from the sunlight and carbon dioxide, and more mobile animals, which evolved from free-moving, unicellular eukaryotes, and fed on other organisms for survival. These developed into an array of corals, sea anemones, slugs and worms. About 550 million years ago some developed into shelled arthropods like trilobites and crustaceans; molluscs like shellfish, snails and squid; and later fishes, the first vertebrate, or back-boned animals.

Some coastal plants began growing more out of the water, reproducing with spores and seeds, evolving into larger land plants like mosses, weeds, ferns, bushes and trees, which later spread into huge forests.

Bacteria and fungi came too, breaking down the decaying plant material in the nutrient-rich soil. Many groups of animals gradually made a successful transition to this new environment as well. First were small crustaceans like woodlice, mites and sandhoppers. Arthropods, like centipedes and millipedes, and larger arachnids like spiders and scorpions. Insects evolved and gradually prospered in this new terrestrial habitat in a multitude of forms – ants, beetles, bees and butterflies.

Later on, about 400 million years ago, some coastal fish in brackish and fresh-water habitats developed leg-like lobed fins to help them crawl along the sea-floor, like the lungfish, giving birth to the first tetrapods – four-limbed animals. Some, like modern mudskippers, spent increasing amounts of their lives on land to avoid marine predators, and for the abundant new food sources there.

Some evolved into amphibians like caecilians, newts, salamanders and frogs, born in the water but growing air-breathing lungs in adulthood. From the most advanced amphibians came land-born, air-breathing reptiles like lizards, snakes, turtles and crocodiles. About 230 million years ago, some reptiles diverged into dinosaurs, a diverse group of herbivorous and carnivorous reptiles like the diplodocus and tyrannosaurus, some growing huge in size, which topped the food chain for millions of years. Some of these developed into winged birds with the power of flight.

About 200 million years ago, small rodent-like mammals gradually evolved from amphibians too. Most species' offspring were born without an egg. They had more erect limbs, different ears, jaws and fur. They were warm-blooded and mobile, and would eventually become more intelligent than any animals that had existed before them.

FIVE

Back to Bangkok like a fly to shit. My little dream of love put to bed now, I was back at the crossroads, where all paths lead to and from, the city you always get dragged back to, the centre of Thailand, of Southeast Asia, of my new world, the black hole at the beating heart of this Universe from which I had no intention of escape. Here lay the temple of the new dawn, the great invisible mountain which I aspired to climb. Where the found go to get lost, and the lost go to get more so. Chiang Mai was over, Laos was over, so what next? Infinite possibilities but only one reality. Was I leading myself or were events leading me? Could I ever say no or was it all just yes yes yes? I still had over a week till my friends arrived. What was I going to do next?

Plodding along with my backpack at dawn there were already familiar faces around. I saw my Irish buddy I was drinking with here over six weeks ago, slouched in the bar of his guesthouse with half a Baileys clamped firmly in his hand. I checked back into the laid-back sleaze of Papaya Guesthouse. A lot of the cleaner guesthouses didn't allow 'night visitors', but the friendly folk at Papaya didn't give a shit. Had bacon and eggs for breakfast which always felt quite luxurious instead of my usual fried rice or noodle soup. Back on the beat all day, the massage girls, burger girl, the junk carts, the stray dogs, the mad bag lady, the juice woman cooing "O-lenz dooce ten baaaaaht," all at their usual spots, *farang* coming and going but life unchanged round Banglampoo. I was bored already, back in the old routines of Groundhog Day. Should I move on or get into it again?

I saw Alan down the arsehole of Soi Rambutri, that depressed alcoholic English teacher I'd met that horrible night down the alleyway of Backstreet Bar. He was sitting at a fold-away metal table drinking warm Chang alone in the hot Sun. I averted my gaze but he remembered me somehow. "Alright mate?" He seemed rather pleased to see me. So I sat down and opened a fresh bottle of Chang Beer instead of lunch.

Alan had been here for four years and overstayed his visa by four years as well, never leaving the country. So if he wanted to avoid jail he had to save up enough money for a flight back to England plus the large fine he'd have to pay to get out the country. However, he only worked two days a week teaching weekend classes, making just enough to fund the other five days a week drinking dirt cheap Chang round the dirt cheap bars of Rambutri. In a word, he was fucked. Now it was early afternoon on a Thursday and he was a mess. He wouldn't go home for days at a time, just crashing in the rooms of other drunks and hussies he knew. He kept rambling away at me. Maybe I was the only person bored, lonely or stupid enough to listen to his bitter and twisted rants. But I sensed a warm heart drowning away in there somewhere.

He took me to a laundrette cafe near East Gate Bar where the hardcore Rambutri pissheads hung out in the daytime. The craziest guy on the street, the scarred-up punk It, was there of course. A few fucked up old working women, two figures past their prime, some one-armed skinhead and a couple of dodgy Aussies. They were all hammered, been up on it all night and day. They were all haranguing and taking the piss out of each other, though they left me alone. Alan whispered to me that the Aussies were involved in procuring visas for Thai girls to get into Australia. If I knew any girls that were interested I'd get a monthly percentage on their earnings over there. I didn't like the sound of it and paid for my beer.

Alan followed me out. I seemed to be the only person willing to put up with him. He was jovial and friendly towards me, despite his apparent bitterness towards the rest of the world, spitting vile at all the locals over bills and any other issues that came into his head. Beware the beast they call Chang. Many many hours later I was clinging onto a tree branch as my vision failed me on the way home, throwing up toxic puke everywhere. Welcome back to Bangers you drunk fuck.

The following day I bumped into my mate Reggie from Laos, now sporting a dodgy bandana, tie-on dreads and wooden beads. I reprimanded him for his foray into the unforgivable world of backpacker fashion before visiting the Grand Palace and the Emerald Buddha Temple by the side of the river. A complex of ornate palace buildings, religious structures and statues, with shining gold stupas rising up into the sky alongside the red-tiled roofs of the temples, all decked in gold, jewels and murals. This was the real Bangkok, the old Bangkok, the travelling that I could be doing more of, exploring the land, history and culture, instead of trawling the gutter by night.

So I proceeded to drag my friend through the gutter with me. Usual rum joints, dripping with scrubbers and mess-heads. I went looking for some girl but was told she'd gone off with her new friend or some crap. It was hard to know what to believe here in the land of smoke and mirrors. I came to, slouched in some late night dive full of spitty joints, degenerates and ladyboys dancing on tables. Sunrise at crossover hour, as the last wasters go home and tonight's arrive off the buses.

We bumped into Samuel Odobo, the guy from Sierra Leone I'd met in East Gate Bar before. He remembered me and we had a few drinks in the early evening. Now he was sober, he was laid-back and friendly, a nice guy. There were quite a few young African guys in the area it seemed. They mostly kept themselves to themselves, but he was out mixing with all the Thais and Westerners. He was pretty well known in Banglampoo, as I was becoming too. I asked him what he was doing here. He said he was a refugee, and produced some scraps of folded paper from his pocket. I'd never met a refugee before. I vaguely knew there had been some kind of war in his country a few years ago, but no more than that. I was totally ignorant of the situation in fact. He told me his father was well-off though, and was sending him money to stay here.

We ended up back at Hell's Pass outside Backstreet Bar, drinking with the unfortunates from upstairs and the undesirables from outside.

One young girl called Wan sat with me. She looked kind of cute in the dusty neon, with puppy fat and a chipped tooth. And despite everything she was strangely eloquent, telling me about the root of the Thai word *farang*. Some of the first Westerners here were French, who called themselves *francais*, which gradually turned into *farang* in Thai. This became the word they used to identify all Westerners to this day. I didn't know if it was true, but it sounded plausible at 4am.

Back on Khao San in the loony late night hours, some old hippie twat mouthing off drunkenly at everyone whilst ranting on about peace and harmony. Another group of tie-died, blond-dread Aussie kids were banging bongo drums and offering free hugs. I swerved through them and the marshlands of stiletto-shoed, crocodilian he-bitches grinning in the shadows and made it home in one piece.

One more night. All I can think about is my next drink. Back to East Gate Bar, my new local, SangSom sets with Samuel, It and the other regulars, before going to EGB Club nearby, quality house music in an unpretentious intimate club. Some little lady called Tangmo, friend of a friend, dances nearby. Cute, short, likes a drink. Power cut. The lights go off and she leaps up and kisses me suddenly. Next thing we're in my tiny windowless room as she bounces on top of me like a semi-conscious water mattress.

I wake up. The girl's gone but I'm definitely not alone. I bounce out of my sweat-drenched wooden box to the toilet in delirious morning bewilderment, the Chang throwing the old soft grey matter around my skull like an elephant on musk. One stench of the rancid piss and the floating semi-turd in the toilet and I was coughing up thick chunks of vile kag. Gotta get out. I quickly checked out the guesthouse before realising I had no idea where I was going, so I dumped my bag and stumbled down the street like a concussed giraffe.

The SangSom had me in her grip though, the heat wringing the life force out of my body. I tried watching one of the fake DVDs in the tourist restaurants, but the shit quality and subtitles just screwed my head up even more. I tried reading a book, but the words turned to spaghetti. Intolerable Thai pop music was blaring out from somewhere. Consciousness closing in.

I cut through a back alley to Phra Athit Road and headed for the white fort park by the river to chill out. I just needed some Sun, some peace, some tranquillity. I sat on a bench, eyes on the murky river, sweating miserably. No such luck. Two giant wasp things wouldn't leave me alone, hovering and buzzing around me ominously. I moved benches. Just a few moments reprieve . . . please! Some friendly old Thai man came and joined me on the bench with a frail smile. I could barely speak English myself by this point, let alone Thai or anything else. But it didn't matter, because neither could he. But he still tried his best to befriend this sweaty fuck-up staring out over the river. My brain rattled continuously. All we could manage to talk about were the boats. He spent the next 30 minutes pointing out every single boat that went past and telling me what it was, looking rather pleased with himself every time. "Ferry boat . . . boat taxi . . . long-tail boat . . . boat taxi . . . boat taxi . . . " and so on. It felt like karmic retribution for some criminal act in my past.

I eventually peeled myself away and fled to Khao San. Luckily there was my friend Reggie. When I told him I needed to get out of here, I think he could tell that I truly meant it. He checked out of his room and we jumped in a *tuk-tuk* to the station.

★ ★ ★

We caught a train north for an hour through the flat golden heartland of Central Thailand, past factories and temples to Ayuthaya, the ancient capital of Siam, feeling a lot calmer by the time we arrived. We got a funky-looking *samlor*, a three-wheeled taxi contraption, across the river to a street of guesthouses, then went out and ate some sizzling *pad Thai* on hot plates in the street. It was nice to come to a normal Thai town, enjoying the easy company of my old friend as we reminisced about a certain trip the previous year.

The next day we hired some cranky old bicycles and went out to see the ruins around town. Ayuthaya was the centre of a Siamese Kingdom for over 400 years until it was destroyed by an invading Burmese army in 1767. The capital was eventually relocated to Bangkok. In its prime it was said to be one of the largest and richest cities in the world, its power and influence spreading beyond the country's modern day borders. The ruins were inter-meshed with the modern town, all set around a natural island formed by the confluence of two rivers. It was a pleasant town, roads dissecting grassy areas with the scattered remains of once great palaces and pagodas, temples, towers and walls. Busloads of Asian tourists mixed with merit-making Thais and hoards of white-shirted school kids in the blazing inland heat. Giant elephants adorned in traditional gold harnesses and red robes carried tourists past the melee, wild dogs and beggars lazing in the shadows. Some of the best-restored areas were magnificent, showing glimpses of the city's glorious past. Buddha statues lined the temples, dressed in golden robes, surrounded by offerings of flowers and joss sticks from the faithful. At one temple a Buddha head lay embedded in the roots of a tree as if it were born of the Earth itself. In the evening we ate five rounds of meals and snacks from a delicious night market by the riverside, taken aback by the selection of fish, shells, meat, internal organs and chicken foetuses in the ice tray.

It was good to see regular Thai people, families, couples and kids, with beautiful fresh-faced women that weren't out to get you. Good to see something new again too. It was very quiet after dark though. After huffing and puffing around another day we got the train back to Bangkok. It seemed wherever you went, all roads led back to Bangkok. They did for me anyway.

I was still reeling with possibilities. My friends were arriving soon. And then? Perhaps back to Ko Phi Phi for the high season in the winter. And next year? I had no idea. Bangkok, Tokyo, Sydney, London? It was all good. My mind revelled over the infinite maelstrom as the train chugged down the tracks.

★ ★ ★

As we've seen, both the nature of causality and the workings of the human brain still remain areas of mystery. Where else can we look in order to gain a better understanding of free will? Perhaps we must focus harder on the nature of human consciousness itself in order to unearth its essential structures and qualities that are common to us all.

Sometimes when people analyse or make judgements on things, they make the mistake of seeing that thing only as it is now, a snapshot, frozen in time. They forget to take into account the temporal nature of all things, the fact that everything has a causal history before it and ripples of effects to come after it. In understanding something's present state, one must take into account its history and its future too.

So what can we all agree on regarding human consciousness? The most obvious thing is that it is temporal – always changing and flowing, never static nor fixed. There is always something going on in our consciousness, as our brains pulsate with explosive energy. So too with our bodies. Our mind is our own, but our bodies are our outward expression of ourselves in the world. And so since we live in a temporal world we can say that there is a necessity of action in our lives. We necessarily have to do something at all times in our lives. Our days are punctuated by sleep, but even in this low-action state we're temporally bound. Even if we choose to lie motionless, or hide away from the world in a darkened room, we are at all times necessarily *doing* something.

And so back to my original question. Why do we do what we do? One of my earliest philosophical intuitions was that, at all times, people necessarily always do what they want to do. Or to put it another way, at all times, it is logically impossible not to do what you want to do. In human action there is a necessity of *action* and a necessity of *intent*. Human beings always do what they want. It is impossible not to. Of course we are limited by physical constraints, but even the prisoner can choose to submit or struggle.

To some this may sound completely obvious. To others it may sound counter-intuitive. Maybe you'd love to quit your job and follow some lifelong dream. Go around the world or whatever else it is you secretly desire. And yet up to this point in time, you haven't done it. If you desire it strongly enough in the future then you *will* do it. If you don't, then you won't. Dreams only come true with action and we can only act in the present.

But surely there are times when we must do things we don't want to do? Perhaps going to work, household chores, an undesirable event we must attend, or a desirable event we don't attend. Your job, ironing, shopping or the pub – whatever's relevant to you. And yet in every example of something you didn't want to do but did, the fact remains that you did it. Perhaps you don't like your job, but you still get up and go to work every day. You clean your home. You go to the unpleasant meeting and get it out the way. You say no to the enticing invitation and choose the sensible option. We experience these situations every day as life presents us with a constant array of choices.

Whether or not you look back on your previous actions with gladness or regret is irrelevant to this argument. You can't change the past, only the present. If you take a different course of action in a similar situation next time, it is nonetheless a different situation in time. You still necessarily do what you want to do at all times.

So why do we do these things that we appear not to want to do, and yet do? At every moment in time we are faced with a necessity of action in a mind apparently free. We are at all times bombarded with an array of choices, yet can choose only one. So why do we choose one course of action over another? If we necessarily do what we want at all times, then it must be that we want to do that action more than any alternatives that come to mind. We think it's a good idea. In fact, we think it's the best idea out of all the options at that moment in time. And so we do it.

Something new has come into the equation. The word *good*. The word *best*. In our lives we are constantly making judgements about what is good, what is bad, what is better, and what is the best thing to do. For more important decisions we do this consciously, evaluating our various options and making a decision. Often it's done subconsciously, as the data keeps buzzing through our brains, guiding us through our daily activities. We decide what we think is the best course of action at all times and we do it. If we didn't think it was best then we wouldn't do it.

So we can also now say that the human mind and human action are necessarily *evaluative*. This means we are constantly evaluating the various options before us, deciding which ideas are good and which are bad, and always choosing what we think is the best one at every moment in time.

Evaluating is about deciding what is good and bad. Good and bad are values. I use the word *value* in its broadest possible sense, relating to anything that has a positive and/or negative value attached to it in any way, be it moral, aesthetic or whatever else. Anytime we talk about *good* and *bad* we are talking about *values*. I don't mean it merely in any of the narrower senses that people often use – that of something being important, useful, or a principle, or anything to do with monetary value; though all of these narrower senses of the word are relevant. When I say the human mind and human action are necessarily evaluative, it means they are always evaluating what is good and bad, comparing the options and doing what is thought best.

So to re-examine our examples of apparently unwanted actions. How do we decide what to do? When the alarm bell rings and we force ourselves from our beds and go to the job that we think we don't want to go to – why do we do it? Because at that moment we value going to work more than not going to work. We value keeping our job, getting paid, having money and security for a more comfortable future, working our way up the ladder, progressing with our lives. This outweighs the short-term benefits of staying in bed or calling in sick. Or perhaps, from time to time, you decide that it doesn't outweigh it. In which case you stay in bed.

Why do we clean the house? Because we value its cleanliness over the short-term inconvenience of the chore. Why do we attend the undesirable meeting – a place, people or activity we don't like? Perhaps because we value the feelings of another person present and the long-term relationship of love, friendship or work you share, over the short-term displeasure of the meeting. Why do you reject the desirable invitation to some leisure activity, however much it pains you? Perhaps because the expected negative consequences outweigh the short-term pleasure. For example, we value going to work on time with a clear head over the quick drink with friends. We value saving money over going on holiday. We value one relationship over another. All the time, these multi-faceted decisions are happening, constantly weighing up the expected positive and negative outcomes of possible actions, deciding which is the best one, and doing it.

So throughout our lives we are always doing what we think is best at the time. We work because we value the expected long-term financial benefits of our career and the positive effects it will have on our lives. We study, valuing education, knowledge and the future benefits it may bring. Perhaps we exercise for the positive mental and physical health benefits. Perhaps we don't, preferring the benefits of rest and play more. Perhaps we spend social time with partners, family and friends, valuing their treasured company. Perhaps we value being alone and pursuing other activities. Often we do something at the request of another, in which case it can be said we are valuing their views and the relationship. All the time, decisions are made based on the shifting scales of values we hold at any given time.

What becomes obvious is the existence of conflict and tension between these contrasting options and values. We value so many different things that it's impossible to satisfy all these desires without neglecting others. This happens to us all on a daily basis. It may not always be a painful conflict but there is always a choice of options, the winner being the one we value the most at that time. Perhaps these decisions are more common and tortuous for some people than others, but even one whose life is simple must make decisions.

★ ★ ★

The day had finally come. The day I'd been waiting two months, and many years before that for. My brothers were arriving today. This was part two of my journey. I had friends to travel with for the first time. I would no longer be alone. From now on events were going to be very much less under my control. We'd be a team now. I'd have to sacrifice some of my independence for the pleasures and comforts of travelling in a group. Something I hadn't really done yet, but was looking forward to for a change.

Charlie, Joe and I had grown up together. We'd been friends since we were allowed out onto the streets. We were three of a bigger gang who'd grown up together from childhood, through our teenage years and now into young adulthood. There wasn't much to do where we lived. Growing up together like that you learn how to make your own fun. It's the only way. You do it together. And we did everything together. Exploring the limits of our little world for years and years. Climbing trees and riding bikes gradually turned into drinking and smoking, getting out of our little minds for a lack of anything better to do. Talking about everything, staring out at the sky at night, looking into the centre of the Milky Way, seeing the Earth rotate, meteors fall and satellites fly. We were locked down in nature back then, like a thicket of trees sprouting up from the earth and flourishing into maturity. Sharing all our experience and wisdom, by the time we were 18 we knew each other inside out. We grew up as one. But the time had come to go our separate ways. We could stay no longer in that never-changing world. We had to leave.

I got a minibus to the airport and waited by the exit amongst the excited greeters and touts. An hour or two passed, my joy gradually fading. I looked around at everyone on their mobile phones, from all four corners of the world at this gateway to the region. I didn't have a mobile phone with me and neither did they. These were the final hours of Man's freedom when one could walk the Earth alone and anonymous, unknown and undetectable. This was *Achilles Last Stand*, the final dying gasps of a dead century in this new world. A world of information, everything at our fingertips, all connected and contactable, all getting richer and more homogenous, all wearing the same clothes and listening to the same music.

I returned on the airport bus with all the new arrivals, feeling like an imposter amongst them – not living here but no longer on holiday, a boat set adrift on windless seas. I'd just have to tramp around checking my emails till I heard something. A few years ago I wouldn't even have had that option.

It wasn't necessary because swerving through market stalls of Khao San crap I suddenly bumped into Joe. We stood there in shock for a moment before laughing and hugging each other. I'd missed them at the airport. We went to their guesthouse and there was Charlie fiddling around with his camera gear in their dingy box of choice. We threw all our immediate thoughts and feelings around the room, then I showed them round, pointing out this pub here, that girl there, and so on. We caught up over beers and food. I was doing most of the talking, trying to fit the last six months into an animated two hour rant, tripping over my own sentences with new ones. This was it! The adventure of a lifetime! The day we'd always talked about, all those years you think will never end.

They looked bewildered but excited, absorbing the sensory overload on my favourite street, the music and clamour, people from around the world, flashing neon, beggars, touts, market sellers and dirty slappers. Travellers and Thais, bores and whores, hustlers, bustlers, tickets to ride, rich, poor, perceptional doors, thousands and millions crossing the Earth, surfing the present from death unto birth. Men and women and all in between, fags, hags and dirty bags, Jack n' Jill, bent old bill. Butterfly? *Mai pen rai.* Buddhist monks and drum n' bass, beggars rub shoulders in millionaires' face. Amputees on Rambutri, what you get ain't what you see. Wham bam, thank you Maam, a couple of buckets and a dozen Chang, lipstick gangsters out for a buck, boys and girls all looking to fuck. Music, sweat, incessant heat, where are we going, that endless beat? Boom-tit boom-tit boom-tit boom, how much for a double room? Wanna-bes and wanna-dies, everybody flirting with a different guise. Paradise alive and dreams manifested. *Tuk-tuk*, boom-boom. "Where you go?"

Charlie Barker's eyes were boggling with the humid neon overload. He was 24, tall and skinny as a rake apart from a little beer belly. His hair was a mousy straggle of a barnet with a wispy little beard he'd grown despite not having many hairs on his boyish cheeks. He was the artist, the story-teller, the comedian, the party loon. Joseph Conway was 23, small in build but physically strong, rugged with cropped black hair. He was the player, the man about town, the boss, the party king. I was the youngest of the group, usually going along with whatever the others were doing. But now I was the one with the experience.

I led them towards the temple, every step forward determining our shared destinies. This was it, yeah . . . but what was it to be? We crossed the road. Who would make the decisions that determined the outcome? Who is truly the master of one's destiny? As we entered Soi Rambutri, it was already too late. I'd already thrown the first dice.

We got a table outside and hit the SangSom. What else? They took to it like fish to water. Everyone does at first. One by one various apparitions came out the woodwork and joined us. A shit-faced Alan, the marooned teacher, sat with us swearing and spluttering, drunken filth and idle despair oozing out of his every pore. My friends were shocked, having this casualty of the jungle thrust upon them so early. There are drunk fuck-ups the world over, but the drunk fucked up expat is a special breed. A pirate on a desert island without a ship. Woozy women waved as they waltzed away. The lunatic punk It, self-professed Mohicaned boss of the *soi* came past boggle-eyed and intense, introducing himself to everyone. "So these are the people you hang around with now?" I could almost hear my old friends thinking to themselves. There were definitely some wrong 'uns round here. And I knew most of them.

I took them to East Gate Bar. Alan followed, abusing the staff in a mixture of obnoxious English slang and bad Thai before collapsing in a salivic mess on the bar. The small girl Tangmo I'd shagged not long ago joined us next. Not sure what to do about her, but she was friendly and fun, so I let it go. Down the lane further to EGB Club, full on drum and bass surging through the brickwork, rum bottles emptying fast. It's already got hold of the lads – Charlie's doing Russian folk dance star jumps, crashing into everyone, Joe's accosting strangers and trying to look into their souls through sprays of tobacco spit. I laughed like a champion. We'd made it, we'd really made it! Top buzz bass lines, build ups and breakdowns, manic-dancing and crazy liquor!

Back in another dirty coffin, wrapped in a sweaty heap humping Tangmo. This one actually had a window. Nice girl and all, but looking at her for the first time without a glass in my hand, I saw she was no Da Vinci. Head-pounding flashbacks and echoes from last night slice through my butter brain. Charlie accepting her invitation for us all to visit her family today. The innate wrongness of the idea. I played it quiet, till she eventually left of her own accord.

I found a mentally brutalised Charlie and Joe washed ashore in their guesthouse. Charlie had woken up in a random room, his first ever morning in Asia, staring into the turbine of a fan in a hard-hitting psycho-epiphany, random Thai woman next to him, having some kind of moral apocalypse now, before being violently tossed off all over the wall. Joe's hangover was beyond physical description. Simian perhaps. We got straight back on it, hatching plans for the future. The Full Moon Party was coming up in about a week. It seemed the natural place to break the boys in and get some steam out of our system before the big trip . . . to Vietnam.

Tangmo found me again and started tagging along. She was pleasant enough but her presence was a bane on my ever-precarious state of mind. I just wanted to hang out with the boys. I broke into an anxious alcohol-sweat and left Charlie to flirt with her as I showered and re-gathered the broken pieces of my soul in my dark box for a few moments. No rest . . . We made it to Rambutri, but that was as far as we got. Sat at the street bars all night, me and the boys, It and his dodgy mate Antoine, Sammy from Sierra and some of his African friends, a gaggle of street sluts and other random, fucked up, young guys all living in Bangkok and suffering with various women, drug, alcohol and mental problems. I was in the middle of it all, Mr fucking popular, hooking people up like some voluntary gutter pimp. A pretty, young, Chinese-looking girl with goofy teeth and dyed red hair called Kookie was entranced by Joe. Charlie pointed out the girl he'd woken up with – a notorious old tart I'd seen with a dozen guys before. I kept the details to myself. Under my kind stewardship the boys were sliding down the greasy pole of moral abandonment with ease. Banter, booze and bollocks!

Another morning, another couple of hours gently braising in my own juices. I finally mounted the will to climb out of the microwave and into the oven – the ruthless gutters of Rambutri where the ghosts of last night took no prisoners. Smiles and smirks everywhere. I found Charlie holed up at his guesthouse alone taking photos through tinted glass of people and cars on Khao San Road below. He hadn't slept all night. Jet lag, chemical-booze and culture shock had got the better of him. He was on edge, his mind grating. "I've never seen anything like it," he said, "the people, monks, taxis, street-sellers, temples . . . " So here he was, hiding in the shadows, shooting paranoid future memories. A slightly worrying development but not wholly unexpected. We'd already spent years poring through each other's minds, exploring new horizons and narcotic states, me the apprentice, he the master. Not anymore though.

I dragged him out to the river where we jumped on the dirt-cheap ferries that dot their way down the Chao Praya River through Old Bangkok. We stood outside at the back where people got on and off frantically. The boats only stopped briefly, anchored loosely by a sling of rope thrown over the harbour hooks. No safety regulations, complaint procedures or legal action here. Thailand was still of the old school, where people lived hard and died fast, and where money talked regardless of any laws that came and went. We whizzed past the Grand Palace and *Wat* Arun; the Temple of Dawn opposite, the steep central tower pointing deep into the cosmos. Past sky-high condos and shanty river slums, me playing with Charlie's mind, "getting revenge for all those festivals when I fucked with your head," in his own words.

I told him something that had been on my mind. "There's no going back for me." I wasn't going home anytime soon. Wasn't settling down back home or anywhere. Not now. I'd gone too far to turn back. Despite everything, I still loved it here with a passion. It was all a big game to me, and I was getting better and better at it. Charlie stared into me in strained silence.

We passed the five star riverside hotels and got off at Taksin Bridge, transferring to the Skytrain which flew through the offices and towers of Satorn Road, the entertainment district of Silom Road, past Lumphini Park named after Buddha's birth place and onto the shopping centres of Siam Square. Charlie shot off more camera rounds of the break dancers on the overpass, the trains and taxis and Oriental city sunset. His mind satisfactorily blown, we went back.

Charlie collapsed in bed and I moved onto Joe. We hit the juice. This new girl Kookie was stalking him like a shadow, slowly twisting his mind with her inane crap and pigeon English. Tangmo appeared too but I had nothing to say to her. Eventually she clocked on and got up. "See you later," I murmured. "Never!" she snapped and was gone. It was taking me about six hours to get drunk these days, throwing back the Changs and SangSom like an endurance athlete. We went deep, re-syncing ourselves, talking about life, the past and the future, a lot of questions but fewer answers. Two young men unsure of where to walk in the world. Just hearing myself speak and remembering how I used to speak with Joe, I could feel the differences between then and now clearer than ever. After a long drunken emotional debate about life, the drinks hit home and we both agreed on the conclusion: "Fuck it!"

We met up with Sammy Odobo, his usual stoned, friendly self.

We talked about the upcoming Full Moon Party which I'd mentioned to him before. He'd never been south before. "Okay man. I will come with you guys." It was all good. Joe went home and Sammy led me into the black crack outside Backstreet Bar, sat on the concrete table with the usual full-stop of society. Hours passed and morning came. I was next to Wan, the friendly girl with the chipped tooth. She looked cute.

We screwed all morning in one of the Hell's Pass guesthouses that could only be entered via the dark depths of the Backstreet Bar alleyway. Hidden away from the smiley face of Khao San, deep in its dark inner rectum. Wan's big soft titties bounced around as I ground her into the sweaty mattress. Nok long forgotten now. Room like a murder scene – empty except for a dirty bed, filthy graffiti and pictures scrawled all over the walls. How many people had been here before? A question barely worth asking. "You know she's a whore," read one line, flying through my mind as I fucked her again. Black marker cartoons of ladyboys with gigantic cocks. Thai script and phone numbers written in scratchy biro on the wood board. The place was deeply wrong. I double-checked her, the jittery ladyboy paranoia checks that always went through my head the morning after. Definitely a real vagina, I was sure. Despite my latent terror, we got on rather well and I found myself strangely attracted to her vulnerability and her laid-back, un-clingy attitude. Or maybe it was just her big tits. A man can rarely discern such things. I felt a strong urge to leave though. The room stank of evil and the midday noose was tightening round my neck. The corridors were strewn with off-duty ladyboys in t-shirts and no makeup, the same ones I always saw harassing guys in the early hours. They all knew me now. This was the hornets' nest, the epicentre. This was Ladyboy House, or *Yabaa* House to others. There were loads of young African guys there too, decked out in their bright urban gear. What was this place? It was the roughest, dodgiest place I'd been to on Khao San. I felt satisfied to have seen it and escaped while I could.

On the way back I saw It and Antoine drinking in the laundrette as usual. Couldn't face any afternoon insomnia in my guesthouse oven so I started drinking again. Antoine was a shady character in his 30s with all kinds of dark, half truths about drug-running and Asian prisons. It was the *soi* hard man. And they both loved drugs. Antoine paid for them, It got them, and they both did them. The same courtship between the dollar and the street that plays out all over the world.

Evening came but Charlie and Joe had fallen into a state of deep confusion and exhaustion and didn't stay out long. I was disappointed, but the merest whiff of rum and I was a mad bull again. I was with Sammy all night. We got on well. "You are my brother now," he told me in the passionate and direct way that many African men speak. He had an easy, positive view of the world, enjoying the simple pleasures of food, drink and women. He was excited about the Full Moon Party. I was happy to have a new friend along for the ride too. It and Antoine were on it, charging round on *yabaa*, meta-amphetamine pills, wide-eyed and super tense.

A posse of girls were with us, including Kookie and her older friend Sin. Not sure exactly who they were, but they all looked vaguely familiar as everyone does when you're getting drunk in the same street every day. Sin gave me a look. "She's fuckin' rich man!" Sammy whispered excitedly in my ear. She had her own little bar near Khao San Road apparently. It sounded intriguing. I could tell she was the boss of her gang. We chatted a bit. She wasn't exactly young and she wasn't exactly pretty, but she had a bit of spark about her as these fast women often did. She had a shiny diamond sticker on one of her canine teeth, giving her a slightly evil-looking glint. She was in charge and up for it, buying bucket after bucket for everyone, which we all lapped up like puppies to a bitch's teat.

By dawn we were drinking in a 24 hour guesthouse bar. Sin was flirting with some smooth-looking Swiss guy. Then she was back with me. I didn't know what was going on. There was some tension brewing. Some guy accused me of looking at him funny, though by then I was having trouble looking at anything. But Sammy stood up in between and they all backed down. I had no idea what had happened but he'd saved me. We were brothers now. There was talk of this new girlie gang going to the Full Moon Party too. Events I'd set in motion were spiralling out of my control.

Mid-morning by now. Sammy dragged me away semi-conscious to Backstreet Bar for more. Wan was there. Through the scattered fragments of another drunken dawn, a spark still flickered. "I'm just going to the toilet," I slurred.

I heard shouting, voices arguing all around me, but I was too fucked to open my eyes. Where was I? I felt a girl next to me, a man's deep voice. I wrenched my eyes open. I was in the dungeon again, in bed with Wan, both naked under a little sheet with some butch ladyboy trying to peer under the sheet at my knackers. Sammy was in the doorway arguing with Wan who was trying to kick him out the room. "Get up man. We have to go," he was shouting. Consciousness crashing in surging waves, I laughed *ad absurdum* – relentlessly, unstoppably off my head.

We stagger out, Sammy acknowledging all the African guys watching silently in the corridors, and zigzag off, buying 6pm tickets for Ko Phangan. I lose Sammy. My vision seems to be permanently blurred. Check out my guesthouse having not stayed there for two or three days. Beer in the laundrette. Antoine with a broken nose from last night and It getting violent tendencies. I quickly leave. Three hours to kill but I'm homeless. Bed good. Tits good. I slip back to Ladyboy House for a third time, collapsing into the soft breasts of Wan. She accepts me without a word. We kiss and fondle each other before fucking passionately and falling asleep in each other's arms. She never wanted anything from me.

Eyes open. Who am I? Light fading. What time? What day? By some miracle it's 5:30pm. Something about a bus. I shoot off, grab my bag and find Sammy, Joe and Charlie waiting for me at a travel shop. The Khao San bus network's running late as usual. We wait till there are 50 of us and are led down the side-alleys to the bus. We all lose the guide, but I think I know the way, leading the whole group to the car park and getting on an empty VIP bus. A massive scene soon erupts as it turns out I've led everyone onto the wrong bus. Highly strung backpackers and surly bus drivers lock horns. After much consternation and backpacker rage, the tour girl finds us and puts us on the right bus.

The VIP night buses are big double-decker things with most of the seats upstairs. Trying to simultaneously apologise to the girl and chat her up, I was the last one on the bus. I had to sit downstairs next to the toilet in a little windowless room with four seats all facing each other. I was in a fucking mess, drinking non-stop for days and not sleeping properly. Sammy was in another of the four seats, an excited stream-of-conscious commentary pouring out his mouth. On another seat was an even more fucked up-looking, grey-faced, middle-aged, Aussie junkie mumbling nonsensical twisted crap. On the other seat was a respectable-looking, jovial, old Frenchman in glasses. He didn't seem aware we were all speaking in English, if you could call it that, and kept chatting away to everyone in expressive fluent French, hands going everywhere. The room had bumpy reflective metal sheets on the walls in all directions. So the alcoholic me, the smack head Aussie, the catatonic Sammy and the genial old Frenchman were reflected, multiplied and merged into an infinity of misshapen images in all angles and directions. No one was making any sense to each other but we all kept talking anyway; trapped in some metallic, ultra-surreal, absurdish, nightmare hell-bubble, an infinity of echoing images and voices colliding and dissipating into nothingness. The bus eventually departed for the 12 hour journey south. It was a long night.

★ ★ ★

A bright dawn in Surat Thani, backpacker interchange hell. But I wasn't alone anymore and things were good. Good to get off the bus at least. Sam called Sin's mobile to see if they were coming. They were but not till after the party. "Man, she likes you," Sam reassured me, "you can have her, I will have her friend Far, she's coming too. Sin's very rich

196

you know! She can take care of all of us." I couldn't remember who this girl Sin was by this point. Whatever, I was happy to go along for the ride and let someone else take the lead.

Out in the smooth morning light on top of the ferry, cruising to the legendary island, bathing in the low Sun, grateful to have escaped the city, though the city hadn't escaped me. Joe and Charlie seemed strangely withdrawn still, like they weren't quite in the zone yet. Charlie bumped into two girls he knew from home, expanding our group. Sam was jubilant, chatting to everyone, clowning around, dancing with our morning beers. He spotted two pretty Chinese-looking girls. As we were trying to decide where they came from, he suddenly went straight over there making things happen. I thought they were going to run a mile from the nutter, but they didn't. He seemed to be getting somewhere. I went over. Fiona and Joyce from Hong Kong, early 20s. They were pretty and cute, polite and charming, shy but curious. Real girls . . . no, angels compared to the girls I'd been hanging around with recently.

By the time we got to Ko Phangan we were eight in number. We got a truck to a small beach resort near the village of Ban Thai on the south coast. It was quiet and serene, just some bungalows and guestrooms on a quiet stretch of beach. The four guys got four individual little wooden shacks in a row, while the girls took the more comfortable double rooms in the main building. The owner of the little resort looked like an elderly Bruce Lee, a handsome, tough old guy with long hair and an emotionless expression on his face. His son was a teenager, halfway to becoming a ladyboy, with spiky hair and touches of makeup here and there. The beach was long and serene; overlooking Ko Samui to the south, but the water was too shallow to swim in. We chilled out all day and night, getting to know each other, exploring the beach and village and fading into a well-needed sleep in the warm evening.

I slept for 16 hours, eventually staggering to the outside toilet in the bright morning like a newborn mole, unable to see or speak.

Another day of calm on the beach. I was slightly entranced by the beauty and innocence of the girls from Hong Kong on this picture-perfect stretch of sand, so shy and polite but friendly and interesting. Joe and Charlie seemed to be getting their strength back too. Sam kept us all entertained with his jokes and lust for life. This was what it was all about – peace, beauty, relaxation and friendship on the beaches of Thailand. But it was just a temporary respite, another fleeting calm.

Darkness soon fell. Got some over-the-counter diet and sleeping pills in Thong Sala. An upper and a downer. Something for everyone. Bruce Lee drove us up the steep hills to Hat Rin. And then the Full Moon Party was back on, people flying semi-naked with props and paint, music booming round from every angle.

We immediately all lost each other. I found Sam and the Hong Kong girls on the beach. Fiona had thick long hair and a darker complexion, a little more confident than Joyce who looked like a lost little angel with her innocent eyes and bobbed hair. We were both slightly besotted by them. Me and Sam light-heartedly discussed who was going to go for whom, but we were gentlemen, knowing these girls were a different breed from Khao San. Their innocence almost overawed me; they appeared untouchable, ethereal, visions of purity I was no longer worthy to consider, carrying the stench of the city with me everywhere I went.

Buckets, beers and diet pills disappeared as I found the others in the clubs. On it now, purple orchids and white gloves. Me, Joe and Charlie went old school, tongue in cheek but loving it, the girls getting into the vibe, Sammy dancing round happily.

Then I passed the blueys out to the guys to spice things up. Bad move. Memories fading, downers on uppers, our psyches thrown into yo-yonic cycles, reality appearing in mere glimpses, half-images barely understood or comprehended. Music and emotions, dancing, friends and faces, sand, fire, lights and darkness combined in a flickering synergy of phenomena, all control swept away with the tides.

A sudden gasp of clarity. Alone in a beach restaurant, Sun up, party still pumping. I knew where to go. Up to Cliff Top Bar, flying over the paradisiacal seas below, the pinnacle of Utopia, the crown heights of the greatest party on Earth. Charlie and Joe were there, someone selling us some white capsules, pure MDMA he said. We were soon whooshing up a one-way glass elevator into the burning heart of the Sun, life appearing in flashes before slipping away into a non-existent dream space of feelings and nothingness. But I know everyone there, all seemingly familiar faces from Bangkok, Chiang Mai, Laos and Phi Phi, everyone knows me too, all my friends, talking to strangers from the bottoms of our hearts, all in bliss as one, we are E, can barely stand anymore, but my best friends are here in all their jaw-chewing, eye-twitching glory. I've got my arms round them, it's real, this is it, we made it!

Another snap of clarity. Sky fading to night. Lanky Charlie lying unconscious in a ragged heap on the dance floor's edge, inches away from rolling off the cliff. I grabbed him, found Joe and dragged them away to get more cash from home, souls still floating a few feet above our bodies. Sammy was at the bungalows with the girls. He was excited to see us, telling us what he'd been up to, though I was still too far gone to understand anything. I gave him my passport as a deposit for him to rent a motorbike and find some Irish girl staying up at Thong Nai Pan Beach over the wild mountain road.

Back to the Cliff Top, night now though I could barely recall it being day. Lights, pounding beats and shadows, memories non-existent, the drugs got our minds hung, drawn and quartered. Stumbling around lost in a building site on my own with a cig and a Chang. Confusion reigns. I'm a smouldering mess, barely human by now.

Like two angels, Fiona and Joyce appear, taking me to a quiet wooden restaurant somewhere, lying me down on the soft axe cushions, feeding me sweet Malibu and pineapple. The others appeared too, rolling on the floor switching between lapses of life and death. The party thinned away as a second sunrise broke over the ocean, the madness tentatively subsiding. I was with my little angels, sent down to protect me in my hour of need. They would take care of me now. The three of us went back and I lay on their big bed with them, though I dared not touch them, too pure were they for this exonerated wreck. I drifted away for a few blessed hours.

Suddenly Sammy bursts in the room like a raging tornado, crazy and hysterical, cuts and bandages all over him. "I crashed the bike!" he wailed. He'd come off on that crazy dirt road up to Thong Nai Pan Beach. He was in shock and panicking, not making much sense. The girls were scared out their wits. My rest very much over, I took him away and got a *songtaew* to a small doctor's clinic to get him patched up. Then to some dodgy repair shop where he's dumped the damaged bike, asking for thousands of baht to repair it. Sam says he can't get any money. Meanwhile my head's pounding like an 808 and my passport's trapped in the bike rental shop. I wasn't sure what was going on, but I was pretty sure it was going wrong whatever it was.

We were both too battered and exhausted to make any decisions so we collapsed on the beach with the girls. Sammy was trying it on with Fiona despite looking like he'd been on the wrong end of a riot stick. Joyce was looking like an angel in her white bikini as we bathed in the still warm waters together. Her voice was so soft and delicate it broke my heart. I wanted to kiss her, but I knew it would only ever be a dream. The four of us chatted in their room in the evening. I couldn't be sure if they wanted us there or not, as they conferred in Cantonese. I slept on their bed again with Joyce in the middle and Sammy on the floor. He kept inviting Fiona down to join him but she didn't move.

The next day we waved goodbye as the ferry took Joyce and Fiona away from us, across the azure waters like two illusions from another world. I doubted I'd ever see them again. But there seemed to be a sadness in their faces as they faded away. Although I'd never touched her, my relationship with Joyce felt purer than anything I'd had with any other girls I'd met here.

I'd hardly seen Joe and Charlie recently. They'd gone on a boat trip with the other two girls around the island. The little split between us was growing and I couldn't see it being repaired anytime soon. I'd brought Sammy here, I'd given him my passport, he'd crashed the bike, he had no money, and now we were both stuck in the shit together. Spent a miserable day, bored, frustrated and exhausted, going up and down the south coast, to the bike shop trying to rip us off, the rental shop holding my passport, and various internet and call shops trying to get hold of Sammy's friends and relatives in Africa to send him some money. No joy.

The next morning I emerged from my hut. Charlie and Joe were packing their bags. They were going to the next island of Ko Tao. They didn't invite me, rushing off hurriedly, barely saying a word. And then they were gone. I was confused and saddened, but not really angry with them. We all knew I was stuck with Sammy, a chain of events I'd set in motion myself, giving him my passport off my head. What was I thinking? They had to find their own path. So now we were two.

Another couple of wasted days passed, the blue haze gradually replaced by a red one. We got hold of Sam's father but he couldn't send any money here as there were no big banks. The bike was repaired. To speed things up I got money out on my credit card and paid for it myself, driving Sammy around the island on the back. I wanted some money off him before I gave the bike back, unsure whether to trust him all of a sudden. The rental shop was asking for more repairs to be done. Fucking nightmare, going back and forth in the incessant heat. Everyone trying to rip us off everywhere we went. I was getting sick of Sam too. The relaxed happy Sammy of before was gone. Now he was angry and bitter with everything, ordering me round, go here, go there, stop, start. I was helping him and he was fucking ordering me around. I snapped at him on the scorching roads more than once, but we were stuck together like bickering Siamese twins.

He was still ringing Sin everyday and eventually it seemed she was coming with her friend Far who he liked. Suddenly he was excited again. "I know these girls very well. Sin is rich! She can take care of us. You fuck her and I will fuck Far!"

I finally found some time alone in the afternoon and lay brooding in the hammock, looking at the beach where Joyce and I had spent those fleeting moments playing together in the gentle lapping sea. But she was gone now. Only the memories remained, and they were few in number. She was soon to be replaced by a brazen Bangkok hussy. The opposing poles of contrasting desires were pulling me apart. I stared out onto the horizon, my mind unravelling. My old friends had gone, deserted me, and I was stuck with a new friend I was no longer so sure of. With the arrival of these bad bitches, coupled with Sammy's inimitable presence, I felt like Bangkok's tentacles were coming to suck me back into the pit.

Everything that had happened was my fault, my responsibility. I was travelling here alone, totally free to do what I wanted. And this was the path I'd chosen. Going round and round creating little homesteads for myself all over the place. New friends, flings, lives and possibilities in each, splitting myself into these various alter-egos. Paradise and its dark underbelly in Ko Phi Phi. The more sedate charms of Ao Nang but with its own road to madness. The intoxicating lure, filth and energy of Bangkok. The failed romance and culture of Chiang Mai. And the emboldening power of nature in Vang Vieng, the ideals of health and vitality. Each place seemed to represent different parts of me; different values I couldn't decide were the most valuable. The one to pursue remained unknown.

★ ★ ★

Our supposed love matches were arriving. I didn't know whether to laugh or cry, as the city's presence loomed ever closer. I couldn't even remember what they looked like. We rented another bike and went down to the port. Soon they were here. Sin wasn't as hot as I hoped, looking somewhat world weary. The chubby Far was her more respectable friend, a plump, plain-looking University student I vaguely recognised. Sammy was alight with excitement. We went to get his stitches out at the hospital before taking the girls back to the bungalows, much to Bruce Lee's bemusement. "Sin put your bag in his room, Far in my room," which they did as instructed.

We explored the west of the island, touring the beaches and cliff tops to Hat Yao Beach by sunset. I swam in the warm waters admiring the views of another picture perfect beach. Gradually, inevitably, despite my better judgement, something twitched and we drifted closer together, the weight of expectation coupled with the lusty romance of the setting. We floated in the sea, bobbing around, soft skin playing in the water, as I picked her up and threw her in the warm tropical sea. Sammy was enjoying being with his favourite girl Far on the beach.

The atmosphere was pleasant but slightly on edge, as we were sober now and barely knew each. We spent the evening up some jungle trail at a quiet half-moon jungle party before returning home and pairing off into our bungalows. Tired and drunk, Sin and I passed out quickly on the bed before being woken by Far, who'd escaped Sammy's advances in the night and joined us.

The next day Sammy looked a broken man again after last night's rebuttal, barely speaking to the girls at all. We picked up their friend Kookie from the port, all mini-skirts, daft grins and idiocies. There was something ridiculous about the girl, her blatant and unabashed sluttiness, with all her talk of "I want boom-boom *farang!*" Things were getting absurd.

Back at the bungalows and the time came to consummate the relationship. It felt more like a duty than a pleasure as we slipped into the sweaty afternoon beach hut, I bagged up and Sin unveiled her dark saggy body and faded tattoos. She was quite intimidating, a point intensified by her hard and aggressive fucking. She was a good few years older than me, and clearly a lot more experienced. I was starting to feel like a little bitch. Stuck between an old tart and an outstanding debt.

A psychological battle developed as the girls tried to borrow one of our two bikes to meet some other 'friends'. I ordered Sammy not to let the key leave his pocket. We didn't dare let the little devils out of our sight. We drove them to Hat Rin for the evening, laughing at Kookie's failed attempts to pick up any young Western guys, who all scarpered in fear of our strange gang. A twisted family was born, tied by choice and circumstance. The matriarch Sin paying for us all with her new he-bitch in tow. And our kids, the unpredictable Sammy chasing Far, and the brazen slut Kookie chasing anything with a set.

Sin wanted to go to Ko Tao the next day, though we suspected they were meeting some other guys there. I didn't know what to do. Sammy owed me a lot of money so I wanted to stick with him, and I also wanted to catch up with Charlie and Joe who might still be there. But my old instincts were just telling me to run. I contemplated making a break for Ko Phi Phi. But I'd never been to Ko Tao before, and I must admit I didn't mind the idea of someone taking care of me for a little while. It was nice to let go of the responsibility. So after taxiing everyone around and finally getting my passport back, the five of us boarded a high speed catamaran to Ko Tao, the remote Turtle Island, me and Sammy plotting away at the back of the boat, water churning behind us in frothy white streaks in the midday glare.

★ ★ ★

Ko Tao is much smaller than its more famous neighbours, a green hump bobbing in the Gulf of Thailand. The boat came straight into the main tourist village on Sairee Beach. We found some bungalows at the north end of the beach, all on Sin. They were the nicest beach bungalows I'd stayed in, large deluxe things on stilts, with a high wooden roof and air-con. We hired two more bikes with my passport again and drove the girls around, though there only seemed to be one main road with little dirt tracks going off it. The island was cute though, with little huts and red hot Southern curry restaurants everywhere.

We veered right on a rough track down a steep hill, bouncing off rocks and gravel to an isolated little cove on the south coast. We swam in the still warm waters as the sky turned a deep maroon. The little bay was surrounded by smooth grey boulders, the slopes layered by the green canopy above. Back on the beach, Sammy had befriended everyone in the Jamaica Beach Bar. It was just a little square bar run by foreigners smoking joints rolled on the bar. They were mostly laid-back Dutch hippies, straggly hair and tattoos. Kookie was flirting with some young Dutch guy called Dirk. He was my age, had been in the country the same time and we got on, but he had a wild reckless look in his eyes. He'd caught the Thai bug worse than me – was full of big ideas about setting up bars and discos all over the island.

We went back, the afternoon's sexual tension unleashed in a torrent of wild fucking in the bungalow. Nice hotel rooms can do that to you. I had no emotional feelings towards her, I knew she was a Khao San warrioress, but that just made it all the more physical. By the time we'd finished, the kids had gone. We found them back at Jamaica, a rejubilant Sammy happily smoking everyone's weed, though perhaps in a manner slightly more direct and aggressive than these stoned beach bums were used to. The night continued and the place developed a surreal blur, an outdoor room you can't remember how you entered and aren't sure how to get out of again.

We moved to Sairee Beach where the more mainstream backpackers and divers seemed to be. The main joint was one of these big wooden fluorescent-painted places on the beach. Sure enough, Joe and Charlie were there, both off their heads. I jumped on them. "I said I'd find you, you bastards!" I joked. Joe nearly jumped out of his skin when he saw his stalker Kookie from Bangkok suddenly standing there, declaring her love for him! Charlie was drowning in a bucket trying to conduct a weed deal with six rough-looking locals till I dragged him away. I was social juggling, trying to chat to the shitfaced Charlie and Joe, keeping an eye on Sin who kept disappearing into the crowds of horny young backpackers, and keeping Sammy calm as he did the same with Far.

Early hours and we're milling out into a dark alleyway shitfaced and blurred. People trying to borrow my bike for this and that, girls everywhere, Sammy shouting at me. I'm getting pissed off with this whole farce. Kookie and Far have paired off with two other guys. Sammy's furious and takes off on his bike, throttling up the steep hill loudly. I lose Joe and Charlie again.

Me and Sin snake through Sairee Village towards 7-Eleven. Then appearing out the darkness, like some vision of hell incarnate is Sammy on his bike, blood gushing down his face and all over his white t-shirt. Here we go again. Drunk as hell, a big gash on his chin, his eyes have gone, all reason abandoned, angry and hysterical. He jumps off the bike letting it collapse loudly on the road and grabs my shirt in an aggressive clench, his blood smearing all over me. "You are my only friend and you have betrayed me!" he boomed in my face, hard in voice but weak in spirit. He was broken. His tears, heartbreak, pain and despair hit me in my stomach. I'd brought him here with tales of paradise. And now here he was, bleeding in my arms and lost in the world. He'd come off his bike braking down a steep slope. Was it all my fault? I didn't know, but I felt guilty all the same. "I'm dying slowly," he said melodramatically. "You're not dying Sammy," I replied. He let go of me dejected. "Why must my parents suffer for these girls?" he deplored. It was a horrible scene. He was tying all the loose ends of his current predicament into some kind of tangled emotional web and using it to rub salt into his fresh wounds.

We managed to get Sammy and the bikes back to the bungalows by dawn. Then I drove him round the deserted island looking for a doctor in the violet skies of 6am, my head throbbing. We found a tiny clinic and woke everyone up banging on the door. Inside, a nurse stuck a needle right in his wound and sewed six stitches into his bloody chin. Sam screamed in agony, tears running down his cheeks as he clenched my hand tightly. I felt bad for him, but I was starting to think he was over-doing it a bit. There were no ATMs or anything on the island, so I paid again. As the heat welled up, Sam's cuts were all patched up and he eventually calmed down into a depressed silence. He slept in my bungalow as Far and Kookie were in the other one. Sin seemed genuinely concerned and upset having seen the whole thing. I lay between them both, gazing at the fan on the ceiling, unable to sleep much. I felt responsible. The whole chain of events started with me, though Sammy had done a good job with the baton. Why did these things keep happening?

The next day he took the boat to Chumporn on the mainland to return to Bangkok, owing me 11,000 baht from his two crashes. I didn't have the will to follow him any longer. Dirk emerged from the other bungalow with Kookie, looking pleased with herself at last. Dirk took us down to the site of his new bar due to open in two weeks. It was just a wooden shell, all belonging to some locals he'd just met, but he was pumping lots of money into it all the same. He told us the island was a former penal colony, and all the local islanders were their descendants. I was sure he was going to get robbed. He was too hungry for the *farang* dream, the dream to come and make it here in Thailand, a hunger that consumed any caution or wisdom. I'd heard dozens of stories of people investing all their savings here and getting robbed by their new wife or business partner. We drove round the pretty bays and up to the picture perfect Ko Nang Yuan, where a sand bank ran over the sea to other rocky outcrops. Again, all too beautiful to comprehend, especially in contrast to the darkness all around.

Joe and Charlie had finished doing their PADI course to get certified for scuba diving. It was something I'd vaguely thought about doing, this being one of the cheapest and best places to do it in the world, but I'd never stopped drinking long enough to consider it a realistic option. Apart from the diving community here, there were a lot of long-termers, mainly attracted by the laid-back beach life and permissive drug atmosphere. People seemed to be doing them openly here. Apparently Ko Samui was once like this, before over-development moved the scene onto Ko Phangan. Over-commercialisation there had now moved the scene onto Ko Tao.

That night we all went up to a big jungle party in the hills in the centre of the island, lots of wooden huts and platforms built into the enchanted forest. We partied till the early hours in the strobe-lit garden wonderland.

I woke up in the morning Sun in the top of a tree house with Sin where the party had once been. It was a beautiful heavenly morning, the light rising up through the tree tops, overlooking the expanse of shimmering ocean down below us. I felt blessed to open my eyes in such a place. I spent the whole day with Sin, going to a couple of secluded beaches on the east coast. The Swiss guy from Bangkok was on the island. They said hi to each other but she never left my side.

We'd now been together nearly 24 hours a day for a week and had grown closer through recent events, although I still didn't have any strong feelings for her. As with Nok, Jeab and all the rest, they profess their innocence, but the weight of evidence against them makes it difficult to swallow – the holes in their stories, the mysterious phone calls and missed calls, the unanswered questions, the plotting and suspicious behaviour, the skeletons in the closet, the bullshit and lies. I could see the stretch marks hidden under the horrible tattoo on her stomach, and could sense some pain from her past. But I didn't ask many questions this time. I didn't wanna know. I didn't care anymore. I just wanted to break free again after all the trials and tribulations. In the end you have to trust your instincts. Except this time I never really gave a fuck. It had been a game – me and Sammy getting one over the butterflies for a change. We'd grown closer than expected but still, I couldn't wait to get away from her. Then she started asking for 5000 baht to go to Krabi. Maybe I was getting the cheque bill at the end of my 'free' trip. I gave her 2000 and called it quits in my mind. It wasn't over though. I had to track Sam down, get my money, and hopefully find Charlie and Joe again who'd left for Bangkok too, though it seemed they were trying their best to get away from me.

The next morning we ate some insanely hot jungle curry for breakfast. I was sweating like crazy, my whole face numb, head pumping from the chemicals in the chillies. We didn't speak much. She asked me to stay with her just the once. I didn't reply and she didn't push it. I wanted out. She waved goodbye and I boarded the six hour slow boat to Chumporn.

There were only a handful of tourists on the old wooden chug boat. When my heart stopped pumping from the curry, I passed out on the deck for a couple of hours before waking up a free man on the open seas, no land in sight. I wasn't sure what had happened on those crazy islands, and I wasn't sure I'd ever get any help with my rising credit card bill, but I was pleased to be away from everyone for a few hours, free to breathe the fresh sea air in uninterrupted silence.

As the afternoon eventually drew to a close, we entered a long estuary lined with hundreds of brightly coloured fishing boats, local men washing themselves and their boats down with buckets and hoses. It must be nice to be a fisherman out at sea I thought. A simple life, out in nature. But I still caught a public bus to Bangkok.

Halfway back we stopped at a late-night service area and some Norwegian girl stuck a joint in my mouth, sending me off on a journey of philosophical introspection as the bus continued north past psychedelic multi-coloured strip lights on the side of the mysterious road. I decided I needed to chill out a bit. I was taking everything too seriously again, getting too involved with everyone I met, too emotional. I needed to step back and enjoy the moment. Through Hua Hin and Petchaburi, dark industrial fields and into the metropolis, that great force of gravity I could never resist. I dreamed about island-hopping south through Thailand, Malaysia, Indonesia, onwards and onwards all the way to the Pacific Ocean and the end of the world. I wanted escape. I wanted to hit the road.

★ ★ ★

Bangkok at midnight, chasing bad debt and drifting friends, my dreams evaporating in the tropical heat. Papaya Guesthouse, *pad Thai*, emails. One from Sammy. " . . . see you in some part of the world." Surely not? He mentioned his guesthouse though. Another email from the guys said they were leaving for Cambodia soon. Damn it.

Up early the next day. Shit to do. Back on the beat, looking for Sammy. I checked the book but he'd never checked into the guesthouse he was supposed to be in. I went round about 15 back-alley guesthouses off Khao San and down Samsen Road where the African guys stayed, asking receptionists and guests if they'd seen him. Couldn't see his name anywhere. The African guys all denied knowing him. Working up a full body sweat, tramping the streets, anger pulsating through my body with every footstep.

I eventually found him in East Gate in the evening. His face had cleared up a bit. He was sounding rational again, but not pleased to see me. Said he'd have it on Monday, five days from now. He was talking about relocating to Hong Kong to see the girls. I suddenly contemplated the idea myself, dazzled by the bright lights of new possibilities. We didn't chat much more than that.

Four hours sleep till the orange alarm bells shook me awake violently. I got an email out of the blue from Nok. She and Bow were in Bangkok for one night only. I went straight to their hotel near the train station to see them. She looked beautiful, dormant feelings stirring. They had some silly story about going south for two months. Suddenly they sounded like Sin or Jeab to me now. I didn't bother asking any questions. I was getting hardened to all these dubious stories and half-truths. They wanted to go to Khao San. Sin was back tonight too. I knew what was coming.

Sure enough, we arrived, turned the corner, and there was Sammy with Sin and Kookie. There's no hiding on Khao San. Sin didn't look too impressed. I kept it brief and we carried on, feeling far more comfortable with Nok. We finally found Charlie and Joe in a street gallery for a brief catch-up.

I ended up back in Nok and Bow's hotel room, cuddled up with Nok like we'd never been apart. Her soft lips touched mine in the dark, as we slept in each other's arms. A part of me may have wanted her, but I couldn't go back. Never back. I was sure she was some other arsehole's girl now, and in the morning they were gone.

Joe and Charlie left that morning, overland to the Cambodian border and onwards to Siem Riep to see the legendary ruins of Angkor Wat, the centre of the mighty Angkor Empire. But I wasn't going with them.

Sammy took me to Sin's joint, Cheeky Bar, for the first time. It was just a hole in an alleyway with some bar stools in front, basically just a pick up joint for Sin and friends and any solo male backpackers who fancied a bit. I told her the girl from last night was my ex-girlfriend. She wasn't smiling and we didn't speak much, but the free beers kept coming. "Last night Sin was fucking crazy man," Sammy whispered. "She was hysterical, crying and screaming all night. She went to wait for you outside Papaya till morning, but you never came back. She loves you man!" It seemed she liked me more than I thought. As for me, who knew? I was riding the Changs all the way into battle. By closing, I was barely conscious, memories dissolving into the gutter.

A dark room. A woman's whisper in my ear. "Do you still love her?" "Maybe . . . I don't know." Silence . . . "It's okay." Hands rubbed my neck and back. I didn't know what I wanted. I closed my eyes and let go.

I opened them some time later. A pitch black room, duvet, air-con, Sin lying asleep next to me. There was a strange, timeless atmosphere. I felt relaxed, away from the clamour of the streets and guesthouses. Too easy to sleep here.

I woke up hard in her hands, as she seduced me invisibly, pushing all the right buttons. Any reservations and memories of Nok I may have had soon faded as she climbed on top and ground the life out of me. I stayed for hours, body too tired to move, but still wary of her unnerving presence. Eventually I escaped her apartment, down the stairs, out the door, finding myself right at the top of Khao San Road, mid-afternoon.

Found Sammy with more dubious delays, waiting for his father to return home. Another night at East Gate, even It buying me a drink after hearing my woes. Tangmo was there, blanking me.

I needed to save my dwindling funds for Vietnam, so I checked into Mama Sin's commune along with Sammy, Kookie, Far and another girl Mon on the floor. All afternoon with Sam and four squawking birds, riddling my patience in this windowless pit. Sin had taken pity on me and Sam. She told me some guy owed her a large amount of money too.

The girls went to open their bar, so we went back to the office, me chatting with It just to avoid seeing Sammy's miserable face for five minutes. It was hustling drinks with his fear-inducing charm, telling everyone about his rough upbringing. "But I only friend with people who bring me money, you know?" he then tells me. Not sure what to think. Then he starts hassling Sammy about some money he owes a *farang* friend of his. I hadn't heard about it before. I didn't know who to believe. The psychotic, drug-addled hustler It, or the lying, thieving Samuel? Fuck this! I went to Cheeky Bar. I just wanted to get some sleep and escape these fucking horrible streets. The bar was closed, the steel shutters locked down. Marched to her room, banging on the door. Lights out, door locked. In a phone box sweating intensely, fumbling with coins and my crumpled up list of numbers. Got to get the coins in and dial within ten seconds flat or the machine spits them all out again. No answer. Again. No answer. Fuck it!

I staggered around looking for salvation. Eventually saw Sin and the girls down Khao San with a group of Western guys. I tried to follow, but lost them in the crowds. I went alone to the drum and bass club and late night roof top bar, but I was far from fucking happy. Checked her room and called her again but nothing. I wasn't exactly surprised, but I at least thought she would've waited until I'd left town.

Back to the gutter. Sam's there looking even angrier than me. I keep my distance from everyone. It's off his head, charging round intimidating anyone that looks at him funny. Suddenly he turns on Sammy, pushing him into some steel shutters, metal clanging loudly, and pinning him there, asking for his friend's money, his glaring maniac face millimetres from Sammy's. Sam doesn't react, just trying to calm

It down. I step in to mediate. It pushes Sam away and turns towards me, fists clenched, shouting, "You want same same?" like some mad pit bull. I definitely didn't. I looked around at the crowd watching us. The whole *soi* was petrified of him. Things calmed down and I fucked off alone. Just wanna sleep but nowhere to go. A friendly Thai guy I knew from Daeng and Alice's old bar gave me a free Chang as I sat alone despondently, feeling sorry and pathetic. I had become an object of pity, another Soi Rambutri waster.

At 4:30am Sin answered my call. She said she was on Khao San, but the background was silent. Couldn't believe a word of anything. She said Mon was in her room. I charged up and Mon let me in, exchanging bitter pleasantries; but I couldn't sleep, my anger greater than my exhaustion. Eventually Sin, Sam and Kookie all came back together. None of us said a word to each other. Sam cut a pathetic figure, but no more than me, lying there waiting for him. I lay next to Sin but no words, looks or touches were exchanged. Slept a little before being woken by Kookie and Mon squawking on about boys. Bitter memories of Ao Nang and Chiang Mai. I got my bag and left without a word. I found a new guesthouse behind the Thai boxing gym at dawn as the SangSom unleashed its claws.

Whatever time I slept, I always woke up at 9am as the heat baked my bones awake. All I wanted was to get out the fucking city, hit the road, and be with my real friends. But I was stuck here chasing debt, surrounded by people I no longer trusted or liked. I didn't want to see anyone, but staying in those box rooms alone and hung over in the heat was an even worse proposition.

So I was stuck on the streets, a stray dog in the urban swamp of Banglampoo. Saw It in the laundrette trying to set his eye on fire. He seemed to have no recollection of last night, not that I brought it up. The streets were closing in on me – It teetering on the precipice, huge young African dealers staring me down in the street. I felt like something horrible was going to happen if I stayed any longer. Portensions of doom. The days were as endless as they were pointless, killing the hours looking for Sam, eating *pad Thai* and drinking 5 baht bottles of water to save money. All I can think about is Sam and the money and getting out of here.

Monday came. I found him in his office. He phoned his sister who was apparently out looking for their father. When I was with him I wanted to believe him, but once we separated I started stewing over things again, the evidence against him too much to ignore. Sam put the phone down. "The money is definitely coming next Monday." Rage spread like radiation from my guts. "Where's all your fucking money for drink coming from you lying cunt?" He said he'd pay me whatever he could with what he had today.

A week wasted in Bangkok while my friends explored Cambodia. An email said they were leaving Phnom Penh for Ho Chi Minh City any day now. I'd missed the whole trip through Cambodia. I had to make a decision today. My mind reeled. I couldn't stand this any longer. I'd heard about a night bus from Bangkok which went to a coastal border crossing with Cambodia. Or I could head for the main border crossing inland, and take the notoriously slow road to Siem Riep and see the famous ruins of Angkor Wat. I could even fly to Ho Chi Minh and meet them there, though it would burn my credit card. I needed the money back from Sam, but if I waited any longer I'd never catch up with the guys as they journeyed north through Vietnam. The dream would be dead. Everything was up to me.

Fuck it. I wanted out. I checked out and dumped my bag at Sin's again intending to leave town soon. Then to find Sam at his guesthouse but he's not there and the others outside deny having heard of the guy. I didn't believe a word of it. People told me a lot of guys were over here dealing drugs and whatever else. Sam was doing the same though he didn't talk about it with me. Convinced he's done a runner. Scanning the streets I find him again and he promises half tomorrow. One more fucking day. Ten hours of Chang later and I was back at Sin's.

Angry hate-sex in the morning. She said she would be lonely when I left. I told her she could find another boy tomorrow. That was the end of the conversation. Fuck it, it was true. What else could I do? The last three weeks – what else could I have done? Sam comes over. "2500 baht later today," he says. Always fucking later. Fuck it, I've got to get out of here. If I'm going to go, just go.

I went all the way to Ekamai bus station and back to buy my ticket for the 11:30pm public bus southeast to Trat, near the border with Cambodia. Back to Cheeky Bar, eating with the girls. Sam had left a scribbled note on some tissue paper telling me to go to his office. He was there. He gave me 2500 baht of the 11,000 he owed me. I didn't care anymore, I just wanted out. We went back to Cheeky and he, Sin, Kookie and the girls came out to Ratchadamnoen Road to wave me off. I hugged them goodbye, got in the taxi and drove off. I watched them fade away into another Bangkok night as I cooled down in the cab. I tried to see the best in people, and despite my scepticism and paranoia, I genuinely believed Sammy would pay me back one day and that Sin cared for me.

But suddenly I didn't care. Suddenly I felt happier than I had done in weeks. Happy to be rid of the pair of them. Happy to have escaped intact. Happy to be out of there at last. It was over. I was free. As the taxi drove me east I smiled the happiest smile I'd smiled in a long time. I was back on the road.

★ ★ ★

All organisms seem to be driven by the same two related goals: survival and reproduction. The reason to live seems to be life itself – an inner desire in all organisms to survive, and then reproduce and create offspring, who in turn desire survival, reproduction and their own offspring. Thus there is a dissemination of successful organisms' genes, characteristics and species. But are these two goals of survival and reproduction distinct from one another, or actually part of the same process? At what level does this instinct for survival work on? Or does it work on more than one level? Is it our genes themselves that, carrying various information about species' physiology, are attempting to perpetuate themselves through host bodies? Or is the individual organism trying to survive as best it can and reproduce offspring in its own image? Or is it groups – at a family, colony, species or higher level – that seek to survive as best they can? Or is life on Earth better understood as a holistic global ecosystem, constantly evolving in order to survive its changing conditions? Some even say that all life has an eternal soul connected by our shared genetic heritage, an idea which physicalises the spiritual idea of a collective consciousness.

Although many species would exist for millions of years, life on Earth has always been fragile, and of the billions of species that have ever existed, 99.99% are now extinct, some disappearing gradually, others more suddenly. There have been many periods of mass extinction in Earth's history, which are usually followed by periods of swift evolution in the surviving species. These extinctions can be due to climate change, changing sea levels, diseases, meteorites, volcanoes and various other cataclysmic events, killing species or their food sources.

The last major mass extinction occurred 65 million years ago, wiping out 90% of land species, drawing to an end the age of the mighty dinosaurs. This was probably due to a giant meteorite hitting the Earth and dramatically disturbing the climate.

Once the dinosaurs had gone, the mammals prospered, growing much larger, more varied and intelligent. Some now-extinct species grew much larger than their modern day relatives, such as the mighty paraceratherium, giant sloths, sabre-toothed tigers and mammoths. Huge ranges of species came and went leading to the many varieties of mammals that exist today, such as pigs, elephants, cats, bears, wolves, cows, horses, mice, kangaroos and monkeys. Some mammals adapted to live in the sea, evolving into seals, dolphins and whales, and some to fly, like the bat.

One group of mammals was the primates. Some still living today include species of monkey, macaque, lemur, orang-utan, gorilla and chimpanzee, though many more species came and went before them.

Around 5 million years ago, a new strand of primate evolved, the *Hominina*, branching off from human's last common ancestor with the modern chimpanzee. Many species grew, evolved and died out from this split until around 2 to 2.5 million years ago when a genus, or group of species, named *Homo* developed, bringing in the Stone Age era.

Whereas their ancestors had lived mainly in the trees, gradually these various species came down and based themselves on the ground, probably due to climactic change drying up the jungle. Gradually the different species spent less time moving on four legs, and more time standing up straight and moving on two legs. And so their arms grew shorter, lessening their upper body strength. They developed locking knees and their spines entered the skull at a different position, gradually enabling them to walk truly upright. Their jaws grew smaller, they grew less hair, they developed opposable thumbs and a better grip with their hands, and their larynx lowered making more complex noises and speech possible.

Their skulls and brains grew much larger and they gradually used stones, wood and animal bones as tools. They made hammers, hand-axes, cutters, scrapers and picks, and used them for killing prey, cutting meat, wood and other objects, building shelters and clearing forests. They became better at hunting in groups with increased tool use, thus eating more meat, gaining more protein and energy and fuelling their brain growth. Tool making and usage seems to have accelerated their brain development through an improved appreciation of cause and effect, and by creating representational images in their minds of how completed tools would look. The use of tools became more widespread and complex, and so the tools became more highly valued as they became more sophisticated and useful. They gradually learned how to create and control fire, to create warmth and light, cook meat, create more tools, hunt, burn and kill.

It seems various related species of *Homo*, or human, were developing simultaneously across Africa, Europe and Asia, notably *Homo erectus*, and later *Homo neanderthalensis*. But by around 200,000

217

years ago, a new species had developed, *Homo sapiens*, Latin for 'wise human'. This is who we are all directly descended from, our species, modern humankind. They first developed in Africa, and spread out, migrating *en masse* towards Europe and Asia about 70,000 years ago, coexisting with populations of other *Homo* species. Others say *Homo sapiens* evolved simultaneously across Africa and Eurasia from existing *Homo* populations. Perhaps there is some truth in both theories. Migration and interbreeding may have been widespread. Whatever happened, *Homo sapiens* would eventually outlive their cousins to become the only surviving *Homo* species.

In fact, the DNA of all humans today is so alike, that it seems we are all descended from the same small group of common ancestors. 70,000 years ago there was a gigantic super-volcanic eruption in Toba, Sumatra, which disrupted the Earth's climate so much it may have nearly wiped out the *Homo sapiens* population altogether. We may all be descended from a population bottleneck of just a few thousand survivors. As they spread in number globally there were gradual, minor changes in physiology such as body size and skin colour, in order to adapt to varying regional and local environments. But despite the physical and psychological differences between people, our species *Homo sapiens* is remarkably uniform in its genetic makeup. In fact, on average, 99.5% of the genetic makeup of any two people on Earth is identical. It is the 0.5% that gives us our uniqueness.

SIX

A busy night market at 4am, heaving with traders in shorts and woolly hats in amongst mud-stained, wooden stalls of meat and fish, fruit and vegetables, herbs and grains. The temperature was in the early 20s, chilly for Thailand; the air thick with the locals' animated bargaining. I'd reached the provincial town of Trat. I edged through the market crowds in a sleepy blur unsure of where I was in this strange but busy hour.

I found a minibus which took me an hour down the coastline. Empty silvery beaches to the right, and a steep, gloomy mountain ridge to the left delineating the Cambodian border. The dark eerie road ran along the cutting edge of the two old enemies and neighbours. The gap between the ridge and the coast petered out till it was just 1km across, like the road to the end of the world.

I reached the border as the Sun broke across the horizon ahead of me. I stamped out and walked the long no-man's land in the pastel dawn with my bag on my back, the sea appearing through the trees down to the right.

Every day started and ended with the heat. It was everywhere I went, all around me, inside of me, bearing down on me like a dead weight. But as I looked across at Cambodia, I saw there was no escape ahead. No 7-Elevens on the corner, no Toyota taxis or plastic franchise restaurants. Just the heat and humidity. Every minute of every hour of every day. Wringing you dry, slowing you down, draining your energy, dulling your senses, sucking the life out of you, altering your very reality.

Whereas Thai people in the street tended to ignore you, suddenly I was the centre of attention. Hoards of guys in cheap flannel trousers, shirts, flip-flops and baseball caps surrounding me, offering me visa services and taxis, kids and beggars with missing limbs flailing towards me for assistance. I weaved through and found a cramped old minibus headed for Phnom Penh.

It took the whole damn morning and afternoon. Weaving along muddy roads through the impoverished land, tired and sweaty, the engine breaking down three times. Four times we had to disembark at muddy river banks while the bus drove onto a rickety floating wooden barge and we chugged over to the other side. There were no bridges and little infrastructure; the country was clearly very poor. We passed ramshackle villages, over gentle hills and flat plains of endless fields, punctuated by tall palm trees and temples in the distance. It was beautiful. Despite being so near Thailand it looked very different. Perhaps it was just the lack of development that was so noticeable, or perhaps that this very lack of development brought the panoramic views of the natural landscape so prominently into view. I felt that raw, heart-pumping thrill of entering a new country for the first time, the more mystical the better.

We approached the capital by dusk. The long straight roads and concrete government structures on the outskirts reminded me of other former centrally-controlled countries I'd been to. The main roads were humming with old mopeds, while the city centre's buildings contained remnants of the city's French colonial past, with peeling, faded, pastel walls and rotten, wooden shutters. The smaller streets were unpaved, bikes weaving round potholes and patches of sand and gravel as best they could, the streets lined with little stalls selling bottles of gasoline, snacks, noodles and whatever else they could sell.

I got dropped off at a backstreet guesthouse. No idea where. I checked my mail. Just one from the boys saying they were due in Saigon tomorrow. Quick think and I decided to leave tomorrow too. I didn't want to leave Cambodia having just arrived. I liked the feel of the place. It danced to a different beat from Thailand. It was a whole different time and era here. I wanted to kick back and explore, but it wasn't to be. Not now. I had to see my old friends again before I lost them for good. I booked a tourist bus ticket to Ho Chi Minh City. I had a beer with the friendly Khmer man running the guesthouse and crashed out for a few hours, the culture shock and lethargy preventing me from really knowing where I was.

I climbed aboard the battered old tourist bus. Vertical seats, no leg room and a wobbly door that swung open from time to time throwing in wafts of hot gritty air. Some little plastic roof vents puffed in some more warm air, the ever-present heat pressing down on me like a disease of the damned. It was crammed with backpackers, young kids from the West all searching for something different. Escape from home and the promise of the new, chasing pre-conceived images of Asia – throngs of bicycles, wooden-shack markets, little farmers in pointy hats, yellow tracks in the jungle and giant scythes cutting through burning fields.

The bus bumped tortuously over the ruinous road towards the border; the fields now flooded as far as the eye could see as the rainy season reached its climax. Trees and wooden huts poked through the endless grey waters like a vision of doomsday. Bouncing around for hours on end, nothing but my ever-meandering thoughts for company. Still searching every town, mountain-top, beach and sunset for an epiphany that wouldn't come . . .

We stopped at a crowded ferry terminal at a wide river crossing. The bus was quickly surrounded by the window-scraping hoards of the hungry – food and drink vendors and old beggars, some with babies, desperately trying to catch the eye of those inside to communicate their starving need. The young backpackers inside sat there silently, shifting uncomfortably in their seats, trying to ignore the small stampede as best they could, as a few of the crowd tried to force open the sliding windows, grubby hands poking through the gaps. All except for this big, pumped up, young Australian guy with his shirt off, a mop of curly brown hair and a toothy grin, arguing with a Cambodian guy through the window over the change for the can of Coke he'd just bought. The seller was trying to short-change him a tiny sum, but the Aussie wasn't having it. It was the kind of exchange I saw a lot, one where you're not sure where your sympathies lie. We eventually crossed the river and continued trundling along the dusty, pot-holed roads of Cambodia.

Later on we stopped by the side of the road in a little village. While the others queued up for the stinking brick toilet, sucking on their Marlboro Lights in silent disgust, the Australian guy marched up the road headed for a little market shack in search of food. I didn't see guys like him very often, far less than I'd expected. I met far more people eating out of tourist restaurants than going to the local market. Far more flying between towns than getting local buses, let alone hitch-hiking. The guy obviously enjoyed the sniff of his surroundings, had a thirst for the new. I followed him up the road and got chatting over a potato and ginger baguette we rustled up from the empty stall. His name was Vince, 22 like me, and like me travelling on a one-way ticket to a destination unknown. He was an easy-going and friendly guy, and we both shared a desire to do things differently somehow, get away from the majority following each other around in herds with as little contact with their surroundings as possible. That was how we met, on the side of the road there.

After two days of travelling overland from Bangkok, I finally reached the Vietnamese border. I left Cambodia regretfully, vowing to return and explore it properly one day.

★ ★ ★

Before me lay a huge red archway with five Khmer towers crowned above it with some faded yellow twirls of Cambodian script. Through the arch lay 200 metres of no-man's land and then another white arch, glimmering in the distance like a mirage, a yellow star and one word in giant red letters – Vietnam.

Vietnam! A country I'd never imagined going to till this day. A country known only to my young mind through the iconography of American pop culture – *Adagio For Strings,* choppers, gunshot, blood and tears. The beauty and the horror. It was October, the end of the rainy season. What was I doing here?

We crossed the border and changed bus. Instantly the pace was more frenetic. Endless streams of old mopeds buzzing around our bus like bats, brick-houses by the road, lines and squiggles all over the letters of its Romanised language. More built up than Cambodia, though no Western brand names visible anywhere, just long terraces of shop houses by the side of the road, and occasional billboards for Asian companies. We barely saw any open countryside the whole way, just endless people, bikes and buildings.

We soon came to Ho Chi Minh City, formally known as Saigon. The city had a raw buzz, a feeling of unfinished business, case unclosed. The scarred beauty of tree-lined boulevards and tin-shack alleys, her arteries clogged with the burgeoning weight of humanity pumping through her soul. People everywhere, the streets electric! The energy grabbed me and squeezed my imagination like a vice. Thousands and thousands of 50cc rusty bikes and rickety old bicycles swarmed the streets, moving as one, each an individual atom in the large amorphous mass. When the lights went green they came at us like a swarm of bees.

Me and Vince found a cheap room in the heaving Pham Ngu Lao area of town where all the action seemed to be. That evening we went out for a few beers, taking in the buzz of the city, charged by the current of people out making money. It seemed like everyone was out to get you. Constant harassment from people following us down the road trying to sell us stuff we didn't want; street-smart kids trying to charm and hustle money out of tourists, beggars and amputees lying in the gutter, and grinning motorcycle taxi drivers on street corners offering "Boom-boom? Marijuana?" under their breath. Little women scuttling round in big pointy conical hats. Others selling their wares off motorbike side-cars, or carrying around two baskets of produce balanced on their shoulders with a heaving length of wood. Baguette ladies, noodle soup and sugar cane juice presses. Kids playing in the alleyways, the anxious mother, men unloading blocks of ice with metal hooks, pale white prostitutes driven round on mopeds, men cycling round with loud rattles, families eating by the road, the angry old grandmother, bandits in face masks, old hunchbacks, faces well worn from a thousand woes, the blind, the deaf, the mentally dispossessed, the missing limbs, the loss of kin, the chemical scars, twisted feet, human meat, lesser lives for the greater mass. A whole population living, working, eating and sleeping out on the streets.

And through the concrete madness of honking horns and beep-beep-beeps, the shuttlecock, the raggedy dog, the yellow-scarved soldiers in green, the docking ships of night and the smog of modernity; silently cruised the noble old cyclo drivers in shorts and rag shirts, bobbing on forever over their chariots – these three-wheeled rickshaws with a large passenger seat at the front, like a bicycle attached to a wheelchair – visions of serenity and melancholy calm. They were powered only by the old drivers, many of them homeless war veterans, out of sight, out of mind, destined to pedal ever onwards until the day their knees finally buckled and they died penniless in the gutter.

I knew I'd find them. I've got a nose for these things. Round a corner and we suddenly came across Charlie and Joe wandering the streets with their backpacks. I sneaked up and gave them the shock of their lives. Turned out I'd actually arrived a few hours before them since they'd come by river ferry. I introduced them to my new friend Vincent Garrett and put them up in our room which had three beds and space on the floor for another mattress. Not a bad room by my usual standards, with an en-suite bathroom and a balcony overlooking the busy lane below.

We went out and ate, avoiding the fried snake and steamed bull's penis, and had a few bottles of weak Vietnamese beer outside taking in the buzz at a busy intersection. Everything was incredibly cheap. I was overjoyed to find Joe and Charlie again. We barely mentioned Sammy and the misunderstandings on the islands. I knew Charlie only had a short time in Asia before going to Australia, so he had to fit everything in. It was all irrelevant now. We were in Vietnam together here and now; that was all that mattered.

The next day Vince went out exploring while us wasters were still asleep. We eventually got up and strolled to The Revolution Museum, inhaling the heavily-fumed scents of the city. Inside the gates a few buildings and old Vietnamese fighter planes, tanks and US bombs. Amputated survivors showed visitors round, beggars and kids following everywhere. The museum gave the Vietnamese Government's side of the story, the one I hadn't seen before, the story of what they call the American War. Photos and video footage of war atrocities, napalm and Agent Orange attacks, grinning American GIs displaying decapitated heads, and whole deformed babies pickled in large jars. Everyone was silent in shock. It was hard for me to understand, but the horrors of war seemed to stir up a normally suppressed part of our nature. Anger, hatred, survival, warfare. In war, was anybody, in any land, at any time, also capable of such atrocities?

What on Earth had happened here? What unknowable horror had torn this land apart so violently? I only knew the basics. After years of French colonial rule, Vietnam fell under Japanese occupation during World War Two. The Viet Minh, a communist and national liberation movement, emerged in Hanoi led by Ho Chi Minh, initially with US and Chinese backing. After the Japanese left, the Viet Minh captured Hanoi and set up a provisional government, whilst the French also returned to re-establish control. Thus the First Indochina War, the French War, began in 1946. This ran till 1954 when the French left and the Geneva Conference declared a provisional division between the Viet Minh run North and the French-loyalist South. The civil war between North and South continued with funding and military assistance from China and Russia to the North, and America to the South. It became the major battle ground in the Cold War. America feared a domino effect if the country fell to the Communists, spreading communism further round the region. By 1965 the Communists were gaining ground so the US sent in combat troops which would eventually peak at 500,000 in 1968. But not only were they fighting the North Vietnamese Army, but also various affiliated groups based in the South known as the Viet Cong. The war escalated and spread to Laos and Cambodia. With no victory in sight and increasing losses and opposition, US involvement was scaled back till they withdrew under a peace agreement in 1973. But the war continued, ending in the Fall of Saigon and the communist North's victory in 1975. The following year the country was reunited.

Once outside I felt reassured that life was still very much going on here, despite all the horrors of yesteryear. Travelling in Vietnam wasn't going to be a continuation of the unbridled hedonism of Thailand. We sank Tiger Beers in cafes all afternoon to perk us up again. As night fell, we found Vince and patrolled the Pham Ngu Lao area looking for some nightlife. It didn't seem up to much though – one bar was rammed full of young backpackers drinking to Western music, the rest mostly quiet. We wandered over to the more upmarket Dong Khoi area with its expensive French hotels, boutique shops and ordered streets and found some bad discos with middle-aged Western men picking up young prostitutes.

We were getting worn down and drunk, tired from traipsing round in the heat all day. Giving up, we hailed down a legion of four cyclos, sat down at last and suddenly cheered up. We glided through the city, just above the tarmac, passing cans of beer and cigarettes between us like some floating street bar. Back in the backpacker area we were hit by a sudden wave of intoxication, steamy streets with wise-cracking local guys, encrazed looking expats and street-corner sin merchants, trying to get home, gangs of little street kids following us everywhere, unnerving us with their near-fluent English. They say they're 13 but look younger and malnourished. One forces me into playing paper-scissors-stone for money. I lose every time, money gone, memories end.

Wake up in a mental cesspit to a four-way morning chorus of unconscious flatulence. Streaks of light and city noise are streaming through the curtains. Stagger to the bathroom to unload the last beers.

One of my eyebrows was missing. I shouldn't have slept first. Marijuana breakfast in our room taking in the roar of the street below. The heat, history, beauty and tragedy of the place were starting to stir our imaginations. Strange new fantastical alter-egos were developing. Joe began growing a handle-bar moustache to go with his aviators. Charlie was on some kind of self-assigned photographic mission with his combat shorts, hat and rucksack full of cameras and lenses. Though I looked like an alien, I decided to keep my remaining eyebrow instead of removing it too, and donned a green army vest.

We eventually stepped out into the city, all red-eyed and hazy, and began to walk. We needed constant 360 degree awareness just to keep from getting mown down on the streets where shop-fronts spread out over the road at different levels, dodging gutters and drains, the endless hassle from beggars and vendors following you round, trying to charge you ten times the real price and never taking no for an answer; as ever dodging the endless waves of motorbikes, coming in waves 20 bikes thick. Watching the locals, we worked out that the only way to cross the street was to dive in and simply keep walking slowly in a straight line and let the little mopeds swerve around you.

We came to the Presidential Palace, where in 1975 North Vietnamese tanks famously stormed the front gates, a few soldiers entering the building and waving their flag from the balcony, ending the long civil war between North and South in Communist victory. The interior had lain virtually untouched since then, an unchanging snapshot of high-end '60s chic. It was like walking into an old James Bond movie – oval-tabled conference rooms with microphones and flashing red buttons, pompous assembly halls now adorned with the red national flag with its yellow communist star, huge busts of Ho Chi Minh, dusty war rooms and a groovy orange and brown bar, complete with a helipad on the roof. We were rather taken by the interior design. We entered a fantasy world of movies past, characters in a film never made, released from reality, whizzing off photos of each other grinning madly on the roof.

We carried on through the manic avenues and came to a long wide road with bikes sifting round each other, fruit and spice stalls spread all over the road, paraplegics crawling through the dirt, no Westerners in sight, heads as far as the eye could see, a canopy of pointy hats. Thousands of people all on the go, movement, noise and heat overwhelming our enreefed little minds. It looked like a social uprising. A fear suddenly slashed through me like a switchblade. Where are they all going? What's going on? Do they know something we don't? Is there some kind of revolution going on? Jitters of panic in the echoes of history.

We continued onwards to a muddy little canal, traffic just inches from us till there were no pedestrians left, just relentless motorbikes blowing smoke and grime at us as we trudged along the side of a bypass road, often faster than the gridlocked motorcade. The heat, noise, smoke and exhaustion were starting to get too much to handle. We eventually climbed up and stopped on a pedestrian bridge over the muddy canal lined with slum shacks, exhausted by it all.

The faded colours of dusk and the dancing shadows eased the over-excited twinges of paranoia into a smooth appreciation of it all. It hit us then – the sheer beauty of the place. This was it! Vietnam! Asia! We'd found the picture of the East that we'd been looking for, here in Saigon. It had an insane, desperate clamour in the air, more than any other city I'd been to in Asia. No tourists, no Western shops or restaurants, just millions of bicycles, dusty roads, old temples, hand-painted signs, street markets, pointy hats and crushing poverty. This was the image of Asia I had in my head before I'd come here. That vague notion of the old Orient from the movies. Saigon was Asia as I'd imagined it would be.

The heat, the energy, the 24 hour noise, history, violence, excitement, weed, rum and crazy dreams were all conspiring to drift us further from that which we knew. And we loved it. We let ourselves slide away into our imaginations, into a world of unlimited possibilities where fiction and dreams met reality, a world where we could do anything we wanted to. All we had to do was stop thinking about it, stop talking about it and just get out there and do it! The triumph of the will, Man as his own master.

We felt enlivened again. That night the four of us found a little bar with a pool table and a rack of cheap rum. We drank with gusto, liquor flowing through us fast into the gutter, little kids peering over the table moving the balls around playfully, Rolling Stones busting out the speakers. Joe had just fallen in love with a girl back home before he came out, and was missing her badly. Her name vaguely resembled *Angie*. When it came on, me and Charlie changed the words, ripping into him mercilessly. What are friends for? But still we continued, coloured balls rattling round our minds, talk of fake passports and multiple identities, Joe raising toasts, Vince's booming laugh, Charlie cracking gags, *Jumpin' Jack Flash*, tequila, pot, *smash*!

We bowled out into the midnight tropics in twisted spirits and weaved through the crowded streets looking for some action. I stopped for a street vendor's steamed dumpling and quickly lost the others, faffing around by myself in a drunken stupor. I sat down staring at the endless motorbikes, wondering what to do next. Then, out of the traffic appear two cyclos tearing down the road at high speed, Joe driving Charlie in one, and Vince steering the other. What the fuck? Joe and Vince have a look of positive insanity in their faces. Charlie looks terrified. No idea what they're doing but I had no option. I burst out the shadows and jumped into the passenger seat of Vince's cyclo, everyone cracking up at the seams!

We speed off, laughing neon maniacs of the night, trying not to stack the things as we zigzag across lanes, out of control through the traffic. I don't know what's going on, assuming they've nicked them. Seemed impossible to keep them in a straight line at this speed with the weight of the passenger attached to the handlebars. Next thing, we turn onto a larger road, and judging by the amount of cars and motorbikes, suddenly realise we're on a highway. We're dodging traffic, trying to keep the things in a straight line, hoping not to get mown down by the passing trucks, when the owners drive up alongside us on a moped screaming at us to get off the road. Somehow managing not to get hit, we turn off into a quiet side alley, but we ain't done yet. Me and Vince swap places, and I chase the others through the alleyways, amazed onlookers cheering on the crazy foreign bastards, till I see Joe's crashed his cyclo into a parked moped up ahead. Getting closer. I look at the handlebars. "Shit! Where's the brakes?" I scream. There are none. A sharp clattering screech of crashing metal. I smash into the back of the other cyclo, twisted spokes of bike everywhere, sending everything tumbling over. The moped driver's standing in disbelief. The furious cyclo owners appear on their bike. Only then do the boys tell me they had just rented them for a short while. We left the situation with the vehicle owners and scattered into the bowels of the city like rats.

★ ★ ★

That night Vince had a dream. He was the outdoors type you see – sporting and athletic, but an adventurer too, up for a challenge, self-confident and highly motivated. And we all liked Vince – straight up bloke, no bullshit, up for a laugh. And Vince liked us, these three lads plucked out of wilderness edge . . . different somehow. But whatever happened that next day, there is no doubt that the seed was planted by Vince himself. We merely . . . cultivated it a little, that's all.

We awoke still laughing from the night before, when Vince suddenly announced that he was going to buy his own cyclo and travel out of Saigon on it. The man was a genius! His plan was the stuff of legend – buy one of the rickety old contraptions, put his backpack in the passenger seat and cycle to Mui Ne Beach 200km to the east, sleeping in the chair at night. Vince didn't want to be shepherded round with all the other tourists you see; he wanted to break free, scratch the surface, do it himself. He wanted to do things his own way, to carve his own trail through the jungle. Although lacking the inclination or physical grit to join him, we were nevertheless inspired by his mission. Brave or stupid, we didn't care, the guy was a hero!

We followed him round in awe that day, planning out what he'd need for his trip over more smokes and beers. The first thing would obviously be a cyclo. He asked a few drivers and soon found one willing to sell his livelihood for the modest sum of 500,000 Vietnamese dong, and arranged for him to meet us at our guesthouse later that night. After a hard day's cycling, he would obviously need to wind down in the evening before settling down to sleep in his mobile death trap. Sorry, chair. So we persuaded Vince to buy a fresh bag of weed from a moto driver for his trip, along with a bottle of cheap Vietnamese rum to wash it down with as he dropped off by the side of the road. And obviously he'd need one of the ubiquitous Vietnamese pointy hats, "for disguise, so the police don't see you," Charlie explained, half-believing himself. The strange thing was that, as ridiculous as all our suggestions were, Vince kept lapping them all up excitedly, eager to please his new fans. His plan was so crazy, yet so inspired, that we all got swept up in the anticipation of it all.

Now, Charlie could see the line fast approaching, but he decided to cross it anyway. "You're gonna need a meat cleaver," he said, "for . . . protection, and . . . chopping up coconuts and shit." Vince thought about it for a moment. "Yeah, yeah, you're right mate!" He lapped up every suggestion with such unrelenting conviction that it seemed almost rude to question their wisdom. We weren't out to trick him; we just kind of got a bit carried away.

So we set off, charging round the streets asking fruit and noodle soup vendors if they had a large knife for sale. Nothing caught the eye, the confused-looking vendors only producing little chopping knifes. Only a fuck-off-big meat cleaver would do. We then asked our long-suffering guesthouse owner, a kind, but nervous, spindly, little man. He tried his best to humour the crazy foreign fucks by offering us a knife from his kitchen. "No, no . . . err . . . you have big?" He went back in his kitchen and returned with the fuck-off-big meat cleaver

I OF THE SUN

we'd been looking for. One of those shiny monsters with a hole in the corner to hang it up. Vince bought it straight away.

Later that night the old cyclo driver returned. We were laughing like mad men by this point. The crazy bastard's really going to do it! His plan was to take off in the middle of the night when the traffic was low and nobody would see the big grinning Aussie driving down the expressway on a cyclo. We checked out the vehicle, the guesthouse owner translated, and soon Vince was the proud new owner of a second-hand Vietnamese cyclo and cyclo license. The little driver then removed his worldly possessions from under the seat, a heartbreakingly small amount, and scurried off. I assumed the money he received was more than enough to buy a new cyclo with. Either that or to retire on. I didn't know. I liked to think he had somewhere to go.

Charlie started taking psychotic photos of us and our anxious guesthouse owner posing with Vince's new equipment. He had a cyclo, a cyclo license, a bottle of rum, a bag of weed, a pointy hat and a fuck-off-big meat cleaver. He was ready. He seemed slightly nervous, but his confidence and our enthusiasm were far stronger. It was 2am by the time he had hidden his secret provisions under the seat, strapped his backpack on top and donned the pointy hat. He was sure he could get out of the city by dawn before getting out onto highway 1 and out into Nam. We waved him off, a huge grin on his face, optimistic as ever, and then he pedalled around the corner and was gone . . .

We went upstairs and skinned up. He'd really done it. Would we ever see him again? We didn't know. His plan was bordering on the insane. We weren't sure if the foreigner-cyclo-highway combination was legal or not, but we were guessing it probably wasn't. Strict communist government here. We'd already found out that you weren't supposed to ride cyclos on certain major roads. And he's going to ride it on the country's main highway in the slow lane, sleeping in the passenger seat at night! If he doesn't get arrested, he'll surely get run down by a truck or mugged in the night. That's all assuming the rusty metal frame holds together without falling apart as he crosses five lanes of traffic! It set us off choking uncontrollably with laughter and the strong smoke and this crazy city and the mad brilliance of it all. And the craziest thing was, he'd just agreed with all our stupid suggestions without question. If we'd told him to take a chainsaw and a pack of wild dogs he would have agreed! It was as if we'd found this nice impressionable young lad, befriended him, filled his head full of crazy ideas, drugged him up, armed him, and sent this brainwashed time bomb out ticking into the streets of Vietnam. In fact, that was exactly what we'd done!

Crying with laughter now, our stomachs aching from it and then *bang!* "Oh my God! What have we done?" The morbid realisation of our actions pulled the rug from under our feet, guilt like a hammer to the face. We'd just sent this poor boy to a certain death. Either that or a lengthy stint inside Ho Chi Minh prison. This poor naive young man who'd accidentally fallen in with us, followed our every word, and then, corrupted and tricked, fallen into a one-way descent into hell!

It was too much to bear. We burst into laughter again, and then another deathly silence, and then more laughter, up and down, up and down, like the Devil's yo-yo. "No, no, he's going to make it, he's a tough lad." And then, "Who you kidding? He's a goner!" He'd have been better off if I'd never bumped into him in the first place. Hang on a minute. I didn't bump into him did I? I . . . *chose* him! *Shit!* Back there on the side of the road in Cambodia. Picked him out from the crowd, a fresh, young specimen on which to work our magic. Poor bastard. Filled him with our madness and sent him out like some piece of performance art, our protégé, our son! Fly my precious fly! It was unbearable.

We didn't talk about Vince much the next day. We went on a minibus tour to the Cao Dai Temple, the centre of a modern hybrid-religion, dressed up like a gigantic pink birthday cake. We then drove on to the Cu Chi tunnels, where Viet Cong soldiers spent years living and fighting the American army just outside Saigon. Though now enlarged for tourists to get through, the entrances were just little post boxes in the ground and the tunnels incredibly claustrophobic in the darkness. We shuffled through in upright foetal positions, trying our best to freak each other out in the pitch blackness. Charlie and Joe then hit the nearby shooting range, firing off rounds on assorted automatic rifles.

Back in Ho Chi Minh, we copped out and took the easy option, deciding to follow the herd and buy tickets for the Happy Tour buses (including free Happy Tour t-shirt,) which drove all the way up the country to the capital Hanoi in the North, stopping off at major tourist sites. It was an open ticket so you could stay at each place as long as you wanted and get the next bus each day. We found it to be a very cheap and convenient option.

Vince wouldn't have liked the Happy Tour, but then he wasn't with us anymore. We might have forgotten about him completely if it wasn't for the fact that he still had a reel of photos of us in his camera, swinging a meat cleaver round in pointy hats inside a Saigon guesthouse with the name clearly written on the wall behind us. When they caught him, they'd go to the guesthouse and get our passport details and track us down for sure. We were worrying for ourselves in this strange and hostile land. Even more worried for poor Vince. Or were we just thinking too much? I could see in my friends' eyes that we were definitely all starting to feel pangs of guilt now, though none of us dared say it out loud. Guilt and paranoia.

★ ★ ★

The next morning we finally left town aboard the Happy Tour minibus, first stop Dalat. Following Vince east down highway 1, we were shocked at how wide and busy it was with traffic. Thousands of motorbikes, buses and huge cargo trucks. Not the kind of place for a leisurely cyclo ride. Nothing was said however.

In time we were rising up through hills and breezy plantations and later into cool temperate pine forests, eventually weaving round steep, wooded corners, 1500 metres high, to the hill station town of Dalat, the "Paris of the East" according to some guidebooks.

It certainly felt like a different world alright. Kind of like any number of cold, damp, grey towns back home in fact. Looking over the rooftops from a hill, it resembled a Soviet-bloc town, with its uniform houses and tower blocks. We all got that soul-sinking feeling from the chill in the air, like we'd come back home but in some strange Vietnamese parallel universe.

Inside the hill top hotel the receptionist asked us for our passports. The receptionist looked at Charlie's old photo with his long hair suspiciously. "You are Charles Barker?" Charlie suddenly flipped out on a paranoid schism, muttering, "What do they want our passports for? They'll give them to the police!" Joe and I didn't know whether to laugh or believe him. We handed them over and hid in our room till the voices subsided. Vince had gone but he was still very much with us, a ghost of decisions past, following us round, a memory we could never forget. A quick walk around the town confirmed there was little here for us, so we drenched ourselves in beer in a tourist bar, not having much to say to the other backpackers there. They all looked a bit straight-laced and serious compared to the Sun-worshipers and thrill-seekers of Thailand.

The next morning we checked our emails. No word from Vince. We put on our warmest clothes and rented out two motorbikes to see all the sights and get it over with. The bikes were old Honda scooters, probably as old as us and just as reliable. It took some getting used to riding on the right-hand side in the kamikaze Vietnamese traffic. I soon realised why all the bikes kept beeping their horns. Because none of them had rear-view mirrors and used the horns to let everyone know when they were overtaking. So I kept beeping my horn and swinging my head around everywhere the whole time to avert danger.

We got a few kilometres out of town, parked the bikes and hopped down a steep path to a small waterfall in the peaceful coniferous forests, dotted with bright colourful flowers. The stream leading to it ran between two large rocks. Me and Joe jumped over the small gap as we explored the scenic area. Charlie looked at the rocky gap hesitantly, never the surest bloke on his feet. Eventually he took a shaky little run up, panicked at the last moment, and fell way short smashing his shin onto the other rock and falling back into the stream. Completely fucked it in fact. We cracked up laughing. Charlie was hurt, staggering out the stream soaking wet and hobbling away into the bushes. He'd smacked his leg pretty hard, but he'd live. We decided to carry on and took turns taking him on the back of our bikes.

Soon we were in the country, feeling good on the open road, cool wind in our faces as we drove through mountain valleys and woods. We reached Chicken Village. We knew we'd made it on account of the giant concrete chicken statue. The local community lived in little wooden huts but had a few shops for any passing tourists, with girls weaving brightly coloured cloths. We moved on deep into the countryside, headed for another waterfall. It was a long drive down a dusty track, not a foreigner in sight, hardly anybody in fact. Charlie spotted a little shop at the park entrance and bought himself a crooked little walking stick. It was far too short to be of any use to him, but he liked it all the same and it made everyone that saw him piss themselves laughing. The waterfall was stunning, 100m wide with dozens of streams of water pluming over the rocks into various levels, pools and rapids.

Satisfied we'd seen enough, we drove back through rain showers and into the night, through burning fields and rising black forests gritting our teeth in concentration to avoid crashing in the massive potholes or plummeting down a ravine. It was cold, wet and pitch black but exciting as hell.

We made it back in one piece and were met by what looked like a young Hells Angel standing in the hotel reception. His name was Roland from New Zealand – big, well-built bearded guy, been working as a doorman in flashy London bars. He was a fun-seeker and not the kind of guy to hold back when talking to strangers, such as when describing smashing drunk customers' heads in or his sordid group sex experiences for example.

Charlie cheered up and decided to make the best of the situation, donning his bright red tracksuit for the first time. He bought it from some charity shop and had been lugging it round the Tropics the whole trip, waiting for the right time to wear it. That time had come. We drove down to the tourist bar and he entered with the tracksuit and walking stick, a young man with aspirations of old age, another alter-ego born. The bar was full of hot-looking women, English and Canadian, and they were all laughing at Charlie. We introduced ourselves. The hottest was a Canadian travelling alone, Chanelle, older than us but pretty and friendly. A few beers and it was story time, the whole room cracking up listening to Charlie's embellished tales of the waterfall jump, crap tracksuits and of course . . . Vince and the cyclo. It was mostly true with generous helpings of exaggeration and the odd Barkerian garnish here and there. The word was out. But we didn't yet know how the story would end. There was still no word from the man himself.

★ ★ ★

We spent another day biking round the wet melancholy of Dalat before hitting the Happy Tour to Mui Ne, apparently one of Vietnam's best beaches. We were in good spirits as we descended the steep mountains by bus, slapping on some vintage '92 hardcore, the Sun appearing again as we escaped down the beautiful winding road with our new friends. Stopping at a picturesque corner, Chanelle's laughing at our stupid t-shirts – my "Happy Tour", Charlie's "Danger! Cambodian Mines" and Joe's riddled with bullet holes from the firing range. A quiet French couple are about to tuck into some frankfurters. "It's all lips and arseholes of course," Roland helpfully reminded them.

Mui Ne Beach was pretty quiet though. The sky was grey over the long palm-fringed beach with dozens of quiet bungalows and guesthouse operations stretched along the coast. The beach was littered with dead palm leaves and debris washed in from the South China Sea. The redeeming features were the steep shoreline and big swell. The three of us and Roland dived straight in, rolling round in the waves, grateful to be washed afresh by the ocean.

We got out and checked our emails. It was Vince! "Subject: Secret mission Cyclo!! Done! Yeah!!!!!" He'd made it! A wave of relief hit us all. He was still in one piece. We pored over the details. He'd spent two nights in the cyclo by the side of the road and one in a friendly local's house. Had people chasing him down the road asking for English lessons and to marry their daughters. He even had to wave the mighty meat cleaver to shake off some freaky guy that wouldn't leave him alone. He made it to Mui Ne with just a handful of change and a sore arse, and sold the cyclo for 250,000 dong. In fact he was a day ahead of us and had left the day before. We were lost for words. Except for one. Legend.

We hired out some more death-bikes the next day. These ones were so knackered that they stalled every time you stopped, be it at a quiet lay-by or a busy junction with the lights turning green. We rode along the coast to some massive, desolate sand dunes stretching high inland. We started hiking up past the spiky grass tufts, but every time we thought we were near the top, another summit appeared. We gave up and looked around. We were in the middle of nowhere. We started laughing at ourselves in our crap clothes stuck up in the dunes, looking like some failed rock band's promo shoot. We rode to some more bright orange dunes where some little boys were hiring out boards to surf down the sand. So off we went, puffing and panting up the dunes. Whenever we tried sliding down the dunes we'd end up flying over the front of the board and rolling down through the sand. By the end of the afternoon I looked like a monster, covered head to toe in bright orange sand.

There wasn't much in the way of nightlife, so the four of us, easily the biggest and loudest group of travellers on the road, took over a bar with our music, jokes, pool and booze. Oh, and the latest instalment of the Vince story. All guilt appeased, Charlie was in full effect now, spreading the Legend of Vince, the story getting more over the top every time. I was getting bored though. There was little going on in Mui Ne. I yearned for some real action.

I was sometimes catching myself feeling down for no good reason. Was it me or Vietnam or being with my friends? Or was it the anti-malarials I'd been taking for almost three months now since my first trip to Laos? I wasn't sure. They contained warnings about their possible adverse side-effects like depression, anxiety and panic-attacks. I felt fine when I'd first started taking them, apart from the mind-bendingly surreal and vivid dreams. But now I wasn't so sure. I was enjoying myself, and yet at times I was feeling miserable and down for no good reason, sometimes silently blaming my companions. I felt quiet and withdrawn at other times, like I had nothing to say to the people I met. But then the next minute I'd be fine again. Charlie and Joe occasionally said similar things about themselves too, though they were on the dailies. I didn't know much about malaria other than I definitely didn't want it, so I kept taking them.

★ ★ ★

Rain fell heavily all the next day. The grey fields and hills looked bleak and sadder than regret, the Tour no longer Happy. We got to the coastal town of Nha Trang by nightfall. Checked in and straight off to the beach looking for action. This was supposed to be Vietnam's premier resort town, but it looked pretty dead to us, with a distinct lack of pick-pocketing hookers on the beach, despite the guidebook's promises.

We found the Boat Club, the biggest joint on the beach, but it was a cheesy indoor bar full of nasty pop music and drunk backpackers. We were far from pissed enough to deal with the place. We wandered back along the beach road and found a little snack stall by the side of the road with a kind old Mama at the helm. She looked in her glass cabinet and produced two dusty bottles of vodka. We drank them straight in the one glass she had, passing it round quickly with malicious intent, as we sat on little plastic stools by the side of the road. Pretty soon Charlie was chucking up on the street. Roland filled a bucket of water and helpfully threw it all over the sick to "mop it up," spreading it everywhere. A picture of class, the four of us. Sufficiently anaesthetised, we returned to the Boat Club. More drinks, dancing like twats, trying it on with the prick-teasing blondes. Roland, in some kind of doormen's code, pays off the security guards "for free drinks and protection," he explains. On and on we went; the cheese rotten but it was all we had. Eventually succumbed and were delivered home by four cyclos like dead chickens in a basket.

Scraped ourselves out of bed and onto the beach. It looked nice in the daytime. Golden sands, clear crystal waters and blue skies, the waves gently rolling in with the tide, islands shining on the horizon. We relaxed as best we could, but the vendors were out in force – drinks, umbrellas, deck chairs, ice cream, crabs and kites – you name it. We were soon back out on the piss through the night, checking out all the bars we could find in town, happy to have found some nightlife, however basic. Everyone from Dalat was there too. Due to the long thin shape of Vietnam, it seemed that everybody was going to the same places on the same route, either south to north like us, or vice versa. So we kept bumping into the same people again and again.

Wake up still pissed in good spirits and stagger to the port, having booked ourselves on Mama Nhu's famous boat trip. We board the little wooden boat with two outdoor decks, one on top of the other and collapse on the lower deck as some reggae kicks in. No Mama Nhu though; apparently she's inside on marijuana charges. There seemed to be a strong heritage of dodgy Mamas here in Nha Trang. Despite her absence the boat was full and the Sun was shining. Beers for breakfast. Soon everyone was feeling good, out burning on the top deck as we chugged around the outlying islands. Music, lunch beers and some reefer. I spotted a couple of likely lads and said hello. Victor, the suave young Sydney business man and his friend Eddie Diamond from

London, with his long curly hair and chequered history as a porn cameraman. Soon we were diving off the boat drunk, looking at fish and coral with misty masks, back on the boat, joking and smoking. Everyone's comparing their experiences and getting rid of their shared grievances of the hassle and rip offs. Everyone is kind of glad they came to Vietnam, but no one goes as far as saying that they really like it here. Charlie tells the ever-burgeoning Vince story, before losing his flow and trailing off about snakes and lakes. Others join in. It was that kind of day.

Next thing we're bobbing around the sea in rubber rings. The crazy guides from the trip have got a big polystyrene floating bar out, and we're all downing plastic glasses of sweet fruit wine on counts of three, trying not to drown. Getting messy now, cup in hand, piss-takes and banter, the Sun beating down hard. A small window of self-awareness passes for a moment and I notice that we're far drunker than everyone else on the boat. We stop at an island; and the lads dive in and swim through the flotilla of moored boats to the beach to avoid the entrance fee. Don't know what we're doing now. A brief attempt at beach volleyball and I pass out on a sun lounger. Wake up in a pool of dizzy sweat, and we're back on the boat, a giant climbing frame now, swinging round the edges, climbing up one side and down the other, talking shit to anyone that'll listen. I'm suddenly stopped in my tracks by the pretty doe eyes of a brunette English girl called Nadia. She's smiling at me anyway, so I must be doing something right. We spot Chanelle and the other girls on another boat and we're diving off the top, swimming over and hanging off anchor lines. Laughing little kids appear in basket boats, basically little floating semi-spheres of weaved bamboo, and me and Joe are swimming over, clambering in and throwing the kids overboard. Oh dear, oh dear. And it continues . . .

Nighttime all of a sudden. I'm lying in a heap of rubber rings on the back of the boat. Confusion and darkness descend my mind, still deeply hammered. Back at the hotel we're shouting at each other about something, so I charge into town alone. I bump into pretty Nadia from the boat, still surprisingly friendly despite me being dangerously off my head. We go down to the Boat Club. Lights flashing, the place packed. Charlie, Joe and the others from the boat trip are coming and going. Everyone's shitfaced. Nadia and I sit on the beach just outside the club. We're soon drunkenly kissing and rolling round in the sand together. Yeah, I'm the man . . . I'm suddenly woken up by a wave crashing over me, soaking me all over. I pick myself up, no Nadia, no idea what's going on, looking like a beached whale. Wander back inside the club, soaking wet and covered in wet sand, a right royal mess. Can't find Nadia or anyone else so I start dancing again. But the wet sand's chafing my arse and strangely I don't seem to be attracting any more women. I take it as a sign to go home. Trudge back alone along the beach road to the hotel where I'm greeted by the sight of Joe's hairy arse staring up at me.

An unremitting pain dawns with the Sun. Bad hangover. Very bad, the three of us like death warmed up. Images from yesterday flash through my mind like subliminal messages. Dehydration, an unquenchable thirst, a throbbing head and undertones of surrealism plague my every step. Joe and Charlie manage to get up and rent a bike out to find a famous local photographer Charlie's been hoping to track down, followed by a trip to some monkey zoo with little monkeys dressed as clowns riding bikes and jumping through hoops and shit. I can't face any of that right now and opt out.

I eventually make it to the beach where I sit trying to grasp my way back to reality. But it's hot and I'm wasted. I stare at the long sea. It seems to be drifting into shore in slow motion, waves slowly peeling over for little eternities. Small bits of rubbish dance in the sand. Tiny crabs keep emerging from nowhere in front of me, little nibbling claws and antennae eyes, before popping back into the sand. Did that really happen? Are they trying to communicate with me? Christ I'm losing it. No end in sight as we're off on a 12 hour night bus north to Hoi An tonight. I manage to get some knock-out pills from the market without attacking any of the hawkers that claw for my attention. I meet the others. Their trip to the monkey show seems to have turned them over to the dark side as well. We start joking about spiking each other's drinks and climbing inside other people's rucksacks. Until it becomes true. The bus is bad. Seats don't go back, it's full and cramped. It gets dark; the stupid jokes turn to conversation, then the odd remark and soon to silence. I can't rest my head anywhere as there's no space, and I'm knackered and rough, the bus bobbing along slowly over the ruinous pot-holed roads. I go through six pills before the night is out. Don't really sleep as such but fall into a state of head-nodding oblivion, the pills lobotomising me sufficiently to get through the long lonely night without losing the plot completely.

★ ★ ★

Open my eyes somewhat surprised to still be alive by the morning, feeling slightly aggrieved to have to get off the bus due to the sedatives. The others seem to be coping better than me as they are ready to go out as soon as we find a room. I want to crash out but decide to push through. We rent some bicycles and head off. Hoi An was a quaint little town full of old buildings, Chinese temples and faded French pastel townhouses. Cobbled streets, networks of alleyways, street stalls and little stone bridges over canals, wooden boats bobbing in the river by the side of the road. Further out of town, through verdant paddy fields and we're soon at a gorgeous white sand beach stretching out as far as the eye can see in either direction. It looks fantastic and the swim wakes me up a little, but I'm still shattered, my mind still lying in a ditch by the side of the road last night. I try to relax but get ceaseless hassle from restaurant owners, pointed hat women and yappy street kids. If they just shut up a minute I might actually have a desire to listen to them. But they don't. I know they're poor and just trying to make money from the rich tourists, but they won't take no for an answer; they stay on your case for five minutes each, trying to engage you relentlessly. You can't get away, you can't relax. My head fills with nasty negative emotions. In amongst the tirade of sales pitches, one woman in a conical hat selling seafood stops my train of thought. After our fifth no, she seems to pick up on our feelings. "People always want what they have not got," she said cryptically before carrying on.

Sunburnt, confused and cursed with the memories of goldfish, we head back into town. Everywhere we go: "You come my shop? . . . You come with me. You come to my clothes shop. You pay dollar," and "You want my postcard? Why you not buy?" and "Two for $5 . . . three for $5 . . . okay, five for $5. You buy from me five for $5. I said five for $5 . . . okay, only one for five. Give me $1 for five." My mind crumbles from the constant stress. They're driving me round the bend. We're trying to eat a meal and kids are trying to grab food off my plate, while every five minutes another little grubby urchin will come along blowing these horrible wooden whistles in my ear, bartering themselves down between peeps. Damn whistling piercing my brain! Make it stop! I was really losing it now and I wasn't alone. Sick of it. I can't handle it in my present state. With this many tourists packed in such a small town the harassment was worse than Saigon.

A decent night's sleep and I felt calmer in the morning, but this place was putting bad thoughts in my head and setting my nerves on edge. The people were poor, that was plain to see, but when the constant harassment was mixed with all the other factors, it was enough to send my mind into dark new territories.

Joe and I went out, dodging all that approached, hired more motorbikes and picked up the still-hobbling Charlie. We needed the rushing wind to cleanse the dark thoughts and the grip of the Happy Tour from our minds. So off into the searing heat we drove, inland to My Son, through shining wet paddy fields, tin shack villages, and far away mountain tops shrouded in glistening silver mist. We eventually came to the red ruined temples of the old Cham civilisation, sitting in a bowl surrounded by steep mountains and thick jungle, many of its ancient carvings still intact. We seemed to be the only people there until a fashion shoot from Hong Kong turned up. Checked out the models a bit before cruising back slowly taking photos of the houses, shops and trucks. One strange building stopped us in our tracks. A huge furnace, a brick factory maybe, toxic clouds pluming out and workers with pyramid hoods and giant overalls.

We were getting confident on the bikes now, overtaking all the loaded trucks and boy racers at top speed, trying to reach the Marble Mountains on the other side of town. We hit some kind of rural rush hour as the afternoon progressed. I lost the others but carried on alone as the evening drew in fast, past more farm trucks and armies of school kids in spotless white uniforms, weaving onwards ever more through the dusky fields. I saw hills far ahead of me on the horizon but it was getting too dark. I turned right, over sand tracks and grassy little dunes, nobody here now, reaching the huge expanse of untouched coast at China Beach as the sky faded into smoky grey violet. I got off the bike and stood there alone for a while. The beach was empty as far as the eye could see, stretching on beyond the horizon in both directions except for three empty basket boats in a triangle on the flat sand, a little flag fluttering alone in one of them. I breathed in the stark salty air, bracing winds rolling in from the eastern sea.

We decided to keep moving and get the bus to Hue, the penultimate stop on the Happy Tour. We had our usual meal of noodle soup, adding all the fresh leaves and herbs that were served with it, and strolled around Hoi An for the final time. It was a beautiful town, but the harassment was too much to handle. I wanted to explain to them that if they kept annoying the very people they're trying to sell to, then there won't be many people wanting to visit. Are they desperate or just over-zealous? It seemed that everyone you passed wanted a piece of your wallet.

I saw Nadia wandering alone in town. I went over to join her and we had a final walk along the beautiful riverside, talking about Vietnam and why we're here and where we're going. She was a rather deep thoughtful girl. We sat on a stone bench by the water's edge, five sad, grubby, little kids surrounding us, all trying to sell us the same wooden whistles. They didn't give up, but they were so young and tiny it was suddenly heartbreaking. I realised they *were* desperate. They had nothing, and I with my dirty vest and credit card had everything. If I knew what it really meant to be hungry I'd be doing the same.

★ ★ ★

The tour continued north through the city of Danang, and over a steep mountain right next to the sea, a natural wall cutting the coastline in two. Giant clouds rolled in as we headed through flooded fields and mud-soaked settlements, the rain pouring down from the dark grey sky, streaming across the bus windows in streaky torrents. I developed a sad respect for the people, but realised there was an unbridgeable chasm of misunderstanding between us, a chasm of poverty, war and suffering that I couldn't comprehend. This sad land, shat on by the outside world and left to reform alone. The dark streets of Hue were flooded when we arrived in the rain and lightning. We waded through the wet streets to stretch our legs, crossing a huge bridge lit by lines of multi-coloured lights contemplating the cool damp night.

The rain was still falling the next morning as I lay in bed, fantasising about escape. We looked around mournful Hue, past the formidable-looking, old Imperial palaces, but they failed to inspire in the grey damp. We booked our tickets for the DMZ tour and Hanoi the next day. The day would have been completely forgettable if it wasn't for suddenly bumping into Vince on the streets. We'd kind of forgotten about him, but there he was alive and well. It was great to see him again. Since the cyclo mission, he'd been attempting to kayak and mountain bike other parts of the journey north with mixed success. We listened to his tales in respectful wonder.

Up at 5am in silence, the black night gradually turning a dark grey. A minibus takes us round what little remains of the Demilitarized Zone, the area that lay between North and South during their separation. It's dark, grey and drizzly all day. We see a bombed out church ruin, a former US camp, and then to the DMZ where nature no longer lives, dunes of grey ash, petrified remnants of jungle and a decimated mountain side, sliced open by bombing. Over the Ben Hai River which marked the old border, to nearby tunnels where locals hid, and past military statues and memorials. We stop at a hill tribe village, the poor villagers in rags virtually dragged out for us to photograph and buy things from, like some human safari. It's a sad addition to the trip. Up to the Khe Sanh military base, high up on a rocky plateau where one of the war's bloodiest battles took place. There is little there now but the ravaged hills, this sad wasteland, testament to the failures of Man. Back through villages where we are only met by generations of mistrustful glances.

Back in Hue, after the long day's misery, we had nothing to look forward to but the final leg of the Happy Tour, an all-night trip to Hanoi. Vince introduced us to Ruud, a gravel-voiced, pony-tailed Amsterdam bar owner. Very laid-back, deadpan kind of guy. He'd been mountain biking with Vince along with Rosie and Ian, two young friends from Australia. We got the two back rows of the bus, as it grunted along over the pot-holes. The night got messy. Lots of big noisy lads cramped together on the back of the pitch black bus, three plastic bottles of rum and Coke we'd mixed up, three different types of sleeping pills – blue, white and yellow – and one very big bump in the middle of the night sending us all flying into the ceiling. As the hours wore on we all descended into head-rolling oblivion. Murmurs throughout the night of "Who's got the old rocket fuel?" and "Let me try one of them yellow ones . . . "

* * *

If there are answers to the questions of free will, then it seems for now we must look within ourselves to find them. A human consciousness of time, action and intention, always doing what we want at every moment. And it seems the human mind and actions are necessarily evaluative, constantly evaluating the possibilities for action, deciding which one is best, and doing it.

All of this begs the question – where do these values come from? The first answer would appear to be oneself. It is you that decides what you do next, so it is only you who decides what is good and bad for you at that moment. They are ideas in your mind, though they also have a physical representation in the brain through the ever-changing complex workings of our neural networks.

So how do we make these decisions? How do we decide what to value? Well, ask yourself. What do you value? What do you think is good? What are the most important things in your life?

After a little thought your list may include some of the following things: life, health, love, your children, partner, family, friends, pets, religion, God, spiritual fulfilment, being-at-one, peace, balance, meditation, beauty, art, music, work, money, wealth, status, career, your organisation, your country, ideology, happiness, fun, sex, food, drink, holidays, freedom and truth . . . to name but a few possibilities.

So why are these things important to you? Again, ask yourself. I guess they give you various kinds of positive feelings. They make you 'happy' in the most general sense of the word. So it would seem that these positive feelings must be strongly linked to our emotions. We like what makes us happy, and so we think it is good, at least while we are doing it at the time, otherwise we wouldn't do it. We do things that give us positive emotional responses, and avoid things that give us negative emotional responses. Of course there is often conflict between these desires as we've seen, such as forgoing an immediate pleasure for the sake of a future one. Or suffering in the present in order to accomplish a future goal and gain future positive emotions. We can hence see a distinction between short-term and long-term values, or *objectives* in more natural English. But overall in life, we strive to achieve the things we value positively, and avoid the things we value negatively. The decisions we make are entirely up to us, and they can only be made in the present moment. The past is gone, and the future never comes.

So if there is this strong link between values and emotions, where do our emotions come from? Some seem to be hard-wired into our physiological make-up. We are hungry, we feel bad. We eat, we feel good. We are tired, we feel bad. We rest, we feel good. When we are damaged, we feel pain. When we are loved, we feel joy. The list of situations and possible emotional reactions goes on and on. That rush of adrenaline, the warm glow of serotonin and the yes yes yes of dopamine. These and other neurotransmitters send signals around our nervous system, some of them manifesting as conscious emotions. They seem embedded in us.

For what purpose do these reactions exist? I think the answer is obvious – for life itself. Our emotions exist in order to steer us towards survival, and a better life in order to better sustain that survival. Whether this is purely survival of the self or of one's offspring also, or maybe of our family, friends and larger social groups, is for you to decide. Survival is usually the strongest desire people have, an urge duplicated in the urge to mate and bear children. This is transferred into the parents' children whose survival usually becomes just as or more important than their own. However, many people freely choose to pursue other survival strategies in various manners from selfish to altruistic. To claim all humans pursue the same survival strategy would be difficult to substantiate given the diversity of evidence.

Most positive emotions are therefore subsidiaries of this yearning for life – survival of oneself and the desire for, and survival of, one's offspring. So we eat to sustain our bodies, seek shelter to rest, socialise to enjoy the many benefits of family, friends and society. That which pertains towards a better life, better body, better mind, is generally associated with positive emotions – health, safety, exercise, play, learning, wealth, accumulation, progress . . .

And of course sex and love. Those compelling urges that pull us towards one another like two stars on a collision course, if only there were just two stars involved. More like a little galaxy, billions of stars circulating and chasing each other down in ever-decreasing circles, till their gravity pulls them together and they consume one another in celestial ecstasy, creating a new star, or are repulsed by each other's gravity, and flung back into the cosmos.

So what of negative emotions? If positive emotions are there to steer us towards life, then negative emotions must be there to steer us away from death. If fear deters us from death, then pain repels us from it. Negative feelings about oneself can come about when one feels dissatisfied with the decisions one has made, such as disappointment, shame, sadness and regret. Negative feelings towards others can manifest through any action that has a detrimental effect on the well-being of oneself, such as irritation, envy, anger and hatred.

So these two poles of life and death, positive and negative emotions, guide us through our lives. We strive towards that which sustains life through positive emotions, and avoid that which diminishes life and brings on negative emotions. Why then do people do things that harm themselves, like over-eating, not exercising, drink, drugs, harmful relationships, dangerous activities and so on? Because at the time of doing the action, the positive emotions outweigh the negative ones and so the action is deemed the best thing to do at that time. We always seek to satisfy our desires for positive emotions and any reasoning that goes on as to which desires to satisfy next is our decision to make.

But of course, values go deeper than these simple emotional reactions. In our everyday lives, our emotional responses and reasoning are very complicated things, more a sea of colour than a world of black and white. We don't live alone in a solitary world of solipsistic emotions. We are strongly affected by the world we grow up in also.

We grow into a world of people – billions of people constantly making decisions. They can be grouped into cultures – groups of individuals with common values. We all belong to many co-existing cultures since cultures can be defined and analysed across many different variables, such as time, location, region, nation, continent, religion, gender, age, generation, class, race, sexuality, fashion, musical tastes, technology use and pretty much anything else you can think of. These cultures can be characterised by their different values on family, friendship, society, gender, age, race, education, religion, politics, art, love and life and endless other things.

Every day we are barraged by the contrasting views of others, often people representing various cultures. What are we to think? Who are we to agree with? The answer, of course, is up to you. The degree to which we agree with the values of others is ultimately our decision to make. There are instances where people are manipulated into doing actions by others. However, it is always one's decision whether or not to follow them, even in extreme life or death examples. We always have a choice.

★　★　★

We were all losing our minds. Something about the trip was bringing out the worst in everyone, tempers fraying, dark emotions simmering away. Maybe it was the tragic history of the land and its present day echoes. Maybe it was the constant harassment and rip offs whenever we stepped onto the street. Maybe it was travelling in close quarters in uncomfortable conditions. Or maybe it was the malaria drugs twitching the wrong nerves deep in our psyches. I'd been feeling increasingly downbeat, withdrawn and paranoid, horrific nightmares of unknowable evil forces and fear plaguing my sleep like nightly trips down Elm Street. Was that really it? Maybe it was the lack of women and the difficulty of finding a good night out anywhere. And of course there was always the heat and fetid humidity squeezing little drops of our souls away minute by minute. I guess it was all of these things.

Finally here we were in the capital Hanoi, sitting by the side of a busy road at dawn, passing round cigarette butts and the last warm spitty dregs of rum and Coke from a plastic bottle, bodies weary, minds dulled by the pams and whatever those yellow ones were. Cyclos and moto drivers, street kids, pointed hat women with goods on their shoulders, the homeless and disabled, the hungry guesthouse owners – we were oblivious to them all by now, initial annoyance turned now to resentful acceptance and rancour, as we were ripped off and duped into an expensive guesthouse somewhere, taking our grievances out on each other, snipes and suspicions.

I slept the pills off, then went out alone to clear my head. We were staying in the Old Quarter of Hanoi just north of the serene stillness of Hoan Kiem Lake in the centre of the city, a much-needed sanctuary of calm around which the city swung. It seemed similar to Saigon, only less extreme. Hanoi was slightly cooler, slightly calmer and more ordered with its lakes, wide leafy boulevards and old pastel-walled colonial buildings. I say slightly because you were still putting your life in the hands of the rush hour every time you tried to cross the road, and the constant hassle on the streets was still chipping away at me. But I was more used to it all now.

The Old Quarter was where artisans plied their trades, whole streets containing nothing but a single trade industry. So as you cut through its twisting alleys and market stalls you passed the hammer and clatter of the metal-workers' street, the sweet pong of flower street, the macabre chippings of tombstone lane and the quaint uselessness of little wooden dangly-thing alley. Noodle soup stalls everywhere and little old ladies heaving round baskets of fresh baguettes. The streets were humming with economic activity, a country once on its knees, now standing up and walking tall.

We sat on plastic stools by the roadside that night, trying to get drunk on the cheap rum in preference to the piss-weak, piss-tasting local beer. There was me, Charlie and Joe, along with Vince, the amiable hippy chick Rosie with her blonde dreads, her platonic friend Ian from Australia, a very laid-back, droll kind of guy, and Dutch Ruud. We ended up in a dead tourist club. We tried our best, Charlie's drunken break-dancing ending on his back in the middle of the dance floor, slowly pushing himself in a circle with his legs. Eventually notice we're the only people there and give up.

★ ★ ★

A plan formulated. We were going to get some bikes and drive off into the mountains of northwest Vietnam. Hanoi, though beautiful and hectic, lacked the raw intensity and novelty we'd buzzed off when we arrived in Saigon. We needed to break out again. Joe, Vince and Ian hired these big old Russian Minsk bikes. Looked like something out *The Great Escape*. They were going to tour the whole region up to the mountain town of Sapa and back. Me and Charlie, not having a driving license or real experience between us, hired a little Honda Dream. We'd do one night in the mountains before returning and visiting Halong Bay on the coast. Ruud and Rosie, who'd got it on at some point, doubled up and joined us for the shorter trip.

Getting out of the city was intense. Very fucking intense. Four lanes of traffic, nearly all motorbikes scooting along with no mirrors, just horns beeping in all directions. Throw in the occasional slow-moving, smoke-belching truck, bicycles, cyclos, and wheeled market stalls crossing the road, oh and the fact that these big four lane roads would often cross other big four lanes roads with no traffic lights, just thousands of vehicles weaving round each other as best they could. We soon lost the others in the chaos and I'm driving, sweaty and hung over, with Charlie clinging on my back snapping action shots, screaming like his hero Hunter S. Thompson, as we swerved through the two-wheeled moving metal jungle.

But fuck me if it didn't feel good flying past all the traffic as quick as we could out of the city and into the green fields of the country. Aviators on, flying high and fast along the busy country roads past forests, fields, villages and lakes, the rush of air alleviating the heat on our skin, bright Sun shining on us as the cooler winds of winter came down from the north. The gradients rose from hills to mountains and eventually we came to a big junction where we turned left up a steep road, twisting and turning round U-bends upwards, temperature dropping, exhilaration rising. Overtaking a truck on a blind turn to reveal two buffalo standing in the road which I only just weave round without flying off the side of the mountain. Giant rocks jutting out of nowhere, little tin huts with expressionless farmers' faces staring out at us, buffalos grazing in fields. Downhill, floating round endless bends carefree and happy, sweet release, life is beautiful, all the darkness gone, God damn, it's '69, I'm Captain America, Dennis Hopper cracking through reels hard and fast behind me. Swooping down into valleys, farmers burning crops by the side of the road, thick smoke rising through the humid afternoon Sun, over yellow fields and conical hats, gracing the fields with an ethereal fog of ages. The land was alive again, our hearts blessed in favour. Out of the city and into the Sun. Up past a mountain ridge, passing motorbikes with wooden benches and giant bushes tied on their backs, solitary men walking the road with rifles slung on their back, past paddies and pyramid mountains. Down the valley side into the cool evening dusk, we eventually reach the small town of Mai Chau by nightfall, finding a beautiful wooden dorm-hut on high stilts among the local people.

It was a relaxed place. The people, good people living off the land, kind and friendly. None of the hassle and bad feeling of before. That night Charlie and I chatted to the thoughtful proprietor about the effects of tourism on the land and people. He worried for the future of the hill tribe people here. We were shivering in the chilly mountain air, though I'm sure it wasn't that cold. We had no idea where the others were, till hours later through the silent night we heard grumblings approaching. Spotlights grew bigger until the big growling Russian motorbikes appeared by chance at our guesthouse. We greeted them all happily and ate and drank till the long day and cold night put us all to bed.

The guys packed up their bikes for the long journey ahead, the mountains looming ominously in the background. The atmosphere there in the rural idyll was ageless. It could've been any time, any place. We said our goodbyes, hoping the guys would make the week-long journey safely through Vietnam's highest mountains on their rusty old bikes. Part of me wanted to go with them, but other glories awaited. It was all good. Soon Joe, Vince and Ian roared off along the dirt track and up the valley.

Charlie and I rode back slowly in tandem with Ruud and Rosie, less rushed now, taking in the views and waving to kids by the side of the road. Halfway back, we stopped off for lunch at a village restaurant by the hot road. At the next table some middle-aged local guys were throwing back snake wine and shots of rice whiskey. The sudden appearance of these Western kids from down the hill only added to their exuberance as they staggered around our table happily, trying to get us drinking. We said no at first, but eventually caved in to their insistence, clinking glasses at every other sip, the absence of any common language no hindrance to the festivities. We humoured them as best we could as they forced shots of the potent liquor down our necks. Then they went into the back room and started bringing out all their war memorabilia, posing for Charlie's camera in their green army caps and jackets and shiny NVA badges. In decades past we would have been enemies, but now we were friends. Strange, surreal encounter. We eventually got out, back into the baking Sun, just about able to drive in a slow straight line.

We were inspired by the rush of freedom in the country. Young Westerners in the dense uniform sea of the Vietnamese population, one of the last remaining ripples of Marxism. All this talk of freedom and will burned even stronger when set against the society around us. A free will that can never be proven but one which the brave know to be true, for it is the one thing that gives us the possibility of Man's greatness, the possibility that we can make our own way in life, that we can write our own destiny.

★ ★ ★

Charlie and I decided to ignore the tour bus option and make our own way to Halong Bay on the north coast of the country, dotted by thousands of little limestone islands jutting out the sea. We found a bus to Halong City port, bought the 'sightseeing ticket', and finally we were back on the ocean. It cost more than the tour bus in the end, but we were grateful to escape the clutches of the tours. By now, just the sight of other travellers was sometimes enough to send my wrought mind flying off in irrational anger – their arguments and complaints, their choice of vocabulary or crap haircuts. As the islands slowly grew into view from the horizon, our first stop was at a large cave. However naturally beautiful its caverns were, inside it had been lit up in garish multi-coloured lights like Santa's grotto, complete with fountains and handy hotel booking desks.

Back on board we carried on and were soon sailing into nature's bosom, feeding on her milk for the soul. Sea salt filled our lungs, endless great tombstones of steep rock rising vertically into the sky in a myriad of formations, lifting me out of my Mefloquine soup. Hundreds of eagles circled the skies high above the beautiful statues of limestone, covered in layers of green velvet, the flat sea under the deep cloudless blue of the sky, gifting us brief glimpses of Heaven. We swam around the boat in the open seas and afternoon Sun feeling good to be alive again, free in a beautiful world.

As the evening drew in we passed dozens of islands before landing at Cat Ba Island, the largest in the bay. We found a hotel in the tiny Cat Ba Town, not much more than a strip of hotels, bars and restaurants along a narrow ledge in between the harbour wall and the sheer cliff face behind, fake metal trees flashing their fairy lights through the night. Hundreds of fishing boats peppered the harbour and all the way out to sea. More kids on the street with their jive-talking English, a girl threatening to kill us for not buying something from her. We threw back a quick bottle of cheap vodka in some God-awful homemade karaoke bar, trying to get over the curious type of shock that being threatened with death by an eight-year-old girl can give you.

But after that everything clicked into place. We came to the local backpacker joint, packed to the rafters. We found Ruud and Rosie inside, very much the couple now and very drunk already. It was Ruud's 30th birthday tomorrow and he *was* going to get laid as he'd assured us the week before. I saw Nadia again too, butting in past some random fucker that was chatting her up. A few more drinks and it was time for the birthday party. Nadia came with us and we went to a nearby shop where Ruud forced the guy to hand over a huge cool box full of ice, Coke, glasses and of course five bottles of rum. We could barely lift the thing. We took it in turns lugging it a mile through the village, over the hill at one end and down the steep cliff steps in the dark, eventually getting to the nearest beach at 11:55pm. Ruud and Rosie suddenly stripped off naked and ran into the sea with a bottle of bubbly to celebrate. We sat on the beach getting wasted on our favourite cheap rum, and soon I was rolling round in the sand with Nadia again. As if by magic, two Swedish hippies appeared in the darkness with a large bag of weed which me and Charlie took care of for them. Staggering round the silvery beach, hammered in the dark, staring up at the million stars so bright in the dark night, talking about the Universe and God knows what and kicking up big whirlpools of shiny blue bioluminescence in the sea, swirling round like the millions of shining little stars above us in the dark ocean.

We spent another couple of nights on Cat Ba Island. Ambling down the scenic wooden walkways around the cliffs and beaches, chilling out in the Sun and swimming out to nearby rocky crags. It was great to finally stop and relax after constantly moving for so long. Our last morning came and we got up at dawn to admire the huge flotilla of boats one last time. It was a hell of a long way to Vang Vieng, where everyone had agreed to meet up. Baguette and bananas for breakfast and we were on the slow boat back to port, past the floating homes with their fish farms and guard dogs pacing the wooden planks, and through the gigantic labyrinth of Halong Bay in the pea green sea one last time, blessed by nature's grace.

★ ★ ★

Back in Hanoi we found Joe, Vince and Ian. They'd completed their marathon trip in a week, thankfully with no major mishaps, and returned the bikes in one piece. From their descriptions of the mountains and from what I'd seen of North Vietnam, I knew I'd missed a great trip, but the stunning warm waters of Halong Bay more than made up for it. We all knew that this was the end now. Through the many highs and lows we'd now spent a whole month here in Vietnam and our visas were due to expire in two days. It was finally time to go. The other lads excitedly got their bags and boarded the truck from our guesthouse. Word on the trail was of a hellish 24 hour bus trip to Vientiane in Laos, driving halfway down Vietnam again, then over the mountains into southern Laos. But they didn't care. Everyone was happy to be leaving here at last. I knew that everyone would love Laos' smiley, relaxed, stress-free environment, especially so after a month here.

However, I didn't go with them. Perhaps I needed some time to reach some conclusions and make peace with the place. Perhaps I just needed some time alone again after the stressful compromises of group travel that I wasn't used to. I decided on one last day in Hanoi and waved them off.

As usual I was released from my nightmare grip at 6:30am. The end theme to *Red Dwarf* was going round my head on loop. That island, the impossible dream realised. I lay there imagining my return. But I was still here in Nam, the last man in the Universe. It felt very far away.

I drifted to the calming grey waters of the lake, mist rising from its surface, cooler now as winter was approaching. I watched the swirl of Vietnamese people circulating her banks for the final time, trying to fathom them, trying to make peace with the nation; but they float by in faceless whisper, you cannot understand them, you cannot break them, for they are untouchable. I admired the colourless scene in silent calm, my mind burning with colour. Time for the Sun.

I finally succumbed to the smiling insistence of a street trader with a giggle of surrender, and bought a bright red Vietnam t-shirt. Early evening it was my turn to leave. I put my new t-shirt on and boarded a dilapidated bus with a few backpackers and local people piling in boxes and huge bags full of mysterious goods to trade, all pushing things around and grunting at each other. We passed a truck piled high with caged dogs on the road.

At some point in the night we suddenly stopped without any explanation. The grumblings of confusion and anger faded as the backpackers tried their best to sleep pressed up in between the seats and piles of boxes. After many restless hours, dawn broke and we found ourselves by the road in grassy hill lands, the driver reappeared and we moved on again, making the short drive to the border, everyone moaning about why we had to leave Hanoi so early to then stop here for hours.

I thought about all the anti-Vietnamese sentiment I'd seen and felt in myself at times too. All this anger in good people. I'd never seen it before. I felt ashamed to have felt such things. All these little events, the pushes and shoves, the hassles and scams, the piles of boxes, the dogs in cages; it made all the anger understandable but yet so sad. Two cultural fronts unable to mix overnight. It depressed me to see all the irate Westerners fighting through the echoes of this war-ravaged land, but I knew I had seen so much beauty here, and also so much hope. With my belief in the free will of all people intact, I knew that things would change in the future. It was all in the people.

In the cool misty morning, some local children in their glowing white uniforms cycled along silently on their way to school, their grace and calm in stark contrast to the shouting and shoving of us adults confined on the bus. I remembered all the poor streetwise kids we'd met. And I knew then that if there is hope here in this land, it lies with them. Ride on children of Vietnam, ride on . . .

★　★　★

We reached the imposing border gate high in the cool misty mountains that marked Vietnam's border with Laos. A European couple on the bus had some minor issue with their visa and were told to go back to Hanoi to sort it out. The last of countless arguments I'd seen here. But I wasn't going back.

We crossed the border and the haze literally lifted away in moments, replaced by a calm blue serenity as we weaved down the shiny mountains, past rocky passes and sandy banks, the urban mass of Vietnam giving way to the rural charms of Laos. I felt my tensions sliding away. It was good to return to the natural wonders and simple pleasures of this dreamy land. Time to relax.

On a dusty highway we stopped at a police checkpoint. The five remaining foreign tourists on board stood by the side of the road sweating silently in the midday heat, while the dozens of well-wrapped boxes were unloaded by the Vietnamese traders on the bus. The packages were inspected at length and photos taken. After two hours we left again minus two passengers and all the boxes.

After a 26 hour journey I eventually arrived in the familiar surroundings of Vientiane. I soon bumped into Joe and Vince who'd done the same trip in 36 hours. They'd lost the others somewhere along the way. It was a long road from Hanoi.

The next morning, the Sun was shining and the weather was sweet. The clouds were parting and everything was starting to make sense again. My shaven eyebrow, which had taken a lot longer to grow back than I'd expected, was looking just about normal again. Time to embrace the joys of life in Vang Vieng with good company, the high season shining on the horizon. I couldn't wait. The Sun, *the Sun*! The partying to be done, the joy, the love, the pleasures above. Why was I being such a miserable twat and not appreciating the moment? Perhaps never in my life would I have such freedom again.

Even four hours crammed on a rickety old bus, six people per row, doesn't dampen my new enthusiasm. Passing gaps in the bushes I'm afforded brief glimpses of Heaven, soft feather down clouds over majestic peaks. And the joyful people of Laos, all smiles, no hassles.

I got a room at Somsak's place again. He seemed pleased to see me, but didn't have much to say. I didn't bother asking about the kayaking. I soon found Charlie and Joe, the now infamous Vince, Chanelle, Victor, Eddie Diamond, Ian and Rosie, plus various other friends and friends of friends that we'd all met along the way, manifesting in a big extended network of Nam-heads here in Vang Vieng.

Next morning, we all dined on the local cake and shakes in our worst clothes. Picked up some massive black inner tubes, piled in a truck up the road before jumping in the river back towards town. We were all smiles and laughs at first, bobbing around the deep river, the end of the rainy season, splashing and joking with each other. We started to drift apart as the varying currents took us off at different speeds. Soon I noticed I was stuck in the slow lane on my own. My mind started to wander and drift in tangents unforeseen. I paddled round to face the giant God-head mountains looming over the far side of the river, faces forming in the cracks, wondering if the Earth really does have ears after all. I begin whispering to them, words of intrigue and awe. Suddenly notice the large group of purple dragon flies swirling above me. They are their messengers, transmitting my thoughts to the Earth gods. I was joking with myself at first, but then pangs of reality-doubt poke me in the eyes, throwing me into metaphysical panic. I tried laughing it off, letting the movie reel roll by in front of me. Animism – the belief that non-human entities have a soul or spirit, that objects are animated – wasn't something I'd ever taken seriously before. But now I wasn't so sure all of a sudden. Everything seemed so . . . alive.

I caught up with the others at Sleeping Cave in a mute panic. I threw my ring into the big pile and made towards the entrance where you waded through the water before heading into the darkness. I should have been leading the way, being the only person who'd been here before. But I could feel a dark one coming on. My knees were starting to tremble, my nerves jittering. Charlie had already abandoned the idea, sitting on the river bank, staring at the clouds and gently rocking. I followed the others in slowly, unsure of myself. At the first sight of one of those flimsy battery packs I was getting flashbacks to that solo cave trip last time I was here. The one when I went in alone and nearly didn't come out again. Fear slices through me like a lightning bolt. I retreated to the river bank in silence where Charlie was going through his own private hell, throwing up in the reeds. We rode out the storm, clinging onto the little fluffy clouds above.

The others eventually emerged successful, apart from Vince who'd got greedy and doubled up his breakfast servings. He was hiding in the middle of the group in green misery.

We bobbed on till we heard shouts up ahead. There was a new wooden bar floating by the side of the river, big bottles of Beerlao in the hands of every sunburnt kid on it, as empty rings floated downstream. The town was evolving into a fun-filled psychedelic water park for the young and foolish. Luckily, coming down off the river was more enjoyable than coming up on it.

I bumbled round town with the guys. Everyone seemed happy here. Charlie perked up and said he'd found his spiritual home. Vince was still looking green. We spent the afternoon drinking at the island bars where the ring floaters came back into town. I still wasn't feeling very sociable though. Didn't know if it was the Mefloquine, shrooms, sleep or what. Me and Vince went off into town together. It was good to chat to him again. We went back to how we were when we first met on the road in Cambodia, berating the sacrifice of our freedom for the fun, ease and safety of hanging round in the huge group we were now in. I could see the inextinguishable fire still flickering in his eyes, that wild, youthful vigour burning away inside him, urging him on further. I knew he had more in him.

Another good friend from home, Johnnie Drummer, passed through town. Same gang as Adam and Reggie. It was good to see him in this surreal valley of starry-eyed psychedelia, but he'd just arrived in Asia and we were headed in opposite directions. He too had to forge his own path for now. We agreed to meet later in the year when the time was right.

We spent another five days there. Long mornings spent in a barely-conscious delirium from about 6am to midday, trying and failing to get back to sleep. Brain dead at first, but soon flickering into life, buzzing round in fluctuations and increasing spirals of self-analysis. Sometimes I'd fall into trances staring at newly-animated inanimate objects, studying the intricate patterns of wood grain, the behaviour of lines of ants, water drops coalescing on bathroom tiles. Sometimes the hours of over-analysis got so much that all I wanted to do was get out my own head, let my mind dissolve and evaporate into the world as a collection of atoms – a pile of earth, a pool of water or a gust of wind.

Once the midday Sun made the trying too painful, I'd get up and wander round with whoever I bumped into first. People were drinking all afternoon, rolling joints smeared in opium and eating mushrooms. I was still feeling uneasy. I tried to navigate the socio-narcotic minefield as best I could. Went tubing again, conquering my fear and marching through Sleeping Cave like a miner. Late afternoons drinking beer, rum and Vang Vieng specials, smiling faces dissolving into silhouettes as fire smoke drifted through the burning sunset over the face of the mountains. Some nights I'd be alright, but my mind was divided, sometimes content in the company of all these friends, old and new, at other times pulling away, resenting them for no reason, going into inward dejection. I decided I had to get back to Thailand and get off the anti-malarials.

Every morning I vowed to leave, planning a solo escape south. But there was talk in the group of going north. We looked into getting bikes to do it ourselves but they weren't roadworthy. Then by chance one day, enough of us found ourselves gathered in the street at once to organise our escape. Then more and more gormless mugs started turning up. I started losing it, trying to organise a dozen dope heads in the hot afternoon Sun. Eventually about 15 of us boarded a *songtaew* for the trip north to Luang Prabang.

It wasn't comfortable with us all cramped up together on the two benches in the back, but the tensions were soon swept away as stunning views rose uphill over the horizon, craggy dark peaks jutting through the violet sunset and clouds of apricot rain. We blasted out music in the back, passing doobs, singing nonsense, hanging off the back and on top of the truck as it careered round the mountain curves by twilight. We were happy again, together in our travelling commune in the beautiful mountains of this earthly Eden.

About 10pm we arrived in Luang Prabang. I wasn't over the moon about being back in this remote backwater, but I'd chosen to stay with the gang. We all bunked in together, sleeping on mattresses on the floor. The next day while people looked round town, Joe, Ian and I went out looking for bikes but there wasn't much on offer. We tried getting some kind of group consensus on what to do next, but it was hard when nobody knew what they wanted to do and everyone said they "don't mind." We eventually agreed to continue to a village called Muang Noi to the north.

★ ★ ★

The next morning, we got another *songtaew* from the muddy bus station and headed north, winding around the fresh green countryside, the warm wind rushing through our creased-up clothes. The sky was a warm blue, the valley sides a brilliant dazzling green. We had lunch at a little restaurant balanced on a ledge on the side of a lovely steep-sided river valley. The water reflected the sky's gaze as we boarded some low boats, their sides barely above the water line. We zoomed off into the wilderness, past sets of gentle rapids, local kids playing on the river bank, passing other boats with families and monks on board.

After a day of travelling we came to the remote village of Muang Noi on a picturesque bend in the river; only accessible by river, with little wooden huts perched on the side of the muddy bank. It seemed like life in the village was unchanged in generations. Sacks of rice and other produce from the market were unloaded from the boats, as well as a big, black, live pig tied to a stick. The locals came out wearing their simple clothes and brightly-patterned traditional sarongs. It was a perfect rural scene, the kind of place you imagine existing out there in the wild world, far from globalised modernity. And so we 15 intrepid explorers climbed up the river bank onto the main road of the village and suddenly found ourselves in yet another backpacker ghetto, here in the middle of nowhere. Guesthouses, bad restaurants, banana pancake stalls and the rest. We obviously weren't the first people to find this place. Still it was a shock to find this development in such a remote location. We found some charming little huts overlooking the river bend as the Sun set on this little corner of Earth, before an early night, as was the norm out here in the country.

But they get up early in the country too – a piping morning chorus of roosters and off-key frog harmonies croaking by the riverside. The village looked even more unreal in the crisp morning mist. Men loading boats, kids playing round in the moist, earthy, morning air. A craggy old wrinkled woman hunched in front of a doorway, her permanent presence like an oil painting. Cock fighters goaded their prize roosters into battle by the side of the road. We rubbed our eyes over glasses of thick black coffee with condensed milk.

We found a guide to take Joe, Charlie, Ian and me into the jungle. He was a small-built middle-aged man, but incredibly agile and sprightly. He didn't speak a word of English but led us off to the back of the village to a valley where scant rice paddies lay, to see the remains of bomb craters from the American War. Then we headed into the jungle and up a steep slope, our guide hacking a path through the web of creepers and undergrowth with his rustic machete. It was good to trek off the beaten track, literally in this case, cutting our way uphill through spiky vines, and climbing razor-blade rocks to reach a view point overlooking the village and valley. Puffing and sweating like mad we realised how tragically unfit we were compared to our nimble guide, despite being in the prime of youth. He then led us to a large, pitch black cave within the belly of the hill with his gas lamp. He and his fellow villagers hid here during the bombing campaigns, the Vietnamese border being just 50kms away. Hard to imagine such horrors taking place in such a remote and beautiful little corner of the world.

Everyone packed their bags in the cool fog the next day. A part of me wanted to stay there and really relax – sink into country life and melt into the warm pool of nature. But it was always a minority voice, one that lost out to a bigger beast. I had itchy feet, a yearning for my old independence and a deep desire to hit it hard. The rainy season was over, the high season nigh, and there was only one place on my mind now. Golden beaches, bright lights, free liquor and loose women. The Jungle was calling.

★   ★   ★

After yesterday's respite, another day of self-interrogation. Despite the beauty of my surroundings I was still feeling quiet and withdrawn, with bouts of depression, paranoia and hatred. The constant cycles of joy and misery seemed endless and unstoppable. Was this the way it was supposed to be? I said nothing, not wishing to give my feelings away to anyone. I just wanted them to go away. Maybe they felt the same. I didn't know.

We journeyed back to Luang Prabang in silence having no more to say to one another. I'd had enough of it. I plotted in silence.

First bus to Vientiane with Charlie, Joe, Ian and Victor. Got placed on a plastic stool in the aisle of the packed bus, my legs crammed in between other people and their massive suitcases and packages. All the locals on board appeared to be emigrating, the amount of stuff they were all taking with them. I could barely move. Charlie and Joe put on their headphones in silence as I stewed over my anger. I chatted with Victor as he took the piss out of the locals, the Sydney yuppie never really getting carried away with the whole travelling vibe. Hours passed. I calmed down, falling into dozy introspection in the closed, confined shadows of the bus as it climbed down the invisible mountain range. Charlie got off at Vang Vieng. We carried on.

4:30am in the suburbs of Vientiane, crammed up tight, my eyes unable to stay open though my senses were alert. Eventually the punishment came to an end at the bus station. Joe and Ian quickly split off. They were headed for the border and a trip to North Thailand. We all needed to get away from each other I think. The joys of the road were coupled with regular bouts of silence, confusion and claustrophobia. I said goodbye to Victor and saw a 6am bus to the city of Savannakhet in the south of Laos. On a whim I got on it.

Suddenly I was alone again. That sweet bite of freedom. It felt good to follow my will unrepentant again. Another endless bus ride with no leg room but I didn't care. I was alone at last. Repressed thoughts flooded my mind.

It was strange. Before Joe and Charlie came I was looking forward to having friends and travelling companions with me all the time. Sharing experiences, thoughts, fun and jokes with them instead of doing it all alone. But as our trip progressed, their presence was having a negative effect on my confidence, not the boost I expected. Whether it was through losing my freedom to the group or feeling inhibited by their presence or issues from the past or something else, I wasn't sure. Perhaps we were just growing apart. We'd all flown the roost already, and there was no going back. There never is. We live in an ever-changing world and we can only move forward. Occasionally with sadness and regret, but that is our choice. The only thing we can control is what we do in the present. We have no choice but that.

After this extended period following my own free path in life, free from the self-imposed commitments of immersion in the group, I was feeling more and more exposed to my uniquity – that feeling of being a unique lone individual in the world. This is a uniquity we all share, but one most of us shy away from by engrossing ourselves in the rigours of society. Exposed to it here, then taken back to the past with my friends, and now alone again – I felt more and more certain that every decision I made was mine and mine alone. I remembered Brad's words by the fire in the mountains of Chiang Mai. I was falling ever further from that which I knew, cutting myself off from the normality of the past. And I knew that was what I wanted.

After ten hours on a night bus and another eight in the day, I made it to Savannakhet. I caught a glimpse of myself in the mirror at the mud and wood bus station. I looked like shit. Dirt and stubble on my tanned gaunt face. But I didn't care. I was on a southern directive and I'd made good ground. There was a Thai consulate in Savannakhet. I could get a three-month Thai visa to see me through high season, then head further south to see Si Phan Don, The Four Thousand Waterfalls, where the Mekong River split into a turbulent rocky delta. I got a room in some dingy hotel at dusk. I looked around in the evening but the place was a ghost town, so I sat in an internet shop for hours staring back into the outside world like a kid in a goldfish bowl.

I slept so well I had trouble working out where I was upon waking, though it was a feeling I was used to. The room was huge, but filthy dirty and decrepit, some worn rag of a curtain billowing over the iron-barred window. I looked outside to see the mighty Mekong River again, wider and calmer than upstream, floating along in silent grandeur towards the sea back in South Vietnam. The river marked the border here too. Over the other side was my old friend Thailand. My loop through Indochina was nearly over.

I quickly found the Thai consulate; just a little office in an old building, nobody there, and handed in my application form. Just 24 hours to kill. I drooped about Savannakhet, a pretty old town, with dilapidated temples, faded old French colonial houses and worn out streets with a certain still charm. Despite being one of Laos' largest towns, the streets were virtually deserted. It felt like it had been abandoned 100 years ago. Once I'd circumnavigated it in the midday heat, I soon realised there was nothing going on here at all, just killing the hours in fruitless dusty pacings.

I sank some Beerlao on a wooden table overlooking Thailand and the wide expanse of the Mekong in the shade of the trees. I planned what I needed to do – see Charlie off in Bangkok, get that money off

Samuel, maybe some job enquiries. Then the sweet promise of the high season in Phi Phi beyond that. Why was I going back? To relive former glories or discover new ones? Both. I wanted it all. Back to the place I loved the most. No more looking for rooms and packing my bags in the morning. I just wanted to follow the Sun south, kick back and let loose.

Perhaps after the high season a few months' teaching work in Bangkok to settle down and sort my shit out. It was about time. And then one last epic trip. Either south, island hopping through Indonesia as far as I dare, or north, overland all the way into China, Mongolia, Russia and Europe! The madness of both trips excited me beyond belief. Maybe summer at home and then back to Asia, a year in Japan perhaps! I couldn't wait any longer. After 24 hours bored as hell, I decided to cancel my trip to the waterfalls, cross the river and get back to the action ASAP.

Another long sleep in that big dusty attic. I looked at the remaining pills I was supposed to take for another four weeks. All that time with Sammy, Sin, Charlie and Joe, and all across Vietnam – a dark cloud had been following me, an invisible devil whispering foul lies in my ear. I binned the rest of the pills with a big smile.

Down to the consulate, collected my passport and excitedly jumped on a long boat over the choppy Mekong. Through a concrete gateway by the river into the town of Mukdahan. The faded pastel charms of Indochina were replaced by the 7-Elevens, bundles of electric wires and faceless concrete shop houses of Thailand. But I wasn't here for the architecture.

I got a four hour bus through rural towns and muddy paddy fields, groups of school kids getting on and off, till I reached the city of Ubon Ratchathani. Bussed across town at dusk to the old railway station at the end of the eastern line. It seemed a big lively city, but I wasn't for the stopping. My mind was already racing way ahead of me now. Shared some grilled chicken and sticky rice with a mangy dog on the platform before getting the all-night train back to Bangkok, headed for the big time.

★ ★ ★

At around the same time as the global proliferation of *Homo sapiens* 50,000 years ago, there is also evidence of an acceleration in mankind's cultural development. Let's now call them Man, mankind, human or humankind, for they are our direct ancestors, and this period marks their transition into behavioural modernity.

Tool manufacturing and use had developed slowly in the past, but now more advanced tools from different materials were crafted such as knives, needles, buttons and fish hooks. Clothes were made from animal hides. Jewellery and body adornments were worn. Modern humans developed more advanced hunting techniques like fishing and trapping, and by working together could prey on animals physically stronger than them. A material culture developed – sharing, bartering and trading food, commodities and services. More organised living spaces were constructed, and the dead were carefully buried with rituals and ceremonies. Cave paintings and carvings representing images of reality and ideas show evidence of symbolic behaviour, a socially-constructed picture of reality. All of these developments suggest an increased capacity for creation and innovation, for abstract thinking, cooperation and planning. They suggest they saw themselves as individual beings in the wider community.

There were undoubtedly high levels of communication between people by this point, the complexity of which had gradually evolved through their *Homo* ancestors. Different groups of humans were developing systems of gestures and sounds which referred to objects in the world, their positions and qualities, to actions and times, memories, feelings and ideas. Different groups understood these sounds and agreed upon what they represented – their meaning. Sounds grew into words, and words combined into sentences with ever increasing depths of meaning, conveying their shared experiences of living in the world. They could share and discuss their different ideas and opinions not just with brute force, but by explaining their reasons too. Humans were developing social languages far beyond any form of communication that had existed before them on Earth. With language they could overcome the challenges of life together.

Animals, though often sociable, are usually thought of as being trapped in a world of sense perceptions and cognitive functions, unable to think of themselves as being distinct from their own consciousness of reality. Perhaps this is not true, but certainly the nature and complexity of consciousness differs from species to species, if one defines consciousness broadly as the total subjective experience, or how it *is* to exist. Everything we perceive and think at all times in our lives is through our consciousness.

However humans had developed a new way of perceiving the world with these representations of reality understood and communicated through sounds and symbols. With complex languages, humans possessed a new shared representation of reality with which they could communicate and empathise, step outside themselves and see the world through another's eyes.

They became aware of there being not just a world and their own consciousness of it, but of themselves as separate beings to their own consciousness. They were no longer locked within their own consciousness – they could become aware of it in-itself. They had developed the capacity for self-awareness or self-consciousness. It is this quality of self-awareness, of seeing oneself as being in the world separate from one's own consciousness, which defines human consciousness. By developing the ability to free oneself from the selfhood of one's consciousness, one gains the possibility of a greater control over it.

Through language, this shared representation of the world, they developed a shared human consciousness, and hence could act collectively in ways not possible in other species. From this bud grew the great tree of human civilisation over the last few thousand years. This is a stunningly short period of time in comparison to the millions of years it took for humans and other species to evolve biologically. In acquiring complex language skills, early humans could interact, learn, create, educate and enact change in a generational progression that operated far quicker than biological evolution did. Through language we handed down our shared knowledge and culture for successive generations to build upon. This simultaneous development of human consciousness, language and free will gave rise to the emergence of human cultures, with forms of behaviour far more complex and varied than those seen purely from the evolutionary development from which they came.

Though languages and cultures were incredibly varied across the myriad of different groups over different times, commonalities existed across most human groups. For example, singing and music developed alongside linguistic skills. Art in paintings, sculpture and body adornment grew more complex.

Groups grew beliefs in supernatural forces, spirits and gods. Possibly to explain the cause and behaviour of unknown forces in nature – the Earth and sky, the Sun, Moon and stars, the weather and seasons, the nature of the elements, plants, animals and dreams. Possibly to deal with the grief felt by the death of loved ones. Complex burial ceremonies suggest a common belief in an afterlife to which the deceased passed to. These beliefs may have developed as a means to organise group's symbolic and cultural behaviour, beliefs and morality. A wide variety of spiritual beliefs, faiths and religions grew, with some growing and others dying out.

The complexity of social groups also grew. Early humans lived as hunter-gatherers in small nomadic groups. They prospered through cooperation in hunting and home building, not just at the immediate family level but by organising interfamily groups through which communities could grow; learning, working and living together, pooling their knowledge, skills and experience for common goals of improving their lives. Conflicts over food, home, sex, wealth, status, land and other matters would have occurred, both within and between groups. The different standards of behaviour in cooperation and conflict within and between different groups may have led to the concept of moral behaviour. Good moral behaviour being that which was in accordance with the agreed values of the group. Bad being that which went against them. Individuals would have to restrain their selfish impulses in order to remain within the group, aid cooperation and thus gain the benefits of living in a society.

In time, technological advances facilitated further exploration. Humans continued to explore and migrate, eventually crossing seas by boat to Australia and the islands of the Pacific Ocean. Others gradually travelled into North America. Later generations moved all the way down the Pacific coast into South America, eventually colonising all hospitable corners of the world, a world that was now ours.

SEVEN

I'd only been away for six weeks but Bangkok felt different now. December had arrived, the winter was here. 30 degree highs instead of the usual 35. Fresh air blowing through the streets, the sky clear and blue. The rains were over and the humidity had gone. And most importantly of all – the high season was here. Khao San Road was packed full of hungry new sun-seekers headed down to the islands. Nearly there.

That feverish anticipation of a night out in Bangkok. I'd forgotten about all that crap from before, but now I was back, the past had become the present again. I put my shirt on and hit the streets, hunting down the ghosts of my past.

First to Cheeky Bar. Kookie, Far and friends were there. "Anybody seen Sammy recently?" I asked. "You not see him?" Far said, surprised. "He left like five minutes ago! Said he go to bus station." The old rage flared back. He must have spotted me, or got a tip off and done a runner. The streets have eyes. Or was I just thinking too much again? They said they didn't know where he'd gone. Sin was apparently in Ko Phi Phi with her new boyfriend, having gone "crazy butterfly" in their words. Fuck this. I hit the streets.

The heaving neon clamour of a Khao San dusk, soaked in icy booze and garnished with strange attire. See Wan and the sisterhood in the streets, plus It and the regulars of East Gate Bar looking surprisingly clean and sane. But I wasn't getting back into all that again.

I soon found Charlie with Vincent, Victor, Eddie, Cornish Jim and others from Vang Vieng dressed up in stupid shades and tracksuits, necking buckets like Laurence of Arabia. Hit the Khao San bucket bars, my old sweetheart passing my lips with a smile. Threw some old Prodigy on at a CD shop and soon we were all raving in the street.

There were dozens of friends, friends of friends, and random acquaintances from the Indochina loop here too. Hot Euro chicks everywhere. I hadn't seen such things in a long time. Hit the clubs, my sexual appetite reawakening in the steamy Bangkok night. Chatting to some Scando lovelies, but Eddie Diamond and Cornish Jim stole the honours.

24 hours later I felt myself falling into the old drunken life again. Back in the city where sex floats heavily in the air, my lust had returned with a vengeance. But no joy. I was starting to think I'd forgotten what to do. Not getting any furtive glances either. I saw Sin and her latest toy boy, plus Sammy's friends claiming not to know him. Got shouted at in the street by various ladyboys and street scutters who all seemed to know my name. Home alone in frustration.

Another problem was the money. My bank balance was coming in to land just as my credit card bill was taking off. I had to get a real job. Bangkok was the only sensible option. It had the big city life, better money and more options than anywhere else. And I loved it. But I was still hesitant about living here. All I really knew of Bangkok was centred on my life in Banglampoo, one of booze and shady characters. I didn't trust anyone I'd met here. What kind of life is that? I was still worried that if I lived here it would consume me entirely.

Nevertheless I arranged some interviews for teaching jobs at language schools. There was of course one immutable clause in my terms and conditions – I wouldn't be starting anything till next year. That final run through the Jungle had been chasing through my thoughts for weeks now. I was doing one more stint. The high season. No doubt about it. Nearly there. If I had a job ready for afterwards then even better.

I put on the unused shirt and tie I'd been carrying around since my first trip to Chiang Mai and headed off, sweating twice as much as usual. I felt like a charlatan in the gleaming shopping malls and office towers of Chitlom in the city's commercial centre. Smartly attired Thai-Chinese families and immaculate women behind cosmetic counters. The first interview with some grim-faced expat seemed to be going okay till he asked me how to form the present perfect simple tense. The answer eluded me. I was told to try again next year.

Outside an old Thai man befriended me. He was polite and friendly, saying he liked to practise his English with foreigners. I followed him through the busy streets and we talked amiably, till we mysteriously arrived at some gem stone shop in Pratunam. I'd heard of people getting brought to these places by commission-hungry *tuk-tuk* drivers offering 20 baht tours of Bangkok. I slipped off and carried on to my next interview at Victory Monument, my shirt soaked through. The school was a dingy little dive though. Took the Skytrain down to Siam Square for my third interview. I wasn't really sure what I was doing by this point though. The whole shirt and tie thing wasn't really me these days, especially when marching the hard-baked streets of Bangkok. I was flitting between feeling excited about living here, and questioning my reasons for staying at all.

More nights out on the strip, but the crew gradually dispersed. Charlie's last day came. Despite my attempts to get him to stay, he decided to stick with his plans to fly on to Australia. He'd never quite taken to the overwrought pleasures of Bangkok. I was sad to see him go. Despite the ups and downs of our trip he was always my brother. I'd thought this was to be our time to fly together. But in fact, it was our farewell. A farewell to childhood, farewell to the past. We had to fly alone for now.

I went down to Pattaya for one night to see Bob again. Another night round the packed out *sois*, thousands of scantily-clad angel-vamps on heat for the high season. I was exhausted, drunk and horny as hell. I needed to get out of here. Fleeting glimpses of the sparkling ocean between the giant umbrellas and mini-skirts of Pattaya Beach. The Sun was shining, the sky a never-ending blue. Nearly there my son, nearly there.

A week since Laos. The clouds of confusion gradually dispersed. Everything was making sense again. I felt my old positivity returning.

Bussed through the smog back to Khao San and booked the next bus south to Krabi with a connecting boat to Phi Phi. I had a good seat with leg room. I laid back with a weary smile of contentment as we drove out the city into the setting Sun. No more travelling, no more cities, no more paranoia or madness, just the beach, the magical island and the job from Heaven. I smiled and stretched my legs as my head emptied; the lights of Bangkok fading to black.

★ ★ ★

I opened my eyes. Goodbye city, hello blue skies, palm trees and lapping waters. We were at an open-sided restaurant by the sea outside Krabi Town, used as a hub for the tourist-transport companies. Backpackers piled out of the VIP buses in their usual weary silence, with the odd random nutter spouting crap to himself. I quickly found some space and cleaned my teeth in an outdoor sink in the fresh morning Sun of the South. I looked at myself in the mirror with a satisfied smile. I wasn't one of them here. Tiny whispers of waves lapped against the grass and rocks behind me. I turned around and looked out at the sparkling radiance of the Andaman Sea, where the blue waters shimmer with diamonds and dreams. It was time to shine.

As my boat skirted across the magnificent vista of the ocean I felt like a conquering hero returning home from war. The shadow of Ko Phi Phi loomed into vision, a lurid rainbow of colours gradually flourishing from the dark silhouette. We curved round the headland and Ton Sai Bay spread into view, pulling me back to where all men want to go. The golden Sun above, the warm sea, the shining beaches, towering cliffs, mysterious jungle and the party that never stops. The island of fantasy, dreams and illusion, a light so bright it burns into your brain. The island that exists in a bubble, too perfect to be real, too real to comprehend.

I couldn't hide my joy as we approached the pier, wondering who I'd see first. But soon I got that strange feeling returning to an old place you once knew – that mixture of familiarity and the new. You know the place, but it's not personal anymore. Any minor changes are glaring. There was nobody there to greet me of course, just a procession of familiar local faces. The young boat man from Trang, the hotel touts with their picture boards, the internet girls, the divers, the morning cleaners, the sandwich and pancake stalls, massage women and locals on their BMXs.

After five months away, I arrived at the downstairs bar of Jungle Bar again, full of high dreams and expectations. The old artist Pablo was there. I *wai*-ed him in reverence. He was pleased to see me, but said there weren't any rooms available. Ning was sitting there too with her old puppy dog eyes, but nothing was said in public like this. She said she'd retired from the Jungle and worked in a shop now.

I found a room near the concrete steps to the viewpoint and spent the day wandering around. But I didn't know any of the Westerners there apart from Jimmy in Lucky Star, Mitch who was running the show at Predator Bar now, and Joey the climber.

"My brother!" Chai the boxer greeted me outside Jungle Bar in the evening, pleased to have me back. Loads of English and Swedish youngsters trying to hand me flyers at night. I was the new kid, back to square one again. Though I had a little history to my advantage. I said hello to everyone and hung out with the girls at Jungle, but not much going on. It all looked a bit silly in fact, dancing round with buckets to shit music, chatting about the latest gossip on the island as if it were of great consequence. After my initial excitement, I felt an anticlimax.

The next day I considered sacking it off and going somewhere new. But then I went for a swim in the warm waters of beautiful Lodalum Bay again. As I swam, the Sun cut through the clouds, the great bubble erupted into mind-blowing garish iridescence, colours so lurid they have to be seen to be believed. Suddenly I knew it was good to be back. It would just take a little while to get back into the swing of things. Back into the laid-back island life, no worries, no problems. Back to the insularism, the great significance of little events in the island's microcosmic society. This little island in the Andaman Sea, inhabited by the descendants of fishermen and sea gypsies, where Thai laws have only the loosest of power. Now invaded by mass tourism, people from around the world welcome to visit, and more, if they dare take a sip from the Devil's cup.

Eye Of The Tiger, boxing, free buckets, cheesy music. The Rasta Green goes by giving me a friendly jab in the gut and a "You fat!" New girls behind the bar. The hardcore climbers say hi. I drank with Jimmy in Lucky Star, then down to a packed out Coco Loco. Crawling round the dark alleys later on, when who should round the corner but Ning and . . . Chainmail, my metal-clad stalker from Ao Nang! I forgot it was only two hours from here. Turns out they're best friends. We sat in some dark recess as Chainmail reasserted her desire to fuck me while Ning laughed her head off.

I wandered to my room in the shadowy subterfuge of Phi Phi afterhours. I noticed her following me at a distance, without a word, quite naturally. After all the heartstrings, trauma and unrequited lust of my previous stint here, suddenly Ning was in my room, ripping each other's clothes off and humping like long lost lovers. I was just glad to get laid. Relief lightens the load on a man's mind.

A dull light emerged in the bare room by the side of the bristling jungle. Ning suddenly shot up. No words, touches or warmth. And then she was gone. I lay there flicking through the memories. "*Jep, jep, jep!*" I guess it wasn't that great after all. All cigarette breath, wriggly worms and dry rubber.

That evening I went to see the boss. "Okay, you start work tonight," the boss laughed. "You work with these guys." I'm introduced to Danny and Stu, two straight-up English lads. Sound. We clicked straight away. We did the old flyer circuit, strolling slowly up to Ton Sai Bay and doing a right up to 7-Eleven, handing out the little paper flyers and giving it the cheesy chit chat. The boys had just started here too, but obviously didn't take the job quite as seriously as I used to. It seemed the right way to go, so we got some big Changs and slipped off to the blackness at the end of the pier as the lights from the boats bobbed in the invisible sea around us.

Stu and Danny had met for the first time in Ko Samui after coming to Thailand with other friends from home. When their friends went home, the new duo decided to carry on, travelling round the country, drinking, partying and shagging. They'd been in Thailand for the same length of time as me, so we all knew about as much or as little as each other. However, they'd just arrived in Phi Phi for the first time, so I filled them in on my last stint here and what I'd learnt, as they regaled me with tales from the beer bars and back-alleys.

Danny was 24, a big strong lad with a slight Northern twang in his accent, but he'd grown up all over the place. Most of his tales were from his teenage years in Wales – raving, fighting, thieving and fucking, then off slaughtering cattle in an abattoir. He was mad for the women, and they for he. He'd just shagged three Western girls the day before – one in the morning from the night before, a quickie off the streets in the evening and another at the end of the night.

Stu was only 19, friendly young lad from London, worked in construction. Been here since he was 18, fresh from adolescence, now losing himself to the wilds of the East. Not quite as corrupt as Danny, though he was well on his way. Laid back, kind guy. Turned out he was also well acquainted with Wan from Khao San, and had already heard of me through her! They made a funny pair, similar interests despite their different backgrounds – hard living, hard drinking guys. I could see they'd quickly developed a close bond out here together. I'd ravaged the wilds of Thailand alone mostly, picking up a few scars along the way, visible or otherwise. They'd done it together, forming a strong bond. Pretty much straight away we became a trio.

Back at Jungle I met more staff. Doing the flyers with us was Rin, a cheeky little teenage Thai girl, very friendly with the punters and spoke fluent English in a strange cockney-Thai accent. Swore like a trooper and had a rampant thirst on her too. Ann was in her late 20s, running the downstairs bar, pretty and classy. Behind the bar was a handsome Thai guy, stacked with rippling muscles all over him, young blondes swooning. They had new DJs too, the tattooed, long-haired DJ Edge from Bangkok and his best friend Tony from England. They'd been DJ-ing together in Phuket for years and moved over here for a change of scene.

It was December, the high season in full gear, the place packed with happy punters. The boss gave the nod and Ann passed us some buckets of the old rocket fuel. The holy trinity was back! Me, Danny and Stu hooked up and sucked the old sacred loopy juice down with gusto. That metallic, sickly sweet toxic taste, the instant rush of triumph! The old roar returned with a vengeance. The streets were packed with beautiful party people, skipping along in holiday bliss. We were handing out flyers, giving the spiel, free drinks, flying on our feet, drinking buckets and Chang with that old Southern delight, the high season was here and we were the new crew running the biggest gig on the island! Ha ha! Welcome to the big time baby! The only way is up!

Then out of nowhere appears Joe Conway. I couldn't believe my eyes. I'd emailed him to say I was coming here, but I didn't know where he'd gone since his trip round the North with Ian. I was thrilled to see him again, here on my old stomping ground.

We went upstairs and I showed him round. Young Rin tried ordering us all to dance. Danny and Stu weren't really the dancing types though. Luckily we had DJ Edge and Tony now mixing proper new music, so I didn't have to do any stupid party-starting tricks anymore. The night drowned in an intoxicating river of heavy booze.

I opened my eyes. An empty disco at dawn, the cleaner nudging me with her broom. I dragged my carcass home through the 6am trannies, weirdos and wastrels.

Soon back into the old swing of things, waking up rough as hell and not knowing what to do till 7:30pm. 200 baht wages a day to spend on food and 7-Eleven beers. I got an afternoon job of sorts in an internet shop, clicking stopwatches and collecting fees in return for free internet time. It was normally two baht a minute, so I'd hang out there a couple of hours a day to kill time and meet tourists. Otherwise just wandering around chatting to anyone I vaguely knew. In the course of the day you would usually see everyone you knew at least once, and often a lot more than that, leading to long afternoons of aimless walks and hung-over chats. Ning and I were no longer talking. I guess friends shouldn't sleep together. Though if that friendship was only based on an unrequited mutual lust, I guess it doesn't really matter either way. You both got what you wanted.

Pretty soon there were more *farang* staff flyering at the bar. Two square young English boys straight from school, a couple of young Canadian girls and a brazen Swede named Cornelia. She was throwing it round the island, former clinches passing by every few minutes. Rin unsuccessfully trying to assert some authority over us in between drinks, fags and sexually-charged tantrums with Stu. After a few drunken shags, they'd developed a tense relationship that had bypassed any honeymoon and gone straight to the warring couple phase. Over at sandwich corner was a big gang from Lucky Star, lots of loud pot-smoking Canadian guys led by the big bad crazy Yank Doug, two more Swedish girls, Lena and Fanny, and a Dutch girl we called Double. Joe got a job there too and was now on the circuit.

Soon a room was free at Jungle house, so I moved my stuff into dank little room 4 on the ground floor. Just a bed, some bits of wooden furniture and a wet grimy dungeon of a toilet. Even the midday sun could barely penetrate the darkness. The light barely worked. Ants everywhere. I pulled the cupboard back and found a nest with hundreds of them crawling around. I got a brush and swept them all into the courtyard. I was back in the fold now. Back inside the house of ill-repute, back on the sweet poison, back on the job, selling dreams in the space between Heaven and Hell.

One night I was introduced to Helena, a beautiful young Swedish girl with an athletic body and long blonde hair. She was going to work with us too, I was told. I smiled and said hello. She did the same. As luck would have it, all the other lads were having a night off. I only had

24 hours till the hounds were unleashed. We were getting on well, dancing and sharing our buckets, though it took me a while to get used to her European sensibilities. At closing time the two of us went down to the courtyard, and she challenged me to an arm-wrestle, saying she usually beat most guys. I beat her . . . just. She raised her eyebrows and smiled, sufficiently impressed by my manliness it appeared.

We moved on past the bobbing moonlit boats on the bay front to Coco Loco Bar. I thought my luck must be in but I still wasn't sure. The Thai girls I'd met in the tourist areas usually made it pretty obvious if you were in there, and tended to cut to the chase if you were. But now I had to go through the whole dance of chivalry and charm. So we drank and bopped together but she kept drifting off, dancing away from me towards other groups of drooling guys brandishing two o'clock semi-ons. I stood my ground, not wanting to show any jealousy. But eventually I tired of all the crap. I saw her go to the toilets and positioned myself near the door. On her return I scooped her up in my arms and kissed her young lips. Thankfully she didn't recoil, so I led her out the mating pit and off into the night. I hesitantly asked her if she wanted to go to the beach. "My room is nearer," she calmly replied. "But no sex." Those three words men dread.

I drifted into consciousness like a slow kiss, a soft breeze blowing through the sky blue curtains in the warm yellow room. Helena lay by my side, a sarong wrapped loosely round her hips, her body firm, smooth and supple, tits hard and pink, this bronzed blonde Princess of Gotland. I slipped into a lusty myriad of erotic dreams and sensual visions. I awoke to see her standing by the door with a smile, shower-fresh, water glistening on breasts of iron. I pulled her onto the bed and kissed her passionately, drunk on her foreign scent. I moulded my hands over her supple contours, but whenever I made a move for the pearl she batted my hand away.

We ate creamy pasta at an outdoor Italian on Lodalum Beach. It felt very extravagant compared to my usual diet here of rice, curry and foamy baguettes. That night the hounds returned, eyeing up their new colleague voraciously. I told Danny and Stu I'd pulled her already and they laid off, but one of the other English lads kept chatting her up all night. I watched them in consumptive silence, an intense bucket charge brewing up inside me.

After work Helena wanted to go back to Coco Loco. She was up to her tricks again, dancing away from me, various guys waving their genitals at her and whispering in her ear. This close to the prize I wasn't going to give up on the little prick tease just yet though. Not wanting to be part of the circle of crotch-shakers, I stood my ground by the bar pretending not to look at her. After what felt like an age, she suddenly shimmied up to me through the corridor of suitors with the words, "Shall we go?" The gods were smiling again! We waltzed out together through the bitter sea of green.

Back in her room I kissed her again, clothes falling away, running my hand round her back, across her stomach and down her velvet hips. I reached for the money. Her defences ceased. That warm wet touch of soft gratification. She was ready. I turned her over and penetrated her like a fighter jet taking off an aircraft carrier, flying up vertically into golden clouds of manna! I licked, sucked and fondled every inch of her divine body, the firm flesh, the tanned skin, her little blonde quiff, consuming every moment of a pleasure I knew would be fleeting.

The next day I beamed down the road like the end of the rainbow, target intercepted and destroyed, Mr Stud Muffin, King of the Hill, *Señor* Fuck Daddy himself! I found the guys blowing up balloons at the front of the bar and did a little jig as they cheered. Loosened up by a couple of free buckets, we were persuaded to wear some long white togas, topped with green vines in our hair. Soon we were upstairs dancing round in our rags, getting carried away with the whole Roman theme, people dancing on the stages, in the boxing ring, everywhere. Helena was starting a diving course the next day unfortunately, so went home at 2am. She kissed me goodnight, doing my toga up as I tried not to get an erection through the thin layer of cotton. The night wore ever on, conducting the mob from my parapet, salt, lime and tequilas, birds in bras, fade to black.

Paralysis in the morning. The mind flicks on and off like a switch, but the body doesn't move, the red rum consuming brain cells like a virus, rechanneling my neural networks into a tight knot of twisted phenomena. I was chased around my taut imagination, running round the island chatting to all and sundry, then intensively debating the pros and cons of fleeing the island. Mouth's so dry I can't even swallow. I flail around with my eyes closed but can't find any plastic bottles with water in them. Two hours of this before gathering the inner will to get up. I suddenly throw myself off the bed, fall into the wall, have a long piss all over my feet in the pitch black bathroom, before opening the door to the blinding interrogatory light of the midday Sun. I was falling back into the rot.

Maybe some exercise would break me out of the early cycles of my re-affliction. I found Joe and we caught up on antics. He seemed to be getting into the vibe of the island gradually, though some unknown urge was bubbling away in him. He moved his stuff into my room.

There was a kayak trip I'd always wanted to do – starting in Lodalum Bay, going all the way around the western cliffs of the island and into Ton Sai Bay before dragging the kayak 100m across the thinnest bit of the isthmus back to the starting point. I'd never heard of anyone doing it before but it seemed feasible to me. Joe was up for it, so we rented a kayak late in the afternoon.

We set off, our arms revolving as one, pulling us through the flat warm waters beyond the shadow of the cliffs and out the bay where the sea opens up in all its spectral glory. Past Monkey Beach and the ragged coves on the northern edge of the cape where exotic birds fly across the water's edge. We kayaked on alongside the great vertical cliffs, out of sight from the rest of the island.

Eventually we came to a mysterious gap in the cliffs. We entered a curved opening and found a deserted little secret beach, invisible from the open sea, surrounded by vertical cliffs on all sides. We saw a bamboo ladder going diagonally up over some jagged rocks before disappearing into the dark jungle beyond. It was daring us to continue, but it was getting dark already and the Sun fell quickly here.

We continued on, alone with only the sky, sea and beautiful flickering spectrum in between for company. But soon it was dark – really dark, stuck between the black cliffs and the undulating shadow of the open sea, the winds picking up as we approached the southern tip of the island, swells rising and falling, bobbing around in our little plastic float as waves crashed violently into the hollowed out ridge at the base of the cliffs. The conversation stopped. We were getting concerned. Our arms sped up, cutting the blades faster into the ocean's surface, pain spreading through our upper bodies. We seemed to be going against the wind and waves now, nearly smashing into the rocks as the waves pushed us towards the cliff. Yet another leisurely trip descending into the danger zone. It was slow progress. Every time we reached what looked like the southern tip, another stretch appeared. We soldiered on defiantly, as humans always do in such situations; that yearning for survival, that essential need to live stronger than any other. Eventually distant lights appeared ahead and the waves calmed as we rounded the cape into Ton Sai Bay and the safety of the island, pulling our paddles through the anchored boats in the darkness, exhausted but satisfied.

★ ★ ★

Back on the beat with Danny and Stu. First past the Lucky Star and Predator flyer crew. The Canadians whooping and Swedes throwing their orange-tanned bits about. Doug was off his head on all sorts, swinging Fanny around like a big plump overfed doll much to her delight. Past the restaurant with the Viking-hatted Thai chef, cock-a-doodle-dooing over the barbecue. Past the massage shops with the flirty older women sitting outside all day, giving the old chit chat in our terrible pigeon Thai. We all kind of half-believed we spoke pretty shit hot Thai, having been here all year. We were wrong. Very deeply wrong. Then down the grey brick road, doing the Phi Phi shuffle, swaggering along at 1mph, gut out, proud as punch, handing out flyers to tourists, avoiding divers and locals, chatting to newcomers telling them what's going on.

And the girls of course. We were always looking for girls, scoping out single ladies fresh off the boats, trying to nudge each other out of the way without looking like complete twats, getting in there first with our flyers. Beautiful girls from all over the world, serenading around every night, here on the world famous, tropical paradise island, and us with our VIP passes.

There was a gaggle of slappers from Coco Loco that Danny was mad for, always out flyering with their buckets. We'd pass them a couple of times a night. "Alright boys," said some Northern English girl we called Whistler, due to the gap in her front teeth. "I were fucked last night. Fucking buckets! Mental! I shagged some lad, shagged his mate the night before . . . " And her chubby colleague Pom Pui, tits swinging about everywhere. "Where's your bucket?" Danny asked her. She grabbed her crotch, "Right here love!" and off they went cackling like witches.

Down to the front of Ton Sai Bay, past the banyan tree, more flyers, laughing at the divers watching their fish videos, dodging the "beep beep" locals on their bikes. A couple of cheeky 7-Eleven beers with the friendlier boatmen who were there 24 hours a day, transporting star-struck tourists to distant bays and beyond. Back to the free buckets, adrenaline surging, the bells and the boxing, charging up the hill, dancing in the Jungle, up on stage, friends everywhere, hot girls and crazy guys. Two buckets at once, pouring the sweet nectar down my throat, chin and shirt with maniac eyes, that liquid injection lifting me to ever higher heights.

And so the nights rolled into days and into nights again and on and on as they always do. Plans to slow it down or pace myself always put to an end by one incendiary sip of the juice. But what goes up . . .

Every day began with a pit trap of bottomless doom, mental graffiti, dark deliberations and endless tribulations. Seconds feel like hours. The approaching buzz of mosquitoes in the dark, hungry for my blood. Spiders' webs dance in the corners from the wind of the filthy plastic fan. Lines of ants crawl in all directions. Creatures suck my blood. The dirty gobble gobble of chickens scrambling through the rubbish in the gap outside. Cockroaches appear like scouts of death, before creeping off to report their findings. All is horror, but I'm too fucked to even get off the bed, let alone the island. Worst hangovers ever. No sign of Joe anywhere apart from his bag on the floor.

Danny and Stu banging on my door, dragging me out into the accusatory stare of the equatorial Sun. They were usually up before me, as I would refuse to go home till I couldn't remember doing so. The eyes burn. Tuna and cheese baguettes. All the familiar faces from the shops and restaurants laughing in our faces, "Ha ha, you very drunk last night." Slaps of flashback shame. Dart through the Thai market to avoid everyone. We start eating red hot *som tam* papaya salad and Beer Chang to kick us awake again. Breakfast of champions. A bitter pill to swallow, but one that sets you up for your midday roasting.

Down to the designated swimming area by the pier on Ton Sai Beach, a deep area roped-off from the anchored speedboats. We dive into the soothing warm bath salts and drift into silence. The pain of the morning forgotten as we float into nature's tender embrace. Bobbing around in the crystal clear sea, the three of us look at each other and start laughing hysterically like mad men, struggling to keep our mouths out of the water, half-drowning as our bodies convulse. "Look at the colours! Look how blue the water is, how green the jungle is, how blinding white the sand is! It's so . . . *intense*! Look at the little turquoise fish nibbling at our feet! The fit drunk women everywhere! We're in fucking paradise! It's too good to be true, but it is! It's insane! How can you leave?" This was the Land of the Gods, the dining table where the divine came to feast at the banquet. And we were the ones serving the food.

We're living in paradise . . . *for free*! Everything you want is here at your disposal. Beauty beyond your wildest imagination, free flowing wild water rapids of intoxicating liquor at the biggest club on the island, thousands of beautiful party people coming and going every day, great friends and loose women! This is the world! Everything is here on this one island. This is the world and everything outside a pale imitation. Everyone is here, from the millionaires and celebrities on their yachts down to the penniless fisher folk living in tin shacks on the rocks. All nationalities, all races, all here together in this little glimmer of Heaven on Earth. This is the world!

And it *was* insane, it *was* too good to be true, and we were laughing till we nearly drowned. We were living in that movie. As the ferry brings you to Ko Phi Phi, you cross into an invisible dome where reality ceases to exist, and you enter *The Truman Show*. The perfect island, the perfect job, living the perfect life.

Only the darkness haunted you, the fears and doubts grabbing you by the throat every morning (and at other random moments in the day,) just to remind you that you weren't invincible. Just to remind you that you were slowly killing yourself. Just to remind you that you were losing your mind. Just to remind you that you didn't have a fucking clue what you were doing, and that there were a million and one dangers waiting to pounce.

But how could you leave? How could you ever leave? Whenever the darkness got too much and you started formulating a plan to do a runner, Truman would send in a gift to divert you and dazzle you with His brilliance. "Send in the biting fish," He would say, "Send in the circling eagles. Send in the hot girls in bikinis. Give them free buckets, beer and tequila. Not enough for you? Okay, send in the 2am drunken slut. That'll change his mind." He knew what He was doing did Truman. He had us in His grip. And we loved it. We were contestants on the craziest show on Earth.

But why us? All the tourists said we were lucky. But we weren't lucky. We were tourists too. We'd brought ourselves here. No luck

I OF THE SUN

about it. We'd done it ourselves. Come to the island and got the job. Entered ourselves into the game. The greatest game on Earth.

Was everybody on the island a contestant on the show? We weren't sure about that one. Or was it just the foreign tourists who came here? Or . . . was it just us three? I looked at Danny and Stu laughing. A pang of doubt. Or was it just *me*? Where did they draw the line? Am I the hero of the show? Or am I Truman? Am I the player or the played? My sanity was unravelling.

As night fell the exhaustion set in again. A few moments' rest in the dank room, red lights and music coming through the gaps. Bob whispering at me to *Turn Your Lights Down Low*. 7pm, right on cue every evening. Morale sinks deeper into the cess. Piss in the hole. Flush with the scoop. Shower in a dribble of brown water, keeping an eye on the nasty-looking spider hanging above me. Occasional electric shocks from the light switch in the bathroom. Look in the mirror. Not sure who I see. I start pulling crazy faces, grimacing off the strain of the bucket comedown, playing hardball with my psyche. I look wilfully insane. Step outside and the sweat starts before the shower water's dry.

I tried to take it easy but Truman was having none of it. In came two pumped-up ex-marines from the States and a young English lad, Kung Fu Ken, the three of them fresh from a stint studying at the Shaolin Temple in China. One of the marines had a partial lobotomy from a training incident and was living on disability payments. I was only getting 200 baht a day for my lobotomy. I briefly considered the alternatives. He celebrated life by buying five bottles of tequila for us and all the front bar staff at Jungle. Staggered on till 2am to get my 200 baht, kissing some ginger Israeli girl all the way to her doorstep till she slammed the door in my face.

Another heart-racing morning crusher. Got to get out of here. Death feels imminent. Realise I haven't seen Joe for like a few days or something. Hard to keep track of time here. No one else has seen him either. Check emails but no word. He must have left the island. The mind jitters away. Up to the viewpoint in the midday Sun to see the islands floating in the infinite ocean. Suddenly everything makes sense again.

Stu, Danny and I watch *Braveheart* and *Gladiator* in the DVD restaurants. Talk of freedom and eternity. The self-seduction of the grandiose flames our egos ever higher.

Strut down the street like a superstar, with the occasional panic attack and rib-jab of paranoia. Just gotta ride it out. The Phi Phi arrogance was back in full bloom, and I started to notice it wasn't just me. Every other guy on the island had a certain strut in their step, chest out, lips pouted, an island of gigolo peacocks proud of their roost, the pungent scent of testosterone spray on every threshold.

On the beach with Pom Pui and Whistler. They're comparing who they've shagged on the island and where. I'm pretty turned off by it all, but Danny's salivating, lining them all up in his sights before Pom Pui waddles off suggestively with two guys in trunks.

Back on the job, cool as fuck, with our little tickets to nowhere. Helena's still working, still hot, but keeps going home early for her diving. Occasionally some angel would descend from the heavens, too divine to be of this world. Whoever spotted her first would position themselves to get in there, the others clocking on and fighting their way through the crowds to do a pincer move. Chatting about all the girls on the island, trading names and information.

Another 6am wake up nudge from the cleaner. Nothing like waking up on a plastic chair to start the day. Go up to Stu and Danny's in room 8 to get revenge. Danny's off shagging Whistler. Me and Stu manage a throat-busting joint till I crash out on Danny's bed.

Danny barges in the room with three Changs. "Fucking get on it!" Me and Stu still stuck in semi-conscious crosswords. Senses doing a 360. Downstairs, Joe still AWOL. Attention span ever decreasing. Can't keep my mind on anything for more than five seconds. Body starting to rebel too. Random pains everywhere. Don't wanna work anymore, the Thai staff blowing hot and cold for reasons unknown.

But there are no nights off in the Jungle. Not when you're living in a nightclub. What're you going to do? Have a quiet night in? In your music-pumping, sweat-dripping, insect-crawling hell-hole of a room with nothing but the voices in your head for company? Fucking no chance.

Hot Israeli girl gangs. I recognise one I was necking the other day. I tell the others. "That's the same one I was with!" Danny says. She approaches. Me and Danny look at each other like who's she going to choose? "Hey guys," she says coolly, taking us both by one hand before gliding away. Upstairs I'm losing my cool with Helena, telling me she didn't like anyone but me, till I turn my back and she's necking with this guy and the next. Whatever, fuck it. Who needs women when you've got mind-bending liquor? Enter the maelstrom.

Something clicked in my head the next day, like a switch stuck on 'ON'. *Kee-mao*, perma-drunk, can't snap out of it. The boys drag me out again. Morning beers in the surreal Sun, then round the burning rubbish tips near the cliffs, foul smoke and burning detritus polluting the atmosphere. Reality's taken on an added intensity, significance embedded in every little detail. My skin is burning. It's too much to handle. Feel like I'm going insane.

I needed escapism, so I hid in one of the DVD restaurants playing movies all day. Any movie would do. Anything to escape my own mind. *Khao pad gai kai dao*. Chicken fried rice and a fried egg. *Gai, kai*, chicken, egg, egg, chicken . . .

Exercise! A healthy body for a healthy mind. I jogged down Lodalum Beach as the Sun fell behind the cliffs. I felt enlightened – the realisation that I could stop the pain simply through the power of my mind, hopping along like some jolly jogging Buddha. This must be how people run marathons, I thought. I managed one length of the bay and went back to the bar.

Hiding in the shadows, slacking off work, taking the piss out of every fucker. Two buckets in front of the boss, soaking our shirts in sweet honey. Upstairs Helena's with another guy. Fuck it, have another bucket. We're howling like sea lions in the asylum, on one leg cocked doing the spit roast dance.

I come to, me and Stu with two Thai girls up at 7-Eleven. Then in Stu's room, Danny's off shagging again, rolling round in the dazzling darkness, slobber and limbs flailing around, into the tiny bathroom, see it's one of the fruity massage girls, pants down but no space to do anything, the door's locked, won't open again. I slip over on the dirty wet floor, with my jeans clamped around my ankles and a hard-on.

Sink into the mud of morning like a lame horse in quicksand. A voice tells me to get the fuck out of here now before I flip out completely. Then the moderator telling me to take it easy and relax. Then the strips of evidence ripping through my consciousness – the flashbacks from yesterday, the girls and the glories, the pain and the shame, the ghosts of last night echoing round my head as if they're right here now, speaking to me clear as day. And so I respond, and they respond and we discuss the current situation in such precise Parliamentary detail I forget it's all in my head. Then the overwhelming knowledge that I'm not going to leave the island and I'm going to do it all over again tonight and it's going to be even worse than this 24 hours from now. And the knowledge that I love it, the masochistic demon laughing, urging me to push it ever harder beyond the limit. My mind is the stage to a theatre of the grotesque, one to which I have exclusive and uninterruptable access each morning. Eventually the unrepentant repetition becomes too much and the show reaches its zenith – I must either escape this black pit right now or flip out completely. Sunlight breaches through the crack of the door. I manage to make it to Ton Sai Beach alone, the cliffs of Phi Phi Leh floating symbolically before me, staring out onto the unreachable horizon in irrepressible awe of the beautiful horror of it all. Starting to think I might die here. Because I can't leave.

And as sure as night falls and morning rises, 20 hours later Truman turns up the heat dial sending me into a feverish sweat, the cat's eyes of conscious twinges flicking on after four hours' sleep. Oh God, please not again. I'm dying. Can't think. Can't speak. Got to get out. Dodged my way to the beach trying to avoid Danny, Stu,

Swedish flyer girls or any other deviants, knowing they're part of the problem.

Stuck in *Groundhog Day*, wandering round the village, same people, same conversations every time. Wander from beach to beach; lost in the aimless beauty, overcome by the wonders of nature's glistening jewel till the late afternoon jitters kick in and I feel myself peering into the chasm of nothingness beneath my feet yet again. More emergency Changs.

2am, Danny was nowhere to be seen. I asked Stu where he'd gone. Him and Helena had slipped off together. I'd given him the green light, but hadn't expected him to claim it so quickly. Horny bastard.

Danny describes bucking the shit out of Helena last night. We hit the buckets, the night full of promise, Brazilian women slinking by in floral dresses, a samba spirit on the streets, the Rio carnival surging through my veins.

The world is spinning ever faster now, light and dark merging into one, the cycles of alcohol use making more sense than those of day and night. Only the Creator's little surprises differentiate one moment from the next. Bring on the caged gibbon! Bring on the hanging shark!

I stir my coffee, spinning ripples of bubbles in centrifugal inertia spiralling like little galaxies sucking my warped psyche into a freeze-dried wormhole.

There's a buzz in the air all of a sudden. It's Christmas Eve I'm told. The evening is long and wet, beers flowing harder and faster than normal, the streets packed with excited punters. Boxing in the sky and the golden cock. Shitfaced already. Flashing Santa hats, plastic mistletoe and cheesy trance. DJ Edge in a red skirt. Upstairs, music, sex, booze and violence. The disco counts down to midnight and everyone starts kissing each other in sweaty, drunken fervour. I seem to have ten potentials on the go at any one point, but in between all of the comings and goings, my work, drunkenness, indecisiveness and unwillingness to be seen with one by the other nine; I end up prancing through the middle of them all empty-handed. A girl's looking for Danny. I send her up to room 8 where The Chaser lies in wait with a spliff and a hard-on. An English woman chats me up at the bar, before some drunk fuck acquaintance squares up to me. Then a rumble in the air. Some bloke's climbed over the railings by the side of the bar and fallen off the side of the hill. But he's alive. Nurse Stu drags him all the way to the doctor's shed on the other side of the island. Meanwhile Rin and Co. push me into the middle of another fight. I drag some fuck-up off the floor and escort him down the stairs.

Stu nudges me alive. It's 5am, the place still heaving. The party pours down the hill, yellow light spreading over the dusty pavings, the streets a-babble with drunken nonsense. Everyone's your friend, a star, a comedy legend! DJ Edge chases some clown down the road in his skirt waving a smashed bottle for calling him a ladyboy. Carry on drinking out the convenience stores till me and Stu look around and realise we're the only ones left. Merry fucking Christmas!

Danny bursts in my room, howling like a madman, before the Sangers had a chance to get hold of me. It was the best Christmas present I'd get all day. Then a wasted Stu, face red and slack, passing me a rejuvenating Chang. Then Rin comes in with Kung Fu Ken who she's shagging now. Then his US Marine buddies and some other girls, one after another while I lie sweating in my pants. We reconvened down at the designated swimming area, the marvels of colour infusing our faces with smiles. Christmas in Technicolor paradise.

That evening we had a full Christmas dinner with all the staff and friends from Jungle and Lucky Star together in a Scandinavian restaurant. Halfway through the meal, the rain started.

Afterwards, I went off alone through the muddy puddles to contact the outer world. Amongst the festive emails was one from Joe's family. I clicked it. It contained a short message saying Joe had had an accident at the Full Moon Party, broken his leg and was now in Phuket hospital. What? I read it again and again. Oh no. This was real and this was bad. The first bit I could understand, as he had a long history of getting into scrapes. But why was he in Phuket hospital, on the other coast from the Full Moon Party? Whatever, I couldn't leave him on his own. I had to go there and find him tomorrow.

I then called my family from a busy internet shop full of revellers clattering around happily. "Hello?" I blocked my other ear, trying to hear their voices through the glaze of party noise and my thick helmet of alcohol. My family's faint voices appeared like a distant whisper from another world, echoes from another life. To hear them brought joy, joy to know there were people who remembered me, loved me and cared for me, but also mystification, the disclosure of the glimmering horizon drifting further away from me, not closer. A faint voice said goodbye, a barely audible voice drifting away through the decades out of some plastic holes on the other side of the world, invisible, intangible, gone. "I love you," I said. But all I could hear was the sound of gibberish from all the people around me.

I forced myself up at 9am to get off the island and help Joe. It was more important than all this shit. His backpack was still in the room so I packed a few of his things into a plastic bag. I lay low, avoiding the guys and their morning beers. Had breakfast in an English restaurant watching the world tear itself to pieces on the BBC, before escaping on the ferry to Phuket with a heavy heart, not sure what was what anymore.

★ ★ ★

So it seems that the human mind is necessarily evaluative and these values' origins are rooted in our emotions. So what is the nature of these human values of good and bad? What do 'good' and 'bad' mean? Where do they come from? Are they subjective? Just the views and opinions of individual people? Or are they objective, an intrinsic part of the world, the same for all of us, regardless of any disagreement we may have on them – one side being right, the other wrong? Both views seem enticing.

If we have free will then surely values are subjective? Our own views, with no influence from other people or the world, and no meaning outside our own mind? Surely this is the consequence if we are to consider ourselves as free-thinking individuals? A world of no good or bad beyond what we as individuals think. Everybody's views their own; nobody's better or worse than another's. A world of no meaning beyond what it means to us. Is this indeed the definition of the human condition? To live in a human consciousness of absolute meaningfulness in a world of absolute meaninglessness? It might seem logical, yet there is so much agreement between human beings on our values. Surely values aren't just our own subjective opinions with no relation to the outside world?

It seems that the values of good and bad originate in life and death. Life is good and death is bad, and all things that pertain to one or the other are thought of as good or bad to varying degrees. So if these values are the same for all of us, or universal, then can we say that they exist objectively? Surely there are some universal human values?

It's tempting, but if only human life were that simple. For any example we give of a value that everyone might agree on, there is always an exception. People's reasoned value judgements manifest themselves in action, not thought or speech. Nearly all of us will agree that life is worth living, as shown by the fact we all yearn to survive and improve our lives. Even the negative or depressed keep going. Therefore, is life itself a universal value?

Not to the suicidal, those sad souls who will their own death due to the unbearable misery of life. Not too for those who decide that the life of another is worth less than their own, or some other value of theirs. The murderer, the euthanasia doctor, the abortionist, the soldier, army general, dictator, or democratic leader elected by millions, sending others to death for a higher cause. Whatever you think about these various cases, the fact remains that intentional man-made death is a common occurrence.

It seems life is almost a universal value, but not quite. How about some other examples? We all want to be happy don't we? Is happiness always good? Not to some pessimists, cynics or misanthropes. Is love good? Not to the hater. Are family and friends good? Not to the loner. Is faith good? Not to the atheist. Is wealth good? Not to the ascetic. Is hard work good? Not to the idle. Is sex good? Not to the celibate. Is truth good? Not to the liar. And so the list goes on. For every single example you can give of a possible universal value, you will always find someone that disagrees with it, their values manifested in their actions.

This even applies when going back to the biological question about what level the human instinct for survival operates at. There is simply not one answer. If we have a freer will than any species before us, then the answer is up to us. Some avoid all procreation. Some willingly choose to have no children. Some take care of their children in a family environment. Some have many children with different partners. Some abandon their children. Some lay their own life down for their children. Others sacrifice themselves for other family members, friends or even strangers. Some even willingly sacrifice themselves for a larger cause, be it their nation or religion or other movement. We are free to choose such things.

There is no value which we can say has absolute universal status because there will always be those who disagree. With so many things to value, if you were to question everyone's opinions in enough detail you would eventually come to the point where there was always a variation between the views of any two individuals. No two people have exactly the same values. But this doesn't necessarily have to be considered a problem. It can be considered a marvel that the human mind can develop its own meanings and freely choose its values, though some may not always be seeing the world as clearly as they could.

So if human values are not subjective or objective, what are they?

★ ★ ★

Arriving in Phuket was like being shaken awake from a long sleep. Back in the real world again. Motorbikes, cars, shop houses, market stalls and normal-looking people everywhere. I was in Thailand's largest island, a province in itself, and the largest centre of tourism in the South. I came to Phuket Town, away from the tourist development on the beaches. It seemed pleasant, with dashes of old wooden and stone colonial-style buildings, built by waves of Chinese and European traders. I found a pretty old white arched hotel in the old part of Phuket Town, which seemed like a palace of luxury compared to my room in the commune. I never had TVs on my budget, but it was large and clean. After a long walk I found the international hospital on the edge of town. I was nervous, walking into the unknown, unsure of what was going on. Not sure if he was even here or what condition he would be in.

The blank anonymous faces and sterile atmosphere of the hospital were alien and disconcerting. The stink of chemical hygiene. The receptionist confirmed he was here. My heart beat harder. I was directed to his room but his bed was empty. I was told he was having an operation. A young woman was in the next bed with a broken spine, the joy washed out of her eyes. She smiled at me benignly but told me my friend was in a bad way. For her to say this . . . I felt a gravity closing in around me from every side of the room. I took a deep breath and thanked her.

I wandered round slowly for hours, feeling useless, stupid and confused. I eventually returned to the room and there he was, my long lost brother unconscious in a foreign hospital bed, both legs in casts. He looked thin and weak, but he was okay. He was alive. He opened his eyes and murmured a little but soon passed out again, whacked out on medication. The nurses said it was best if he slept. Another long walk back through the suburbs into town. I wrote to his family to tell them he was okay, deliberating over every word.

I woke up to unfamiliar urban noises with no hangover for the first time in a long time. That long horrible walk again. Approaching the gleaming gates of life and death, through the electric doors and the wave of cool conditioned air, the halls, strip lights, lifts and corridors, nearing the door with trepidation.

He was awake now. His face was grey, creased, stony and miserable. He looked much worse now he was awake, like all the life had been drained out of him. Both legs were heavily wrapped up with his skinny torso poking out the top. There were some terrible bloody infected areas on his body too. He tried his best to explain what had happened though he was confused and I could barely follow anything anyway. I sat frozen. I couldn't take my eyes off his shaking contorted face, the words struggling to come out. It was horrible to watch him like this.

He'd gone to the Full Moon Party in Ko Phangan with various random people he'd met in Ko Phi Phi and others from Laos. Obviously the whole period was a blur. Then he'd gone to Ko Lanta with some other people and at some point throughout the non-stop partying, music, lights, culture shock, chemical blurs and mass confusion found himself lying in a wreck on the ground. He remembered being in an ambulance and now he was here in Phuket, his legs badly broken in various places, skin horribly torn up and infected, concussed, shell-shocked, in constant unbearable pain, drugged up and far beyond the point of safe return. And through all the confusion and pain all he could worry about was his family and how he would hurt them and how they would be burdened by him now. He was worrying so much he couldn't sleep unless he was knocked out with drugs. The doctors told him he was extremely lucky he only broke his legs and not his back or skull. They said he should be able to walk again though it would take many months.

I sat there, sinking in silence trying to take it in, failing to take it in, little idea what was going on or what to do or what to say. Trying to appear optimistic when he fell silent, trying to get more information, trying to get the doctors' help, telling him I'll sort out any hospital issues, his insurance and travel arrangements. And I knew I would, though I had no idea how. But it was a mess, a big, big, horrible mess. It didn't seem real but there was no avoiding the realisation that it was. It *was* happening, it *was* real. And I had to cope with it because my brother was in a far worse position than I. I felt terrible for him, lying there broken, scraped off the floor, moments from death. I stayed there all day, helping move him to a private room and assimilating all the information coming in from him, the foreign representatives and the doctors, trying to make sense of the situation.

I made my way back through the lonely night, gradually accepting and digesting it all. I couldn't help but feel responsible. He may have gone off alone, but it was my actions that had brought him here. I was the one who'd persuaded him to come here with my dumb stories. The one who'd pushed him on and toyed with him on our travels. The one pouring the liquid evil in his glass. The one who helped him get a job on the island. The one who abandoned him when he got there. The ugly truth consumed me. I realised now that I'd hardly spoken to him the whole time we were on Phi Phi together, so wrapped up and smug I was in my own little world. We'd worked in neighbouring bars and even shared a room for a few nights, but apart from our kayak trip I only ever saw him in passing, wandering around drunk and bedazzled. A quick chat and we'd continue on our separate ways. And when he disappeared unannounced I'd barely noticed, assuming he was off to find his own path. And now he was alone in a world of pain. Our childhood dreams had finally come true. And we blew it.

I lay in my hotel room with the lights off for hours. I felt like I should cry or something. But I couldn't. Nothing would come out.

I stayed with him all the next day though we spoke little. There was nothing left to say. We both knew each other's thoughts. I wanted to be there and help out however I could, but I felt useless and uncomfortable as I didn't really know what to say or do. He had barely slept through all the pain, but the doctors were waking him up at 6am and rationing his medication. I got some extra sleeping pills from a pharmacy to knock him out. How could he deal with everything stuck in a hospital bed all day with no sleep to ease the mind?

I didn't know how long he would be here but I had to stay with him. So I checked out of my hotel, came back to the hospital and slept on the sofa in his private room. It was a thin little sofa and I wasn't used to the freezing cold air conditioning, but I felt so exhausted I slept okay. Though it gave me little peace since I knew he was usually awake, legs crushed, spirit defeated, tubes sticking out of his body.

I spent the following days in hospital, trying to sort things out with the doctors and insurance, and emailing his family. Long hours watching crap on TV or reading books in cold silence, sleeping on and off, and emptying his piss pot in the night. The days were long and joyless for us both.

After various conversations, documents, photocopies and red tape, the insurance company said that they would pay all the bills. But conversations with doctors and international coordinators about flying him home went round in circles as they weren't sure he could fly with his legs in casts.

On the night of the 30th I smuggled in some beers, cigarettes and Diazepam for us both which seemed to perk him up a little. I told him I was going back to Phi Phi tomorrow and I'd come back the next day with the rest of his stuff. We opened up a little and had our first decent chat in days before the pills came down over our heads.

I woke up in the morning before Joe for the first time. I watched him asleep. He looked calm and at peace. Though I knew it was fleeting, I felt a little hope for the first time in a week. He was pretty out of it by the time he did wake up. He'd necked the whole bag.

Motorbike back to the port area. Then on the ferry, packed with happy New Year's Eve revellers. The contrasts between what I was seeing and feeling were tearing my head apart. But the sky was thick with cloud and it began to rain hard. Everyone packed inside for the journey through the choppy waves in the turgid green sea as we neared the great red cliffs of Phi Phi's western wall.

Back on paradise, everyone setting up shop for New Year, happy people everywhere, some in costume, music and fun, people kissing and spreading joy. I drank with the guys for what seemed an eternity, but I couldn't get into it.

The day drew into night, this long year on the road finally coming to an end and a new year arriving. On and on it went. I kept drinking in silence and watching the joy of the people living here on this Earth, all too aware that it could all end in one moment, one decision, one movement, one slip, one fall, one gulp, one thrust, one jump, one step, one false move and it was all over.

I remembered all the stupid shit I'd done on my trip. The list went on and on. I'd had some close shaves but no major accidents and I was still alive. My friend had come even closer. He wasn't okay but the intricacies of cause and effect had given him another chance.

We live a life of infinite possibilities, but only one certainty. A certainty most of us shy in the face of. A certainty, a fact, a truth most of us can barely comprehend or accept, but one which we will all acknowledge in time. It's very precarious this short life we have here on Earth. Very precarious and very precious. Use it wisely.

I returned to Phuket the next day with the last of Joseph's possessions. A few days later he got the all-clear and we were driven to Phuket Airport in an ambulance. We said goodbye with few words, sad but hopeful, as he was pushed away into the departure hall in a wheelchair with two white casts sticking out in front. The automatic doors closed behind him, leaving a murky reflection of myself in the world. I had no idea when I would see him again. He was alone but he would be home with his family soon. I told myself he would be okay. There was nothing more I could do. It was over for me. So I let go.

★ ★ ★

Earth's last glacial period ended over 10,000 years ago. By this time humans had developed a greater understanding of nature and were better able to manipulate it. They developed sustainable agriculture and could farm the land, sowing and harvesting plants such as wheat, rice, grains and beans. Other vegetables and fruit followed. Animals like horses, sheep, goats, pigs and chickens were domesticated as another resource for labour, food and other materials. Humans also began forging metal tools made from smelted minerals, and created new technology like bows and arrows, shadow clocks, ploughs and the wheel.

Food surpluses allowed for a greater division of labour into other areas. This led to permanent settlements growing in desirable areas, often in fertile river valleys. The complexity of trade, cooperation and social structures henceforth increased till around 6000 years ago when the first city-states and states began to develop in the region now known as the Middle East. These became centres of population, trade and manufacturing. Permanent military forces were created, as well as different forms of government to administrate.

Pictographs and ideograms were gradually refined into signs and symbols that came to represent parts of spoken languages. Written language developed, aiding the flow of information, communication and taking permanent record of mankind's history for the first time. Generations of oral knowledge and story-telling were set in stone for the first time, and from heroes were born legends.

Governments, economies and societies grew with their populations, states cooperating, competing, and sometimes waging war for land and resources. Around 2000-3000 years ago, states grew into empires which conquered, reigned and fell across Africa, Egypt, Arabia, Persia, India, China, Greece, Rome and Mesoamerica.

Philosophical ideas and religious beliefs evolved. Some were polytheistic, worshipping many gods and deities; others monotheistic, worshipping one God. Some were more focused on human actions. There were countless pagan, animistic and local traditional beliefs, along with larger movements like Zoroastrianism, Judaism, Greek philosophy, Hinduism, Jainism, Buddhism, Confucianism, Taoism, Christianity, Gnosticism, Islam and Sikhism and many other religions, all subdivided into various sects and denominations. Some died out, some continue to this day.

Eventually the Roman Empire expanded across Europe, gradually converting to Christianity and breaking up into small states. Hindu beliefs rose to prominence in India, Buddhism spread East, while Islam rose to become the main religion across North Africa and the Middle East. Dynasties rose and fell in China too, often under attack from nomadic tribes from Central Asia and Mongolia. Great kingdoms and centres of learning and trade also came and went across Africa, Southeast Asia, Japan, Korea and the Americas.

Over the centuries, great advances were made in technology – irrigation, mining, metalwork, textiles, printing, architecture, engineering, roads, compasses, chariots and gunpowder. Advances were made in science, anatomy and medicine, mathematics, logic, geometry, astronomy, navigation and cartography, economics, art, literature and education. The world and humankind's possibilities within it were exploding with energy and ideas like never before.

EIGHT

Charlie's gone. Joe's gone. But I'm still here. Irresponsible and free. Low on cash and high on time. Anything was possible. For now though I had little choice but to get back to my free room until I worked out my next move. Little choice but none. Would I learn any lessons from this experience? I didn't know. Lessons aren't learnt overnight. I just wanted to escape the pain and forget. And what better way to forget.

So I returned, back to the circular rhythms of life on Ko Phi Phi – the morning hangovers, breakfast beers, afternoon meanders, evenings at work and nights of bucket-fuelled madness. The joy and the suffering, up and down, round and round. And as the days turned to weeks, the amplitude and frequency of the oscillations increased . . .

The Truman Show was moving into primetime now. The rains were called off and the colours burned through the screen. The piercing bright skies, the brilliant blue ocean, the screaming green trees and the blinding white sands. Jungle Bar was the busiest on the island and it seemed like I knew everyone here. Mr Popular on Paradise Island, where the booze flows freely and the girls are easy. These were the Days of the Senate and we walked the streets of Rome like centurions. Everyone knew us. Everyone wanted to be our friends. For we ruled the Empire. Men gave offerings of food and drinks, pleading to join us. Women would massage our backs and offer themselves to us. As pretenders to the throne came and went, we passed judgement with an extension of the arm and a raising or lowering of the Imperial thumb. Submission or death? Judgement passed, fate sealed. We were gods.

One morning I was sat on the stools at the front of the bar having a sandwich when suddenly Kookie from Khao San turned up, looking for work in her miniskirt and dyed red hair. She was alone and assured me Sin wasn't going to follow. So I asked the boss and soon she was flyering at Jungle's. She was very grateful, giving me the odd backhander when she came into any sudden influxes of cash. They started doing female boxing which she got into too, beating up someone's girlfriend to further the bottom line.

Danny and Stu had an idea which we put into action, organising the island's first ever wet t-shirt contest on stage upstairs. Cornelia, Double Dutch, Lena and Fanny got stuck in plus a wasted Rin. Danny and Stu were already both humping Rin and Cornelia on unfruitful nights. Danny had already had a go on Double Dutch and Lena as well. Only the silicone-titted Fanny remained.

Stu and I were chucking water while Danny was on stage helping relieve the girls of their white t-shirts. The mob roared with appreciation for the Senate's gift to the people! They cheered for their favourites. A few looks between us and we announced the winner as Fanny, on account of her tit job and the fact that Danny hadn't banged her yet. She'd get her prize. On the wooden walkway outside room 8 a few hours later. Rabid beasts! Wet t-shirt contests, boxing promotion and pimping. We were branching out in all directions.

But this wasn't enough for my ever-swelling ego. One lunchtime me, Stu and Danny were wandering around when my old friend Mr Kit suddenly popped up; the guy I was vaguely planning beach parties with on my first stint here. He remembered me and invited us to go to Maya Bay with him. I hadn't been to Maya Bay since my return, so why not?

So we boarded a long-tail boat. He knew all the boatmen on the beach. All excited I started to give it the big'un about how we were hanging with the big boys now. The merest whiff of power is sufficient to corrupt. Stu and Danny said little all afternoon. On the way he started telling us about how he was the boss of the island and how it was worth hundreds of millions of baht and generally scaring the shit out of us. We got there and swam beside the most photographed beach in Thailand, the pearl of the Andaman, 'The Beach', surrounded by towering cliffs in a majestic goblet of warm salt juice. Tourists only went there on day trips, so there was no accommodation. It was protected by the locals who collected the valuable swiftlet nests from the cliffs.

Mr Kit beckons us over to the little huts on the side of the beach and gives us food, beer, joints. The mind loosens. Then he pulls me over for a chat. "I want you come work for me on Maya Bay. You sell . . . ice cream," he smiled, passing me his joint. Says I can live there in the tiny huts with the local family that tend to the beach, sell cold drinks and 'ice cream' and have everything taken care of for me. Realisations of *Robinson Crusoe* form in my mind. "Why me?" I asked. "Because . . . I think you have good heart." Contemplations stirred in me, delusions of ever greater grandeur spiralling out of control. No Westerners live on Maya Bay. It is 'The Beach'. The global symbol of escape, of paradise. It *is* paradise! Beauty beyond compare. And for me to be the only foreigner actually living there! I would be some kind of legend. So . . . shall I embrace my destiny? Then the negatives kick in. Stuck on an inescapable island in the service of the dodgy island boss. Not cool. It all sounded too good to be true. "You can go fishing, catch lobster, go kayaking," he tells me. "We have guns. You can shoot . . . for fun!" Okay, nervous smile time.

But the offer was seductive, as the dangerous often is. We went back on a speedboat as the Sun set over the western ocean, the gigantic cliffs of Phi Phi Don looming to our right, then round past Monkey Beach and into Lodalum Bay, a ride so beautiful it stays ingrained in your mind forever, a beauty that will haunt you for life. Stu looked at me with some awe after our free trip around paradise. "What was that all about then?" I had no answer, for I had no idea. But from that day I believed myself to be the chosen one, the newly self-anointed King of Paradise. That was until I returned to the evil of room 4 and the gates of paranoid insanity banged shut. What was I *thinking*? Crawling under the thumb of a gun-toting mafia boss! What have I done now? Panic racked my body whenever the thought bobbed above the flood waters of anaesthetic.

I had to avoid the pier area from now on, as this was where he and the boatmen usually hung out. But Phi Phi ain't big. He saw me a couple more times, closer to where I worked in the middle of the island. He kept asking when I was coming, looking increasingly disappointed each time I stuttered out some dubious delaying tactic. My paranoia became geographic, half the island off limits now.

More 5am piss ups, high season, bars all packed, and me and Danny are flyering the streets in the early evening as usual. A middle-aged Thai man in smart casual clothing, who I don't recognise, comes up and asks for a flyer. This never happens. I smell trouble immediately. He looks at the flyer and sees where we work. "You know who I am?" he orders. "Immigration." He's undercover from the mainland looking for foreign workers. We'd heard about it but hadn't seen it until now, and now it was too late. He orders us back to the bar. We are told to fetch our passports and wait at the front of the bar. Stu and the others disperse while me, Danny and Jimmy have to sit there while the management thrash things out. We have a final beer and mull over how to get hold of a large sum of cash, deportation or a sobering stretch in Krabi prison. "We've had a good run mate, but nothing lasts forever," says Danny with a thousand yard stare. But after an hour everything is sorted and we're free to go. I'm relieved but starting to feel the coastline closing in.

A few days later, curiosity took me for a long swim along the western cliffs of Ton Sai Bay past the climbing wall. The same place the stingray got me. I swam alongside the massive vertical cliffs until I came to a deserted beach which is visible from the bay, but few people venture to. Looked around the thin beach, cliffs and coconut husks. On the swim back I passed a tiny wooden hut perched on the rocks, where the cliffs meet the sea. About eight local guys were there now sitting on a wooden platform by the hut, their boat bobbing on its mooring. And this being The Truman Show and me being the star of said show, they call me over. Not one to say no, I swim over and sit with them tentatively. They have that wild lawless look in their eyes, intense bullet-eyed stares that cut through your soul. And so they pass me their bamboo bong. Too intimidated to say no, so I say yes, sucking up the old anti-reality fumes.

"We mafia," they tell me straight-faced. Here we go again. Hold it together. More logs to the fire of my burning paranoia. They are the bird nest collectors of Phi Phi, they tell me, and this is one of their camps. They tell me all about their work, how they sell the nests on to the government who sells them on to China and other countries. Oh and how they kill anyone who tries to steal the nests. Nice enough blokes apart from that, but I'm being told far more than I want to know. I eventually calm down and tell them about my work in the bar. After a while I make my excuses and leave.

Why can't I just sit on the beach and travel the easy way like all the carefree holidaymakers I see around me? Curiosity and the cat. I returned to my room stoned and paranoid but still in one piece. I went to work telling the guys about my latest run-in.

After another heavy night I awoke in my usual mental turmoil, mosquitoes whizzing around my ear. Eventually opened my eyes, and through the ants noticed a little paper note that had been pushed under my door. What the . . . ? I unfold it. It's got my name on it in English, followed by some Thai script. Shit. Shit! *Shit*!!! Soul implosion. Mind overdrive. What does it say? Who wrote it? The bird nest collectors? Mr Kit? They all knew where I worked. It wouldn't be hard for them to find out my room number. Oh God . . . What's happening? No . . . I'm just paranoid. I calmed myself down. But just a little. Maybe it was from someone in the bar. A jealous boyfriend? An angry boxer? Or perhaps it's just a love note from a girl? I gotta find out. But who can I ask to translate it for me? I racked my brain for answers. I didn't want to show it to anyone at the bar in case it involved someone else from there. I needed help.

I went up the rickety wooden stairs to Danny and Stu's room and explained my predicament. They had no idea what to do either. We avoided the girls at the front of the bar and went to the little shack where we had our hangover breakfasts of *som tam* and Chang. I decided to show the friendly woman the message. She read it and looked at me strangely. "It says – I don't want to see you again. If I see you again . . . I kill you. Birdman."

It's a death threat. This is it. I've fucked up big time. Gotta get off the island! Right now! I sat there shaking in white terror, planning my rat run through the quietest alleyways to my room and the pier. Just grab my bag and get the first boat out of here.

"So what ya gonna do?" Danny's voice trembles. I look up. Fluids are leaking out of Danny and Stu's strained red faces, trying to hold their laughter in. They see I've caught on and explode in breathless laughter, snot and tears pissing down their faces. They'd got up before me and asked Ann to write the message. It showed me what kind of state I was in, that it never occurred to me it could've just been a wind up. The tricks the mind can play on itself . . .

The Senators' evil plot thwarted, that night the King of Paradise drank himself into oblivion before retiring to his quarters and falling into a deep dream. Back on his throne, the sublime beach of Maya Bay. But it was different now. It had been developed, the dunes and jungle replaced by concrete buildings. And the cliffs had been carved away to make space for the gigantic electricity generators that now stood there, built into the very walls of the bay, buzzing away for the tourists' convenience.

I emerged from the delta of semi-conscious narratives and half-thoughts and was whisked away by my companions onto a wooden boat, over turquoise waters, shiny as the eyes of God, and I sat there on Long Beach, my head a turbulent fog, and looked around at the water and the land, the floating crown, the impossible beauty, this paradise alive and me living here in this impossible life, contemplations of the Mastermind up above, soaked in the rays of the Sun, and suddenly it felt as if that dream, the dream of the beach felt more real to me than this consciousness here now. Bobbing in the sea, my eyes cut across the surface, the bottom of the ocean and the top of the mountains are one, fish swimming with eagles flying with fish. Is this real life? The world was pulsating with energy and spirit, everything moving, everything changing, there was no doubt about it anymore. The world was alive in waves and I just a mere ripple.

The beauty, the job, the status, the life you've always dreamt of. Why be a little fish in a big pond when you can be a big fish in a little one? And what a pond! Too good to be true. Why me? I looked down. That dark abyss lurking underneath. The feeling that the carpet could be swept from my feet at any given moment, if not by the world then by myself. So tired, so unfit, an expanding gut, rampant alcohol abuse, a creeping towards death, gnawing sexual desire, not knowing where you're going, memories of the past, the ghost haunting my mind, and the sudden pangs of absolute horror as you feel that at any moment right now your head is going to fucking explode. Sometimes it feels too heavy a burden to bear. All I have to do is leave.

But Truman wouldn't allow it. That night, in is thrown a hot young Danish girl, shaking her buxom titties up to me on the dance floor out of nowhere. No friends, no competition, she's all mine, a beautiful gift from above. I slammed the door behind me, ripped her clothes off and ate her out like a free buffet at a Michelin restaurant, juices dripping down from the bridge of my nose to the bottom of my chin, like the blood of a lion's prey. How can I leave? I mean, what do you want? King of Paradise or another ant in the ant hill? What do you *want*?

★ ★ ★

The switch goes on again. I'm alone except for myself, a self screaming at my mind. Causal laws no longer apply, a consciousness strobing under siege from a twisted melee of unconnected mental phenomena – colours, faces, conversations and pains. Can't think or speak. I'm going mad. Gotta get out of here.

I make a break for it, relishing the simple application of my will.

312

I take a trip on my old favourite, the late afternoon boat to Ao Nang, past the ancient island monuments of wonder, soaking up the Sun, trying to move on. Move on into the past. I hadn't been in Ao Nang for six months, my old training ground and scene of my lowest ebb. I was pleased to escape the relentless revolutions of the island, but apprehensive of what I might find back there, my chemical-riddled moods alternating like the flapping of a mosquito's wing. Arriving at the jetty on the edge of rural Ao Nang, I got the large *songtaew* past the grassy picnic areas and soft strands of the casuarina trees of Nopparat Thara Beach, past Moon Bar, over the bridge, round the bend to the beachfront and the shops hiding the entrance of Spicy Park, memories flashing past me clear as day.

I booked into Mermaid Guesthouse again but the staff had all changed. A bit like entering your old home with a new family inside. But a bigger shock hit me further up the road towards the girls' old house. Just six months on, I recognised only pockets of the quiet old ghost town whose dusty strip I once strutted. Three new high-rise hotels pierced the once-sacred palm tree line, new side-streets dug out to serve them. I turned into the *soi* where Shamrock once was. The empty waste ground opposite was now a gleaming bank. Only the shell of my old street theatre remained. The corrugated iron and wooden frame now a makeshift camp full of workers, all eyeing me over accusingly as they carpentered wood in the shade. I felt like telling them this used to be my playground, my temple.

But the biggest shock was to come. Very recently I'd dreamt of a future Ao Nang, with a massive new shopping plaza where the village lanes once ran. Further up the road I couldn't believe my eyes. Large new commercial blocks had been erected from nowhere, almost exactly as I had dreamt it, large posters promising a McDonald's coming soon. Tourists, mostly couples and families everywhere. Fervent traffic. This was a fast-developing tourist resort, not the sleepy holiday village of before. The Thais had told me it used to be handfuls of wooden huts ten years ago. Every beach in Thailand used to be handfuls of wooden huts. Not anymore. Pattaya, Phuket and Ko Samui were all over-developed, polluted urban sprawls now. Would Krabi province go this way too?

I went to Ao Nang Beach, my first beach in Thailand, and went for a long swim towards the cliffs. At least the beach hadn't changed. As I pulled myself through the waters again, a different man from ten months before, heartfelt memories came pouring back to me, and I was back there again – newly arrived in Thailand, a young man on the road, full of hope and expectations of a future unknown, innocent and naive. Before it all melted away in the heat of the Sun.

I caught up with my old diver friend Nick, who told me Sally had been forced to move on due to all the new hotels. Round the usual bars till I was ready for Spicy Park. It had been a while now and I was curious to see it all again. Inside the gathering of quiet beer bars were a few familiar faces and the odd hello. Did they really remember me? I'd been down that road so many times before I almost laughed at my own stupid paranoia. Almost. A few drinks at Dream Bar till my booze-laden serenity was sliced through with Jeab's spine-tingling growl and razor sharp smile. There's little conversation between us, though she calls me her 'ex', as she works the room, eyes like an eagle, lady drinks, dancing and pool. Young Noi is there too. I couldn't help but feel sorry for her as I caught her staring into space occasionally, a look of hopelessness embedded on her face. She said Lek and Dear had left town.

The following day I took a longboat around the cliffs from the mainland to the hanging gardens of Railey Beach, where macaques swing from trees and tangles of electric wires. I then double-backed, over the rocks at low tide and on to Ton Sai Beach. Whereas Railey was an exclusive beach resort, here had more of a laid-back traveller feel to it. Climbers dotted the dripping cliff faces and a TV commercial was being filmed at the large overhang where the cliffs met the sand. I looked across the sea for a moment, seeing the silhouette of Phi Phi on the horizon. I missed it already. Here I was nobody again.

Beach bars merged with wooden bungalow operations as I went inland along jungle paths looking for my old friend Bird, who Nick told me was here now. I soon found him in a climbing shop hidden in the trees. "My friend!" he beamed, skipping over and poking me in the belly, "You're fat!" He laughed his head off. Not exactly the reception I'd hoped for, but it was good to see him again. He was calm and balanced again, not the confused, sexually-frustrated bucket casualty of before. He couldn't believe I was still here. He was happy and content, helping out with the tourists at a climbing centre. It was a beautiful spot in the jungle, surrounded by surreal cliffs leading down to one of Thailand's finest beaches.

Bird led me down to the beach at night and I met some of his buddies in the quiet beach bars. This was nothing like Phi Phi. An older more mature crowd, many staying for months at a time, most of them rock climbing at these world class sites. There was a kind of pseudo-hippie-yuppie vibe about the place. People into nature and travelling, drink a bit, smoke a bit, but not to the extremes of the party crowd. They had real lives back home, from which this was a temporary escape – high flying city jobs, or maybe a trade or freelance work they could go back to anytime. While Bird was chatting up some Western girls, his American friend suggested I stay a while and learn to climb in these beautiful surroundings. I looked at the people around me, all shiny and healthy, untroubled but slightly dull. And I looked at myself, beer bottle surgically attached to my hand, a burgeoning gut and bogged up brain. I felt a little envious. Was it really that big and clever getting drunk for free every night, clowning around on stage, slowly drowning my sorrows with every passing turn of the Earth? I wanted to know what it was like to be fit and strong, to swim with dolphins, climb mountains and run like a wild animal. I told them I'd be back, before going to a little Full Moon Party at a bigger bar and getting leathered. It was nowhere near being the underground rival to Ko Phangan that I'd hoped for. Eventually Bird pulled me out of a deckchair and we went back up the hill through the silvery shadows of the moon-lit jungle.

I woke up in Bird's tent which he'd kindly lent me while he slept outside in a hammock. Good old Bird. It was a joy to wake up in this enclave, surrounded by the sounds and aromas of the verdant jungle with fresh moist air and animals cooing. But it wasn't enough for me. I said goodbye to Bird and carried on up the hill along a narrow mud track as the jungle thickened. Over fallen trees, sweat dripping, insects whirling, taking in the sensations of this isolated wonderland. I eventually came to the muddy flats and mangrove trees of Railey's east beach and took a long-tail boat on to Krabi Town.

I loved this corner of the world. But still the visions of paradise and the inner abyss of imminent doom, these poles of life and death, were pulling me apart. An acknowledgement was growing that this must end soon. I was going back to Phi Phi for now, but there had to be changes, I had to exert my own will over myself. After just two nights away, I'd gone from seeing my perma-drunk antics as comical to pathetic. A young alcoholic slouched in a deckchair, blind drunk every night. Blind. Sometimes you've got to take a step back in order to go forward again.

As I returned across the Sun-kissed effervescent waters and back into The Truman Show, I could hear Danny and Stu goading me back with their buckets and japes. And I did love it, for it was me to a large extent, but not all of it. And as much as I loved the delusion, the suntan, the beer gut and swagger, the laughs, fame and adoration, the booze and the birds, the fact remained my mind was hanging on tenterhooks by its last sinews. Half of me wanted to stay here forever. But I knew it had to stop pretty soon before I A-bombed my own brains with the over-stimulation.

★ ★ ★

Back to Phi Phi in good spirits and even better intentions. The ferry was packed. Pleasure craft filled the bay. I chatted with a Thai guy I knew from the little Bamboo Bar on the beautiful sands of Lodalum

Beach where we sometimes hung out in the afternoon. He spoke of his worries about the future of the island, how it was sinking under the weight of development here. "You come back here to Phi Phi in 20 years, you old man, nothing, just water." I looked at the rising plumes of toxic smoke where the rubbish was burned. I thought about the brown water that came out my tap. I looked at the endless lines of tourists and buildings. On the pier I looked down at the shoals of tropical fish through the oily slicks on the water's surface. Pearl of the Andaman, victim of her own beauty, consumed, raped and abused by every hungry tourist here, hungry for their own slice of the cake.

Straight off the boat I'm accosted by Mr Kit, all impatient and business-like. "Where you go? Okay, you come work for me in three days. You sell ice cream for me okay?" he said smiling that unnerving gold smile. Says he'll buy a tent for me, I can go fishing, kayaking, and shooting of course. "I boss here. Some people don't like me, want trouble with me, but I good man." "Why me?" I ask, despairingly. "I think you have good heart. You my friend. I want to help you. I give you good money if you help me. Three days and we go." And then he's off in one of his boats. My instincts are telling me to run a mile, getting involved with this guy. I mean, what does he really want from me? All the talk of guns, drugs, money, mafia and police is freaking the shit out of me. And yet . . . the dream won't die. King of Paradise, the Legend of Maya Bay, waking up to perfection, an island outlaw, a life beyond your wildest imagination. It might be the best thing I ever did. But my friend from home Johnnie Drummer was coming soon and I wanted to spend time with him. The pier area was therefore well off limits. Welcome back to the show ladies and gentlemen.

I wasn't 100% pleased to be back at work, my mind still seduced by the escape of nature. My old colleague Katie was back, so I had more voices of reason around me than before. I cut down on the booze a little, holding back on the buckets till after midnight at least. The next day I went skipping along the rocks on the east side of Lodalum Bay like a mountain goat, before hammering the front crawl back to the beach. The next afternoon, played football with the locals at low tide. More *som tam* with the boys, gradually egging ourselves on with more chilli peppers every time. We were up to five peppers each now, sweating profusely with the wake-up buzz. And I hooked up with the woman I'd met on Christmas Eve. My strength was returning.

To combat the sleep deprivation and morning madness I decided to start chewing on Diazepam as soon as I got my first wake up of the morning. One morning I was rolling round in brain-dead slovenly delight till I heard a sudden knock on the door. My old friend Johnnie Drummer had found me. We'd been housemates back home, so he knew me as well as anyone, but was more level-headed than I, often acting as a voice of caution for my more wayward plans. I'd only seen him briefly in Vang Vieng a while back, but he'd obviously been enjoying himself. I was pleased he'd travelled alone before meeting me, so we could hang out on equal terms. I was tired of being the tour guide. We celebrated with a cold Singha lunch at Bamboo Bar.

Johnnie dragged me down Lotus Bar after work, a chill-out bar on the way to Long Beach where people lay on the sand smoking and watching fire shows through the night. I generally avoided the place, as it inevitably involved joints being stuck in my mouth, before stumbling around nauseously in the dark at 5am on the wrong side of the island. Dangerous place.

Stu and Danny suddenly tell me they're leaving the island to travel a bit before heading off to New Zealand in a couple of weeks. I'm surprised they're leaving so suddenly, so we head straight down to Bamboo Bar at 11am and get tanked up all day with Mad Doug and Johnnie, till we're blind drunk in the scorching afternoon Sun, wrestling in the shallow waters, pulling Stu's trunks off and trying to drown each other in front of the sober sunbathers. We hit it double hard that night, torrents of booze, Doug getting out the gear till dawn.

Danny and Stu drag me out of bed for the final time, flashbacks of the clowns' parade in Lucky Star last night clearer than my current vision. We have our final three *som tams* with ten rat shit chillies in each, the culinary equivalent of French kissing the Devil, face burning, body sweating, masochistic rage! We've all lost the plot. One minute laughing uncontrollably, the next minute staring into the abyss. I can see the boys have had enough. Months and months on the constant piss. Stu knows he's got to get off the booze. He looks permanently screwed, all red eyes and expressionless face. Danny's a shaky bag of nerves too. I saw them off at the pier, as their boat took them away to new adventures. Farewell my friends. Until the next time. Though like everyone else I'd met on my trip, I had no idea if we'd ever meet again.

I wandered back to Bamboo Bar and sat alone feeling confused suddenly. What was I doing here? Wasting away, an aimless, crazy alcoholic. Don't know what to do or where my life is going.

But the game wasn't over yet. Truman had yet more tricks up His sleeve. The mysterious bald Swiss man who'd been on the island alone all high season was a Bamboo Bar regular too. He was obviously well-off as he had his own speedboat which he used to go wake boarding. He came over and we got chatting as best we could through the boundaries of our languages, eccentricities and hangovers. We were joined by Johnnie and Katie with her female friends. Then it came. "Why don't you guys come with me on my speedboat to Bamboo Island?" I love it, I fucking love it! The flyer crews from Coco Loco and Pirate Bar were having a little beach party there today which we'd swerved to see the boys off.

And so we boarded our host's speedboat and shot off out of Lodalum Bay, around the long northern cape of Ko Phi Phi Don before heading across the open seas, past the rugged rocks of Mosquito Island towards the beaches of the desert island of Bamboo. Me and Johnnie stand at the front of the boat, gripping onto the metal bar, bouncing up and down like bucking broncos in the waves, the raw power of the beast and the beauty going straight to our heads like a shot of adrenaline to the cerebral cortex. Insane laughter, ego eclipsing the Sun, we arrive at Bamboo Island, my competitors having their little party. They gaze at our speedboat in wonder as I give the royal wave from the bow of the ship, chest out, pouting like some Roman demi-god. The Days of the Senate were over. The Emperor now ruled alone.

They looked at us in disbelief. All I needed was a bottle of champagne and a supermodel. And the keys to the speedboat perhaps. One day . . . So we stepped off and joined their little party, arrogance beyond belief. Some looked on in admiration, others in jealousy. Such things are to be expected. One of the Pirate guys refused to sell us any beers from their cool box, but eventually relented. We sank one can each and left. The crazy Swiss man, spliff hanging out his mouth, cut up one of their rented long-tail boats, waves sending it crashing round on its anchor. One of the girls tries to take a photo of me and Johnnie but complains, "The Sun's between us." The Swiss man laughed like a maniac. "There is nothing between us!" he proclaimed, before powering off towards the horizon. The Emperor's coronation ceremony came to an end, strangulating narcissism, consciousness like a frozen lightning bolt.

As the Sun set, I returned to the squalid reality of my damp insect box for an intense panic attack in the dark. What goes up must come down. Then I got on it again.

★ ★ ★

Little blue breakfast in bed and soon I'm driving a gigantic cruise liner down a big skyscrapered street, turning the ship's wheel, deliberately bashing it from side to side of the road taking out everything in my path. I find a coconut, break it open and a dozen large chicklets come out with multi-coloured, bobbled fur, blue, pink, yellow and green. Then a beautiful blonde appears in my room, sex so vividly sordid I wake up questioning whether it actually happened or not. I go for a long swim across the dreamy bay, occasionally laughing hysterically to myself, sea water pouring into my gullet.

Opposite the Jungle rooms, the old resident artist, Pablo, was painting a huge mural along the inner wall of the downstairs courtyard, about 15 metres long. It depicted a scene that struck an unnerving chord. In the centre was a huge tree of life, naked women lying in its shade, covered in long coiled snakes and empty booze bottles. To the left were a multitude of sharks, rays and turtles, the sharks devouring the bodies of errant scuba divers, blood and severed limbs everywhere. And to the right were the twisted, skinless bodies of tortured souls, their muscles and agonised faces contorted and entwined together. At the far right was one figure, his skin burned away, just his red muscles visible, eyes closed but trying to escape the scene. One afternoon I was admiring Pablo at work. "When I feel crazy . . . I paint. When I not crazy . . . I not paint," he explained wide-eyed. He pointed at the figure on the right. "This man . . . is you. I see you in Jungle Bar upstairs, you stand up, you eye not open, you sleep. I paint you here." I'd never been painted before. I felt kind of honoured, though the portrait was less than flattering. The *hedonista*, suffering in Sun-drenched hell, led astray by the tantalising pleasures of paradise. It summed up the state of affairs perfectly.

Two more English lads and a Hungarian guy had started working at Jungle, but I didn't speak to them much at first, missing the old crew. Johnnie got a job singing with the band at the Rock Bar, on the island where all your dreams come true. Just be careful what you wish for. Every few nights the band played the outro of *November Rain*, the lyrics and electric solo coaxing the solipsistic hubris to ever greater heights.

Up at 8am again. Not again, please God. I pop another pill to lull me through the morning chorus of schizophrenia. I'm drifting into chemical peace again when my alarm clock suddenly goes off. What the . . . ? Why did I set my alarm? . . . Oh shit. I forgot. I've got to go to Krabi Town Immigration Office today to extend my visa for another month. Contemplate fucking it off but realise it isn't going to go away. Drag myself up and zigzag the streets as the Diazepam battles my rampant hangover for supremacy of my consciousness. Get a boat ticket and KFC orders from the travel agent girls. On board, downstairs, air-con, pass out across four seats.

Still feeling wobbly disembarking in Krabi Town. It all looks dangerously normal here. Get a set of passport photos done, unnerved by how positively insane I look in them. Dirty tan, dead-looking face, shifty eyes and hair everywhere. Trudge up the hill to the Immigration Office when another realisation hits me like a frying pan. I was walking straight into the hands of the people who'd arrested me two weeks earlier. And I was alone now. Nobody could help me . . . No, no, no, hold it together. I briefly contemplated taking a bus for four hours to the next Immigration Office, before going in nervously and quickly signing the forms, avoiding eye contact with any of the officers. I escaped to the shopping centre a free man and got the KFC order in.

Made it back for work in zombie mode. Things weren't the same since the lads left though. I went flyering with Kookie and the Hungarian guy Gyorgy. He was a handsome athletic guy of 28. He seemed nice enough but was very cocky and sure of himself. He claimed to have seduced one of the massage girls Danny and I always flirted with on the walk of fame. He described sensual scenes of them massaging each other into the night in room 8 which he'd moved into. But they didn't go further as he had a girlfriend back home. He was a former kickboxer with a shady past, and was now cycling around the world intermittently, sleeping in a hammock by the side of the road during his cycling stints. He'd recently got stuck bartending on Ko Tao for a few months, and now he was here. I wasn't sure what to make of him.

Kookie was giving Rin a run for her money now on the cock-hunting stakes. Though they got on, there was a bit of unspoken competition between them. Johnnie was flyering and singing at the Rock Bar. Doug was up to no good, drugging the caged gibbon with a banana full of sleeping pills and getting into late night scraps with obnoxious tourists. I got to know the new English guys working at Jungle better. They were regular young lads, like Danny and Stu, but we didn't quite connect in the same way. Gyorgy was jumping in everyone's faces with flyers and cheesy grins; then showing off, walking down the street on his hands. I felt a twinge of envy with the women swooning over him, his athleticism and constantly cheery nature. It was all a bit too much for me to take in my precarious state.

I went to Lotus Bar with Jimmy after hours, past another late-night brawl at sandwich corner. I never liked going there as it generally involved rolling round in the sand talking crap. We sat in a large group but I had nothing to say to anyone, staring out at the bobbing lights in the bay. Lena from Lucky Star sat with me, and we had a normal conversation for the first time, instead of the usual bucket and flyer crap. She started talking about how she missed Joe and what a great guy he was. Hearing his name spoken was a shock. I realised I'd been trying to block out the whole episode. It echoed like a ghost from a past I didn't want to revisit. I went off into the darkness, down and lonely.

Contemplate another pharmaceutical breakfast but decide they are probably not helping things. My moods were flickering ever faster. Swinging between feeling like an Emperor to a pathetic little piece of shit on the lost shoe of nothingness. Need to get out of here but money's low and I don't know where to go. Still apprehensive about living in Bangkok as memories of the street life in Khao San seem even more horrific than this. Faint memories of family, friends and home. I decide I have to go home by the summer.

★   ★   ★

A trek round the island was organised by Gyorgy, with myself, Johnnie Drummer, the two new guys from Jungle and two Canadians from Lucky Star coming along. Gyorgy was in irrepressible spirits, leading the way with a bandana and big wooden stick as we clambered over the massive grey rocks along Lodalum Bay, past deserted stretches of sand, the village growing smaller behind us. At the end of the bay we found a little trail going up over the ridge through the jungle. Straight up, sweating like soldiers stuck behind enemy lines ploughing on through the trees, then down again to a flat area on the north of the island that

I'd never been to before. Eerily quiet but strangely ordered, trees laid out neatly around empty bungalows. No one in sight, like we'd missed the place's heyday. We clambered over the cliffs to a hidden beach surrounded by craggy rocks, swimming through the coral, letting the Sun's rays permeate our souls.

While the others swam on, I had a joint and a proper chat with Gyorgy for the first time. I quickly realised there was more to him than my hollow first impression. "You are not the same as these other guys," he tells me. "I can see in your eyes . . . Do you meditate?" he asks. "Never," I reply. He spoke to me about the meditation techniques he'd been taught at a retreat in Hungary and their revelatory effects. He spoke seriously and intensely but with a gentle compassion. I tried to talk to him about free will. He spoke so cryptically that I found him hard to understand through my hangover and perspiration, but he stressed the importance of *Om*, the energy that is everything. "It is everything – atoms moving in the Universe," he said.

We cross bridges through the mangrove swamps which give the island its name, and over to the eastern coast of the island where the exclusive hotels lie, far from the madness of Ton Sai Village. Suddenly I feel energised and start to sprint along the wet sand of the beach, feeling the power surging through my body. All this beauty around me, all this potential in my mind, all the myriads of possibilities – they make me feel pathetic for wasting days and weeks of my life doing the same shit over and over again. If I want to do something – I can – I've just got to go ahead and do it. I am utterly free.

Trekking south down the long sands we cross a large area of spiky and wobbly rocks. Gyorgy and I get left behind the others as our conversation broadens across many topics. "When you think bad thoughts, that is when bad things will happen," describing an accident he had whilst thinking bad thoughts. "You must concentrate on the present. If we were to think bad thoughts now we might walk on a rock badly, twist our ankle and fall over," he says.

He picks up some strangely shaped rocks excitedly and shows

them to me with the enthusiasm of a small child. "I love stones. They have so much energy!" He then asks me if I know what *carpe diem* means. "Seize the day," I say. "Good," he says, "you are the smart guy." I knew what it meant but I'd only done it on occasion. Just surviving the day was more at the forefront of my mind here.

We rest at Rantee Beach on the east coast before heading up into the jungle, a 150 metre climb up an extremely steep densely-forested track. I feel heart-pumpingly alive, clambering up the rocks and tree roots in the thick tropical air. We surge up in long strides without a break, thighs burning, the adrenaline of the jungle urging us on. We get to the top of the slope, through a clearing in the trees to some boulders and realise we've reached the famous viewpoint from the back.

It had never looked as beautiful as it did that day – a purple haze framing the sky as the cliffs led down to the two bays kissing the sliver of land in the middle, the mysterious peaks of Phi Phi Leh bobbing in the ether beyond. I knew for certain right then that we are nature. We are of the Earth, not on it. We are not separated by our bodies or mind, but are a fundamental beating part of the whole, an amazing natural life form developed from other amazing natural life forms over countless millennia. We stand on the rocks of the viewpoint taking in the magnitude of the beauty and grace. Gyorgy picks a yellow flower and puts it in front of my nose. "Smell the energy," he says calmly. I inhaled the molecules into my nose, producing a sweet, fruity sensation. I see that Gyorgy is not a philosopher sat behind a desk contemplating the world. He is out there living and breathing his own beliefs and ideas.

We descend to the village all feeling jubilant. The others peel off and I eat with Gyorgy in the restaurant next to Predator Bar. "This is my reality," he says, making a triangle shape with his hands. He then pointed out the three corners. "This is reality, how you see. This is compassion. And this is affinity." Despite listening intently I can't grasp his world view, but I realise it is as strong and sensical for him as mine or anyone else's is for them. He goes on to explain how we are all comprised of physical, mental and spiritual energy, and makes graphs on the table with cutlery to describe the different energy of members of his family. "Some people call it God, some the Universe, but it's all Energy." Then onto people's auras. A year ago my rational instincts would have dismissed such talk as new-age spiritualistic nonsense. Now I was listening.

A young flyer girl from Predator's comes past and says hi. Gyorgy smiles warmly and tells her sincerely how nice she looks. Her face lights up from the simple compliment. "You see now what I mean about your aura? If you give out a good aura, good energy, you can pass it on to the world. She is feeling good now. She will go to her friends and the people in the street with a good aura and pass it on to them. And so on, and so on, passing good energy out into the world."

I try to interpret his language into my own causal view of the Universe. It suddenly seems to make sense in an obvious way. Is this karma he's talking about? By doing good things, good things will happen to you? Or simply cause and effect? Are they in fact the same thing? Can karma be understood in scientific terms as simply acting in a positive way towards others, and in return others are more likely to act positively to you? Causing good events and receiving good effects. It was revelatory. After all his wise words, it gradually dawns on me. "Are you actually Buddhist?" I ask him. "I am Christian, and I am Buddhist," he replies.

I think I understand his view of goodness too, that goodness is simply caring for the lives of others. By choosing to be good, by being good, that goodness and love can spread into the world. It's so simple. And as I have known for some time now, if the world is to change, it can only begin in the hearts and minds of individuals. If you want to change the world, the first place to look is in the mirror.

We look upon each other with mutual respect. Two philosophers of a different ilk but on the same journey. "There is the world, but it is all about how you see." "How you interpret it," I say, rewording him. Perhaps we are interpreting the world in different ways, though both looking for the same thing.

I feel rejuvenated that night, high on life, happy, friendly, helpful and kind. Why would you want to be anything else? I eat with colleagues after work. Pablo presents us with a jet black chicken for Chinese New Year, as Rin and Johnnie slope off together.

Another day of bad quality DVD restaurants and writing dubious love letters for Thai guys. I'm told that I have to move into the double room 8 upstairs with Gyorgy. I go up and Gyorgy welcomes me warmly. His light-weight racing bike is standing vertically up against the wall. So he really is cycling round the world. Not the whole world, he laughs, but just some stages of his trip. He tells me his name is Gyorgy Arany and shows me his photos from Hungary and Ko Tao.

At work we're all still pumped up from the trek. I tell the guys about how Joe and I kayaked bay to bay around the western cliffs. They're all up for it, so the next day we continue our adventures, the same group plus our tall Swedish friend Andreas. I lead the way this time, eight guys in four double kayaks cruising through the flat waters of Lodalum to Monkey Beach. We paddle along the vertical cliff walls, magnificent crags and overhangs spiked with nature's fearsome bite. We carefully manoeuvre the kayaks, avoiding the surges gushing through the narrow gaps in the rocks, so not to smash into the razor sharp points and encrusted shells all around us. Suddenly Gyorgy jumps out his kayak with a splash, swimming to the side of the cliff and climbing up the sharp overhangs, his body in impossible contortions, as we all look on laughing in awe.

We continue along the far side of the cliffs to the secret beach Joe and I found before, invisible from the open sea. Everybody's blown away. A lone bird nest collector is resting in a wooden shelter on the beach, a young afro-haired man I don't recognise. He's friendly, inviting us to look inside the cave hanging just above the beach. We clamber up the rocks and into the hole, Gyorgy marching in first with a candle. There are some ancient paintings of boats inside and some thin bamboo poles strapped together reaching up into tiny cracks in the roof to collect nests. We come out with black soot dripping down our sweaty bodies. The man tells me it's okay for us to go up the bamboo ladder that rises diagonally over the rocks by the beach. I go first, shimmying along on all fours up to the edge of the rock where another rickety ladder plummets vertically down. This was as far as Joe and I got first time round. I'm sure there's no way the next ladder is going to hold my weight. The lads pile up in a long line on the diagonal ladder behind me, till Gyorgy pushes past and turns onto the top of the next ladder. A couple of rungs down, the whole thing collapses, sending him crashing down into a web of bushes and bamboo poles below. We ask if he's okay, but he just untangles himself and silently scampers off into the mysterious narrow canyon that cuts into the centre of the mountain, bordered on both sides by huge vertical cliffs.

I have to see it too, so I turn and carefully edge down the razor-sharp rocks to the canyon floor. I run along and over another giant rock on bamboo poles and I'm alone. My heart is pumping with the hunger for the bait – venturing into the unexplored beating heart of this island. The narrow valley turns a corner and comes to a dead end. I find Gyorgy ahead of me inspecting thick tree roots hanging down the surrounding cliff sides like ropes, tens of metres in length. I can see he's contemplating climbing up, but they don't lead anywhere. We take in the wonders of this hidden world in humbled silence till it's pierced by the hyperbolic whoops and hollers of the other guys catching us up.

The canyon is a dead end, but there is one last place to explore. A few metres up one of the canyon sides is the entrance to an open sided cave, but it seems impossible to reach from the floor. Suddenly Gyorgy disappears into a tiny crack in the cliff face, nimbly shimmying up a narrow vertical tube in the rocks. We are amazed, not knowing where he's gone. We try to follow but none of us can get up it. Then we hear his Hungarian accent echoing from inside the cliffs somewhere. "There is a cave!" he keeps saying. Then I spot a route up the side of the canyon, up some loose earth and stones. I scramble up till I hear Gyorgy's voice getting louder. The cave has two entrances. This entrance is low, and the cave walls and floor are made of loose mud that falls away to the touch. In the mud are large, spiky boulders, also loose, wobbling precariously under foot. I clamber in the cave and see the glow of Gyorgy's cigarette lighter ahead of me, knowing that the whole thing could easily collapse at any moment. The others start piling in behind me like lambs to the slaughter. One false move and we could easily bring down the cave roof with everyone in it. We carry on in the crumbling spiky darkness till the tunnel narrows to a dead end, with just a small hole at the end. It's just big enough to squeeze your head and one arm through. Gyorgy gives me his lighter and I put my head in the guillotine. I flick the flame alive. A small curved cavern rises vertically up, untouched by human eyes, too small to enter. This is as far as we can get into the heart of the forbidden island, deep inside its sacred inner sanctum. Eight of us were squeezed into the dark death pit now, voices, bodies and limbs scrambling round in the darkness. "The ground is moving!" Gyorgy exclaimed, as the mud walls disintegrated to the touch and the rocks wobbled. Heartbeats accelerating from excitement to panic as we scrambled back through clouds of mud dust. We all made it out without the cave collapsing. We huddled together on the edge of the loose rocks by the cave entrance peering out over the canyon, caked in mud and sweat, wide-eyed in childlike stupidity. But we all felt great, seeing parts of the island you should not see, protected by force for the love of money.

We return to the beach, desperate for a swim, but the tide's gone out 30 metres, revealing a bed of sharp rocks, shells and coral. We carefully tip toe over it barefoot carrying the heavy kayaks. Quick dip, then the long paddle round the southern tip of the island, me and Johnnie ploughing on in silent determination, the Sun beating down on our backs, the imposing fortress walls looming over our little bodies, a two-metre overhang and dripping stalactites hanging above, the scars of energy stretching back countless orbits.

We entered the bay again passing families of macaques scrambling along the deserted beaches. This island! The cliffs, caves and jungle, the thin isthmus and perfect double bays. And the animals! Land, air and sea! Monkeys, lizards and snakes, swiftlets and eagles, sharks, turtles and manta rays. It teeters over the brink of comprehension.

Back at work the emotions subside and I look around the disco. Lots of pretty young Israeli and Swedish tourists going crazy on their buckets. I can't be bothered with it anymore. After another exhilarating afternoon, I sink back into the mire. I look at the tourists jigging around with their plastic buckets to shit music in a desperate attempt to get laid. It all looks ridiculous. The ghost of nothingness haunts me, ever present in my mind, the soul destroying truth echoing round my head harder than my heart palpitations, hollow pleasures eating away at me like cancer. I go to bed depressed but not knowing exactly why. Gyorgy comes back later and skins up. He senses my negativity but doesn't mention it, talking about astrology instead. "What star sign are you?" he asks. I tell him. "I am Leo," he says. "We are not the same."

I'm home again. But my family don't want me there anymore as I have become such a disgrace to them. They hate me. We argue until I turn and run away forever, my heart poisoned with rage.

The vivid dream submerges me into my doubtful reality in a state of lonesome melancholy. I mope to the beach to pick myself up; but despite the cloudless blue above, the lush green, the squeaky white and shimmering turquoise, I feel nothing. The abyss looms ever closer, threatening to swallow me up if I dare look down. Everything and nothing, the world and I, meaning and meaninglessness. They are pulling my soul in two and yet just three days ago I felt so sure they were one.

The guys organise a boat trip to Maya Bay. I can't be bothered but decide it would be better than the alternative. My emotions are unravelling, the ecstasy and the agony so close I wonder if they are one. I peel off alone on arrival, swimming across the bay, washing the dead skin from my tattered bones, whilst nervously keeping an eye out for Mr Kit. I've never seen the beach as busy as this, hundreds of people sunbathing, dozens of boats churning oil and smoke out into the bay, punters hungry for their own piece of paradise, just like me, just like all of us. My dreams are materialising before my eyes again. Meanwhile Gyorgy is entertaining half the beach with his one man stand-up routine, interspersed with crocodile walks and gymnastic displays in the sand. Everyone loves the guy. Not often you come across someone that can inspire all they meet.

We return as the Sun descends through its spectrum in the red satin sky. Johnnie is talking about leaving tomorrow as Rin had flipped out on him as she always did at some point. I can see the bucket paranoia taking its toll on him too – all the mysteries, ambiguities and unanswered questions of life on the show. It couldn't be doing his insides any good either. He'd been in hospital twice with serious alcohol-related illnesses on previous trips with me. The island I'd lured him to was rotting him away. I didn't want it to happen again.

We get ready for the evening. Gyorgy suddenly tells me he is leaving for Ko Lanta tomorrow to dry up before cycling down through Malaysia to Singapore. He's been lounging on the islands for months now and is eager to get back on his bike. He invites me to come along. It sounds like a good idea. I tell him I'll bring Johnnie along too.

During work I nip off and watch Johnnie singing a couple of numbers with the band in the Rock Bar. Good to see him up on stage giving it his all. He bounds off stage with two Singhas in his hands to rapturous applause. A hot girl next to me remarks how good he is, the star power of the lead singer hard to match. He hadn't managed to convert much of his singing success though. One random guy he'd never met before even came up and thanked him. The night before a girl had asked him, "Aren't you the singer in Rock Bar?" He said he was and they hooked up. Poor old Johnnie. I tell him we're leaving.

I see the door of room 8 wide open in the dark across the courtyard. I sprint up thinking we've been burgled. I find Gyorgy sitting cross-legged on his bed in the dark. I say hello but he doesn't respond. He's meditating. The guys had been hounding him to fight in the ring and show off his skills before he left. He was unwilling, but the lads from Jungle found two Irish guys on the street willing to fight in a tag team match. Our friend Andreas was up for it too. Gyorgy eventually gave in and was now preparing.

We go up and have a word behind the bar. Being the senior flyer boy, I referee the match. They put on a real show for us, with the lights and sound effects. The stage is set. The boxers climb into the ring, lights beaming hot and bright. I follow. Up in the ring I notice how packed the place is, hundreds of eager spectators crammed together.

Ding-ding and Andreas faces off against the first guy, Queensbury rules. Of course I'd never refereed a boxing match in my life, but you've got to start somewhere. I just copied what I'd seen in the other fights. They were the ones doing all the hard work after all.

So in they go, drunken arms swinging furiously, not all slow and controlled like on TV. I hover in the middle, keeping it clean and even, as the staff look on incredulously. Then they tag each other and Gyorgy comes through the ropes up against the other guy. The crowd goes wild, suddenly getting up on to the edge of the ring to watch up close. I realise how much fun I'm having too, dancing round the edge of the violence like an untouchable sprite, pulling them apart when necessary and throwing my hand down to restart the battle. The thumb of judgement and the old Imperial fantasies again.

Gyorgy doesn't block any shots. He doesn't have to. He shimmies about, avoiding every punch with quick glances of his body, before springing in with lightning fast combos when the opportunity appears. After a couple of rounds he gets a clean hook in and knocks his opponent to the floor, following up with a straight jab to the face as he's going down. The Irishman lies on the canvas, concussed, broken bloody nose, black eyes and a vacant stare. He's finished. I ask his partner if he wants to carry on. The look on his face says it all. I throw my arms out to end the fight. Gyorgy's already climbed out the ring and disappeared without celebration, so I pull Andreas through the ropes and lift his glove in victory to triumphant applause.

★ ★ ★

People come in and out the room all morning to say goodbye while I lie there semi-comatose. We eventually leave with Gyorgy's bicycle, find Johnnie and board the ferry to Ko Lanta in good spirits. We sit on the top deck in the Sun. A little blond toddler runs around the passengers, amusing everyone before returning to his young parents' loving arms. So much energy, happiness and love between him and his parents. We feel the power of the engine as the boat surges through the choppy waters in the blessed space between the sea and the sky with all these happy people around us.

I cruise around the large boat enjoying the warmth of the happy faces, until I see Gyorgy alone at the back of the vessel, a Thai flag fluttering above him. He is staring back at Phi Phi as it fades into the distance, silent tears dripping down his cheeks. "My country is very poor. I am so lucky to be here," he says. I smile and leave him alone, reflecting on my own feelings as the island fades to grey. Why have I been so up and down all over the place? Those regular moments of overwhelming elation, that feel like they could crack open and implode at any moment, throwing me head-long into an abyss of my own making. Perhaps men should not fly so close to the Sun.

I imagine Joe with me as we reach the large but fairly undeveloped island of Ko Lanta. This was the place. Bombarded with touts, we choose one and drive down the main road along the coast, lined with bungalow operations all the way. It seems nice enough, but unremarkable, a large island with a long coastline and hills in the middle. More spread out and sparsely populated than Phi Phi. We get a room with three beds near Khlong Khong Beach. I go straight out alone to the endless beach where the Sun sinks purple into the murky sea. Just a few people scattered on the sand. It seems like more of a chill-out scene than the drunken holiday crap I'm used to. Again, I see Phi Phi's silhouette over the sea and wonder where I'd rather be. *Angie* plays out loudly from a deserted beach bar. Playing just for me.

We eat and all pass out in the room exhausted. Then I'm woken up. Gyorgy beckons me outside quickly. Johnnie's still zonked out. It's a dark windy night. We stumble over rickety bridges crossing grassy streams by the silvery blue moonlight. I've only been awake a few seconds and still feel like I'm dreaming. Patches of beach are illuminated by smoky little bonfires. Fairy lights hang from the ramshackle beach bars, dancing in the warm breeze. We enter a wigwam bar and go through to a hidden back area in the undergrowth. We come to a little clearing, two long-haired local guys and a silent Finn smoking bongs. We join them, both groups a little wary of the other, but the deal is done.

The smoke hits home and reality twists and twirls ever more doubtfully, still unsure of this foreign island. I start gasping for water so we make our way back to the beach, till I notice I've forgotten my flip-flops. I go back to where I thought we'd been, but can't find the clearing or people we were just with. They've vanished in the undergrowth. I'm ploughing through leaves, branches and bushes in the pitch black, stoned out of my mind, no idea where I am. I hear Gyorgy pissing himself laughing, suddenly getting my bearings and shoes back.

We stroll through the soft sand down the near-deserted beach. It stretches on forever, lit only by multi-coloured bulbs and the star-drenched heavens above. It's beautiful, but far quieter than I'm used to. I feel myself falling down to Earth and beyond from the great heights of folly I'd constructed in my head. Damn weed is pulling my head into a negative spiral. The past still preys heavily on my conscience.

Dow-dow-dow-dooooooow . . . *Shine On You Crazy Diamond* opens from the same deserted bar as we lie down on the beach, smoking on the sand, only the galaxy above visible now. Memories of home, of what I could be, should be, would be, if . . . Images of possible worlds flicker through my mind. Everything of the moment here is so, so . . . uncanny, like it was meant to be. Messages and signs everywhere, seemingly unconnected thoughts and ideas intertwine, spurring my imagination on ever further. I don't know whether to carry on or come back.

Gyorgy is talking non-stop about *Om*, the three gods, the five elements, eggs and auras and Hare Krishna. I can't follow half of it, somewhat preoccupied by my own precarious schisms. Gyorgy picks up on my negative energy again. Our backgrounds are too different to easily meet halfway, my mind too torn to easily grasp another's ideas, let alone my own. But everything in his cosmic words suggests a higher force. Perhaps I am wrong. I look at the stars, the ungraspable expanse of time and space before me, and then at my own little life, my twinkling consciousness, and know that there must be something . . . more. All this . . . all this . . . *Energy* couldn't have just come from nothing, a causeless event from a state of nothingness. The idea sounds more absurd than anything else that at least proposes a cause. Be it God, be it Nature, be it *Om* or any other Force, there must be a reason . . . there must be more than . . . *this*.

"Don't think me crazy," says Gyorgy, pulling me back outside myself as the song reaches its crescendo, our eyes pinned to the endless billions of suns above. Contemplations of insanity. "You can tune into the music of the Universe," he continued. He told me to focus on one star. I choose one and focus upon it until all the other stars disappear from view as he said they would. Then too, the star I am focusing on disappears and I am plunged into blackness. "At higher levels of meditation you can see tunnels of light going into the Universe." He was light years ahead of me, stuck as I was in myself.

I couldn't shake the negativity, however self-inflicted it was. These paradoxical poles – the absolute meaningfulness of human consciousness and the absolute meaninglessness of the Universe – were tearing me in two. But I look at Gyorgy, a burning spear flying through the world, and feel sure that there's no need to let dark thoughts overwhelm me. I must hold onto the precious jewels in my heart whilst looking ever outward for their source. We head back, but my mind's electric and I can't sleep till I munch on another pill in the middle of the night.

A distant voice penetrates the darkness. "You got to get me to a doctor's or hospital or something." I can't open my eyes, think, talk, move. The voice is gone. Eventually I wake, musty-headed, alone in the room. What happened? A girl from the guesthouse knocks on the door and tells me Johnnie's been taken to Ko Lanta hospital with stomach pains. My heart clenches tightly. No, not again. I'm sure it's his old pancreatitis come back from too much drinking on Phi Phi. I feel terrible. Why do I keep fucking my friends over?

I get a lift with some guys from the guesthouse, but then we get a phone call halfway to say he's back already. Back at the guesthouse is a parked ambulance. My stomach tenses in fear of what I'm about to see. I approach the back door and see the horrible sight of Johnnie lying in a blue hospital gown, wired up to drips and needles. It's real. It's happening. Gyorgy comes out the room with a plastic bag of Johnnie's things he's packed for him.

I get in the ambulance and we head off for the larger hospital in Krabi Town. I look at Johnnie. He looks at me dozily. He's high on painkillers but smiling and talking. We take two ferries and a bridge to the mainland and after a couple of hours arrive at Krabi's government hospital in an old concrete building. Johnnie's set up in a room. He assures me he's fine, though nobody's sure of his real status yet. I decide to go straight back to Ko Lanta in the ambulance, as both our bags are still there, before returning tomorrow.

I get back at sunset and find Gyorgy rolling another joint. "For me, rolling the joint is like preparing the food." He is going to get up tomorrow at dawn, cycle to the port, get a boat to the mainland and continue his epic journey by bicycle. He shows me his bag of pharmaceuticals and energy supplements to help him cover the 150km he does a day, sometimes overtaking cars at junctions, grinning like a maniac as he passes stunned onlookers.

That night we relax in the guesthouse restaurant with drinks, smokes and a three course meal. This is our last chance to share our ideas. "All my life I have always done what I've wanted," he explains to me, the cosmic gratitude evident in the humility in his voice. His comment strikes a chord. "Why?" I ask intently. He looks deep within himself for a while before answering in a deadly serious tone, "The winner never gives up . . . *never*." His answers always surprised me. I ask him a final question. "What is good? What does the word 'good' mean to you?" He gets up and slowly takes a few carefully measured walking meditation steps before answering. "When you are at one with nature . . . that is good."

Early next morning he is preparing his bicycle as I pack mine and Johnnie's bags. "Don't you have a helmet?" I ask. He laughs. "I have good karma, I don't need a helmet!" When I first met him I wasn't sure whether to believe his tall stories, cynically blinded by his exhibitionism and extrovert nature. But of course it was all true. The shady past, the kickboxing, the cycling, meditation and aura. It was all true. I admitted to myself a touch of jealousy when I first met him. A horrible, self-hating emotion, but one to which we occasionally fall prey. I was ashamed to remember it now. But the dog's jealousy of the lion soon turned to admiration once I actually spoke to him. He was a one man phenomenon, a hero of the road. Although me and the other guys on Phi Phi had only known him for two weeks, he had taught and inspired us all.

I pulled out my red Vietnam t-shirt with the bright yellow star on the front and gave it to Gyorgy. He seemed touched by the gesture. We hugged, said goodbye and he pedalled off down the long road. Gyorgy Arany, the living embodiment of *carpe diem*, and man of good heart and good karma. An enlightened being, leading a life not of ideas, plans and potential, but of actualisation. He saw something in me, but I never really knew what it was. He never seemed very interested when I talked about my ideas. One afternoon whilst hungrily devouring a barbecued chicken on Phi Phi, he looked at me and joked, "That's what you are – an animal, a clever animal!" He said it slightly disdainfully, though I took it as a compliment. Perhaps he thought my lack of belief prevented me from attaining anything higher – a devout spirituality, a perpetually guiding love of life that fuelled him forth across unbridgeable oceans. Perhaps he was right. All I had was myself. Perhaps I *was* wrong. But for now I tried to hold on to his ideas of goodness, aura, the at-oneness-with-nature, and the karmic transmission of this goodness throughout the world by simply being good.

★ ★ ★

After a thousand years of relatively slow development in Europe, came the beginnings of the Renaissance in the 14th and 15th centuries, a rebirth in learning. People were optimistically reassessing mankind's place in the world. Protestant Christian groups began to split from the main Catholic Church. There was an explosion of humanist art and literature. Man was to be the measure of all things. The Earth was no longer the centre of the Universe – we revolved around the Sun. The new printing press democratised knowledge and brought about massive improvements in communication and education.

This was followed by an age of discovery in the Scientific Revolution of the 16th and 17th centuries. This would lead to the Industrial Revolution of the 18th century in transport, agriculture, manufacturing and mining. Mills, looms, railways, coke, steam power and ocean-worthy ships were developed, changing the world. Populations, urbanisation and economic development grew rapidly. Capitalist economies began to develop over old forms of feudalism and the modern nation-state was born. Europeans sailed the world, trading globally. They crossed the Atlantic Ocean, leading to the colonisation of South America by Spain and Portugal, and North America by Britain, France and The Netherlands. This was fuelled by European émigrés and a massive slave trade of imprisoned people from Africa. The Ottoman Empire grew across Turkey, North Africa and the Middle East, and Russia expanded eastwards.

The 18th century was also called the Enlightenment or Age of Reason by some. Through our freely thinking conscious mind, knowledge could be gained through experience and reason. There was a growing feeling of mankind having greater power over themselves and the world, of being at the centre of all things, whilst simultaneously realising the world and cosmos were far bigger than first thought. Notions of freedom, human rights, individualism and secularism became more popular. The American Revolution led to the United States of America, free from British colonial rule. The French Revolution ended centuries of absolute monarchic rule and popularised these new ideas. Various related political ideologies like democracy, republicanism, nationalism, conservatism, liberalism, socialism and communism developed around this period.

Inter-nation warfare over European nations' fledgling empires grew in the 19th century. The French Empire dominated Europe until defeat led to the dominance of the British Empire, which spread east into Africa, India and Australia. Other European nations also expanded their colonies in Africa and Asia. Wars of independence, revolutions and rebellions spread across Europe and beyond. New nation states such as Germany and Italy formed. Latin American countries also gained independence.

Electrical power and light, internal combustion engines, mechanisation and other advances in petroleum, communications and shipping contributed to the rise of 24 hour industry and mass production. More advances followed into the 20th century – cars, airplanes, rockets, nuclear power, lasers, electronics, radar, radio, telephones, computers and television. On the whole, people's quality of life was improving. They were getting richer and living longer due to healthcare improvements and new technologies.

But meanwhile Europe was still a pressure cooker of many closely-linked rival nations, locked in webs of complex treaties. Tensions finally erupted into The Great War centred in Europe. New technologies led to death and destruction on an unprecedented scale. Britain and France were severely weakened and a revolution in Russia formed the USSR, the world's first communist state. Fascist, nationalist dictatorships emerged in Germany, Italy, Japan and elsewhere. Meanwhile the world economy sank into the Great Depression.

Military expansion by Japan and Germany led to World War Two. The scale of destruction was even greater this time as bombs, airplanes, tanks and submarines were used in huge numbers. The Allies eventually prevailed in Europe, and the USA dropped atomic bombs on Japan ending the war in Asia. Communism spread into Eastern Europe, China, North Korea and North Vietnam. A decimated Europe precipitated the dominance of capitalist USA and communist USSR and an ideological Cold War, both armed with enough nuclear weapons to destroy mankind. Colonialism collapsed, creating a plethora of new states across Africa and Asia, but wars and genocides would continue. The United Nations and other regional unions were formed to aid international cooperation. Eventually the communist economies couldn't keep up with the economic growth of the capitalist West, and most of their regimes collapsed. The USA was the world's sole superpower for a while but China, Russia, India and regional blocs like the European Union were growing in power.

The 20th century saw growth in social freedoms, economic development and technological advancements for most people. The world population soared to 6 billion people by the end of the century, as mobile communication and the internet brought about a new era of mass communication and information. The world's people were brought into closer contact with one another, old borders and distances dissolving in a world of increasing globalisation and an explosion of information and opinion.

But centuries of population expansion and technological change also had an increasingly detrimental effect on the global environment. Pollution spread through the air, land and sea. Habitats were destroyed, many species made extinct. The climate itself appeared to be affected by Man's activities. The dominance of free market capitalism was blamed by some for this environmental destruction, as well as being responsible for the unbalanced distribution of wealth in the world, and the rise of materialism and social alienation. The extent of destruction, warfare and murder in recent history was so shocking that it forced many people to pessimistically reevaluate mankind itself. Many increasingly viewed human beings less as free-thinking, autonomous individuals, and more as selfish, violent, causally-determined, mechanistic animals like any other.

Yet despite all the disagreement there always remains one thing that unites us all. One thing we all have in common which cannot be denied. One thing. One word . . .

★   ★   ★

With two full backpacks, I made the awkward journey to Krabi Town and stayed in the same attic room I'd stayed in on my first night here nearly a year ago. I got a motorbike taxi straight to the hospital. Krabi hospital wasn't nice, nothing like the gleaming palace of Phuket Town, more like one of those places wounded soldiers go in old war movies, long wards with no privacy, beds with sick patients dumped in corridors, anxious relatives everywhere. I approach Johnnie's room nervously. He's on a drip, no food, painkillers, but he's in good spirits. I've seen him worse. He doesn't want to go home. He says I can sleep on his sofa, but I politely turn him down. Not again.

Krabi Town was pleasant and amiable, but there was little to do other than wander round the riverside, shops and markets. After months of island madness, it was a relief to be back in normality, with normal people living normal lives everywhere. I remembered the first time I came here, seeing the trail for the first time. I don't think I ever found those secret backpacker enclaves I'd imagined. Just lots of people getting wasted.

I spent the next day in Johnnie's air-con hospital room watching travel shows on TV. Exotic destinations around the world. I began reflecting on my old wanderlust, my desire to go everywhere, meet everyone and do everything. Nearly a year on, is this what I had done? I could have travelled the world, and yet my decisions had brought me here to Krabi hospital, staying in the same guesthouse I was in when I first came here. I hadn't gone everywhere and done everything. I realised that it was the people that had influenced my decisions the most. Faces of the last year passed by my eyes. I'd chosen to spend my time with people I liked. I'd valued them above the places and activities.

Over the next few nights I slept like a baby, the exhaustion and voices fading away, the warm easy light of sobriety and sanity taking their place. Everything started to make sense again. No more uncontrollable trains of thought, cacophony of voices and attacks of meaninglessness. It was all the drink and gear. Johnnie said he was feeling better too, though it may have just been the self-service morphine tap.

I undertook the long-anticipated Krabi night market eating contest alone. A bustling, sensory melee of exotic curries, fragrant seafood, spicy salads, fruits and cakes. After some chicken fried noodles, rice with two scoops of curry, a large barbecue sausage, beef noodle soup and six mini crepes, I called it a day and waddled home.

Fully revived, I wake up early feeling fresh and decide to rent a motorbike and see the province. Johnnie says he'll be discharged that evening. So I take off on some knackered old thing, heading north on a small road out of town, feeling alive again, no more responsibilities, no more confinement, off into the green countryside, wind rushing through my lungs, purging my battered soul. Memories of home flash past me in the green hues and earthy air. The road turns rough as I head west, through remote Buddhist farming villages surrounded by rows of rubber trees, tropical birds singing in their cages, the locals smiling benevolently at the lost *farang*. I smiled back, my brothers and sisters.

I see a turn off to Ao Leuk in the middle of nowhere, vast limestone turrets protruding out of the plantations and scattered palms. I speed northwards up highway 4, on and on, following signs to Than Bokkharani National Park. I find it on the edge of the town, a lovely little hidden valley of paths through thick jungle and natural emerald pools, waterfalls and caves shaded under the forest canopy. An untouched pocket of primordial Earth, seemingly unchanged in millennia. Local families picnic and paddle in the pools happily. I admire the beauty, climbing up the cliff side, avoiding the giant black spiders poised on their huge sticky webs.

I cruise south leisurely, the Sun radiating above, hugging the coastline as best I can. Through sleepy Muslim fishing villages, to the ends of wooden piers admiring the magnificent karst islands floating in the serene Phang Nga Bay beyond. Then I hit highway 4 again and pull the throttle all the way back, going as fast as the clattering bike will allow, 50kms back to Krabi Town, tearing off caution to the wind, swinging the bike between lanes with a shimmy of my backside, overtaking everything in the way, singing rock and rollers at the top of my voice, the wind pulling tears from my eyes.

I carry on through Krabi Town centre towards the Tiger Cave Temple on the far edge of town. Like all large temples it has a car park for the many families who come to make merit. Past golden Buddha and monk statues festooned with colourful garlands, stone chickens and other animal statues, gongs, incense smoke burning the whispered prayers for the deceased. It's overlooked on the left side by a high vertical wall of limestone, made from the compressed dead matter of millions of years of marine organisms from a time when the seas were much higher than today. Yesterday's marine life is today's mountain. These wonders surround me.

No time for the 1200 stairs to the summit so I enter a forest meditation area surrounded by the white walls of crustaceans for a smoke, marvelling at the vines and jungle flora, huge kaleidoscopic 1000-year-old trees, like walking between the legs of dinosaurs frozen in time. My mind flickers into that other mode of consciousness, the hints of ideas and meanings. I'm struck by the greatness of it all again, that rush of existential vertigo, a sudden reminder that my fragile mind could easily fracture again from all its recent batterings. But no, no, no I tell myself. Not today. Not now. The Sun is not yet set. Keep going.

I ride out the temple grounds, back into town, flying past all before me with an urgency, as I charge through my own fantasies. I cruise down to the riverfront and pull over. But the Sun is not yet set; I can't stop here. I must follow the Sun. Through the town I continue, giant shadows charging into me downhill until I'm lost in desolate sandy roads at the end of town, motoring on through the scrubland and purple haze. Still I follow the Sun westwards, driving against the turning Earth, till I suddenly reach a large unused concrete coastal port. The buildings are brand new, building debris and plastic wrap everywhere. A new pier built, but not yet opened. But there is the Sun, burning orange over the water, hovering just above the tops of the limestone peaks far off on the horizon. Nobody in sight, I pull up and stride down the long covered pier leading into the fragrant salt water where the river meets the sea and mangrove swamps; to the end of the pier, birds calling above, and out into the Sun's gaze, shining light unto water, golden stars dancing on the blue ocean's surface, twisting and spiralling in wonder before my eyes.

Overcome by the beauty and magnitude of it all, I instinctively bowed my head and prayed to the Sun, the God of Earth. And at that moment I felt such love and respect for our nature, the nature of Earth from which I came and to which I was intrinsically bound and to which I will return. I felt and knew with absolute certainty that I was of the Earth and not on it. To think otherwise is an abstraction of modernity, an abstraction caused by the great power of the human mind, a fruit born of this very Earth itself. And at that moment it quickly became apparent to me that if I want to change, then I had to take the love, respect and sense of belonging I felt right then and keep it in my heart, capture and hold it there like a flaming torch beating in my chest, and by its light guide my actions through the darkness of this world and be good.

Uplifted and enlightened, I cruised back to the hospital. I knew it wouldn't be possible to keep that feeling in me at all times, but I knew now that as long as the Sun rose each day, it would always be there, always with me, even if it would sometimes be hard to find through the negativity that can sometimes cloud the human heart. I picked up

Johnnie and took him to the night market for another evening of delicious local food.

On his deathbed in 1851, the Romantic landscape painter J.M.W. Turner, at the end of his long and distinguished life, is said to have uttered these final words, "The Sun is God." But for the merest glance at his paintings, it's clear that nobody saw the Sun as clearly as he.

★   ★   ★

So where do values come from if not from ourselves or the world? There is a third possibility. We live in a *human* world, not of subjective or objective values, but of *intersubjective* values. They are values subjectively agreed upon between people in groups, or cultures. These values vary between cultures and over time too, but they are values agreed upon between people. Values don't just spring freely from our subjective mind. Some are strongly ingrained in us from birth, like survival, and some develop during our lives. And these values all change in their strength and character over our lives, often influenced by the various cultural forces in the world, most of which have existed long before us, and in turn have developed over time.

Different cultures' intersubjective values are often grouped together and called *morality*, that which is good or evil, right or wrong. This is a huge topic which we won't investigate now. My point here is that values, what we think of as good or bad, are intersubjective. They are the general agreements between people. Most of these are rooted in our evolutionary urges, such as survival, reproduction, learning and socialisation, but with the increasing complexity of human interaction, so the myriad of values becomes ever more complex.

So then, are our values determined by the social groups to which we belong? Are we unable to form opinions outside these groups? Of course not. Ultimately, as we grow into adulthood, our views are our own. We can change our opinions on things from one moment to the next. We do it all the time. Our mind is our own. So in that case values could be said to be ultimately subjective if we believe in free will, though they are usually derived from objective (evolutionary) and intersubjective (cultural) roots.

So what are we doing when we change our opinion on something? We are changing our values. Human beings have the ability to change their values about anything if they really want to. If we will it, that which was good can become bad, and that which was bad can become good.

How can we control our values? With the power of our mind we can exert a greater control over our emotions. Our basic emotions exist as carrots and sticks to steer us towards survival and reproduction, and away from death. But with practice they can be intensified or weakened at will. These decisions will be implemented physically by the brain and nervous system, releasing adrenaline, serotonin, dopamine and various other neurotransmitters. These affect our body's functions such as heart rate, body temperature, sleep, memory and our mood. Obviously they react to external stimuli, but these things can also be controlled by the power of our mind. Ultimately, we can be as excited or calm, happy or sad, about something as we choose. By changing our emotional reactions and values towards things, we are changing our minds. By changing our minds, we can change our actions.

Of course in reality things are rarely this simple or absolute. We live in a world of infinite options, the actions we take being our own decision. But by freely re-evaluating your opinion of things, you can change your actions. It is up to you. Your 'nature' or your emotions may be telling you one thing, but you have the ability to see them, question them, and ultimately control them if you wish. Of course you don't have to. Our emotions exist for good reasons, and much of the time are there to be heeded and enjoyed. Why not enjoy the good ones and change the bad ones?

(Be wary of those who talk about a fixed 'human nature'. Of course we are natural beings, but anyone trying to define a fixed 'human nature' since the time we became free-thinking, linguistic, cultural beings, will be misguided.)

So by freely changing our values, we change our reasons for action. Our will becomes the reason for our actions. Our will becomes the first cause of our actions. Perhaps *this* is the meaning of free will.

Are there then two modes of being? Our more outward-looking, social, animalistic, emotionally-driven side, and our more inward-looking, personal, rational and freely-willed side? This dichotomy in various forms has been noted since the dawn of history. It still appears plausible to me. It's part of our being. Perhaps these are related to the two modes of consciousness we already looked at that define the evolution of humankind: regular, unreflective consciousness, and the more self-aware, self-consciousness. In our lives, are we constantly flicking between these two modes of being, or perhaps moving between them in degrees? It seems so. Sometimes conscious of the world as we act within it, sometimes conscious of our own mind as we reflect upon it. In the world, in our mind, in the world, in our mind. Perhaps it is only when the two come together that one truly becomes divine, that one truly becomes god of oneself.

So you can choose your own path in life. You can do what you want to do, and in doing so be who you want to be, for you express yourself as a human being and individual by your actions. You can change your values and in doing so change your actions. If you wish, the negative can become the positive. The pessimist, the optimist. The apathetic, the enthusiastic. The lazy, the motivated. The unconcerned, the caring. The hostile, the friendly. The hater, the lover. The beast, the human.

But of course, this is entirely up to you. Only you can act to change your own behaviour. Only you are free to think what you want, consider and control your emotions, change your values towards things and evaluate the world in any way you want. In doing so, only you are free to will yourself and act upon the world any way you choose. You are free.

But this freedom we have in our hearts at all times is nothing. Freedom is a nothingness. An empty space we fill with our actions. It's what we do with our freedom that counts. And of course, we must never forget that every action we take will then have effects in the world. Cause and effect. Cause and effect. Every move you make has consequences for yourself and others. This is how the world changes. So what should you do? This is another huge topic. But ultimately the answer is totally up to you.

★　★　★

I take Johnnie to Ao Nang where he can recuperate in the Sun and sea. I'm feeling strong and confident again too. We take it easy, lounging on the beach, long swims to the rocks.

The old *"Muay Thai, Muay Thai,"* truck goes by in the evening, but it no longer sounds menacing. My old drinking chum Jackpot goes by in his newly kitted-out Scooby Tours truck. Noi's on the front at night, telling me my face has gone fat. I tell Johnnie. "Yeah, but like, when are you going to stop drinking?" he replies dryly. Jeab is there too but the tension has gone now and we chat amiably. Everything's cool. At the end of the night Johnnie and I look out from the balcony of Mermaid Guesthouse. She walks by alone and gives us a wave at the place where it all began. And then she's gone.

I realise I'm missing home more and more. It usually gets me just as I wake, reconstructing the crumbling fragments of my dreams and realising . . . yep, still here. Day after day, still here.

Johnnie leaves for Malaysia in the morning and I'm alone on Valentine's Day deciding what to do next. I can't carry on like this, going round in circles for months on end – no reason, no meaning. That's the problem with the road. It goes on forever. There is no destination.

But I need one now. It's time to work. I go to an English teaching website and absent-mindedly send my CV to some schools in Bangkok. Amongst the ads is a vacancy for a four-month job in China. I send them one too for the hell of it.

Now what? Full moon in a couple of days. Maybe one final swan song before the replies come in. I pack my small bag and leave the other at Mermaid.

* * *

The parched dry leaves are falling from the trees everywhere, signifying not the end of summer, but its beginning. The scorched earth now devoid of all moisture, life waning as the heat intensifies. The cycle was close to beginning again.

Surat Thani harbour, waiting for the night boat with the endless streams of backpackers going round in circles. I leave the tourist depot and tramp past strange theatrical performances in brightly adorned Chinese temples.

I check my emails in a shop full of sweaty teenage boys playing online games. One reply already. A guy called Fabien in Beijing. Says if I phone him, that teaching job in China is as good as mine. It sends my head reeling. A four month contract teaching at a school in a city near Beijing, China. *China!* I'd never really considered going there and now I suddenly have a golden ticket. Opportunities come like passing freight trains to wandering hobos. You only have a few seconds to decide whether to get on or not. You wait too long . . . and they're gone. But it's so far away. I tell him the earliest I can be there is two weeks.

I have another email from Nok's friend Pin, telling me Nok's moved to Bangkok and wants me to call her. I briefly fantasise about getting back together. No, stupid idea. Making decisions based on girls I don't trust. But other things keep me here. The joys of Krabi province. Sammy and my money. Making a go of it in Bangkok. Yet this China thing seems the perfect escape. Get away, somewhere new.

Lying on the wooden floor of the crowded night boat, shoulder to shoulder with two strangers on our hedonistic slave ship. I look out at the stars as the vessel chugs out of port, thinking back to love's lost hopes of yesteryear.

Thong Sala at dawn. My fourth trip. Suddenly realise I could be taking an unnecessary gamble so close to the finishing line, considering my previous trips here ended in heartbreak, dengue fever and motorbike debts. It's a dangerous place for the overenthusiastic.

Hat Rin, backpacker Heaven. Maybe it was before the road was built, but I'd missed that boat. Just lots of drunk kids with UV paint and mopeds now. I soon bump into a huge gang from Phi Phi – Doug, Lena, Fanny, Double Dutch, the Canadian jocks, divers and various friends of friends, clung together in a massive extended gang. I hated faffing around in big groups.

Emails. Fabien tells me to hurry up and ring. I could go to China if I want. I really could go. It's totally up to me. Raw free choice strangles me with its actuality. Can't make my mind up. But I got to.

I swim from Sunrise Beach to another bay cut off by a steep rocky headland and think it over. Only four months, decent money, free room with TV, DVD, PC, internet. A brand new campus with canteen, pool, football, tennis, basketball. And an onward flight anywhere I want in the world. It all sounds very luxurious after a year on the road. Get out. Escape. New country. Start again. I think of the things I'd miss – friends, girls, Songkran, alcohol, sweat, madness. No. Enough is enough. They're all gone now. I'm going to do it. I'm going to China.

I feel fantastic as I stride through the waves onto the uninhabited beach. I clamber back across the giant grey rocks to Sunrise Beach. I ring Fabien. Says the job is mine. I just got to tell him when I'm coming. Amazing. How did this happen? Suddenly an absent-minded email is taking on a life of its own. Some call it fate or destiny. I call it cause and effect. My cause.

I meet the others and tell them I'm off to China. "We'd better celebrate bro!" says Mad Doug. We buy a ten litre mega bucket, add three large bottles of SangSom, bottles of energy drink, Coke and ice and drink it. Life fades to a dream – beach, music, lights, dancing. Morning comes. Solo pilgrimage to Cliff Top. The faintest recollections, pills and spills, familiar faces, new and old, familiar patterns of inebriated perplexity, fuck-ups and four-to-the-floor beats going on forever and ever and ever. The beat . . . never . . . stops. I'm alone in a twisted mess. But I don't care. For I know this is farewell. And I have no fear. I've done it. And I can do it all. I'm free. I will.

Wake up off my head on a secluded axe cushion covered in mosquito bites. It appears to be morning again. Remember I've got to do another damn visa run. No rest for . . . Endless cycles of suffering. Here we go again. The road ahead foreshadows my every thought. Surat Thani, Hat Yai, Malaysia, Krabi, Bangkok, Beijing, China. Fuck it. Let's do it. Go, go, go . . .

A choppy boat, mind spiralling in ever-decreasing circles. Consciousness over-alert, seconds like minutes. Panic attacks and mental schisms, as my immediate past and my immediate future come together to overwhelm my immediate now. Just gotta ride the storm. Hold it together. Keep going.

A cramped minibus, knees embedded in the seat in front, nothing but road signs for company. Struggling to hold it together. Can't turn my mind off, or even turn down the volume. 300 minutes times 60 long seconds of dark, silent introspection. I guess yesterday's lessons aren't learnt overnight.

6am border in a sweaty juddering mess. Border guard induced paranoia. Hat Yai. Another minibus to Krabi, nauseous from my own stench. Grab my big bag in Ao Nang pausing to look at the internet shop where I sent that email. It all started and ended here. Back to Krabi on the evening's last *songtaew*. I take a quick mournful glance at Jeab's old house as we pass by. There was nobody there now. Through the dark jungle and mystical canyons as the light fades on this bewitching land. Just one last goodbye to go.

★ ★ ★

Roof of the morning boat all the way there, basking in the blue rays till she approaches me. We round the cape and she opens her legs for me one final time. She never says no.

351

But the game is over. It's just the same shit going round and round. Doug's back already. He ain't stopping. We empty his ten litre mega bucket again. I end up in the ring with him, Pablo, Chai, Green and the boxers breaking up a mass tourist brawl. Time to hang up my gloves.

A terrible, terrible mess. Madness reborn in hell. I writhe in my bare room, grappling with my own being. Depression. No feeling. Loneliness and self-hate. I've been up and down like a yo-yo, drinking for months on end, but I can't turn this one off so easily. The King is dead, the Emperor exposed. Why? What's wrong with me?

I'm lonely. That's what it is. Like when I got here. No one to connect to, I sink like a shipless anchor. I lie there motionless. What should I do? Get up? No. I think of possible ideas but don't wanna do any of them. I just wanna roll over, let consciousness fade and dissolve. Please let me wake up somewhere else. He haunts me like a ghost. The ghost of consequence. Decisions ill thought-out. A demon deep within all our souls. My heart is crazed with wanton desire, my mind racing round like a rocket on a bungee cord, sparks of realisation instantly forgotten. I want for nothing. I want everything. Is it really possible to be master of one's emotions and not their slave?

I know what it is, that missing piece. Of course I know what it is. Yet it is the one thing I fear the most and understand the least. I dare not even speak its name. All in good time. Desire and suffering. Patience, have patience. This crazy micro-being, Ko Phi Phi, Pee Pee, to be or not to be? Just be, just be . . .

Monday morning. I scrape myself onto a computer. Fabien says if I'm not in Beijing by the weekend, I'll lose the job. Accounting for the time it'll take to get to Bangkok, get a Chinese visa and fly, I have approximately . . . one hour before the boat to Krabi leaves.

My feet sink into the white hot sand as I gaze out upon the living dream, the shimmering turquoise waters shining in crystal brilliance, the imperial cliffs draped in lush green vegetation bursting into the endless blue skies, the vision of paradise you can only truly grasp when the beauty merges with one's consciousness and for a split blissful second become one.

How can I leave? There's only one way. The time is now. Grab my bag, buy a ticket, run the gauntlet, down the pier, over the plank, the ferry leaves and that little cosmos that blew my mind over and over again fades away behind me.

* * *

I took a public bus from Krabi Town, the only Westerner on board. 12 hours on a night bus is rarely enjoyable, but whereas people on the tourist buses would be making noise, complaining and fighting over centimetres of leg room, the Thai people all sat in calm silence, barely moving their seats back.

I began to appreciate that many of the facets and quirks of the culture that had once so baffled me – the laid-back attitude, saving face, smiles and *kreng-jai* – were cultural extensions of the core Buddhist religious values that had existed here for so long. As with any other country, we are all born into a world still reverberating with the cultural echoes of centuries past.

Tuesday morning. Bangkok. ATM, photos, travel agent, Chinese visa forms. It'll be ready on Friday afternoon they assure me. Book a Friday night flight on credit, one-way to Beijing. I'm going. I smile a little smile.

Three nights round Banglampoo. East Gate Bar, Wanderers, Centerpoint, all the usual shit, but can't find anyone I know. Sammy's gone. No It. No Cheeky girls. No massage and orange juice girls. They've all moved on. I feel an anti-climax. The year is up. My time has passed. *Mai pen rai.*

My old partners in crime had all moved on too. Joe was back home on the road to recovery. Charlie was hitting it up in Australia and setting up his first exhibition of his Asian photos. Stu was working with a Maori building firm in New Zealand. Danny went too, but freaked out from the greyness and flashbacks and flew back to the UK. They were both saving to get back to Thailand. Gyorgy cycled to Singapore and flew off for more adventures with an eye on Hollywood. Oh, and Vincent? He was headed to the UK, but he was never one to do things the easy way. He was going overland. To India, through Pakistan, Afghanistan, Iran, Turkey and into Europe. The man was a legend, a hero, a true warrior of the road.

My final night in Thailand. Suddenly an email from Johnnie to say he's on his way. Good lad. We meet under the flashing neon lights of Khao San Road. He's brought Doug, Lena, Fanny, Double Dutch and friends with him. I bump into Rin, Ann and more of the Jungle girls too. My final night alone becomes a happy celebration with friends, laughing, dancing, having fun.

I say goodbye and jump in a taxi to the airport, charging down the home straight towards the chequered flag. I've spent a whole year in Southeast Asia. Now China. Anything is possible. It doesn't seem real. China! What am I doing? No idea. But I love it. I'm as free as a bird soaring high around the world. I'm a little sad to be leaving the land where you can go anywhere, meet anyone and do anything. But after a year of relentless freedom, hedonism, everything and nothing, it's time to retreat and recharge, work and learn. And despite all that's happened I know my journey's barely begun. The road is long, but life is short. Seize the day.

I check in at the airport with time to spare. I sit in the corner of a quiet cafe by myself and consume one final little bottle of SangSom before I give it all up. One last toast to old Jack and the boys. Here's to you.

The beaches, the glory, the girls, love and heartbreak, the endless roads, buses and trains, beautiful people and cultures, the lost and found, smiles and tears, exhilaration and depression, bottomless glasses, limitless highs, mountain tops, jungle life, mental strife, happy days, heart unfazed, we carry on unstoppable, the ever-wanderers cutting their own path, etching their own meaning in a world of boundless actualisation. Forever will they continue.

This is just one tale, one year, one man's journey. The story of I in paradise. But of course it's all bullshit. There is no I, no paradise. They are mere myths in a world of truth. A truth all around us and in us at all times. Just open your eyes, clear your mind and let it embrace you.

I smile alone, pouring the final drops of the old loopy juice into my plastic cup, watching the planes taxiing in the night outside, blurred through the shadowy rainbow of reflections. The flow of time evaporates with my satisfaction. Lights dance with thoughts fantastic. Alone again, end in sight, memories burn as strong as night. A whole year chasing that which was already there, that which always existed yet didn't exist at all, a nothingness, an empty space I must fill by my actions, just as we all do – a black hole in the centre of our Universe around which we all rotate.

I board the plane in a delirious haze, find my seat and the engine powers up, readying for departure as free flowing feelings take off and float into space. Images, sounds, deep emotions and nostalgic dreams combine with future fantasies in an aromatic cocktail of intoxicating phenomena.

★ ★ ★

How remarkable it seems looking back upon all the events which brought us here. Trying to fathom the infinitely-detailed causally-linked circumstances which brought about the Universe and its physical laws, billions of galaxies with billions of stars in each one, our Sun and the Earth existing in just the right balance for life to evolve. The factors which led to the extinction of so many species except for those that still survive today. And the rise of humanity and all that has contributed to our short but remarkable history.

But it's not really remarkable. It simply is. This is the world. It exists. Time and causality only move forward and develop further. New forms of existence emerge with no apparent preconception – the Universe, forces, atoms, stars, planets, life, evolution, humanity and consciousness. And this is what happened.

And then, not long ago, something else hugely significant occurred. Something just as elemental as the birth of the Universe, that great explosion of light. A form of being unlike anything else. Two lines of survival and reproduction – running through evolving species over billions of years – came together. The male released millions of genetically unique sperm into the female, just one of which fertilised her genetically unique egg. And after a period of gestation, a new life was born. A new bud. A new perspective unto the Universe. A new source of being emerging from nothing, zero to one, a new light in the dark, surging forth limitless possibilities for the future. You were born. And this world is yours. And in the years of your life that have passed up to this moment, your actions have been yours and yours alone. And so only one question remains. What are you doing now?